THE ART OF
PEACE

THE ART OF PEACE

PEACE

Engaging a Complex World

Juliana Geran Pilon

Transaction Publishers
New Brunswick (U.S.A.) and London (U.K.)

Library of Congress Catalog Number: 2016024677
ISBN: 978-1-4128-6423-7 (hardcover); 978-1-4128-6444-2 (paper)
eBook: 978-1-4128-6386-5
Printed in the United States of America

Library of Congress Cataloging-in-Publication Data

Names: Pilon, Juliana Geran, author.
Title: The art of peace : engaging a complex world / Juliana Geran Pilon.
Description: New Brunswick (U.S.A.) : Transaction Publishers, [2016] |
    Includes bibliographical references and index.
Identifiers: LCCN 2016024677 (print) | LCCN 2016041616 (ebook) |
    ISBN 9781412864237 (hardcover) | ISBN 9781412864442 (pbk.) | ISBN
    9781412863865 (eBook) | ISBN 9781412863865
Subjects: LCSH: United States--Foreign relations--Philosophy. | World
    politics--21st century.
Classification: LCC JZ1480 .P57 2016 (print) | LCC JZ1480 (ebook) |
    DDC 327.73--dc23
LC record available at https://lccn.loc.gov/2016024677

This book is dedicated to my beloved late parents, Charlotte and Peter Geran, with gratitude for finding the courage to wait with equanimity seventeen years till our family was allowed to leave Communist Romania and finally reach freedom in America.

Like it or not, today we are part of this larger world and must carry out our part. We cannot wait for problems to arrive here or it will be too late; rather we must remain strongly engaged in this complex world. The international order built on the state system is not self-sustaining. It demands tending by an America that leads wisely, standing unapologetically for the freedoms each of us . . . has enjoyed. [We must address] the need for America to adapt to changing circumstances, to come out now from its reactive crouch and to take a firm strategic stance in defense of our values.
—U.S. Marine Corps General James N. Mattis (Ret.)

To believe that at any historical point men will rest content with a peace that deprives them of personal and political liberties is an illusion reserved for those who reap the advantages from a dichotomy in the world politic.
—Irving Louis Horowitz

The Art of Peace is medicine for a sick world.
—Morihei Ueshiba

Contents

Foreword *by Colonel Michael R. Eastman*　　　　　　　ix

Preface　　　　　　　xiii

Acknowledgments　　　　　　　xxv

Introduction: Peace and Strategy　　　　　　　1

I. Sun Tzu's Acme of Skill

1　　Opposites Detract　　　　　　　27

2　　The Art of Information　　　　　　　45

3　　Shaking the Invisible Hand　　　　　　　55

4　　Leadership　　　　　　　63

II. The Founders' Art of Peace

5　　Sovereignty and Self-Government　　　　　　　81

6　　Influencing　　　　　　　99

7　　Diplomacy and Commerce　　　　　　　115

8　　A Brave New World　　　　　　　131

III. Strategic Deficit Disorder

9　　American Self-Ignorance　　　　　　　155

10　　Intelligence Deficit　　　　　　　177

11   Soft Power for Softies   205

12   One-Hand Clapping   227

13   Communication-Challenged   243

IV. Rebalancing to Win the Peace

14   Strategic Dialogue   263

15   Development Engagement   285

16   Peace-Building Reboot   301

17   Exceptionalism as *Realpolitik*   323

Conclusion: Medicine for a Sick World   345

Bibliography   357

Index   371

About the Authors   385

Foreword

Karl von Clausewitz occupies a place of honor among military strategists and practitioners of warfare. His treatise *On War* is a staple in the education of virtually all American officers. It is discussed, read, and studied (often in that order) at the intermediate and higher levels of professional military education. Debates over the nuances of 'coup d'oeil' or 'center of gravity' resound in college academic halls and the headquarters of military units at all echelons of command. Quite frankly, in military circles you cannot go wrong introducing a paper with a quote from Dead Karl, or cleverly inserting a term like "schwerpunkt" to sway opponents to your way of thinking. There is good reason for this, and in no way is it meant to detract from the great Prussian. The foundational tenets of Clausewitzian thought, that war is the extension of policy by other means, or that warfare itself is an illogical thing whose outcome rests on the relationship between the State, the military, and the people, are as close to timeless wisdom as exist in the literature.

Clausewitz's ideas hold considerable appeal to the Western mind and have had a huge impact on our way of war. His emphasis on focusing against an opponent's source of strength, on the critical need to maintain popular support in war, even his prescriptions for victory where they can be found or extrapolated, align well with our desire for rationality in a fundamentally irrational endeavor. Taken in isolation, they provide much wanted guideposts to victory, even as we struggle against the fog and friction of warfare that the author himself warned us against.

In dominating the landscape of our thinking about war, Clausewitzian thought crowds out alternate approaches to both military strategy, and perhaps more importantly, to the way we as a nation conceptualize and employ the vast arsenal of tools at our disposal in the pursuit of national goals and objectives. We sometimes forget that Clausewitz the man is not wholly represented in his seminal work, or that he might have expanded upon the role of economics, intelligence and statecraft had he not died as a result of battlefield service at the age of 51. On these topics and others, *On War* is silent, while Clausewitz the man likely was not.

Dr. Juliana Pilon challenges us to address these biases in our thinking, breaking the conceptual chains that bind us to a rigid strategic approach that has not delivered lasting results. In this ambitious work, she reintroduces us to a thinker of equal renown, the inimitable Sun Tzu. Whether his writings on strategy are the work of a single author or the distillation of centuries of wisdom by many, they encourage us to think differently, to approach strategy and warfare from a different perch that is arguably higher in altitude and broader in vision than that offered in Clausewitz's sole unfinished work. The approach taken here is complementary, opting against the "either this or that" approach so prevalent in our rationalist approach to strategy making. Instead, it asks us to hold two countervailing positions simultaneously, to acknowledge that the complexity of the real world, whether in politics or at the end of a gun, can rarely be reduced to a cost-benefit equation.

At a practical level, this work begins to address the yawning gap so painfully exposed by the Soldiers of this generation. For almost 16 years, we have fought a series of campaigns against seemingly intractable enemies. To be sure, the wars in Afghanistan and Iraq delivered an almost unblemished record of success at the tactical level. Given a mission, we have proven time and again that we have the ability to take any hill or hold any piece of ground. Against enemies unconstrained by concerns over innocent life, we have demonstrated a near-surgical level of precision and reduced collateral damage to negligible levels. For all this success in the field, however, we have very little to show for our efforts.

Despite an immense expenditure, measured not only in dollars, but in American lives, we need turn no further than the evening news to see that there is no stable government in Iraq; no denial of safe havens in Afghanistan; and Islamic radicalism has spread across the continent, swallowing up competing groups as they pledge allegiance to the entity we know as the Islamic State. While we might debate whether or not this presents an existential threat to our nation, it is undeniable that our tactical military dominance has not produced lasting strategic results. This despite the best efforts of countless Americans, in uniform and out, totally committed to the task. The question is, why?

As a career Soldier of twenty-five years with combat deployments to Iraq, Afghanistan, and most recently commanding a brigade in Operation

Inherent Resolve, hard experience offers insights but no answers. As a people, we don't seek to truly understand our enemy, or at times ourselves. Good intentions, whether in the form of liberating a village or building a million-dollar reconstruction project, run aground when they are uninformed by the constraints of local politics, unsustainable in a faltering economy, or cut short and abandoned because they don't immediately deliver results. We can and must do better.

Further, there has been no real distinction in recent years between national and military strategy. Because of its exceptional capabilities, we have turned to our military to address our greatest foreign policy goals, from building democracy in the Middle East to destroying a rising global terrorist threat. In doing so, we blur the lines between what we as a nation can do and what we should.

As a function of these first two, we have allowed perhaps our once greatest components of national power, from statecraft to economic influence, to atrophy. Development work is done by Soldiers in the field, 'heroic amateurs' who lack critical skills and experience necessary for these efforts but are frequently the only ones available to perform them. Diplomacy, when it is practiced, is far more likely to be conducted by a General Officer than an Ambassador, whose movements in a conflict zone are limited and whose culture favors the gravitational pull of the Embassy over meeting tribal leaders in the hinterlands. In the area of Strategic Communication, our country has all but given up, gutting organizations like Voice of America, whether in pursuit of cost savings, or mired by bureaucratic processes, so that we consistently lag behind the news cycle – that is, if we attempt to inform local peoples at all.

This slow, steady decline in our national capabilities has created the perfect vicious circle. When presented with problems of a strategic nature, most viable tools left at our disposal reside within the military. Limited options drive us towards a military solution, not because it is the best way, but frequently the only way to bring national power to bear. In short, we have perfected the world's greatest hammer, and soon enough every problem starts to look like a nail. What we have found as a nation over sixteen painful years of war is that achieving lasting strategic outcomes, much like building a house, requires more than a hammer and a bag of nails.

Fortunately, Dr. Juliana Pilon is perfectly positioned to provide a clear and convincing way ahead. Bringing both formidable academic experience and a professional career spent in the field, she is that rare scholar-practitioner who speaks with equal credibility to our national leaders and the Soldier guarding a lonely outpost in mountains of the Hindu Kush. In *The Art of Peace*, Juliana sheds light on the shortcomings in our thinking about strategy, at the same time demonstrating that things were not always this way. More importantly, they need not remain so in the future. As one who has seen firsthand the tragedy of war, this work could not come soon enough.

Colonel Michael R. Eastman

Preface

The euphoria brought on by the collapse of the Soviet Union and the end of the Cold War led many in the Department of State and Congress to believe that the primary threats to U.S. diplomacy and security had largely vanished. Republican and Democratic Congressmen, as well as political commentators, spoke of a "peace dividend," and one scholar claimed it was "the end of history."
—History of the Bureau of Diplomatic Security of the
U.S. Department of State, 2015

The American tends to be an extremist on the subject of war: he either embraces war wholeheartedly or rejects it completely. This extremism is required by the nature of the liberal ideology.
—Samuel P. Huntington, *The Soldier and the State: The Theory and Practice of Civil-Military Relations*, 1957

After the rapid implosion of the Soviet bloc, the Reluctant Superpower,[1] incontestably the strongest yet also the least belligerent state ever known, felt triumphant. Scarcely noticing the insidious rise of radical Islam, Americans never expected to suffer the most devastating attack on their soil since Pearl Harbor a mere few months into the new millennium. The experience stunned everyone; offended to the quick, the nation reacted fiercely. It was a rude awakening: evil had proved, once again, ineradicable. The political leadership showed itself more decisive than either well-informed or wise.

Two costly and inconclusive wars, billions of wasted dollars, and countless lost lives later, much has been learned, but too little implemented: "America's way of war," wrote the preeminent British strategist Colin Gray a few years ago, continues to be "apolitical; astrategic; ahistorical; culturally challenged; technology dependent; focused on firepower; large-scale; impatient."[2] The freest and most generous nation in history appears bumbling, about to squander its enormous moral and natural resources, with no one to blame but itself, lost without a compass in a complex world.

Having now seen two different approaches to the New World Disorder—those of George W. Bush and Barack Obama—we are no wiser. For one thing, they have been misrepresented. The first, accused of favoring "unilateral militarism" over diplomacy and development, was in practice not much different from the latter, which has rhetorically supported the converse, arguing for patient diplomacy over military action. So concludes US Army War College professor John R. Deni:

> [d]espite unambiguous rhetoric, official pronouncements, and pol-
> icies all aimed at rebalancing toward diplomacy and development
> and away from defense, in fact, there is much evidence to indicate
> that U.S. foreign and national security policy remains militarized,
> perhaps overly so.[3]

We might as well take a deep breath and get used to it. For "[r]egardless of whether militarization is good or bad, the fact that U.S. foreign policy is likely to remain militarized, even beyond the Obama years, carries major implications for the U.S. military as well as for those in the executive and legislative branches that would seek to wield it."[4]

But do we really have to resign ourselves to this situation? The relatively short answer is: not unless Deni is correct that the Obama years have truly given "diplomacy and development" a chance, and it has proven not to work. In truth, that simply isn't so. For, with the exception of a modest increase in State Department personnel, the Obama administration has most certainly not undertaken a serious rebalancing of the national security establishment structure. To be fair, neither has any of his predecessors. The Art of Peace is not even taught, let alone practiced.

Instead, Americans have increasingly turned to the military at the expense of civilian instruments of power:

> [S]everal factors point to a continued militarization of U.S. foreign
> policy, including funding levels, legal authorities, and the growing
> body of evidence that civilian agencies of the U.S. Government
> lack the resources, skills, and capabilities to achieve foreign policy
> objectives. Continued reliance by senior decisionmakers at both ends
> of Pennsylvania Avenue on the U.S. military in the development,
> planning, and implementation of U.S. foreign policy has significant

implications. Foremost among them is the fact that the military itself must prepare for a future not terribly unlike the very recent past.[5]

This is very disturbing, not only because the military cannot be expected to do the work of civilians but also because it shouldn't be. Using the military to do the job of civilians is expensive, inefficient, and ultimately self-defeating. Though seemingly easy to understand, hard power is also easy to misunderstand. The best solutions to a conflict, moreover, often turn out to be a matter of dollars and sense—of the common-sense variety: cheaper may not be faster, but may last longer and actually deliver the desired results. David's slingshot prevailed over the dumb giant knight's shining armor. Let's lose the shine, and get more smarts.

The threat of American "militarism" is actually rather misleading. Defined as "the tendency to regard military efficiency as the supreme ideal of the state and to subordinate all other interests to those of the military,"[6] it does not describe the United States so much as Germany before World War II. True, Deni is simply describing a fact, namely, that decision-makers rely more heavily on military than on civilian instruments of power in dealing with international problems. But there can be little doubt that unless we learn, or relearn, the Art of Peace, the only thing left is the Art of War. That shouldn't have to be. As it happens, Sun Tzu would heartily agree—as would America's Founders.

Whence this book. The nation is not unlike a sick patient who turns to drugs to address aches and pains: sometimes drugs are the only sensible option, but drugs don't necessarily work, and when they do, seldom do they work alone—they need to be supplemented by other remedies. (Not to mention that prevention is the best choice of all.) The military, even if indispensable to national security, as a deterrent no less than as the most radical weapon, should not be the only—or even main—branch of government required to prepare itself for future threats. For, like it or not, the need for diplomatic and other non-hard-power tools of statecraft has not diminished; on the contrary, the steep rise in unconventional conflict has raised their importance.

We face challenges that simply will not allow us the comfort of relying on lethal weapons, however superb; and not even the best, culturally savvy warriors-with-PhDs can make up for an atrophied, sclerotic civilian sector. Nor is it just a question of appropriating adequate resources (although there's that); as importantly, the people working in the civilian agencies have to be equipped with ideas that enable them to succeed. In that, the academy is failing us all, abysmally.

It's wake-up time. America can no longer afford to sit on the proverbial three-legged ("military, diplomacy, development") national security stool where one leg is a lot longer than either of the other two. We aren't so much becoming militarized as *decivilianized* (with apologies to spell-check).

Though absent from school curricula, the Art of Peace is not a new discipline. Nor is there a dearth of data documenting what plagues our nonmilitary or civilian[7] approach to foreign policy, with plenty of recommendations for how to address the appalling weaknesses in the nondefense sector. There is no paucity of smart people thinking about conceptual models, though some of their theories are admittedly esoteric, if not outright inscrutable, making it that much harder to bring them to the attention of policymakers. And while true that bureaucrats have traditionally been more worried about their pensions than about national interest, no one wants to do a lousy job; it's demoralizing, after all. Even the most mercenary of pencil pushers would profit from more efficient interagency coordination, a better allocation of resources, appropriate training, and applying lessons-learned to avoid repeating mistakes that cost lives and money.

No one needs to be reminded that new dangers to the United States and to world peace continue to accumulate with alarming rapidity. But while a conceptual as well as structural reappraisal of America's strategic direction has long been considered overdue, little has happened. Partly to blame is the toxic partisan dialectic pitting hawks against doves, which seems only to get worse with time. So long as the shouting match that passes for a national conversation is reduced to pelting interlocutors with bumper-sticker labels intended as expletives, the chances for a rational national discourse on American foreign policy are minuscule. I suggest it will take a radically new approach—or rather, a radical old one that we can no longer afford to forget.

For starters, to avoid the familiar food fight between the two sets of avian rivals, who each cite the "data" that best seems to support their respective prejudices, oversimplification and easy "isms" must be shunned. For a realistic rebalancing of America's foreign policy to be implemented in fact, not merely in rhetoric, the current dysfunctional strategic culture must be faced head-on. What has to go first is a risibly simplistic hard vs. soft power dualism, which leaves out a wide variety of weapons available in both the private and public sectors.

Equally obsolete is a definition of victory in overly narrow military terms. Though "winning the peace is harder than winning the war" has become a veritable cliché, it doesn't say much and can be misleading. Acknowledging that winning battles isn't everything doesn't imply that hard power should be shunned—far from it. Instead, the notion of peace must be reassessed, and peace-faring taken seriously as a tool not antithetical to warfare but complementary. Sun Tzu will help in that endeavor.—

For many reasons, which we will explore in depth, America's non-military capabilities are in deep trouble. Secretary Robert Gates summarized the problem succinctly:

> if we are to meet the myriad challenges around the world in the coming decades, this country must strengthen other important elements of national power both institutionally and financially, and create the capability to integrate and apply all of the elements of national power to problems and challenges abroad. In short, based on my experience serving seven presidents, as a former Director of CIA and [later] as Secretary of Defense, I am here to make the case for strengthening our capacity to use "soft" power and for better integrating it with "hard" power.[8]

Though he was speaking in 2007, he could have uttered these words yesterday. Our intelligence system suffers from overdependence on technology at the expense of human intelligence, known as HUMINT. The notoriously ineffectual foreign aid industry continues to flounder, rudderless. Public diplomacy[9] has been all but abandoned by the State Department, and strategic communication (as explained in chapter 6) remains MIA (missing in action). Most alarming—the traditional beliefs in individual liberty and free trade have eroded, even as political correctness dominates the academy. What does America stand for? With its leadership seemingly incapable of formulating strategy, the citizenry is confused about its own direction and identity, which is one reason why we must revisit our Founders' ideas and practices.

The United States has slowly become a victim of its great military and economic power, which permits us to flounder for quite some time without dire immediate consequences. (Winston Churchill is reputed to have said that Americans can always be trusted to do the right thing, once all other possibilities have been exhausted.[10]) We would be well advised to remember that our Founding Fathers had no such luxury; though uncompromising in their principles, they had to make up in savvy realism for what they lacked in money and hardware. The upstart republic that improbably gained its independence from the mightiest empire of the day was lucky, for its great *strategos*,[11] the incomparable warrior-farmer and spy-master George Washington, shared the national vision of Alexander Hamilton, benefited from Franklin's knowledge of human nature, along with John Adams's tenacity, Sam Adams's talent for political warfare, Thomas Jefferson's erudition, and James Madison's political acumen. Together they understood that to win, Americans had to be smart, nimble, brave, yet cautious. And they recognized that peace is predicated on power—hard or otherwise.

The continued relevance of the Founders' thinking is explained by David Abshire: "In effect, Washington and his successors implemented the three principles of classical strategy: unity of effort, freedom of action, and strategic proportionality."[12] General Washington, meet Sun Tzu.

Though blatantly anachronistic, this is not as far-fetched as it might seem. In his dissertation published by the Strategic Studies Institute, for example, Major Kris J. Stillings observes:

> Over 2500 years ago, the great Chinese military philosopher, Sun Tzu wrote, 'The good fighters of old first put themselves beyond the possibility of defeat, and then waited for an opportunity of defeating the enemy.' Some twenty-three centuries later at the outset of the American Revolutionary War, General George Washington unknowingly adopted Sun Tzu's advice as he struggled to create an effective strategy for fighting the British.[13]

Stillings is right that Washington could only have adopted Sun Tzu's advice unknowingly. But looking back, it is worth noting what the ancient Chinese strategist who founded the discipline (even without naming it) shares with America's greatest hero.

What links them—and all good strategists, for that matter—is the fact that basic principles of war and peace are transcendent, notwithstanding the great variety of international conflicts across space and time, in different ages and throughout the globe. In this book, I plan to show how Sun Tzu's insights as applied, however unconsciously, by America's main Founders fit today's challenges. His great epic, entitled *The Art of War*, explored strategy in peace no less than that in war, for unless the peace is won, wars will necessarily be lost. Moreover, it is during peace that wars have a chance to be prevented.

It should not surprise that many of Sun Tzu's key strategic principles were in use at America's founding, since they possess a timeless validity, applicable once again in the current, admittedly exceedingly complex, national-security environment. What the Chinese sage shared with Washington and the other Founders was a keen appreciation for grand strategy and specifically for the role of nonlethal power, infelicitously dubbed "soft" by modern-day political scientists.

What they all grasped is the centrality of cultural intelligence and the need for a realistic, accurate assessment of the total, albeit fluid, environment of every conflict, anywhere. That fluidity, in turn, necessitates adapting to constantly changing circumstances. But contrary to self-styled pragmatists, proponents of power politics, and demagogues who pay lip service to ideals while ruthlessly ignoring them, genuine peace cannot be attained without commitment to a moral outlook, nurtured within a culture of trust, and a sense of common purpose.

This book is focused on the strategic deficit disorder afflicting American foreign policy, which in the aftermath of the Cold War and 9/11 has been caused in part by deep confusion about the nation's values and conception of peace, exacerbated by ignorance and misunderstanding of history and tradition. That tradition, however, which dates from the Revolutionary era, defines who we are and what makes this country special, whether or not divinely "chosen," as a beacon of freedom.

"Strategy" may not have been in the vocabulary of the nation's Founders, but it was evident in how they conducted themselves. As Gray points out, "our whole human history," and hence specifically our own, "is a protracted strategic narrative, regardless of what it was called and how it was defined at the time."[14] We must seek to learn from it. Fortunately, as Gray also notes, "strategy has not changed as a broad function through the ages;"[15] Sun Tzu is now as relevant as ever. His wisdom is thus reexamined, assisted by new studies of his thought, in part I of this book: his discussion of intelligence and influence operations, the need for alliances, the importance of recalibration and flexibility, and the primacy of morality and leadership, team-building, and a strong national ethos.

The Revolutionary era is the subject of part II, which examines the philosophical principles rooted in classical liberalism that guided the nation's architects, which included an almost religious trust in the peaceful effects of global free trade. Principles aside, their mastery of strategic communication or "influencing" was exceeded only by their self-confident resilience and adaptability. Though America's Founders were not saints, their strategic acumen and keen appreciation for the critical importance of using every tool of power at their disposal is a legacy worth adopting and applying to current conditions.

Part III describes the strategic deficit syndrome afflicting the United States. We talk about "development and diplomacy" as being on a par with "defense" but we know neither how to synchronize them nor what goals a national strategy is supposed to advance. It doesn't help that Americans are not just ignorant about their own origins, they are often misinformed. Alas, when popular ignorance is too pervasive, and exacerbated by bias in both the media and the academy, leadership is sorely undermined. The intelligence agencies are also deficient, and overly reliant on technology. Good intelligence takes considerable cultural knowledge; and there is no substitute for old-fashioned human intelligence. Another deficiency is the inability to synchronize all the elements of power, the inability to wield so-called "soft power" (an especially ill-defined concept).

Part IV centers on the conceptual building blocks of a realistic yet moral, hard-nosed yet compassionate foreign policy without illusions, committed to engagement guided by our national interest, which cannot be divorced from the natural rights of men and women throughout the world. None of this implies that America should take upon itself the role of hegemon or empire, no matter how benign: for not only is that impossible but also self-defeating. Such concepts are simple enough to articulate; however, it will take patience, honesty, and a renewed appreciation for America's commitment to individual liberty and the generosity of its spirit for us to preserve the peace with liberty for which the nation was founded and hope that it extends as widely as possible.

Finally, a few specific recommendations are advanced to achieve a strategic "reboot" to win the peace. Few, if any, of the suggestions are new; none should surprise. But revisiting Sun Tzu and the legacy of our Founders should provide added conceptual ammunition for a rational and productive conversation. The national dialogue must transcend partisanship, with due regard for fiscal and other constraints, yet in a spirit of commitment to America's original ideals, dispensing with self-righteous rhetoric.

The book's intended audience is anyone[16] interested in national security and everyone who isn't but should be. Impatient readers might dislike my forays into etymology and the occasional biblical reference, but these do offer invaluable glimpses into our cultural DNA; so please grin and bear it. Those who trust hard power to solve most problems—and are allergic to all the talk of nonlethal peace fare—might come to change their minds. So might the soft-hearted, who think hard power inherently jeopardizes peace rather than help win and prevent wars. My hope is that we can all transcend ideological tribalism and find better ways to maintain peace or, when lost, to win it back.

America is the most peace-loving nation in history, but over the course of the past two centuries, we seem to have misconstrued—if not forgotten altogether—what our Founders knew too well. They loved peace, but knew that securing it meant not to forget war's potential resurgence at any time, which requires constant vigilance and doing everything possible to try to prevent it, excluding engagement in wishful thinking. General George Washington as president advised his nation to avoid foreign entanglements; yet in his First Annual Address before both houses of Congress, he warned that "to be prepared for war is one of the most effective means of preserving peace."[17] Complacency invites attack; and peace can never be assumed to be permanent.

Today, Lt. Gen. H. R. McMaster speaks for all those in leadership position who understand that such preparation requires adequate weapons, effectively synchronized, "capable of operating in sufficient scale and ample duration to win, [or else] adversaries are likely to become emboldened and deterrence is likely to fail."[18] But he continues, military preparedness is hardly sufficient. Whether "preparing effectively for war to prevent conflict, shape security environments, [or, should war become necessary] win in armed conflict [always] requires clear thinking."[19] General Stanley A. McChrystal underscores as well the need for a "shared consciousness"[20] by an entire network, a team of teams that must learn to work together against agile enemies in highly complex settings.

Clear thinking is exactly what Sun Tzu had prescribed because he believed that the acme of leadership consists in figuring out *how to subdue the enemy without fighting*. But war is best avoided when the nation possesses both the ability and willingness to use all available instruments of power in peace as much as in war. To that end, self-knowledge is as important as knowledge of one's enemy: for *if you know neither yourself nor the enemy, you will succumb in every battle*. Alarmingly, we are deficient on both counts. And though we can stand to lose a few battles, the stakes of losing the war itself in this age of nuclear proliferation are too high to contemplate. We are certainly strong; but to avoid becoming a hapless Goliath, whose physical strength renders him overconfident, let us recall what we knew when our nation had the energy and savvy of a David, when our superiority lay not in hardware but in political acumen, intelligence, and devotion to ideals that are still relevant today, if only we would remember.

Notes

1. The term was coined by P. F. Holt in his book *The Reluctant Superpower: A History of America's Economic Global Reach* (New York: Kodansha Amer Inc, 1995).
2. Colin S. Gray, *Irregular Enemies and the Essence of Strategy: Can the American Way of War Adapt?* (Carlisle, PA: Strategic Studies Institute (SSI), March 2006), 30.
3. John R. Deni, *The Real Rebalancing: American Diplomacy and the Tragedy of President Obama's Foreign Policy* (Carlisle, PA: Strategic Studies Institute and U.S. Army War College, October 2015), 2.
4. Ibid.
5. Ibid.
6. http://dictionary.reference.com/browse/militarism
7. Not an ideal word; but "nonmilitary" seems to imply its absence, or hostility, to the military, while "transmilitary" carries a peculiar connotation of transcendence. I am simply referring to complementarity. Semantics is never "mere."
8. Robert M. Gates, Landon Lecture, November 26, 2007. https://www.k-state.edu/media/newsreleases/landonlect/gatestext1107.html
9. The State Department's mission of "influencing and informing foreign publics." http://www.state.gov/r/
10. https://richardlangworth.com/americans
11. Greek, meaning "general."
12. David Abshire, in *Forging an American Grand Strategy: Security a Path Through a Complex Future, Selected Presentations from a Symposium at the National Defense University*, ed. Sheila R. Ronis (Carlisle, PA: Strategic Studies Institute and U.S. Army War College Press, October 2013).
13. Major Kris J. Stillings, USMC, *General George Washington and the Formulation of American Strategy for the War of Independence*, Marine Corps Command and Staff College, April 2001. http://oai.dtic.mil/oai/oai?verb=getRecord&metadataPrefix=html&identifier=ADA401347
14. Colin S. Gray, *The Future of Strategy* (Cambridge: Polity Books, 2015), 10.
15. Ibid., 11.
16. Stylistic note: Whenever possible throughout the book I have sought to avoid use a gender-specific pronoun. And unless context indicates otherwise, I have selected to use "he" in a gender-neutral sense, meaning "he or she."
17. http://www.archives.gov/exhibits/american_originals/inaugtxt.html
18. H. R. McMaster, "Discussing the Continuities of War and the Future of Warfare: The Defense Entrepreneurs Forum," *Small Wars Journal*, October 14 2014. http://smallwarsjournal.com/jrnl/art/discussing-the-continuities-of-war-and-the-future-of-warfare-the-defense-entrepreneurs-foru

19. Ibid.
20. General Stanley McChrystal, Tantum Collins, David Silverman, and Chris Fussel, *Team of Teams: New Rules of Engagement for a Complex World* (New York: Penguin Group, Portfolio, 2015), esp. Ch. 6, 115 ff.

Acknowledgments

In my earlier book about the importance of using all the instruments of power in defending national security, *Why America is Such a Hard Sell: Beyond Pride and Prejudice*, my main concern had been to underscore how poorly this country has been wielding its non-military weapons. But over time I became increasingly aware of how much deeper the problem really is. The dangerous polarization prevalent in our political culture between war and peace, and correspondingly between military and civilian power, is far more than conceptual. It is visceral, having insidiously turned into a veritable class struggle, that threatens to sabotage the nation from within, castrating it unnecessarily.

Few people understood this better than the late professor Irving Louis Horowitz, whose death in 2010 left a gaping hole in the intellectual life of this country. Fortunately, his exceptional wife Mary Curtis, long president of Transaction Publishers, shared his acumen in grasping essential cultural rifts that deserve in-depth analysis, which is reflected in the company's fine collection of studies. It was her enthusiasm for the idea of this book that gave me the courage to tackle such a variety of disciplines, including security studies, Chinese philosophy, American political thought, foreign policy, development, public diplomacy and information operations, and intelligence. The Horowitzes had long defined Transaction's approach as the serious study of human action, which must transcend academic stovepipes and narrow professional categories. I was lucky to have found them.

It had also been what I learned at the University of Chicago, many years ago. Thus I cannot fail to acknowledge my first philosophy professor and later doctoral dissertation advisor, the late Manley Thompson, who specialized in American pragmatism, along with the late scholar and wonderful friend Joseph Cropsey, with whom I discussed at length many of the concepts I explore in this book, notably the contrast between Locke and Hegel.

Which is one reason why finding a home at the Alexander Hamilton Institute for the Study of Western Civilization has been such a blessing. Under the able stewardship of the dynamic, erudite and amazingly personable history professor Robert Paquette, most of whose students at Hamilton College deservedly worship him, the Institute is an oasis of informed debate and devotion to learning. Thank goodness for the AHI and its generous supporters, such as founders Carl and Cordelia Menges, the Lynde and Harry Bradley Foundation, as well as Abby Moffat and Diana Davis Spencer. The Institute's mission is invaluable.

I certainly want to thank many of my worthy colleagues over the years, and also my students, especially the exemplary Army Fellows Col. Mike Eastman, Col. Reggie Bostick, and Bg. Gen. Brian Mennes, whose fine minds are matched by their dedication and patriotism. I am honored that Col. Eastman agreed to write the Foreword to this book; his keen appreciation for the critical relevance of nonmilitary factors in warfare is truly impressive. But besides having a first-rate mind and a rare sense of humor, he is a man of integrity and deep commitment. That someone with his military experience and intellectual background appreciates what I have been trying to convey in this book is both gratifying and humbling.

During my long and varied career, I also benefited enormously from students and colleagues, far too many to name, both American and foreign, whose insights and experiences in many parts of the world, whether in intelligence, military, diplomacy, or development, added immeasurably to my understanding of the complexities involved in conceptualizing national security strategy. But specifically, I want to thank Katherine Humphries, who generously read several early versions of my book, and University of Chicago colleague James Freund, whose meticulous editing queries were indispensable in the early drafts, as were suggestions by the brilliant Dr. Steve Bryen, a former high-level Defense Department official and political science professor, not to mention a real *mensch*.

Most important, however, has been my family's support – starting with my son Alex, whose ear for clarity led me to simplify some overly convoluted sentences. While my daughter Danielle was far too busy to read any drafts, it was highly encouraging that she was convinced a book about peace, written by her mother no less, would become a bestseller. I am grateful also to my constitutional scholar and philosopher husband, Roger Pilon, whose own superlative prose always serves as a beacon, even if we have somewhat different stylistic preferences. Much as I hate to admit it, he is often right.

Finally, I hesitate not thanking Sara, my devoted cat (which, I realize, is generally an oxymoron) - strands of whose abundant fur perpetually coated my computer during countless hours of editing - for only seldom seeking to correct my grammar, considering she was never right. Glued next to me on the couch, mostly asleep, her trust has been unflinching, her purring soothing, and her phlegmatic equanimity a welcome antidote to the illusion that any one person can make much difference in the cacophony that is Washington's national security conversation, if one may call it that.

Juliana Geran Pilon
May 23, 2016
Washington, DC

Introduction:
Peace and Strategy

Our world is full of violence, and our daily lives can be marred by conflict and turmoil. But God promises His people a peace that surpasses all understanding.
—Proverbs 16:7

The black-and-white distinction between war and peace, or traditional war and irregular war, makes for nice, simple boxes, but the real world is not so easily categorized. In fact, some adversaries seek to exploit U.S. paradigms and the gaping institutional seams that they create.
—Frank G. Hoffman, *2016 Index of U.S. Military Strength*

Two Jews sit in a coffeehouse, discussing the fate of their people. "How miserable is our history," says one. "Pogroms, plagues, discrimination, Hitler, Hamas, Neo-Nazis. . . . Sometimes I think we'd be better off if we'd never been born." "Sure," says his friend. "But who has that much luck—maybe one in fifty thousand?"

You don't have to be Jewish to think that maybe that's not so funny; that doesn't mean you can't appreciate the absurdity of the endless violence that throughout history has destroyed the lives of perfectly innocent people. Yet, the inability to describe something as inherently elusive as peace hasn't stopped us from yearning for it. Miraculous Peace Everlasting embodies everything good: every religion has promised it to its followers, as has virtually every quasi-religious ideology. War has been linked to evil, death, and struggle. Everybody naturally loves the kind of peace that—from the dawn of mankind—has symbolized ultimate perfection.

It certainly did in biblical times. The Hebrew word that means "peace"—שלם (*shalem*)—refers to wholeness, completeness, or "unbrokenness," like the uncut stones of the altar (*Deuteronomy* 27:6) and the temple (1 *Kings* 6:7), the entirety of a population (*Amos* 1:6), and of course "whole" hearts that are devoted (wholeheartedly) to the Lord (1 *Kings* 8:61). Similarly, if more subtly, it also denotes "full" and just weights (that don't cheat), which are God's delight (*Deuteronomy* 25:15; also *Proverbs* 11:1), and a "full" or hence, too, "fulfilling" wage (*Ruth* 1:12). Interestingly, Hebrew scripture uses the term not only as a noun, to indicate a condition—as in a state of peace or a peaceful situation—but also as a verb, which might be rendered as "to shalem-ize," which would translate as "engaging in peace" or more accurately, if awkwardly, as "conducting peace fare."

The biblical *"shalemizing"* refers to achieving or restoring whole-ness by some kind of payment or covenant; for example, the owner of an accidentally killed ox is to be paid restitution (*Exodus* 21:36), oil is sold to pay off a debt (2 *Kings* 4:7), and the Gibeonites talk Joshua into making a (monetary) covenant with them (*Joshua* 10:1). *Shalem* is also used when vows are to be paid to the Most High, or when days of mourning are to be completed (*Isaiah* 60:20), and ties in directly to the Messiah and his salvific, redeeming work (*Joel* 2:25). Some nouns derived from this root verb literally mean "peacemaker," or perhaps "peace farer"—referring to someone who wages peace, which is to say, offers the requisite fare to achieve peace.

So too, it should come as no surprise that the English verb "to wage" is cousin to the noun "wage," a synonym for "salary," which in Middle English of the thirteenth-century variety, according to the lexicographers, meant "a pledge," or guarantee. The connotation of "to carry on" (as in war) followed shortly thereafter in the mid-fourteenth century, and is most likely derived from "to offer as a gage of battle." Waging war thus originally, and quite literally, meant to deliver a concrete promise, a pledge, a signal that a fight is about to follow.

Wages are equally important in war and peace. This is reflected not only in Hebrew but also, closer to our own linguistic home, Latin. With apologies to the reader whose passion for etymology is at best faint, the word *peace* entered into English in the middle of the twelfth century, having originally meant "freedom from civil disorder," denot-ing the healthy, undisrupted state of social life. Like many other words relating to political organization, *peace* had passed from the original Latin through the French *pais*, whose Latin ancestor *pax* could in turn denote "peace" as well as "treaty" or "agreement," having itself derived from *pacisci* which meant "to bargain for" or "agree upon." Inferring an apparent nod to Hebrew tradition is hard to resist.

Actually, Latin's *pax* also had other non-Western relatives. Its Proto-Indo-European[1] root *pag-/pak-* meant "fasten"—an assurance needed by any credible bargain. Still other forms of *pag-/pak-* developed in other Indo-European languages have more literal denotations: Sanskrit uses *pasa-* to mean "cord" or "rope;" in Avestan, *pas* means "a fetter;" while in ancient Greek, *pegnynai* meant "to fix, make firm, fast, or solid," which could allow for broader interpretations. English words as varied as *fang*, *impinge*, and *propagate*, among others, also derive from this root. The ramifications of peace are broad indeed.

Interestingly, while we speak of waging war yet hardly ever of waging peace, the idea of peace is arguably more closely related to the idea of "wage" than is war—certainly if etymology is any indication. Wages involve bargaining and rational agreement; by contrast, war has traditionally been connected to chaos and havoc. In Old English, *wyrre* or *werre* referred to "large-scale military conflict," which derived from Old North French *were*, meaning "difficulty, dispute; hostility; fight, combat, war"—now *guerre*, in Modern French—itself descendant from Frankish *werra*, from Proto-Germanic *werz-a-* (cognates include the Old Saxon and Old High German *werran*, and German *verwirren* "to confuse, perplex").

In brief, engaging in war traditionally meant, in most European languages, "bringing into confusion"—a somewhat awkward way of saying that disorder has just been willfully, deliberately, commenced. There is a great deal of plausibility to the common, if unverifiable, assumption that Spanish, Portuguese, and Italian all turned to Germanic for their use of the similar term for war, *guerra*, rather than the more obvious Latin *bellum*, to avoid the latter's unwelcome similarity to *bello-* "beautiful." For even as opposites attract—and violence connotes a certain romance, however pathological—they remain opposites.

But it does seem peculiar that notwithstanding the relevance of "wares" qua "wages" to peace, all the attention among strategists continues to be on warfare, or the art of war, while peace fare is hardly ever deployed—let alone studied. And thereby hangs a tale of strategic self-sabotage through linguistic amnesia—or in plain English, by failing to use the word, we have neglected to practice effectively, efficiently, and without illusions, the important and difficult skills for which it stands.

Not that the "art of peace" is altogether absent from our modern vocabulary and experience. The visitor to West Potomac Park in Washington, DC, for example, may be edified by two lovely bronze statues, erected in 1951, commemorating the Arts of Peace: one represents "Music and Harvest," the other, "Aspiration and Literature." Also, googling "the art of peace"—the most reliable barometer of cultural relevance—reveals a plethora of how-to books on relaxation, Eastern philosophy, and assorted pacifist websites. Though an outlier, Ambassador Chester A. Crocker's "The Art of Peace: Bringing Diplomacy Back to Washington," published in the July/August 2007 issue of *Foreign Affairs*, goes some distance in redeeming the term's still-current strategic implications.

The far more prevalent "art of war," meanwhile, has come to be used almost interchangeably with the "art of strategy" in the context of national security. Notes strategy scholar Laurence Freedman: "Through the Middle Ages and into the modern era . . . the relevant reference [to 'strategy'] tended to be to the 'art of war.'"[2] But why is the art of peace not taught and practiced alongside the art of war? Iraq war veteran Paul K. Chappell posed himself the same question when he was enrolled at the West Point Academy. Having learned in the military that training is necessary for waging war, he "was surprised to learn that so many peace activists have little to no training in how to effectively wage peace."[3] And why not, he asks: why had he not learned in school that waging peace had a long tradition in American history? For that matter, why do pacifists abhor knowing anything about war? It makes no sense, writes Chappell; after all, just as doctors must understand disease to promote health, "if our job is to promote peace, we must also be experts on war and violence,"[4] for the two are complementary.

Chappell's medical analogy offers a useful insight into the way the problem is formulated in an international context. If peace is defined as the absence of war in the way that health is the absence of illness, war could be seen as a kind of illness of the body politic. We often think of health as the normal course of events, and hence more or less taken for granted—the *status quo*. By contrast, each illness has its own symptoms, with varying methods of cure. This is reminiscent of Lev Tolstoy's celebrated first lines of his masterpiece *Anna Karenina*: "All happy families are alike; each unhappy family is unhappy in its own way." Health, happiness, and peace—what ordinary people ardently seek for themselves and their families—provide fine greeting-card material; they make for dull reading. Meanwhile illness, unhappiness, adultery, and war provide juicy subjects for long, fine novels. (Tolstoy's other masterpiece is—what else?—*War and Peace*.)

The uninteresting, however, is only deceptively uneventful: inner strife is no less dramatic for being largely invisible to the naked eye. Consider the fact that a healthy-looking person may actually be fighting off diseases that only reveal themselves when they reach a certain acute stage, which a strong immune system may be able to avert before it becomes devastating. Strong immunity, in turn, is enhanced by "waging health"—such as regular exercise and a healthy diet. By no means is health the default setting of the human body: indeed, the body has to work hard at both averting illness and preserving as well as, if incapacitated, restoring health. The same is true of the national health that we sometimes call peace: its establishment, preservation, and restoration, require a great deal of knowledge, and certainly art.

The currently widespread assumption that peace is the "natural" state of a body politic corresponds to what historian of politics and culture Adda Bozeman identified as the modern "Western" approach, which she deplores. For her extensive comparative study of international war theories throughout history "leaves the definite impression that war was both being perceived more keenly and explained more accurately by earlier observers,"[5] who saw international peace as basically remote and at best temporary. Bozeman goes on to observe that in the West, and especially in America, there is an unspoken yet widely shared assumption that if people refrained from fighting, we would all live in harmony. It's somewhat like saying that if it weren't for rain, we wouldn't need umbrellas.

Among those who best understood the unavoidably persistent nature of conflict was the Dutch jurist Hugo Grotius (1583–1645), who laid the foundations of international law. In his seminal book, *The Rights of Peace, Including the Law of Nature and of Nations*, Grotius warned against too simplistic an idea of peace as merely the (apparent) absence of war; peace, he observed, tends to be limited in both time and space. Therefore, just because no battles are fought at a particular location does not mean that war has ended: the common condition is little more than a "transitory peace, in travail with war"—adding "that [truces may be] made too for years, twenty, thirty, forty, even a hundred years!"[6] "In other words," writes Bozeman, "a state of belligerency may well be semi-permanent or protracted."[7] Analogously, as we learn more about the complex mechanism of the human body, we appreciate its constant efforts to ward off toxins, mutating cancer cells, and potential agents of infection—in its miraculous, if unobserved (which is not to say unobservable), routine to stay alive. Hypochondriacs excepted, this is no reason for alarm; quite the contrary: it simply puts the business of life—and hence, by analogy, of peace—in clearer perspective.

"Transitory" peace, to use Grotius's term, is then not so much the "real" thing as a temporary suspension of crisis. Similarly, a state of affairs where fighting does not erupt because the offending party is not met with resistance is hardly what most people consider the true meaning of peace. Lasting or *genuine* peace is not the uncertain lull before the proverbial storm, the unstable respite that precedes an inevitable conflagration, whether through death or destruction, or the mute solitude of the infinite—whether divine or vacuous. Genuine peace is a positive condition of wellbeing, tranquility, and relatively extended, though never permanent, safety.

Most human beings cannot attain this condition without love and integrity in their lives, without the sense of being able to tell the truth and raise children who can do the same, and the ability to thrive and achieve their potential. Real peace is more than mere absence of strife. We have clad the word in splendid illusory garb, bathing it in feel-good ambiguity for adulation; but in a vain quest for Peace Everlasting, we have neglected the hard work of facing facts.

There has never been a shortage of utopians who think it attainable on this earth; but Immanuel Kant (1724–1804) was not among them. Though his notion of "perpetual peace" did indeed refer to a state of mutual respect among nations, he thought such a condition unattainable by human powers. Rather, it was nature that miraculously seems to strive toward a kind of order: "The guarantee of perpetual peace is nothing less than that great artist, Nature," he wrote. You would never guess by observing actual human beings: "In her mechanical course we see that her aim is to produce a harmony among men, against their will and *indeed through their discord*."[8]

Kant was impressed by the way that nature could reach her ends even through war, though especially through peaceful alliances fueled by self-interest. Of course "perpetual peace" could not be literally "guaranteed": the admittedly misleading expression simply reflected the remarkable fact that even deeply flawed, immoral men can (at least in principle) agree to peaceful coexistence for the purpose of self-preservation. Explains Kant scholar Frederick Rauscher: "Kant considered world peace impossible without both individual republican states and an international federation among them."[9] In other words, any resemblance between his theories and the real world, though not unfathomable, is purely coincidental.

It is not a little ironic that Kant's detractors use the term "perpetual peace" to mock the great German philosopher's ideas, using it to paint a caricature of the utopian anti-realist position, when in fact Kant himself was fully aware of its absurdity. In the preamble to his essay, Kant reports having spotted the phrase that he deems a "satirical inscription, on a Dutch innkeeper's sign upon which a burial ground was painted." He adds whimsically that whether "its object [was] all mankind in general or the rulers of states in particular, who are insatiable of war, or merely the philosophers who dream this sweet dream, it is not for us to decide."[10] Even if he never did leave his little Prussian hometown of Konigsberg, Kant was no fool; he was simply engaging in philosophical discourse, and an especially dense version of it, to which the German language is especially well suited.

Kant's presumption is elaborated in his short, influential, if too often misunderstood, essay that international peace had to be predicated on the existence of a liberal constituency, could not be farther from the totalitarian mindset, which is based on universal consensus, the precise opposite of liberal pluralism. Famously adept at semantic acrobatics, Islamists define the realm of peace (*Dar el-Salam*) as the region under sharia, leaving the rest of the world in the realm of war (*Dar el-Harb*) at the mercy of fanatical killers. By implication, as long as there are non-Islamists, there can be no peace. Talk about standing reality on its head. These enemies of freedom do not want the peace of diversity and dialogue, the peace of democratic debate and the harmony of difference; they crave the unanimity that comes from the suppression of dissent and the silence of suppression. If that is absence of war, it is also absence of human values worth living for. To non-Islamists, it amounts to the silence of a living death.[11]

No less adept at promising earthly nirvana are the followers of Karl Marx, whose new-speak acrobatics are nevertheless easy to expose, at least to those willing to listen. George F. Kennan (author of the United States's ambiguously named "containment" strategy against the Soviet Union) did so, eloquently, in an article published by *Foreign Affairs* in January 1960, in his response to Soviet premier Nikita Khrushchev: "There is one kind of peace that is compatible with the true security of peoples; and this is one which is based on the principles of genuine national freedom. There is another kind of peace which represents the silence that reigns where the instruments of coercion are simply too formidable to be challenged by those against whom they are aimed."[12] While "peaceful coexistence" became a code word for unfettered Communist Russian expansion and implied that any resistance to Moscow's march toward global hegemony was equivalent to warmongering, it infected public discourse worldwide—the result of an astonishingly effective campaign of newspeak. It largely explains why today many "peace studies" departments at American universities are home to self-described Marxist and far-left professors.[13]

This is unsurprising. An object of supreme human desire, peace lent itself easily to obfuscation and ideological warfare. All the more reason to understand what we mean by it, clarify it for ourselves and others so as to more effectively articulate national security strategy, and expose its deliberate distortion by those who wish us harm. Not everyone seeks our kind of peace, let alone condone the same kind of tactics. Does it make sense to murder, maim, rape, and commit suicide in the name of heavenly peace while causing havoc on earth? It certainly does not seem reasonable to most of us in the West—and no deconstructionist rationalizing can make it so.

To be sure, Western faith in the universal power of reason is surely a double-edged sword. While it led to miracles of scientific discovery and advances in technology, it seems to have fostered an occasionally too rosy a view of human nature. No doubt, the assumption that all human beings are endowed with reason legitimizes the universality of natural rights—that all people are created equal, that no one has the right to enslave or decide for another—forms the basis for (republican) democracy and self-government. But alas, the power of reason to actually override the passions, which drive so many to keep ignoring the universality of rights, is notoriously faint.

Our ancestors in ancient Greece understood this well. The great Euripides, writing in the fifth century BC, had the chorus in his tragedy *Suppliant Women* lament: "How far peace (Eirene) outweighs war in benefits to man—Eirene, the chief friend and cherisher of the Muses; Eirene, the enemy of revenge, lover of families and children, patroness of wealth. Yet these blessings we viciously neglect, embrace wars; man with man, city with city fights, the strong enslaves the weak." The Greek goddess of peace, Eirene, who also doubled as the goddess of spring (late spring being the usual campaign season in Greece, when peace was most at risk) was daughter to Zeus, king of all the gods, while her mother was the great Titaness Themis, daughter of Gaia (earth) and Uranus (sky).[14] Spring never lasts forever; like the seasons, men turn to fighting, then stop to taste the fruit of the vine.

In brief, Greeks who demonstrated a profound appreciation for the dialectic of opposites were at home with complexity. The use of metaphor, images, aphorism, and the symbolism characteristic of mythological thinking, is a skill we would do well to recapture. As the enchanting ancient Greek stories illustrate, Western thought was more nuanced in antiquity than it is now. It was indeed far closer to Sun Tzu.

And so the story goes that Eirene was the goddess of peace alongside the god of war who was none other than the mighty Ares, who morphed under the Romans into a somewhat tamer but still fearsome Mars. The Greeks had no great illusions about their deities—as on earth so it was in Olympus. Ares was paired, albeit adulterously, with the beguiling goddess of beauty, Aphrodite, on more than one occasion. The rationale for this union of opposites—Ares and Aphrodite, war and beauty—is not far to find. Warlike qualities include courage and idealism, strength and determination, all romantic traits, which may well beguile the goddess, along with the far more sinister attraction of blood. Her own loveliness, in turn, can lead to suffering and death, as too does war. In keeping with the antinomy, their offspring included not only Deimos and Phobos—the gods of fear and panic—but also Eros and Harmonia—the god of love and the goddess of harmony and concord. Opposites are never far apart.

Fear and panic are inevitable in war, but may also cross love's treacherous path. The goddess of harmony too symbolizes the dialectical unity of opposites, as demonstrated by her fate. Though presiding over marital bliss as well as harmonious action, she had been doomed. For as soon as Aphrodite's husband, Hephaistos, discovered his wife's betrayal with Ares when conceiving Harmonia, he cursed the child with a necklace that condemned her descendants to endless tragedy. (Her Roman counterpart, Concordia, was seemingly luckier: seen as the personification of order—concord—and civic unity, she was revered especially by members of the Senate. But Roman harmony, and with it, the Empire, would soon come to an end as well.)

The Greeks wisely believed that opposites coexisted, earthly creation was subject to constant change, the death of one thing followed by another's rise—a worldview best articulated by the pre-Socratic philosopher Heraclitus, famous for such aphorisms as "war is father of all things" and "one must know that war is common and justice is strife, and that all things happen by strife and necessity."[15] Complete peace, or rest, is unattainable on earth: that is only the province of the Unmoved Mover, or God—a belief that continued to resonate in Christianity. Heaven alone could offer eternal peace. Strife is our lot, only occasionally punctuated by periods of temporary respite. Some of those periods, in fact, feel more like war than peace; cold war perhaps, but hardly restful.

We know all about the Cold War, or think we do. The existential divide that was supposed to have ended in 1989 had been so dubbed by the clairvoyant George Orwell as early as October 1945, when he realized that fellow essayist James Burnham's prediction of a polarized world caused by the intransigence of a state—the USSR—based on totalitarian ideology was dead right. Orwell predicted that such a state would be "in a permanent state of 'Cold War' with its neighbors."[16] Yet few people realize that the idea itself of a non-hot war is anything but new. The honor of coining the term actually belongs to the Spanish prince Don Juan Manuel (1282–1349), an astute diplomat and highly talented, prolific writer, who described the conflict between Christianity and Islam as a "lukewarm war," contrasting it with the essentially redundant "hot war."[17]

Eerily relevant for our times, the prescient analysis by Columbia University professor Anders Stephanson is worth citing in full. As it happens, Prince Manuel

> was part of the long and continuing Christian campaign to reconquer the Iberian peninsula from Islamic power. This struggle featured a wide range of irregular engagements and changing frontiers against the backdrop of a "total" political and cultural conflict between religious ideologies. Don Juan Manuel, reflecting deeply on the nature of the antagonism, is said to have called it a cold war. What his manuscript actually says is probably "tepid" or "lukewarm." The rendition "cold" is the accidental result of erroneous editorial transcription in the 1860s. Yet Don Juan Manuel's image of tepid war is not without relevance in the present context. Real war, he says, has real results in the form of either death or peace. Tepid war, by contrast, is not an honorable war between equal enemies and seems not to result in any real peace. The mistake of his subsequent editor in any case illustrates some of the problems with the metaphorical aspects of the term: the opposite of cold may be hot, in this case signifying open war, but a rising temperature can also indicate a "thaw," as in a warming relationship replacing a frosty, frigid, and unresponsive one. The term indicates, then, the absolute, polar enmity of real war without any real fighting: it is warlike in every sense except, paradoxically, the explicitly military.[18]

Whatever its precise temperature, eventually war should end decisively—or at least decisively enough for the threat of renewed violence to greatly diminish, if not disappear altogether for the foreseeable future. Otherwise, its apparent termination is necessarily ephemeral, nothing more than a truce of undetermined, often quite brief, duration.

Don Juan Manuel recognized the dismal chance that "lukewarm" warfare among adversaries whose ends are irreconcilable is able to accomplish much more than the faint illusion of reconciliation. If the parties are intransigent enough, each will seek total victory over the other—which is seldom possible without apocalyptic clashes. To be sure, war is generally waged by using both lethal and nonlethal power, hot and not so hot. Any lukewarm struggle, however, as Don Juan Manuel correctly noted long before the current War on Terror, is a form of symptom suppression; the disease festers when its causes are left misrepresented and misunderstood. He is right that we should understand the peace-war spectrum as a continuum rather than a dichotomy—not unlike health and disease. In brief, as historian Michael Howard demonstrated in *The Invention of Peace*, "Archaeological, anthropological, as well as all surviving documentary evidence indicates that war, armed conflict between organized political groups, has been the universal norm in human history."[19]

Creating a rigid dualism between war and peace obscures their intertwined nature in an attempt to differentiate the impulse for peace and order from the impulse to violence. Those impulses are indeed engaged in eternal struggle: it has always been thus, and continues to this day. For that very reason, however, their coexistence should not be ignored. Thus the bombing of the World Trade Center on February 26, 1993, and later the simultaneous attacks on American embassies in the capitals of both Kenya and Tanzania on August 8, 1998, though events happening in nominal peacetime, were merely a prelude to 9/11. The war against the West had been "officially" declared by Osama bin Laden in August, 1996, and then again in February, 1998, but it didn't register, the United States still basking in its end-of-history complacency. The difference on 9/11 was not qualitative but quantitative. Similarly, a cyberattack demonstrably originating in a hostile state, such as North Korea, Russia, or Iran, which seriously disrupts infrastructure and endangers lives, lands us squarely (oxymoronically speaking) inside the ever-borderless area between war and peace.

Actually, an overly rigid differentiation is not only unwarranted but dangerous. Nadia Schadlow, former member of the Defense Policy Board, is exactly right:

> By failing to understand that the space between war and peace is not an empty one—but a landscape churning with political, economic, and security competitions that require constant attention—American foreign policy risks being reduced to a reactive and tactical emphasis on the military instrument by default. The final aim of all tactics employed in waging a war is to seriously damage, if not destroy, the adversary. This is clearly what traditional weapons, often described as 'hard,' are all about. But wars, even very hot ones, involve weapons that cannot be described as 'hard.' Unfortunately, we lack adequate terminology to describe those nonlethal counterparts.[20]

Not everyone, however, likes the term "hybrid war," which is used to refer to that "space between war and peace," and many have objected to it as one more source of confusion—and with good reason. Professor Damien Van Puyvelde reports, for example, that "at a recent event sponsored by NATO and organized by the Atlantic Council, attendees were told that 'there is no agreed definition of terms related to hybrid warfare.' In other words, the 28 members of the North Atlantic Alliance cannot agree on a clear definition of what they are facing. How can NATO leaders expect to develop an effective military strategy if they cannot define what they believe is the threat of the day?"[21] Indeed. Puyvelde's "recommendation is that NATO, and other Western decision-makers, should forget about everything 'hybrid' and focus on the specificity and the interconnectedness of the threats they face. Warfare, whether it be ancient or modern, hybrid or not, is always complex and can hardly be subsumed into a single adjective. Any effective strategy should take this complex environment into account and find ways to navigate it without oversimplifying."[22]

He is essentially correct that we probably do not need another word;[23] what we do need is to change our mindset, and not allow words to blind us to the facts. That said, being able to approach war and peace not dialectically, as complete opposites, but as coexisting elements in a complex world, and accepting the ambiguity of a gray zone between the two, can be hard to do without radically changing our vocabulary. Frank Hoffman is right that our enemies will use our words against us; they refuse to comply with our acronyms. Writes Hoffman:

> Hardwired and quaint notions of declared wars between states with symmetrically equipped armies and navies facing each other on

defined battlegrounds are no longer helpful. The US must expand its definitions and concepts beyond its history, cultural biases, and organizational preferences. Ultimately, its security is predicated upon its national security community's being aware of the enduring continuities of war and possessing an adaptive ability to counter the many forms that warfare can take.[24]

This is even more true of peacefare: "The United States faces adversaries capable of using strategies and techniques across the entire conflict spectrum. It must not give ground in Gray Zone [25] conflicts if its interests are challenged." Call those "gray zone" conflicts, cold wars, or hot peace, or lukewarm almost-war (ouch), it's basically a conflict spectrum, requiring what Kennan famously described in 1950 as political warfare, which he defines as

> the employment of all the means at a nation's command, short of war, to achieve its national objectives. Such operations are both overt and covert. They range from such overt actions as political alliances, economic measures, and "white" propaganda to such covert operations as clandestine support of "friendly" foreign elements, "black" psychological warfare and even encouragement of underground resistance in hostile states.[26]

Hoffman rightly points out, however, that Kennan's definition of political warfare is highly misleading, for "his concept has little to do with warfare per se; it is largely about *non-military efforts* associated with subversion or counter-subversion."[27] (We will return to this concept in chapter 11.) But one thing is clear: employing "all means at a nation's command is what some people call "grand strategy.""

You may well ask, what is that? Does the United States have one? And if not, should it? All good questions, deserving answers. But first, let's define "strategy."

Good grief, you say. Surely we don't need a new definition of the term: isn't strategy what football coaches work out during a game? Yet for some strange reason, once we turn away from games to foreign affairs, the word suddenly loses all clarity. J. Boone Bartholomees, Jr., US Army War College professor of military history, laments that "[s]urprisingly for such a significant term, there is no consensus on the definition of strategy even in the national security arena." Perhaps he should have said "especially." He continues: "The military community has an approved definition, but it is not well known and is not accepted by non-military national security professionals."[28] More than one definition, alas, is usually worse than none— especially when its users seem unaware of the differences. Given its critical role in defending the nation, strategy deserves better. So does the nation.

It doesn't help that the term was born with a double birth defect. First, from the outset it had an opaque denotation. Derived from the Greek word for "general"—*strategos*, which is a compound of *stratos* ("spread out" referring to an encamped army *spread out* over ground) and *agein* ("to lead")—it was essentially understood as meaning "the art of the (military) leader." This of course is like saying that art is what artists do, or else that artists are people who produce art: the circularity is logically vicious and doesn't help us distinguish between, say, a Jackson Pollock and a relatively indistinguishable (to a mere philistine, I hasten to add) kindergarten production. Admittedly, generals were thought to be like artists—subject to divine inspiration. For even though good generals, like good football players, are assumed to prevail over their counterparts through skill and practice, in ancient times the gods took much of the credit for men's victories in battle. And no wonder, for even the most astute of mortals could never be sure of military success. But if a good *strategos* is more than just a commander favored by the gods of war, that added quality remains inscrutable.

The second congenital handicap is the term's military pedigree. True enough, in war the strategic (goals of engagement) becomes entwined with the tactical (means to those goals)—hence the two can easily be conflated. They are nevertheless quite distinct: a tactical victory (winning a particular battle) that represents a strategic setback (failing to advance, and even detract from, the ultimate goal) is known as a pyrrhic victory, thus semantically immortalizing King Pyrrhus's short-lived defeat of the Romans at Aesculum, in 279 BC, that would soon be followed by his own. To further muddy the conceptual waters, moreover, in sixth-century Rome, strategy referred to skills that today we would classify as tactical and logistic.

As a result, the conflation persists to this day, arguably in an even more pernicious, virulent strain. As Gray points out, "military history demonstrates a rather consistent tension between the levels or categories of warfare that are understood as the tactical and the operational, let alone the distant abstraction of the strategic."[29] Which doesn't make their confusion and conflation any less exasperating; he explains:

> no military action in the field should be considered inherently strategic, rather is it all within the realm of tactics. This means that any and all such military action requires conversion into the different and higher currency of strategy. Given that all military behavior should be sparked by political intentions, it has to follow that the

use of military force cannot even make tactical sense if the relevant action lacks political meaning or even intelligible purpose or sense.[30]

This is not inscrutable to grasp: every action in any confrontation is ultimately deemed strategic only if it can be translated into its political payoff. It may not be rocket science, but that's just the trouble: it isn't science at all, it's an art.

No wonder it took another twelve hundred years for this ambiguous term, *strategy*, to find its way into Western vernacular languages. Freedman credits the timing of its belated eventual adoption, at the dawn of modernity, to "an Enlightenment optimism that war—like all other spheres of human affairs—could benefit from the application of reason. It also reflected the demands of contemporary warfare, with mass armies and long logistics chains."[31] If only reason, alas, were as powerful a motivator as the sages of that era had optimistically expected. And if only mass armies had been able to deliver the definitive resolution of disputes postulated by some erstwhile reputed theorists of warfare—but they could not. Even the most devastating tactics couldn't simply be converted into strategic success. Reality, as usual, turned out to be a lot messier than political theorists had politically theorized.

A truly astute strategist experienced in the way our world works cannot fail to recognize that victory is impossible to win on battlefields alone: Gray is correct again, as usual. Thus Freedman settles on a definition of strategy as "a comprehensive way to try to pursue political ends, including the threat or actual use of force, in a dialectic of wills."[32] He is here echoing the definition of the celebrated Prussian general Carl Philipp Gottfried von Clausewitz (1780–1831) as "the employment of battles to gain the end of war," noting as obvious that "war is politics by other means." It is the single most widely quoted phrase of his oft-cited magnum opus *On War*.

Unfortunately, despite a widespread impression that it constitutes the very heart and soul of his entire approach to warfare,[33] that is more or less where Clausewitz left the matter. For, as Michael I. Handel, professor of naval strategy at the US Naval War College, points out, although "best known for his ideas on the primacy of politics, [he] actually devotes relatively little space (two out of eight books in *On War*) to the analysis of war on its highest level. The diplomatic or economic environment in which war takes place is just not within the scope of *On War*."[34] Although he seems to have become more interested in revising that approach later in life, Clausewitz died prematurely of cholera. His influence therefore has centered on the other, principal focus of his work, which touts the primacy of force. As Freedman describes it, "Clausewitz was of the view, almost taken for granted in his time, that once the enemy army was defeated, the route to victory was clear." And not just the army; writes Clausewitz: "victory consists not only in the occupation of the battlefield, but in the destruction of the enemy's physical and psychic forces, which is usually not attained until the enemy is pursued after a victorious battle."[35] This approach had an enormous impact on Western military thinking, with rather disastrous consequences.

It was left to the other contender for the prize of the Greatest Strategist of all time to take seriously what is considered the core of what we now call grand strategy. Ironically, he never used the term himself. What is more, he lived four millennia ago—and he was of course Chinese. His name means "Master Tzu"—and a Master he was, his reputation having only grown since his book's arrival on Western shores.

It was very late in landing. First brought to Paris by a Jesuit missionary in 1772 and translated into French, the English-speaking world did not have its first glimpse of *The Art of War* until the distinguished British Museum curator Lionel Giles gave it a try, with limited success, in 1910—evidently not soon enough to have an impact on the World War I. It took the influential twentieth-century British military historian and theorist Sir (also, Captain) Basil H. Lidell Hart, a veteran of World War I, to explain the work's importance: "Sun Tzu's essays on *The Art of War* form the earliest of known treatises on the subject, but have never been surpassed in comprehensiveness and depth of understanding. They might well be termed the concentrated essence of wisdom on the conduct of war."[36] High praise, this. And fully justified.

Having become disenchanted with what he had come to see as Clausewitz's unwarranted overemphasis on decimating one's enemy to achieve victory, Sir Basil was traumatized by the ravages of that apocalyptic world war whose greatness turned out to refer mostly to the number of its victims, and its promise to end all wars a tragic hoax. He became notoriously eager to minimize future casualties of battle, which the uber-mechanization of warfare had turned armed combat into ritualistic butchery on an industrial scale. Presciently, he warned against overlooking the devastating effects of an unjust peace, and was especially leery of a so-called "total victory" that destroys an opponent yet inevitably produces the mere "mirage of victory." Once a war is over, after all, one still has to live with one's neighbors.

Thus mindful of the "peace that must follow war," Sir Basil opted for what he called an *indirect* approach, which is said to have "encouraged a new generation of officers to think in terms of achieving success by surprise and superior mobility; and to make full use of science and technology to minimize casualties."[37] Sir Basil fully credited the Great Master of ancient China with inspiring him in this way of thinking.

Above all, he agreed completely with Sun Tzu's observation that "the profoundest truth of war is that the issue of battle is usually decided in the minds of the opposing commanders, not in the bodies of their men."[38] For that principle to apply, of course, the minds of the commanders should be reached long before a battle breaks out. In the case of Sir Basil, unfortunately, the political leader he directly influenced was Sir Neville Chamberlain, who failed utterly to understand the—admittedly deranged—mind of the commander he was opposing.[39]

It is impossible to overestimate the effect of Sun Tzu on Sir Basil, who goes as far as to suggest that "civilization might have been spared much of the damage suffered in the world wars of [the 20th] century if the influence of Clausewitz. . . . had been blended with and balanced by a knowledge of Sun Tzu. . . ."[40] A greater compliment to a strategic thinker is difficult to imagine. It certainly underscores the lasting impression the Chinese sage had made on the great British theorist who, in turn, influenced a whole slew of Western strategists to this day, and deserves still more.

When he first encountered Sun Tzu, in spring of 1927, Sir Basil reports being struck by the "agelessness of the more fundamental military ideas,"[41] which transcend both time and geography. Without minimizing the difficulty of cross-translation both from one culture to another and one type of language to another, Sir Basil appears to agree with Handel that "there is no such thing as an exclusively 'Western' or 'Eastern' approach to politics and strategy."[42] That said, it is worth noting that prior to Sir Basil's book on *Strategy*, published just after World War II, the systematic study of grand strategy was virtually nonexistent in the West, even as it reigned supreme in China.[43]

The lack of systematic study does not necessarily imply that strategy, even grand strategy, was not in use throughout the ages—just as Moliere's Monsieur Jourdain had indeed been speaking prose (such as it was) all his life, long before he knew (or thought he knew) what the word meant. For that matter, conversely, neither is obsession with a word tantamount to practicing what it denotes. Strategy scholar Hal Brands ironically observes that "strategy" is now all the rage, quite in vogue along the corridors of power, both inside and outside government, with no discernible improvement in either clarity or application. Yet Brands, like Bartholomees, castigates it as "one of the most slippery and widely abused terms in the foreign policy lexicon,"[44] to whom a great deal of lip service has been paid without the requisite respect, or at least articulation, that it deserves.

It certainly cannot be ignored. For like it or not, understand it or not, Brands is right to observe that strategy "inevitably shapes a nation's foreign policy"—meaning, everything from diplomacy to foreign aid to the use of military force. Specifically, grand strategy, its lofty name notwithstanding, is neither more nor less than "the conceptual logic that ensures that such instruments are employed in ways that maximize the benefits for a nation's core interests."[45] Accordingly, "it operates no less in peacetime than in wartime,"[46] which makes its absence keenly felt at all times.

At its simplest and clearest, grand strategy refers to a nation-state's overarching direction. The current sorry state of affairs, unfortunately, follows along a downward spiral that started quite some time ago. Writes William C. Martel, Professor at the Fletcher School of Diplomacy:

> First, the United States has become unmoored from the traditions in its grand strategy, and thus is struggling to define core principles to guide its foreign and domestic policies. Second, the absence of guiding principles has led to policies that lurch from one priority to another, often based primarily upon urgent, short-term concerns rather than on a coherent, long-term strategy of what best serves the nation's overall interests.[47]

What best serves the nation's overall interests, however, cannot be articulated unless those interests are defined and communicated, shared and heartfelt, and based on reality rather than wishful thinking. Long-term planning, moreover, implies constant recalibration of circumstances and assessment of relative balance of power, both military and nonmilitary—which implies recognizing that strategy is no less indispensable in war than in peace.

Though experts will argue about the details, the essence of the concept is simple. Martel puts it most succinctly: "Fundamentally, grand strategy describes a broad consensus on the state's goals and the means by which to put them into practice."[48] Such a consensus does not arise simply by an invisible hand waving a magic wand; it takes leadership. Admittedly, in a democracy it is ultimately the people who are responsible for the leaders they want—which means that they end up getting the leaders they deserve. The current lack of any coherence in the conduct of foreign policy is not merely the fault of a clueless administration; it is evidence of a nation adrift.

That lack of coherence has been especially calamitous in the case of the Middle East, which most observers agree is descending into chaos with increasing rapidity. As virtually every country in that benighted region, from Libya to Afghanistan, is involved in some military conflict, one is hard pressed to disagree with the assessment of former Clinton aide David Rothkopf that the situation there is "unprecedented." Strictly for reference purposes, in the interest of accuracy, he notes that the "technical foreign-policy term for this is [sic] cluster-fuck."[49]

This is not all, or even primarily, the fault of the United States, as he readily admits. That said, we Americans bear our share of the blame. Rothkopf's verdict is scathing:

> The biggest culprit is strategic incoherence. We don't seem to have a clear view of our interests or a vision for the future of the region fostered in collaboration with our allies there and elsewhere. 'Leave it to the folks on the ground' is no more a U.S. foreign-policy strategy than is 'don't do stupid shit.' It is a modality at best and in fact, it is really an abrogation of responsibility when so many of these relationships do have trade, investment, political, military, and other elements that give the United States leverage that it could and should use to advance its interests.

The abrogation of responsibility is, obviously, not only to the region, but to the American people.

Admittedly, most Americans do not appreciate the full implications of their nation's predicament. To some extent, it's because ordinary folk would rather not be bothered with foreign policy: why else elect representatives in Washington? It's their job to figure it out what to do, after all. Moreover, pursuing happiness is so much more enjoyable than is worrying about how to preserve the right to do so. Wars in faraway places that are not perceived as affecting Americans in their everyday lives usually fail to interest John Q. Public. This is not only understandable but in some ways also felicitous, considering most ordinary citizens' notable, and noted, ignorance of all history, including, most alarmingly, their own. A generally complacent attitude toward the outside world, however, comes at a price.

It has been and will likely continue to be an awfully high price, in lives lost and treasure wasted. If revisiting the Grand Master of ancient China can help us recalibrate our compass, the journey will have been eminently worthwhile. Sun Tzu offers a refreshing alternative approach to key, perennial national security issues; it just might jump-start the currently sclerotic debate in America to a new—or is it old?—level.

Notes

1. Proto-Indo-European is the ancestor of the Indo-European language family, and is based on historical linguists' knowledge of the vocabularies and structures of many subsequent languages. This family comprises several hundred languages, ranging from modern English all the way back to ancient Sanskrit, including everything from Celtic to Iranian in between.
2. Gray, *The Future of Strategy*, xii.
3. Paul K. Chappell, *The Art of Waging Peace: A Strategic Approach to Improving Our Lives and the World* (Westport, CT: Prospecta Press), 19.
4. Ibid., 18.
5. Adda Bozeman, "War and the Clash of Ideas," *Orbis*, Spring 1976.
6. Hugo Grotius, *The Law of War and Peace: De jure belli ac pacis* (New York: Classics Club, 1949), Book III, Chap. 21, 1.
7. Bozeman, "War and the Clash of Ideas."
8. Immanuel Kant, *Perpetual Peace: A Philosophical Sketch*, First Supplement, "Of the Guarantee for Perpetual Peace," https://www.mtholyoke.edu/acad/intrel/kant/firsTzup.htm (Emphasis added).
9. Frederick Rauscher, "Kant's Social and Political Philosophy," *The Stanford Encyclopedia of Philosophy* (Summer 2012 Edition), ed. Edward N. Zalta. http://plato.stanford.edu/archives/sum2012/entries/kant-social-political/
10. Cited by John Gittings, in *The Glorious Art of Peace: From the Iliad to Iraq* (Oxford: Oxford University Press, 2012), 128. Gittings, however, points out that "in fact, the title to Kant's essay comes not from an inn-sign but from the Abbe de Saint-Pierre's *Project*." See note 10, 266.
11. This dichotomy deserves a much fuller discussion, to avoid the impression that Islam as a whole is at root essentially intolerant, which would be quite misleading, but this is not the place for it—any more than would a conversation about the relative toleration for disagreement implicit in any other religious creed or culture.
12. George F. Kennan, "Peaceful Coexistence: A Western View," *Foreign Affairs*, January 1960. http://www.foreignaffairs.com/articles/71531/george-f-kennan/peaceful-coexistence
13. "It is widely acknowledged that Peace Studies have a well-informed bias, for which they have been widely criticized. . . . ." Randall Amster, Laura Finley, Edmund Pries, eds., *Peace Studies between Tradition and Innovation* (Cambridge: Cambridge Scholars Publishing, 2015), 211.
14. Eirene was especially well regarded by the citizens of Athens, who established a cult for her after their victory over Sparta in 375 BC, and held an annual state sacrifice to her to commemorate the peace treaty known as Koine Eirene ("Common Peace"), invented in 387 BC, which declared peace

between all the combatants in a war. Before that, peace treaties in Greece were ephemeral, with a specific expiration date, and were concluded between two combatants only. Although the Koine Eirene too did not last long, at least it was tried.

15. http://www.philosophy.gr/presocratics/heraclitus.htm
16. George Orwell, "You and the Atomic Bomb," London Tribune, October 19, 1945. http://orwell.ru/library/articles/ABomb/english/e_abomb
17. Anders Stephanson, "Cold War Origins," Encyclopedia of American Foreign Policy, 2002. http://www.encyclopedia.com/doc/1G2-3402300027.html
18. Ibid.
19. Michael Howard, The Invention of Peace: Reflections on War and International Order (New Haven, CT: Yale University Press, 2001), 1.
20. Nadia Schadlow, "Peace and War: The Space Between," War on the Rocks, August 18, 2014. http://warontherocks.com/2014/08/peace-and-war-the-space-between/
21. Damien Van Puyvelde, "Hybrid War – Does it Even Exist?," Nato Review Magazine, May 2015. http://www.nato.int/docu/review/2015/Also-in-2015/hybrid-modern-future-warfare-russia-ukraine/EN/
22. Ibid.
23. There is no shortage of related, if not synonymous, terminology: "in the history of warfare we have seen similar activities under various terms, including for example nonlinear operations, low-intensity conflict, full spectrum conflict, political warfare, unconventional warfare, irregular warfare, asymmetric warfare, and unrestricted warfare. Nevertheless, it is important to keep in mind that the art of war is developing all the time and we often encounter new mutations or rehashes of previously well-known doctrinal approaches." Aapo Cederberg and Pasi Eronen, "How can Societies be Defended against Hybrid Threats?" Geneva Centre for Security Policy (GCSP), September 2015.
24. Frank Hoffman, "The Contemporary Spectrum of Conflict Protracted, Gray Zone, Ambiguous, and Hybrid Modes of War," 2016 Index of U.S. Military Strength: Assessing America's Ability to Provide for the Common Defense (Washington, DC: The Heritage Foundation, 2016), 32.
25. This term appears in the 2010 Quadrennial Defense Review (QDR) and has also been reflected in official Japanese government documents. See U.S. Department of Defense, Quadrennial Defense Review Report, February 2010, 73. http://www.defense.gov/QDR/QDR%20as%20of%2029JAN10%201600.pdf. Japanese Ministry of Defense, Defense of Japan 2010 (Annual White Paper), 61, http://www.mod.go.jp/e/publ/w_paper/2010.html
26. For Kennan's policy memo promoting this initiative under the auspices of the State Department, see "Policy Staff Planning Memorandum," May 4, 1948. http://academic.brooklyn.cuny.edu/history/johnson/65ciafounding3.htm
27. Hoffman, The Contemporary Spectrum of Conflict. 29-30.
28. J. Boone Bartholomees, Jr., "A Survey of the Theory of Strategy," in Theory of War and Strategy, 4th ed., Strategic Studies Institute, July 2010, Vol. 1, Ch. 2, 13.
29. Colin Gray, Tactical Operations for Strategic Effect: The Challenge of Currency Conversion (Tampa, FL: Joint Special Operations University, 2015), 14.

30. Ibid., 1.

31. Bartholomees, "A Survey of the Theory of Strategy."

32. Laurence Freedman, *Strategy: A History* (Oxford: Oxford University Press, 2013), xii.

33. James R. Holmes, in an aptly-titled article "Everything You Know about Clausewitz is Wrong," points out that the phrase 'war is the continuation of policy by other means' was actually mistranslated: "by" should have been "with rendered as "with." Here's the difference: "Declaring that war is a mere continuation of policy 'by' other means implies that diplomatic, economic, and ideological interaction between the combatants screeches to a halt when the shooting starts. Statesmen set nonviolent policy implements aside while armies, navies, and air forces batter away at one another. . . . Pursuing political objectives 'with' other means connotes adding a new implement—namely armed force—to a mix of diplomatic, economic, and informational implements rather than dropping them to pick up the sword. War operates under a distinctive martial grammar, in other words, but the logic of policy remains in charge even after combat is joined. In this Clausewitzian view, strategic competition falls somewhere along a continuum from peacetime diplomacy to high-end armed conflict. The divide between war and peace can get blurry." *The Diplomat*, November 12, 2014. http://thediplomat.com/2014/11/everything-you-know-about-clausewitz-is-wrong/ In either case, Clausewitz did not elaborate further on the continuity of war and peace; while he spelled out a plan for doing it and revising his book, it was "a task that, alas, he never lived to complete."

34. Michael I. Handel writes that "Clausewitz, who is best known for his ideas on the primacy of politics, actually devotes relatively little space (two out of eight books in *On War*) to the analysis of war on its highest level." *Matters of War: Classical Strategic Thought* (London: Frank Cass Publishers, 2006), 35.

35. "Clausewitz, unfinished note, presumably written in 1830," in Carl Clausewitz, *On War*, edited and translated by Michael Howard and Peter Paret (Princeton, NJ: Princeton University Press, 1992), 31.

36. B. H. Lidell Hart, foreword to *Sun Tzu - The Art of War*, trans. Samuel Griffith (Oxford: Oxford University Press, 1963), v.

37. Brian Bond, *Lidell-Hart: A Study of His Military Thought* (New Brunswick, NJ: Rutgers University Press, 1977), 51.

38. B. H. Lidell Hart, ed., William T. Sherman, *From Atlanta to the Sea* (London: The Folio Society, 1961), 14–15.

39. "Some of Lidell Hart's more compelling statements seemed to be hauntingly echoed in the personal letters of Chamberlain to his sisters at the very commencement of the conflict." Robert J. Caputi, *Neville Chamberlain and Appeasement* (London: Associated University Presses, 2000), 118.

40. Lidell Hart, Foreword to *Sun Tzu*, Ibid.

41. Ibid., vii.

42. Handel, *Matters of War*, 3.

43. Derek M. C. Yuen, *Deciphering Sun Tzu: How to Read*, The Art of War (Oxford: Oxford University Press, 2015), 128–33.

44. Hal Brands, *The Promise and Pitfalls of Grand Strategy*, Strategic Studies Institute, August 2012, 1.
45. Ibid., 4.
46. Ibid., 6.
47. William C. Martel, p. 331.
48. William C. Martel, Grand Strategy in Theory and Practice: The Need for an Effective American Foreign Policy (Cambridge University Press, 2015), 339.
49. David Rothkopf, "Operation Charlie Foxtrot," *Foreign Policy*, March 27, 2015. http://foreignpolicy.com/2015/03/27/-charlie-foxtrot-middle-east-yemen-syria-saudi-obama/

I

Sun Tzu's Acme of Skill

*The ancient Chinese sage approached the world with trust in the supreme power of the mind to navigate the storms of life, provided it can learn to follow, rather than seek to abolish, the powerful waves that stop for no one. Adversity and ambiguity, antagonism and contradiction, are intrinsic to change and unavoidable: as night follows day, nature embraces opposites in the service of a greater harmony. Sun Tzu trusted that knowing about the ways of the world would help work **with** it rather than against it, which is doomed to fail.*

Knowledge, however, is far more than a set of data. Above all, human beings must grasp what motivates their friends and enemies, learning to decipher the mysteries of the mind and heart despite a wide variety of cultural and physical obstacles to communication. Besides geographical, demographic, and other kinds of hard information, most important is an understanding of motivations and interests. Otherwise, it is impossible to design effective means of confronting enemies and preventing violence.

Sun Tzu opposed violence above all because it constitutes the most intrusive intervention in the natural course of events. An astute leader could prevent bloodshed by outwitting an opponent bent on conquest, using cunning and adapting to changing circumstances. A strategy predicated on following the natural tendency (tzu jan) of each situation and using it to advantage seemed most pragmatic as well moral.

The astute leader therefore should be not only shrewd, well informed, and intuitive, but moral, there being no conflict between ethics and pragmatism. His power is inseparable from his ability to work with others—in that sense, he must be a team leader, whose task is to inspire the energies of all the people under his charge. A national leader must know how to energize the entire community, enabling it to survive in a complex world.

1

Opposites Detract

'In pace, ut sapiens, aptarit idonea bello.'
In peace, as a wise man, he should make suitable preparation for war.
—Horace, *Satires* Book ii, 30 BC

Ambiguity is not, today, [caused by] a lack of data, but a deluge of data.
—Paul Gibbons, *The Science of Successful Organization*, 2014

We want peace, but we study war.
—Irving Louis Horowitz, *The Idea of War and Peace*, 1957

Who would have imagined, back in 521 BC, that several millennia later, *The Art of War* would become an international runaway bestseller? Eventually rediscovered on every continent, it is breezily cited, if not necessarily read from cover to cover, even in the nation least inclined to revere anything older than itself—modern-day America. This improbably popular slim volume has been translated into just about every language, its aphorisms appealing to political scientists and military officers as much as to salesmen and entrepreneurs, self-help gurus, and ordinary unsuspecting folks who like its aphorisms without being quite sure why. Perhaps the most celebrated how-to manual of all time, Sun Tzu's military guidebook continues to be a publisher's dream. The seemingly self-evident aphorisms resonate, taunting the reader with the feeling—accurate, as it happens—that there is more, much more, behind their bumper-sticker wisdom. Writes Colin Gray: "This short work is far more subtle than it appears to be in its presentation-like form. While concentrating in the main on generalship, it does have much of value to say about political statecraft."[1]

For that reason and more, the little book's relevance is only growing, notwithstanding the great distance from us in both time and space. Born during the so-called Spring and Autumn Period (around 771–476 BC) in Chinese history, Sun Tzu had been witness to massive changes in technology and geopolitics. In the early days of that period, pitched battles were uncommon; "deterrence and diplomacy, rather than warfare, were often the preferred means to fulfill a ruler's goals."[2] But that was soon to change. Wars migrated south, where rivers were plentiful, leading to new types of terrain that now required water transport and fleets. Far more complex joint operations included infantry, chariots, and fleets; war became more protracted and increasingly violent, necessitating radically new approaches to both war and peace. Conscription was introduced, and armies became much larger. Military rituals that characterized earlier, milder confrontations, were giving way to a deception-based approach. Unsurprisingly, as the stakes rose and the danger of massive bloodshed increased exponentially, so did the importance of outwitting the adversary. Though far less apocalyptic in scope than today's weapons of mass annihilation, even in Sun Tzu's time, "war had become a dangerous business; the recourse when other means had failed."[3]

But Sun Tzu recoiled against overreliance on sheer hardware and army size. Should violence be unavoidable, even the most lethal weapons cannot deliver specific desired outcomes in the absence of astute, targeted, well-thought-out plans. Though primarily a military manual, his *Art of War* underscores the importance of strategic communication, political influence, intelligence and information operations, not to mention cultural acumen—in brief, the spectrum of assets, both physical and psychological, required to defend the nation's interests and values. The nonlethal tools, moreover, are deemed indispensable at all times: before as much as during the course of military engagement, and certainly in the aftermath.

His approach is deeply pragmatic. Though hard weapons can annihilate the enemy, only a wise strategy, shrewdly executed, against a well-understood enemy, can define victory, and eventually secure it. Military measures could be compared to surgery: they are ideal if what is needed is excising a tumor. That said, a preferable course is preventing the tumor's growth in the first place; by the time surgery must be performed, the disease is usually advanced. Not to mention that after surgery, there is convalescence and additional therapy—measures that in a foreign-policy context may be called, for lack of a better word, *soft* weapons.

But they are *soft* only by contrast with the lethal *hard-ware* that blows things up or otherwise destroys, sometimes indiscriminately, often causing unwelcome collateral damage. In no way does Sun Tzu imply that "soft" weapons are somehow second-best; on the contrary, the violent variety has many drawbacks. For example, even when they reach their intended targets, hard weapons tend to boomerang in unexpectedly catastrophic ways. These include killing and maiming innocent civilians who are either caught in the crossfires or deliberately planted by cynical enemies, and destroying the property of innocent people, thereby unhelpfully alienating them. Thus tactical success may be undermined by greater, strategic failure. In many ways, so-called soft weapons are actually much *harder:* more difficult to wield, their success less immediately obvious. Also, their effectiveness is invariably less tangible than blowing up a city or fortress. Least obvious is what soft weapons achieve by preventing something from happening; and nonevents make non-headlines. Yet it is usually soft, rather than hard, instruments of power that ultimately end conflicts, that win the peace after either having prevailed in, or succeeded in deterring, battlefield engagements.

What matters to Sun Tzu is the human personality, which he takes seriously as central to understanding conflict—an emphasis nearly absent in today's techno-centric conversation. He believed that nothing surpasses the need to understand both one's enemy and oneself, assessing realistically and without illusions the full dimensions of a volatile situation. Indeed, there are no shortcuts: the whole conflict environment—physical and human, the entire spectrum of relevant factors—had to be grasped astutely and realistically. No starry-eyed idealist, Sun Tzu took it as a given that life is perpetual strife, that winning battles is ephemeral, and that war and peace are not so much opposites as steps along the hard road of survival. His best-known mantra—that the acme of a general's skill, and the highest goal of a true strategist, is *to win without firing a shot*—has resonated through the millennia. It is as true today as ever.

There are no quick and decisive solutions to conflict when the world is always teetering on the verge of war when not right in the middle of it. The notion of a "solution" is itself misleading: all we can hope to accomplish is mitigate the ever-present dangers that lurk into the background in a dauntingly complicated environment. To go Donald Rumsfeld one better, besides the known unknowns and the unknown unknowns, there are, dauntingly, the *unknowable* unknowns. And if that weren't bad enough, the entire conflict environment—including the knowns, the unknowns, and the unknowable—is constantly changing. Sun Tzu had understood that taking the challenge head-on means fully embracing its complexity, always mindful of opportunities to prevail in a fluid setting.

His pithy aphorisms, however, cannot alone reveal fully his underlying, fascinating worldview that differs from our own in ways that are very much worth exploring. Imprecise translations, due in part to linguistic ambiguities, and insufficient understanding of ancient Chinese philosophy generally, have prevented a deeper appreciation by Western readers of his sophisticated work. We thus owe a debt of gratitude to the groundbreaking new book by Professor Derek M. D. Yuen, *Deciphering Sun Tzu: How to Read the Art of War*, written under the tutelage of the brilliant Colin Gray at Reading University, where Yuen received his doctorate. Chinese-born, Yuen also benefited from consultation with fellow Chinese scholars at Hong Kong University, where he teaches. For the first time in two and a half millennia, Yuen's careful study offers English-speaking audiences the opportunity to explore more fully the insights of the world's most astute strategist. Not a moment too soon.

But, the American reader may well ask, isn't Sun Tzu approach likely to be too Chinese? The short answer is: actually, no. Yuen agrees with scholars Michael Handel, Laurence Freedman, and many others that good strategy is not determined by either culture or geography: considerable differences in tactics notwithstanding, there isn't a "Western" or an "Eastern" art of strategy. So while Chinese strategic thinking follows patterns different from those commonly accepted in the West, the wise course would be to blend the two approaches.

In the first place, both system of thought may be described as dialectical, in the sense that both make use of concepts that are opposites in meaning. *Dialectics* (from *dia*, "through," and *legein*, "speak"), refers to a conversation or *dialogue*, usually meant to arrive at some conclusion that reconciles two opposing perspectives, with one proposition followed by another challenging it. The most common way of interpreting dialectics in the Western world is the Aristotelian, based on classical logic, whose most fundamental principle is the law of noncontradiction. In its simplest form, that law states that A and not-A cancel each other out—or, put differently, their juxtaposition always yields a necessarily false statement or contradiction.[4] Accordingly, A and not-A cannot both be true; a possible resolution might state that A is true except when (fill in the blank), in which case it is not-A. For example: "All swans are white except when the color gene mutates, and then some swans turn out a different color. So not (quite) all swans are white."

Another form of Western logic is so-called Hegelian dialectics, after the German philosopher Georg Wilhelm Friedrich Hegel (1770–1831), who applied the concepts of "thesis" and "antithesis" beyond discourse to the material world. To oversimplify a bit (the only alternative to long years of study, preferably in the original German), Hegel's view is as follows: nature and history could be imagined as a sequence of ideas, such that an event, which may be described as a "thesis," confronts another event that may be called an "antithesis," which in turn "negates"—or opposes—the thesis. (A true metaphysical idealist, Hegel tended to conflate reality and the language used to describe it.) And as thesis and antithesis occur in the world simultaneously, they lead to conflict whose resolution entails the annihilation of both. The previous example of "most swans are white" is therefore not as useful an illustration of synthesis as, say, an oxygen molecule colliding with two molecules of hydrogen to yield an entirely new substance—water.

The Marxist application of Hegelian dialectics to history considers the opposing classes that coexist at any historical stage (e.g., feudalism) as a thesis opposing an antithesis, whose inevitably clashing synthesis ushers in an entirely new historical stage—for example, capitalism— which then repeats the process, with the proletariat and bourgeoisie becoming the next thesis and antithesis. The eventual culmination of all history, when it ends with an epic secular finale, is the classless society of humans liberated from property and therefore from all greed—which is viewed as the root of all evil/war/inequality/etc., QED.

What Aristotelian and Hegelian logic do share is the assumption that contraries cannot coexist: whether in a conversation or in the real world (which is at least mirrored in, even if not coextensive with, language), contradiction must be eliminated. Yuen calls this methodological approach "aggressive"—an apt description, as the Marxist application vividly illustrates. In contrast, Chinese *yin-yang* logic is predicated on the world being "at once interconnected, interpenetrating, and interdependent in an uninterrupted manner, [as] the polarity of the situation essentially rests in [the *yin-yang* continuum]."[5] According to this mindset, opposites are not destroyed but persist. By analogy, when autumn follows summer, although leaves die, something lives on, which reappears in the spring: or, to put it differently, every slice of reality consists of opposites. (Think negative and positive charges coexisting inside a molecule; simultaneous attraction and repulsion to a unique object, within the same breast; new cells emerging as dead cells are eliminated.) This type of dialectic, which Yuen calls "holistic," helps explain

31

why "Chinese strategic thought is not military-centered, or at least it is far less military-centered than its Western counterpart."[6] Reality, in Chinese strategic thought, one might say, is intrinsically Janus-faced. Thus hard and soft aspects must be addressed simultaneously, difficult as that sounds—and is.

Another way of distinguishing between Western and Chinese thinking patterns is by describing the former as *causal-linear* and the latter as *cyclical-evolutionary*. The scientific, linear method generally relies on seeking causal relationships that are repeatable, quantifiable, and simplified. The holistic approach, on the other hand, is irredeemably complex, taking all the related factors as contributing to the *evolution* of motion and reality, such that one state may precede another without necessarily being assumed to have literally, let alone solely, *caused* the latter. The evolutionary mindset presupposes the coexistence of apparent contraries without expecting a resolution (at least not any time soon) and without fear of paradox. On the face of it, imagining someone being both friend and foe, or a menacing outburst of anger being accompanied by soothing psychological relief, is not difficult. But holistic dialectic represents a much more all-encompassing habit of mind, predicated on the ability to entertain mutually incompatible or complementary perspectives, and a willingness to be both intellectually and psychologically nimble. That is considerably harder.

Contradiction, paradox, and opposition are notoriously unsettling to the Western mind. The result is a pervasive cultural inability—certainly a reluctance—to embrace the uncertainties, ambiguities, and inherent messiness of the world, specifically the human world of flawed reasoning, rationalized emotions, apparently irrational behavior, and the irksome constant change that defines every society. This near-phobia of ambiguity was clear to social philosopher Irving Louis Horowitz, who explains in *The Idea of War and Peace: The Experience of Western Civilization:*

> The 'dialectical' scheme of human nature, called society, must put aside the idea that either the *anarch* [anarchy—total individual freedom] or the *behemoth* [leviathan state—no individual freedom] can long survive without the other. For the most part, as an optimum outcome, we live in the public space between war and peace, much as we live our private lives between love and hate.[7]

Accordingly, his choice of the thinkers whose ideas on war and peace he proceeds to analyze in his book is based on their grasp of complexity.

Horowitz commends their having "wrestled with the devil of war and worshipped the god of peace—but they knew full well that the[se] giant concepts, like the world itself, were locked in mortal combat."[8]

"Mortal" might not apply to feuds among the deities, saintly or satanic, but what about us humans? Describing the struggle between opposites in such dramatic language captures that aspect of the Western mindset which abhors combat while worshiping peace. Thus unreconciled to eternal strife, however, the pacifist is doomed. Indeed, if the true nature of reality is tumultuous, we have only two choices. We can acquiesce to the confrontation as desirable, as is the lovers' life-giving embrace, or the pangs of birth that precede all creation, and excruciating death which yet morphs into life. Conversely, we can seek to obliterate change and might convince ourselves that we can define it away. Western *hubris*, unfortunately, seems partial to the latter. In truth, all utopias seek to obliterate differences while worshiping consensus, and consider complete harmony to be not merely possible but preordained. In secular utopias like Nazism and Communism, the price of non-dissent is unflinching monologue, whose disruption is forbidden on pain of annihilation. Religious totalitarianisms subordinate this world to the next, but with equally drastic penalty for noncompliance.

There are many good reasons for separating religion from politics. The medieval Christian philosopher (later, Saint) Thomas Aquinas (1225–1274), for example, advised mankind to turn away from this messy world and its passions, to seek peace in prayer, charity, and the afterlife, letting Cesar be Cesar and have as little to do with him as possible. This world cannot hope to escape strife given human nature as it is, rather than as it should be; doing so can only lead to dangerous utopianism. For this reason, Horowitz commends the Thomist approach spelled out by economic historian John U. Nef: "Let us not hoodwink ourselves with notions of perpetual peace and of the millennium. These only increase the danger of war, for they rest on a misunderstanding of human nature."[9] Misunderstanding human nature is ineluctably fatal, as is the conceit that it may be altered by changing economic and other structural circumstances. Horowitz observes that "the values of peace are not divorced from the social, economic, and cultural goals of mankind."[10] Sun Tzu would heartily agree.

It is no coincidence that the very governments determined to obliterate pluralism and rendering it obsolete, allegedly in the "interest of the people" and the ideal of world harmony, pose the greatest threats to world peace today—notably, Communist North Korea, Islamist Iran, Putin's neo-Communist Russia, and the nondemocratic People's Republic of China. They all proclaim allegiance to universal salvation and peace; it is the common rhetorical currency perpetrated by all cynical dictators, whose bank accounts are invariably exceeded in size only by their elephantine egos. Interestingly, while these are not Western countries, their state ideology certainly is, Marxism no less than Nazism constituting a legitimate, if bastardly, offspring of European thought. The same may be said of modern-day Islamism, whose debt to Hitler's fascism and Stalin's KGB has been copiously documented by Middle East scholar Laurent Murawiec in *The Mind of Jihad*.[11] It is unfortunate that a more tolerant strand of Islam failed to prevail over its virulent strain that currently infects both Shiia and Sunni sects, threatening us all with extinction if left unchecked.

Leaving aside the irreconcilably bellophobe,[12] whether by temperament or ideology, too many remain who are gullible enough to be too easily seduced by rhetoric. Many of those who consider the abolition of war as tantamount to the eradication of greed-and-profit believe that dialogue among enemies, however sworn they may be, will help abolish war. It is this mindset that helped create the United Nations (admittedly, with some help from Moscow's agents who had ascended to the highest rung of President Franklin Delano Roosevelt's administration[13]), and other international organizations putatively dedicated to fine ideals that their subsequent performance, unsurprisingly, belied. (The relentless harassment of Israel is but one, if perhaps the most egregious, example of that grossly overestimated organization's deeply rooted hypocrisy.) As if there wasn't already plenty of evidence for the sinister end that dooms even the finest intentions fashioned from wishful thinking, Horowitz observes that the period after the end of World War II "has demonstrated that human beings can construct agencies dedicated to world peace, but also pollute such agencies into instruments for further strife—racial religious, national, ethnic, you name it."[14]

What if the other approach were adopted to address the reality of conflict and, taking a deep breath, acknowledge its necessity? Like the human organism, like it or not, the body politic cannot avoid attacks on its well-being. Horowitz helpfully uses the medical metaphor that I too favor, noting that while we all seek to be healthy, we all get sick and eventually die. But this doesn't mean that along the way we cannot try to stay as healthy as we can to make the intervening journey as rewarding as possible.

Transferring the analogy to the world, we might say that global peace too is achievable, given the right habits. But even what looks like health is but a prelude to the final demise. Cells die every day even as others are born; leukocytes destroy countless intruding microorganisms; precancerous and even cancerous cells are discarded; the list goes on. Similarly, the inorganic world is subject to constant erosions and transformations: tsunamis, earthquakes, volcanoes, abound. It is obvious that no matter how much we may advance in our knowledge of the world we can never find "cures" to everything that can harm us. The same goes for the human world: envy, ignorance, and just plain evil will continue to take their toll. That said, we can and must work with what we have, to try to minimize pain and maximize well-being.

The lesson is simple enough: let not the mirage of creating eternal peace in our lifetime blind us to the need to understand, and address, the necessary conflicts of the world as it is, not as it should be. And let's not assume that the "aggressive" dialectic of life is *ipso facto* bad: some peace is not worth dying for—certainly not the peace of silence and slavery. The main advantage of a holistic approach characteristic of Sun Tzu and his contemporaries, notably Lao Tzu and the other Taoists, is that it enables a more open attitude toward flux and complexity, which is reflected in their attitude toward strategic engagement and hence more promising as methodology.

That methodology leads to specific practical advice. Here is how Sun Tzu makes use of opposites to illustrate how to confront and undermine enemies: "If they are angry, perturb them; be deferential to foster their arrogance. If they are rested, force them to exert themselves. If they are united, cause them to be separated" (*AoW* I. 22–3). In other words, if they are irritated, bother them further; indulge them in their dangerous hubris so they'll make mistakes; if they are relaxed and thus not ready to act, goad them on. *The Art of War* is replete with pairs of contraries: enemy-friend; peace-war; win-lose; life-death, advance-retreat; strength-weakness; attack-defense; move-stop; fear-courage; hungry-full; and so on, almost ad nauseam. These pairs, Yuen explains, are used to describe any situation to help strategists embrace the always-changing environment and stretch their imaginations, opening their thinking to nontraditional tactics, simultaneously encompassing, intellectually and psychologically, the full complexity of the human terrain.

While the reasoning behind this approach seems counterintuitive, it is altogether logical, arguably more appropriate than is plain linear thinking to understand irrationality, encourage self-defeating behavior in the adversary, and exploit his potential weaknesses to prompt a tip-over. Writes Yuen:

> For Sun Tzu and the Taoists, assisting the natural tendency is always preferable to opposing it as everything carries within itself its own seeds of destruction when it overextends, in much the same way as yin-yang works.[15]

On a more general level, in the Tao philosophy to which Sun Tzu's thinking belongs, "natural tendency" is also known as "natural pro-pensity" and "inevitable result," and applies to everything in nature.

> Should you want to contain something, you must deliberately let it expand.
>
> Should you want to weaken something, you must deliberately let it grow strong.
>
> Should you want to eliminate something, you must deliberately allow it to flourish.
>
> Should you want to take something away, you must deliberately grant it.
>
> This is called illumination. (*Tao Te Ching*, ch. 36).[16]

Though some of the flavor of these aphorisms falls by the wayside in translation, their message is fairly simple: a particular goal may require short-term measures that appear to go counter to the ultimate end, but on closer examination it will take us there—just as an induced coma can allow a patient's body to confront the trauma it suffered by letting some of its organs rest and heal. So too, many drug-addiction victims report that only once they "hit bottom" are they sufficiently motivated to do what it takes to go "clean." And so forth—examples abound. The key to the Taoist approach is how to think out of the proverbial box by asking first: What seemingly paradoxical measures that might look like the opposite of what is sought will in fact lead us precisely to where we want to be?

What can make all the difference, especially in a difficult and complex confrontation, is ingenuity. That is Sun Tzu's, and the Taoists', secret weapon. It is also ours. But ingenuity will not succeed unless we take very seriously nature as it is, not as we want it to be. David never deluded himself about Goliath's strength, nor about his own. He did estimate correctly that Goliath would be unprepared for David's unexpected form of attack, reacting with confusion, which proved his undoing. David won against Goliath not because he was so much stronger, but because he knew where Goliath was weak.[17]

The mind is notoriously susceptible to mystifying complexity, to paradox and ambiguity, to unrelenting contradiction. Operating in the realm of psychology requires being comfortable with embracing opposites rather than seeking to obliterate them. Any meaningful human relationship can only be sustained if it manages to accommodate divergent personality traits and values. So too in global affairs. The ability of the Taoists "to draw on contrary means of achieving a goal, providing them with an advantage and additional methods for dealing with complex situations,"[18] is what Yuen believes "marks a real breakthrough in the realm of strategy as it denotes a complete break from the means-end rational framework that is at the heart of modern [Western view of] war and strategy."[19]

Sun Tzu's approach happily challenges linear thinking. This includes not only embracing opposites but looking for the unexpected, for the seemingly unrelated event. Causality is always multifaceted: challenges pop up from the most unlikely corners.

The limitations of linear thinking have long been appreciated best by advocates of "red teaming," notably former CIA Assistant Director Mark Lowenstein, who writes that

> [t]he Intelligence Community should train analysts in how to avoid or to compensate for linear thinking. Yogi Berra captured this when he said, "The future will be like the past, only different." Analysts need to look for discontinuities, if only as an intellectual exercise. They need constantly to be asking "What if?" questions so they can be alert to the nonlinear event when it happens, or so they can ask why it does not happen. The Arab Spring is the most recent example. What about "China stumbles"—instead of "China rising"? If nothing else, it is an elegant mind-stretching exercise.[20]

And there is one other, normative aspect to the linear, means-end rational framework: being straightforward; it is deemed virtuous. Being direct, or "straight," is considered preferable: isn't the shortest distance between two points the proverbial line? It follows then, does it not, that if we want to destroy an enemy, we set upon building the strongest weapons, which is simple and direct. But think again: it might actually be better to try turning his friends and supporters against him, or letting him destroy himself.

To be sure, there is much to be said for "fighting fair," cards on the table; but what if our enemies scoff at our scruples? On another level, suppose we want to handicap an enemy, before he has had a chance to do us more mischief, and decide to harm his reputation. Do we then say things about him publicly, which is more honorable than doing it behind his back? Or might it not be even more effective to simply catch him in situations where he does something embarrassing, without much prompting (though not, perhaps, entirely by chance)? Specific tactics do not have to be inherently immoral—it is indeed far better if they are not. But all these methods of dealing with an enemy fall under the category usually translated as "deception"—and they are by no means without merit.

Deception is a tactic of choice especially when seeking to prevail in situations where violence seems imminent. Sun Tzu's declaration that "war is deception" actually constitutes a departure from a tradition of military confrontation that had just preceded him, dating from the early Autumn and Spring Period, of honor-bound ritual of battle-ground conflict, governed by predetermined rules. A ritualistic tradition would become practice in Western Europe many centuries later, only to be once again repudiated in irregular or guerilla warfare. While ungentlemanly, deception is often very useful, even indispensable, in an especially rough, no-holds-barred confrontation. It is key to victory in modern warfare, and to winning the peace with the least amount of bloodshed, as it can facilitate defeating an adversary by averting battle. The United States has certainly engaged in deceptive practices, much as it often hates to admit it, though not always effectively.

Whatever the merits of Clausewitz as one of the great strategic thinkers of all time, the fact that he all but dismisses the importance of deception in war must be counted as a major blind spot. He advocates instead the concentration of superior force at the decisive point in a war, on the ground that "plans and orders issued for appearances only, fake reports designed to confuse the enemy, etc.—have as a rule so little strategic value that they are used only if a read-made opportunity presents itself."[21] How the great Prussian general could have failed to appreciate the immense value of deception is simply mystifying. The tragic consequences of that failure cannot be overestimated. Focusing on defeating an enemy's army through massive, straightforward attacks, while ignoring the subtler nonmilitary instruments of statecraft, lie at the heart of the West's inability to adapt to the current complex environment.

In truth, "deception" is a very approximate and inadequate translation of the ancient word *gui*, which lies at the heart of Chinese strategic thinking. By no means does it refer merely to lying, or issuing deliberately inaccurate or false orders. For example, when *gui* is coupled with *dao* ("the way"), as in *gui dao*, meaning "the way of deception," it can also mean "strange," "anomalous," even "paradoxical." The point about using a deceptive tactic in the Taoist sense is not to lie, which in any case can be short-sighted and self-defeating, but to turn to the unusual and the unexpected, in a word, rely on the *counterintuitive*. While this tactic is less effective when used in state-against-state contests that test technological prowess in the battlefield, it is ideal in the increasingly common "wars amongst the people," to use British Major General Sir Rupert Anthony Smith's term for what has variously been described as asymmetric, low-intensity, irregular, nonconventional, and guerilla warfare.[22] In the latter case, in fact, it is usually indispensable.

That said, effectiveness, albeit important, is essentially a tactical matter; the main import of Sun Tzu's approach is strategic. For, unlike his relatively myopic Western counterparts, the ancient Master looked beyond the end of battle to the establishment of peace, and was particularly concerned about what *kind* of peace follows conflict. One of the unintended consequences of military success, after all, is the inability of civilian populations to return to their previous lives with infrastructure destroyed, food scarce, and souls scarred. Violence is always to some extent "unnatural"; it amounts to a major, often cataclysmic, interference. A society continues to bleed and stays vulnerable long after the scalpel of war has stopped cutting into its flesh.

Accordingly, one of the main reasons for doing everything else first, such as engaging in deception, before engaging in frontal attack, is to try to go with the flow, following as much as possible the natural course of events. As Yuen puts it, "one of the foremost tasks of a strategist is to limit any action/interference so as to prevent negative unintended consequences from arising and to eliminate any chance that they will lead to a reversal of the tide."[23] It is certainly not preferable to be truthful yet end up killing people, including one's own along with the enemy, when a sly detour would derail the opponent's plans and achieve victory with less bloodshed and greater efficiency. Put differently, deception is a mighty weapon for peace and can greatly minimize violence if artfully wielded. Not that avoiding violence is always a good in itself; neither is deception legitimate if used to undermine a legitimate system of government that serves its constituents ably. But that goes without saying.

It is hardly a secret that the principal enemies of Western liberalism—Communism and Islamism—both happen to embrace the practice of deception in ways that make it awkward for gullible Westerners to confront. During the Cold War, for example the USSR's secret police, the KGB, devoted enormous resources to engaging in what it called "active measures" (Активные мероприятия), which were deception operations against the West. These "measures" were deemed legitimate by its practitioners, since their goal was merely to hasten the demise of rotten capitalism—an eventuality Marxism-Leninism considered historically inevitable.

While never entirely abandoned, these activities have recently reemerged in Russia, with a vengeance.[24] Its current dictator, the seasoned former KGB officer Vladimir Putin, continues to find the old ways as relevant and handy as ever. Speaking before a closed audience at the Russian Academy of Military Sciences in late 2013, the Chief of the General Staff of the Russian Armed Forces General Valery Gerasimov captured the essence of would become "Russian nonlinear military doctrine in 2014 known as the 'Gerasimov Doctrine' . . . [which asserts that] nonmililtary means have surpassed the use of force to achieve strategic and political goals."[25] In a new study released by NATO known as the Munich Security Report, NATO's Commander General Philip M. Breedlove explains that "what we see in Russia now in this hybrid approach to war is to use all of the tools that they have [. . .] to reach into a nation and cause instability, use their energy tools, use their finance tools, use what I think is probably the most amazing information warfare blitzkrieg we have ever seen in the history of informational warfare, using all these tools to stir up problems that they can then begin to exploit with their military tool. . . ."[26]

Similarly, Islamism practices what it calls *taqiyya* (a literal Arabic translation of "deception"), which is deemed "of fundamental importance in Islam. Practically every Islamic sect agrees to it and practices it. . . . *Taqiyya* is very prevalent in Islamic politics, especially in the modern era"[27] and is specifically sanctioned by the Quran for use against non-Muslim states. It is also becoming increasingly obvious that a combination of active measures and Taoist *gui* is at the heart of current Chinese "stratagem."[28] Further improved as a result of KGB training,[29] *taqiyya* tactics are not to be underestimated.

Just as the Communist "perpetual Revolution" against Western capitalism is in effect until the dictatorship of the proletariat is complete, so do the Muslim faithful define the "realm of peace" (*Dar al Islam*) as everywhere that "true" Islam prevails, as against "the realm of war" (*Dar al Harb*), populated by the infidel. Similarly, just as Marx believed that the end of history would render all struggle obsolete, so the Quran declares that war against the nonbelievers (which includes allegedly pseudo-Muslims, deemed apostates) must go on in perpetuity until "all chaos ceases and all religion belongs to Allah." (*Quran* 8.39)

Both totalitarian ideologies—Communist and Islamist—consider that the current global state of affairs is essentially evil, yet both subscribe to a version of determinism that is incompatible with ethics as such. Communism, based on materialist determinism, simultaneously postulates that history progresses through necessity and punishes anyone who doesn't march along with that history. But justification is meaningless if history marches inevitably: where that leaves personal responsibility is, basically, nowhere. So too, radical Islamism holds that Allah controls everything that happens, yet also expects His followers to punish those who disobey Him. (What constitutes disobedience, of course, is as subject to interpretation by the elite in Islamist as in Communist countries.)

Determinism is a cheap way around moral justification. It happens to be incompatible with a tactic of deception, which assumes that man has to nudge history along, but that presupposes respect for reason. Deception evidently plays a useful role when outright annihilation of the infidel is inconvenient: the end justifies the means, which sums up the morality of every form of totalitarianism. The bottom line with both monist totalitarian worldviews is that deception is but another tool alongside violence against everything that stands in the way of their complete, allegedly preordained victory. This couldn't be farther from the approach of both Sun Tzu and the liberal West.

Though deception is a universal practice, the major difference between, on the one hand, Western states and, on the other, both totalitarian states and organizations whose ideologies are predicated on the abolition of pluralism, is that the latter consider themselves to be in a constant, necessarily adversarial situation with everyone else at all times. The apocalyptic ideologies engage in all forms of conflict, but especially deception, routinely until they prevail. The West, by contrast, considers deception a highly anomalous tactic, designed for specific, limited goals, having used it primarily, even if not exclusively, during armed combat (Greece having taken notorious advantage of Troy's inexplicable trust in the adage "Never look a gift horse in the mouth").

During World War II, for instance, a slew of ingenious schemes (e.g., Operation Mincemeat, Operation Overlord, etc.) were carried out by brilliant and courageous people. And deception is a standard warfare tactic of the US military: *The Department of Defense (DOD) Dictionary of Military Terms* defines means of deception as "[m]ethods, resources, and techniques that can be used to convey information to the deception target." This is unsurprising. Were any nation to dispense with tactical deception, it may as well capitulate from the get-go. What makes active measures and *taqiyya* different is their widespread use during periods when there appear to be no signs of "war" in the traditional Western sense of a detectable physical threat, but is only defined by the mere *existence* of different systems of political, economic, and social life. In short, such systems are defined by their totalitarian opponents as intrinsically bellicose. Like it or not, we do not have the luxury of not being at war with them: for they are at war with us.

Interestingly, both *taqiyya* and the Russian use of deception have recently found an echo in Chinese military doctrine—specifically by Colonels Qiao Liang and Wang Xiangsui. Victor J. Morris, a civilian contractor who teaches at the US Army Europe's Joint Multinational Readiness Center in Germany, writes that "[t]he 'Gerasimov Doctrine' contains particular similarities to the Chinese doctrine outlined in *Unrestricted Warfare*, published in 1999, and historical roots in previous Russian doctrine. Both strategies involve using proxies or surrogates to not only exploit vulnerabilities in low intensity conflict, but to also prepare for future operations that may involve high intensity conflict."[30] While the core similarity between the Russian and Chinese doctrine involves destabilization and exploitation of vulnerabilities, other states, as well as non-state actors, have adopted this multifaceted, nonlinear strategy. Continues Morris: "Although this type of warfare is not new, contemporary threat actors are redefining the application by employing 21st century technologies and combinations of diplomatic, intelligence, militaristic, economic, and humanitarian means, and in various domains that are overlapped by cyberspace."[31]

Morris seeks to explain the difference between traditional and nontraditional tactics by contrasting linear with "nonlinear warfare [which] directly or indirectly employs nonmilitary and military instruments through the following means: diplomats, intelligence agencies, professional soldiers, special operations forces, insurgents, guerillas, extremist groups, mercenaries, and criminals."[32] What he omits to point out is that these instruments should not be employed only during a full-scale war as traditionally understood. That is the whole point of setting these apart as "nontraditional" warfare.

We thus find ourselves back in the ancient Taoist mindset of nonlinear logic and the mysterious yet incontrovertible cycle of opposites, of *ying* and *yang* in a strategic context, a fluid view of natural evolution, of reaching one's objectives through all the means possible, and taking advantage of an adversary's weaknesses. To be and yet simultaneously not to be is not a question; it is a condition of change. But to survive change and even emerge stronger, we must have adequate intelligence— which means information, and more.

Notes

1. Colin S. Gray, *The Future of Strategy* (Cambridge: Polity Books, 2015), 119.
2. Mi Zhen-yu, ed., *Histoy of Chinese Military Scholarship*, Vol. 1 (Bejing: People's Liberation Army Publishing House, 2008), 92. Cited in Derek M. D. Yuen, *Deciphering Sun Tzu: How to Read The Art of War* (Oxford: Oxford University Press, 2014), 56.
3. Samuel B. Griffith, trans., *Sun Tzu - The Art of War* (Oxford: Oxford University Press, 1982), 9.
4. So if true that "The President lives in Washington," "The President doesn't live in Washington" is false. Schematically, this looks this way: If "A is B" is true, then "A is not B" is false.
5. Yuen, *Deciphering Sun Tzu*, 16.
6. Ibid., 36–38.
7. Irving Louis Horowitz, *The Idea of War and Peace: The Experience of Western Civilization* (New Brunswick, NJ: Transaction Publishers, 2007), ix.
8. Ibid.
9. John U. Neff, *War and Human Progress* (Cambridge: Cambridge University Press, 1950), 416. Cited in Horowitz, ibid., 41.
10. Ibid., 48.
11. Laurent Murawiec, *The Mind of Jihad* (Cambridge: Cambridge University Press, 2007).
12. "War-hater." Chris Aldrich, *The Aldrich Dictionary of Phobias and Other Word Families* (Bloomington, IN: Trafford Publishing, 2002), 225.
13. M. Stanton Evans and Herbert Romerstein, *Stalin's Secret Agents: The Subversion of Roosevelt's Government* (New York: Simon & Schuster, Threshold Editions, 2012).
14. Ibid., viii.
15. Yuen, *Deciphering Sun Tzu*, 74
16. Ibid., 75.
17. For a fascinating take on that biblical conflict, see Malcolm Gladwell's *David and Goliath: Underdogs, Misfits, and the Art of Battling Giants* (New York: Little, Brown & Co., 2013), "Introduction."
18. Yuen, *Deciphering Sun Tzu*, 77.
19. Ibid., 74.
20. Mark M. Lowenthal, "Intelligence Education: Quo Vadimus?," in *American Intelligence Journal* 31, no. 2 (2013): 10.

21. Clausewitz, *On War*, 89.
22. Rupert Smith, *The Utility of Force: The Art of War in the Modern World* (New York: Vintage, 2008), xiii.
23. Yuen, *Deciphering Sun Tzu*, 95.
24. Peter Pomeranetz and Michael Weiss, *The Menace of Unreality: How the Kremlin Weaponizes Information, Culture and Money* (New York: Institute of Modern Russia, 2014).
25. Victor R. Morris, "Grading Gerasimov: Evaluating Russian Nonlinear Warfare through Modern Chinese Doctrine," *The Pendulum*, May 14, 2015. https://medium.com/@Doctrine_Man/grading-gerasimov-8089ea595851
26. "Hybrid Warfare: Who is Ready?" *Munich Security Report 2015* (Munich, 2015), 34.
27. Raymond Ibrahim, "Islam's Doctrines of Deception," *Middle East Forum*, October 2008.
28. Michael Pillsbury, *The Hundred-Year Marathon: China's Secret Strategy to Replace America as the Global Superpower* (New York: Henry Holt and Co., 2015).
29. Murawiec, *The Mind of Jihad*, esp. 307 ff.
30. Morris, Ibid.
31. Ibid.
32. Ibid.

2

The Art of Information

Sun Tzu . . . is considered by many to be the first "information warrior."
Therefore, it is the fate of the intelligence professionals to know and
understand the adversary's capabilities, limitations, and intent.
—Leigh Armistead, *Information Operations and*
the Hard Reality of Soft Power, 2004

All fact-collectors, who have no aim beyond their facts, are
one-story men. Two-story men compare, reason, generalize,
using the labors of the fact-collectors as well as their own.
—Oliver Wendell Holmes, Sr., *The Poet at the Breakfast Table,* 1872

Ex nihilo, nihilo est: From nothing, nothing comes. Nothing cannot even be imagined—synonyms such as "absence," "chaos," "void," "vacuum," and "before-something" aren't much help. In the Abrahamic tradition, God solves the logical dilemma: He just **is** the Infinite, the One Who Is Beyond Both Space and Time, and He is not supposed to be imaginable. With time comes change, metamorphosis, imperfection, death. The philosophers who conversed more than twenty-five centuries ago in Athens similarly considered all change a sort of imperfection. By contrast, they glorified the Eternal, Unchanging, Unmoved Mover who stays the same even as His creations are born and die, living in convulsions of agony and ecstasy, until they return to dust once again, replaced by equally ephemeral progeny.

According to this narrative, which became dominant in the West, the saga of man is a checkered and spasmodic affair, at once dazzling and terrifying. Humanity spans the spectrum, as men prove capable of unspeakable cruelty, but also complete devotion and self-sacrifice, stunning creativity, and scientific insight. The Great Ukrainian Famine, the theory of relativity, the Holocaust, the Internet—each is but a moment along an oscillating trajectory that conforms to no linear or any other geometric pattern. Collapse follows splendor, terror precedes birth; sometimes they all intertwine, coiled around the space-time continuum. Like an ouroboros—a serpent consuming its own flesh, only to regenerate once again like a new limb—chaos turns into harmony, then cacophony, which still manages to reemerge as prayer-perfect plainsong. The war/peace cycle tantalizes both mind and heart, in perpetual, oscillating recurrence.

If war in its traditional sense of mutual human butchering has been described as chaotic, so have other types of disorder, such as plagues. What distinguishes the two types of disaster—at least from a standard secular perspective—is that, while nature is expected to proceed blindly, morally speaking, human perpetrators are supposed to be endowed with a modicum of reason and choice. In truth, all of nature has its measure of mystery, and man himself is beastly, his reason failing more often than not, even when his moral compass is comparatively sound. But whether caused by *Homo sapiens* or not, chaos is at least partly mitigated by knowing as much as possible about the relevant environment. Just as seismic data helps predict the size and location of earthquakes, so does timely and thorough intelligence concerning the context of a human-propelled conflict.

To translate this in political terms, if conflict is to be prevented with any degree of success, the decision of where and when to start assessing a baseline is critical. All the relevant factors must be included to be sure that the response to a potential danger is adequate. In the words of Sun Tzu, the first step involves a reckoning, a calculation, an "appreciation of the situation:" the title of his first chapter is "Initial Estimates." That appreciation needs to begin at a point in time that is distant enough to allow the appropriate considerations to be included, but not so distant as to render calculation unwieldy. But unless the preengagement assessment is made logically and carefully, the enterprise is doomed from the outset. The potentially war-festering "situation" is like the stem of a weed whose roots rest in the soil of history: to be eradicated, it must be extracted in its totality, lest it be simply dried to extinction. Ruled out is the option of thinking it harmless, or bound to die of natural causes.

Once the starting point has been determined, at least preliminarily, Sun Tzu tells us that the assessment or estimate of any situation of impending crisis includes five elements: "the first of these factors is moral influence; the second, weather; the third, terrain, the fourth, command; and the fifth, doctrine (or, 'law,' 'method,' 'art.')" (*AoW* I, 3).

Moral influence is defined as "that which causes the people to be in harmony with their leaders, so that they will accompany them unto death without fear of mortal peril" (*AoW* I. 4.). Today, this critical function would be considered central to the mission of public diplomacy and strategic communication. A nation's policies can never be guaranteed unanimous support, either at home or abroad, but an effective effort to spell out those policies and seeking to justify their adoption is highly recommended. When people are in harmony with their leaders, even if not asked to sacrifice their lives, they are less likely to sabotage the national course of action.

Next, the geographical realities—including weather and natural resources, arable land, potable water, and access to navigation—must be assessed so as to have adequate information about one's own and others' strengths and weaknesses. Notice how much of this is what we would call "open source" rather than secret "classified" intelligence. That said, even such relatively hard facts as geographical data have a critical human component. The same informational resources in the hands of a kleptocracy bent on squandering it for personal use will render a nation helpless before a sturdy enemy, as compared with another with fewer such resources but a unified, resilient population with a dedicated and committed leadership.

That falls under the rubric of *command* and *doctrine*, the other two elements Sun Tzu states must be included in compiling a thorough "initial assessment" of a situation under analysis from a national security perspective. Though true *command* refers to "the qualities of wisdom, sincerity, humanity, courage, and strictness" (*AoW* I. 7) as necessary in military leaders, the same is implicitly true of civilian leaders. A nation whose leadership is ruthless and oppressive, whose command is devoid of the virtues mentioned by Sun Tzu, is especially vulnerable. For if the needs and desires of the population are irrelevant to the action of their so-called presidents, kings, or Supreme Leaders, the nation is bound to be threatened from within. So too, cowardly leadership might be reluctant or even unwilling to engage in offensive actions abroad, which is equally dangerous for the population at large.

Finally, *doctrine* refers to "organization, control, assignment of appropriate ranks" (*AoW* I. 8) and similar matters related to state institutions and efficiency. Even a benevolent leadership, popularly elected and well-intentioned toward the people, will fail in the absence of viable state structures necessary for governance and without the rule of law. In assessing whether a society is able to sustain itself or is vulnerable and might become a failed state, perhaps on the verge of revolution or sheer chaos, this kind of information is critical. In sum, good intelligence must take all of these factors into consideration before any kind of engagement is contemplated and planned.

In many ways, information is like money and good looks: you can never have enough. Though on second thought, too much money can sap self-sufficiency, good looks lead to vanity, and data overload paralyzes analysis. But still the adage, often attributed to Francis Bacon (1561–1626), that "knowledge is power" reminds one of Sholom Alecheim's poor peddler Tevye citing Scripture to validate some tautology. Only keep in mind that knowledge, intelligence, information, and data are not synonymous. You can have a lot of data and still be clueless about the world.

Both data and information are usually considered best if unfiltered, that is, untainted by messy prejudices and personal foibles. Bad enough that we are all plagued, as a species, by the inevitable epistemological and psycho-neuro-biological quirks that all but confirm the medieval distrust of the senses, which were believed to have doomed fallen man— to say nothing of woman. If the medieval sinner genuflected before the inscrutable Almighty, his modern offspring substituted the false deity of Pure Fact of Transparent Reality, distrusting treacherously imprecise impressions and mere instinct. Excited to use his new electronic toys that make it possible to do "crowd sourcing," for example, modern man (and, why deny it, woman) unwittingly, certainly witlessly, thereby shuns an old asset whose reputation should never have been allowed to sink so low: subjectivity. Some call it "the human factor."

Sun Tzu knew that "[k]nowledge of the enemy's dispositions can only be obtained from other men" (*AoW* XIII. 6). Obviously, no one could possibly deny the importance of intelligence, and of obtaining as much information as possible about an opponent, above all his "dispositions" or intentions. But as Derek Yuen points out, what Sun Tzu is talking about is considerably more complex. The Chinese word for the kind of knowledge that he advocates is *ch'i*: "Though intangible, *ch'i* and mind constitute the 'information' or 'intelligence' that Sun Tzu deems most important"[1] for national security. Understanding the enemy's psychological and spiritual inner essence is the knowledge most worth having. It is also the most elusive—with the notable exception of the possibly more elusive knowledge of oneself.

Knowing oneself is not to be confused with finding oneself—an obsession often associated with the infamous one percent, whom it afflicts disproportionately in late adolescence or after a costly divorce. Rather, Sun Tzu is referring to being in control of oneself, staying composed and realistically aware of one's strengths as well as weaknesses, and using cultural intelligence to compare one's own mindset with that of the enemy. Referring to the last chapter of *The Art of War*, entitled "Employing Spies," Yuen clarifies: "Although Sun Tzu identifies various forms of intelligence, he places a particular emphasis on cultural intelligence in war," adding that "good intelligence alone is still not enough to avoid being 'endangered in a hundred engagements.' But 'know thy self and know thy enemy' [*AoW* III. 18] will prevent this. The line that points to the real meaning of this maxim does not appear until Chapter 7 [of *The Art of War*]: 'That *ch'i* [i.e., morale, spirit, energy, etc.] . . . can be snatched away, the commanding general's mind can be seized.'"[2]

Seizing the enemy commander's mind—meaning, foiling his plans or denying him control over his actions—is principally what is meant by *knowing* him. Hardly a common interpretation of that word, the idea is central to the sophisticated, though not inscrutable, philosophical system of Taoism. "Preserving one's *ch'i* [spirit] is what is meant by 'knowing yourself.'"[3] In this context, "preserving" implies preventing someone else's snatching it away; thus "knowing oneself" implies keeping control over one's actions and thereby not allowing the enemy to prevail over—in some sense, "snatching"—one's spirit, and hence one's self.

Knowing "oneself," especially when applied to an entire community, requires a considerable amount of targeted, deliberate effort. Sun Tzu's concept of *hsing*, variously translated as "shape," "form," "appearance," or most commonly, "disposition" (which, we learn, "connotes more than physical dispositions"[4]), focuses on both the reality and the appearance of one's own strength. Sun Tzu observes, for example: "Anciently, the skillful warriors first made themselves invincible and awaited the enemy's moment of vulnerability" (*AoW* IV. 1). Making oneself invincible is something that must happen regardless of whether or not an attack is contemplated or anticipated; it is the indispensable prerequisite of waging peace. When Sun Tzu says that *invincibility lies in the defense*, he intimates that it refers to a potentiality, a mode of being: one who is said to be *invincible* is fully prepared for an attack (*AoW* IV. 5). But being prepared in no way implies that one should attack; on the contrary, the enemy should not be taken on before he is a clear and present danger, as well as vulnerable. Invincibility is a necessary, but not sufficient condition for prevailing against an adversary; there is still the need to wait for the right moment.

Evidently, then, invincibility, contrary to the word's common connotation, does not refer exclusively to the ability to conquer in any attack. We can make ourselves exceptionally invincible yet still have no control over our enemies. Invincibility, as Sun Tzu uses it, refers strictly to one's own abilities, without implying relative advantage over an enemy. This is a crucial distinction: for the actual outcome of a confrontation depends not only on one's strength, and the awareness of that strength, but on knowing how to (along with being able to) use it effectively. "Therefore it is said that one may know how to win; but cannot necessarily do so" (*AoW* IV. 4.).

With that caveat, let's now focus on the importance of not only becoming the best but also knowing how to project that strength, internally as well as externally. A nation may in fact be exceptionally powerful in relation to its potential enemies, yet not know it. Conversely, it may imagine itself stronger or at least more effective than it really is. Many a Goliath nation has been undone by a more agile, nimble, and clever David. The secret is to possess a realistic understanding of one's powers, and use them to best advantage. Only then can one become invincible in the sense of being actually unvanquished—preferably, if deterrence works as planned, dispensing with the bloody proof.

Intrinsic to invincibility is building a civic consciousness, cultivating a love of country, and pursuing common values. That too is an art, and should not be confused with crass propaganda of the kind perfected by totalitarian dictators. Rooted in a healthy civil society, it connotes respect for the individual. Sun Tzu described the moral dimension of (national) reputation in terms of *cultivating the Tao (AoW* IV. 15), which is further explicated by the ninth-century commentator Tu Mu as "the way of humanity and justice." A people must "first cultivate their own humanity and justice and maintain their laws and institutions. By these means they make their governments invincible."[5] This central element of ancient Chinese thought, of an unmistakably liberal bent, is critical to a solid understanding of the Art of Peace.

Despite the unfamiliar metaphysical language, which demands additional explanation and exegesis, it is very clear that Sun Tzu places enormous importance on psychological factors, on the need to understand the inner workings of the mind and soul. When he talks about "knowing," whether oneself or another, he refers to "interpreting and evaluating the intentions, traits, and thought patterns of the enemy as well as the mental condition of an opponent's troops. As with many of Sun Tzu's other maxims, this again highlights the way in which Sun Tzu viewed war as a mind game, where attacking the enemy's mind is vastly more preferable to other forms of offence."[6] Meanwhile, one's own mind must stay the course, staying "invincible" and focused.

The unduly neglected, nonmilitary component of intelligence that relates to strategy renders the ancient Chinese approach to conflict particularly relevant to our own challenges today. For while technology has advanced with breathtaking rapidity, man's nature has barely evolved: the same primeval fears and desires move our species now as they did our ancestors millennia ago. True, we have far better means of communication, more scientific and presumably more sophisticated ways of probing the brain to access the workings of the mind (if admittedly not of the soul), and avenues of engagement have proliferated beyond count. In principle at least, it ought to be easier to penetrate one another's cultures.

Ideally, however, that should take place not only at a superficial level and only when danger lurks; for if we are to grasp the inner workings of our adversaries' minds, intuit their motivations, and react effectively, we cannot wing it or do it on the fly. This was no news to ancient Chinese strategic thinkers like Li Ching, who noted that a decision to attack our enemies "does not stop with just attacking their cities or attacking their formations. One must have techniques for attacking their minds." The same, he continues, goes for "defense [which] does not end with just the completion of the walls and the realization of sold [solid?] formations. One must also preserve spirit and be prepared to await the enemy."[7] Preparing to "await" the enemy is one of those techniques. It does not imply a preference for passivity. Rather, it refers to allowing time for the enemy to reveal his vulnerabilities, so as to be exploited most effectively.

In stark contrast, Clausewitz advised destroying rather than getting to know one's enemy, which he deemed ineffectual. The noted American strategist who had become a Sun Tzu disciple, Colonel John Boyd (1927–1997), a much admired US Air Force fighter pilot and Pentagon advisor, explained the difference between these two giants of strategic thought in disarmingly plain English: "Sun Tzu tried to drive his adversary bananas while Clausewitz tried to keep himself from being driven bananas."[8] Of course, Sun Tzu advocated both—for he thought them inextricably intertwined. Clausewitz, as far as we can tell, succeeded in staying sane; the same cannot be said of everyone who adopted his losers-lose-all view of victory.

How well Boyd was able to catch the deeper essence of *The Art of War* is especially remarkable given his lack of familiarity with the Taoist context of that ancient work. As Yuen explains, Boyd sought to bring back "intuitive thinking and judgment to the framework of Western strategy."[9] Specifically, he stressed the crucial role of what he called *orientation*, which "shapes the way we observe, the way we decide, the way we act."[10] Writes Boyd:

> Orientation is an interactive process of many-sided implicit cross-referencing projections, empathies, correlations, and rejections that is shaped by the interplay of genetic heritage, cultural tradition, previous experiences, and unfolding circumstances.[11]

In other words, much of this process is unconscious. Boyd's remarkably trans-rational, though in no way antirational, approach to information is spot-on in the tradition of Sun Tzu.

Another way of describing that approach is by comparing it to pattern recognition. Boyd understood that in intelligence analysis the most important asset is not the amount of data available but the analyst's capacity for intuiting patterns, through what he calls "judgment"—an insight confirmed by contemporary research in cognitive psychology. One of Boyd's most astute interpreters, Air Commodore Frans Osinga, identifies the common theme found in both Sun Tzu's and Boyd's approach to knowledge as emanating "not from the attainment of absolute certainty, but from the formation of a correct interpretation of the situation. . . . Without judgment, data means nothing. . . . Moreover, it is judgment of highly dynamic situation."[12]

In a fascinating section on the possible influence of Chinese writing on Sun Tzu's thinking, Yuen stresses its pictorial character, which is far more conducive to innovative visual modeling and analogous thought. Unlike European languages, which are based on categories or sets reflected in alphabetically constructed words, Chinese is able to exploit the rich complexity of image and connotation. This observation deserves very serious attention, and is worth additional exploration for the purpose of expanding our ability to synthesize and think "out of the box." Because pictorial communication is especially well-suited to analogical and flexible thinking, it may be more amenable to capturing evolution and novelty, and less encumbered by preexisting divisions that we humans impose upon the world in an attempt to detect regularities where none exists. This is an especially important consideration given that cognitive conceptualization is a complex neurological process that involves a blend of visual, auditory, and other dimensions. (I hasten to add that any similarity between Chinese pictorial visualization and PowerPoint graphics is not even coincidental. The latter has proved more likely to stunt than enhance creativity.[13])

Though alphabetical writing has many advantages, the pictorial method facilitates a much more holistic, intuitive understanding of patterns. The ability to form a judgment of the evolving environment each of us confronts in the real world is not a mystical quality. It is enhanced by extensive experience, which further hones the ability to adapt one's presuppositions and prejudgments to actual fact, and should raise respect for complexity. Complexity, in turn, underscores the need for humility, which comes from appreciating each individual's insignificance before the unfathomable, infinite universe. We cannot be reminded often enough of the dangers posed by the ever-present temptation of *hubris*.

Notes

1. Yuen, *Deciphering Sun Tzu*, 111.
2. Ibid.
3. Ibid., from "Questions and Replies," in *The Seven Military Classics*, trans. Ralph Sawyer, 353. Yuen undertakes a brilliant explanation of the profound significance of these ancient Chinese treatises which are still all but unknown in the West.
4. Griffith, *Sun Tzu - The Art of War*, 85.
5. Griffith, *Sun Tzu - The Art of War*, 88.
6. Yuen, *Deciphering Sun Tzu*, 112.
7. Ibid., 113.
8. Robert Coram, *Boyd: The Fighter Pilot Who Changed the Art of War* (New York: Hachette Book Group, 2002), 332.
9. Yuen, *Deciphering Sun Tzu*, 146.
10. John Boyd, *Organic Design for Command and Control*, unpublished manuscript, 1987, 26.
11. Ibid., 15.
12. Frans P. B. Osinga, *Science, Strategy and War: The Strategic Theory of John Boyd* (New York: Routledge, 2007), 36–37.
13. Harvey Wallbanger, "The Case Against PowerPoint," *The Atlantic*, January 28, 2010. http://www.theatlantic.com/business/archive/2010/01/the-case-against-powerpoint/34429/ and Elisabeth Bumiller, "We Have Met the Enemy and He Is PowerPoint," *The New York Times*, April 26, 2010. http://www.nytimes.com/2010/04/27/world/27powerpoint.html

3

Shaking the Invisible Hand

It is best to do things systematically, Since we are
only human, and disorder is our worst enemy.
—Hesiod, *Works and Days,* ca. 700 BC

Adapt or perish, now as ever, is Nature's inexorable imperative.
—H. G. Wells, *Mind at the End of Its Tether,* 1945

Our patience will achieve more than our force.
—Edmund Burke, *Reflections on the Revolution in France,* 1790

No longer do we tremble before Zeus when we hear thunder. In truth, even in the fifth century BC, Plato and his disciples dismissed stories of capricious divine escapades as mere fairy tales designed for popular consumption. Both he and his more empirically minded student Aristotle put their trust in the Prime Unmoved Mover, who in time morphed seamlessly into the universal Father. Whether lovingly parental or ineffably detached, the Western mind conceived of Him and His Hand as orderly and rational, even if not always comprehended by the imperfect faculties of lowly mortals. Faith in the divine harmony of the universe, however, did not exclude disorder and tragedy, not long absent from most lives. What did result was a growing confidence in man's ability to discern, aided by reason, the laws of nature—implicitly trusted to be both optimally efficient and morally pristine.

Thus emerged the Invisible Hand, which Scottish philosopher Adam Smith, in his seminal (though sadly no longer very well-known) *Theory of Moral Sentiments,* credits with organizing human affairs felicitously, notwithstanding our species' infamous flaws. Though he did not coin the term, Smith gave it a new and vitally important function: he noticed how the rich "are led by an invisible hand to make nearly the same distribution of the necessaries of life, which would have been made, had the earth been divided into equal portions among all its inhabitants, and thus without intending it, without knowing it, advance the interest of the society. . . ."[1] Smith would later expand this insight into *The Wealth of Nations,* published the same year as the document that launched the political experiment designed to prove him right: the American Declaration of Independence.

Smith's trust in the Invisible Hand (henceforth capitalized here) never implied that human beings are even subconsciously altruistic. From simple observation, he found people to be basically selfish, seldom ruled by their reason. Yet the best overall outcome from their myriad trans-actions emerges almost miraculously: providential order transcends individual predilections. This would not have surprised Austrian-born Nobel Prize winning economist F. A. Hayek (1899–1992), who argued, in *The Constitution of Liberty,*[2] that since no human mind could grasp all the facts required to decide what is best for everyone, it seems far more efficient to allow each person to decide what is best for himself, allowing the "general good" to emerge from the blend of innumerable individual goods. Perhaps even more to the point, a mere mortal would have to be not only infinitely wise, as well as powerful, but morally omniscient—qualities no one could claim without incurring the charge of delusion, blasphemy, or both.

But engaging in social experiments has always been too tempt-ing, especially after the Scientific Revolution exacerbated what the Greeks had long identified as mankind's fatal flaw of "hubris." Called "pride" by Christians and "chutzpah" by Jews, the sin of playing God has repeatedly led mankind to interfere visibly in all manner of ways, supposedly for some desirable end, only to make matters worse. In foreign affairs, this flaw has caused all manner of disasters. We ignore the complexity of the universe, the ubiquity of chance, the unexpected unintended consequences of our actions, the intricacies of the human heart, including our own, at everyone's peril. But rationality invariably loses to nonrational and even irrational forces. Nowhere is this more obvious than in the history of warfare.

It certainly seemed that way to one of the premier students of the subject, British military historian Sir John Keegan, who declared him-self impressed by the evidence that war is manifestly abhorrent: "War, it seems to me, after a lifetime of reading about the subject, mingling with men of war, visiting the sites of war, and observing its effects, may well be ceasing to commend itself to human beings as a desirable or productive, let alone rational, means of reconciling their discontents."[3] One can only wonder, though, what gave Sir John the idea that war has typically been waged rationally. Perhaps he spent too much time with his fellow Oxbridge-educated men of war, and too little with the likes of Mao Tze Tung and Osama Bin Laden. But no one can object to his abhorrence of violence as the best means of settling disputes.

He had a staunch ally in the author of *The Art of War*. The book famously starts off with a warning to leave no stone unturned and reconsider many times over before deciding to take the momentous step of officially declaring the commencement of a state of belligerence: "War is of vital importance to the state, the province of life and death, the road to survival or ruin. It is mandatory that it be thoroughly studied" (*AoW* I. 1). Undoubtedly in agreement with his disciple Li Ch'ing's addition that "weapons are tools of ill omen," Sun Tzu consistently underscores the importance of avoiding violence and bloodshed if at all possible. No other treatise on war presumes as self-evident the proposition that the best victory is achieved without firing a shot.

Mark McNeilly, a former US Army captain and a Sun Tzu devotee, acknowledges how surprising it is for a military treatise to warn against battles: "One may think that this is a ridiculous proposition."[4] Yet McNeilly commends Sun Tzu for advising not to resort to warfare unless and until it is absolutely necessary, and only after having exhausted all other (non-hard) weapons, attacking adversaries by "political, economic, psychological, and moral means prior to resorting to military efforts."[5] And in his own work, McNeilly highlights especially the moral superiority of avoiding bloodshed.

But in a larger context, ancient Chinese thinking assumes the choice of nonlethal means for attaining victory is preferable not only on pragmatic and moral grounds but, no less important, for strategic purposes. Indeed, the deeper, metaphysical rationale for preferring the least intrusive possible options chosen to prevail against an enemy is based on the conviction that man can only be truly successful if he swims *alongside* the current rather than against it. The metaphor is both figurative and literal, testimony to Sun Tzu's humility before nature, his respect for the unknown and the unknowable, without succumbing to either fatalism or defeatism—an approach well worth emulating.

The first sentence of *The Art of War*, which proclaims the need to thoroughly study, or "calculate," the conditions leading to a potential violent confrontation, is based on the assumption that "the way Nature behaves is the most objective and impartial."[6] This contrasts with the "partiality and the rigidity in which an individual point of view"[7] can become trapped, as against "the overall coherence of becoming" manifested in the greater One, also known as the Way, or the Tao. Rigidity is the opposite of fluidity and change; partiality is the opposite of objectivity. In Western terms, the Invisible Hand transcends every visible one, and like the Tao, proceeds impartially toward a larger goal which is "good" in an all-encompassing, global way.

If this is beginning to sound more like spirituality than strategy, it is because the two are intimately interconnected for Sun Tzu. Hence his appeal to the prolific Buddhist scholar Thomas Cleary, as well as the success of books such as *The Art of War: Spirituality for Conflict*[8] and of such websites as Sonshi (www.sonshi.com). Apart from this somewhat niche audience, the notion should resonate with everyone, including the hard-nosed military community, as just plain sensible—neither more nor less than a candid acknowledgment of an ineffably complex reality. Each of us is able to catch at best a glimpse of the awe-inspiring order that surpasses the understanding of any one person, any one team. As General Stanley McChrystal might put it, there is beyond all the leaders of our little teams an even loftier One, whose Hand, however invisible, is nevertheless shaping all reality.

In practical terms, Sun Tzu takes this to imply that we must be fully aware—or at least, as fully and intelligently as possible—of the largest possible number of relevant indicators, which he calls "initial estimates," that would alert us to dangers and opportunities. These include all manner of information from Heaven (or Sky) and Earth (or Ground),[9] together constituting the realm of geography, economic and political systems, demographics, and similar components of the world around us.

Sun Tzu's prescription that all relevant indicators be considered when assessing any particular situation is good managerial advice. It is also rooted in an intricate metaphysics based on reverence for the higher order, which is beautifully illustrated by a deceptively simple image known as "the water metaphor." It underscores how a picture can be better than a thousand alphabetically depicted words at capturing a complex dual concept that includes *shih*, meaning potentiality, impetus, momentum, strategic advantage, combined with *hsing*, meaning disposition of forces, also translated as "configuration." Consider: "That the velocity of cascading water can send boulders bobbing about is due to its *shih* strategic advantage" (*AoW* V. 13). If a boulder is an obstacle one wishes to have removed, the power of cascading water will inevitably do that, implying, as Derek Yuen explains, that "the suitable conditions for something to happen must be created (as a consequence) and that nothing should and can be forced."[10] Though water by itself is no match for a massive boulder, velocity changes everything: the secret is to harness that energy.

What the strategist does is create the potential to bring about a disposition of force (*hsing*) that leads to the intended effect. In Sun Tzu's words: "The combat of the victorious is like the sudden release of a pent-up *hsing*." No wonder Chinese strategists often use *hsing* and *shih* together, as one concept (*hsing shih*), often translated as "the trend of events," or "situation," which captures the idea of "condition-consequence" approach characteristic of Taoist philosophy. The two constitute a twin concept. The third, which encompasses them, is the idea of *tzu jan*, and may be translated as "natural tendency."

Sun Tzu then notes that "water's configuration (*hsing*) avoids heights and races downwards. . . . [and] configures (*hsing*) its flow in accord with the terrain; the army control its victory in accord with the enemy." In other words, just like water adapts to the terrain, one must adapt according to the enemy, and "not maintain any constant strategic configuration of power (*shih*), [just as] water has no constant shape (*hsing*)" (*AoW* VI. 29). The result is nothing short of sublime; for "one who is able to change and transform in accord with the enemy and wrest victory is termed spiritual" (*AoW* VI. 30). In essence, natural propensity can be assisted by encouraging its impetus; one might say, the Invisible Hand may not be controlled, but it can be shaken a little to coax it in the right direction. To succeed in obtain the desired result, it is best to nudge the factors present in any situation in the closest conformity with the course of nature. To do that, one has to be clear about the facts, and respect the constraints of the real world. With the right guidance, those factors will fall into place—quite literally.

At the core of the water metaphor is the concept of constant change—fluidity—in every environment, not only on the battlefield or in a conflict setting, which call for nimble adaptation, but at all times. The need for recalibration, reassessment of plans and tactics, for applying lessons learned and flowing with the evolving situation, is key to his approach. Unfortunately, this is hard to do in so unwieldy and bureaucratic a setting as the US government.

In many ways, Sun Tzu's conception of a natural harmony is eerily similar to the Enlightenment's concept of Natural Law, the notion that the world obeys certain regularities in accordance to a grand design set by a Grand Designer. These regularities, in turn, may be grasped by reason, which is capable of using the knowledge wrested from the highly complex yet orderly universe to ends that advance human interests. No wonder Sun Tzu's analysis would prove resonant at the time of America's founding, when Enlightenment ideas were embraced and applied with enthusiasm by leaders who grasped their importance at a crucial time when history handed us a unique chance to establish a nation like no other before or since.

As it happens, history is once again handing the nation exceptional leaders, like General Stanley McChrystal, who understands the need for strategic recalibration. Through the course of over a decade, he has come to realize that "we had to unlearn a great deal of what we thought we know about how the war—and the world—worked. We had to tear down familiar organizational structures and rebuild them along completely different lines, swapping our sturdy architecture for organic fluidity, because it was the only way to confront a rising tide of complex threats."[11] And he credits Adam Smith with the insight:

> Adam Smith's "invisible hand" of the market—the notion that order best arises not from centralized design but through the decentralized interactivity of buyers and sellers—is an example of "emergence" *avant la lettre* ["the concept preceded the term"] . . . as it relates to our study of the team of teams. . . . In other words, order can emerge from the bottom up.[12]

Could a higher compliment be bestowed upon Sun Tzu alongside Adam Smith than to credit them with having anticipated the most astute leadership model of the twenty-first century, applied by one of the best generals of the most important nation in the world, in the most complex environment that history has ever known?

But the Invisible Hand, or the Tao, or whatever we want to call the Order that we ignore at our peril, can only be enlisted to help us if we grasp its laws and respect them. For that, we must find in us the humility to be transparent and learn from our mistakes. We need true leadership. Here once again, Sun Tzu comes to the rescue.

Notes

1. James R. Offenson, ed., *Adam Smith, Selected Philosophical Writings* (Charlottesville, VA: Imprint Academic, 2004), 74.
2. Friedrich A. Hayek, *The Constitution of Liberty* (Chicago, IL: University of Chicago Press, 1978).
3. John Keegan, *A History of Warfare* (New York: Alfred A. Knopf, 1994), 59.
4. Mark McNeilly, *Sun Tzu and the Art of Modern Warfare* (Oxford: Oxford University Press, 2001), 18.

5. Ibid., 19.

6. Yuen, *Deciphering Sun Tzu*, 36.

7. Explained with remarkable lucidity by Francois Jullien in his *Treatise on Efficacy: Between Western and Eastern Thinking* (Honolulu: University of Hawaii Press, 1994), 72–73.

8. Thomas Huyn, annotated, *The Art of War – Spirituality for Conflict* (Woodstock, VT: Skylight Paths, 2009).

9. These are both complex terms for Sun Tzu; see Yuen, *Deciphering Sun Tzu*, 34–37.

10. Yuen, *Deciphering Sun Tzu*, 78.

11. Gen. Stanley McChrystal, *Team of Teams: New Rules of Engagement for a Complex World* (New York: Penguin Random House Portfolio, 2015), 19–20.

12. Ibid., 105.

4

Leadership

Our patience will achieve more than our force.
—Edmund Burke, *Reflections on the Revolution in France*, 1790

If wise, a commander is able to recognize changing circumstances
and to act expediently. . . . If humane, he loves mankind, sympathizes
with others, and appreciates their industry and toil. If courageous, he
gains victory by seizing opportunity without hesitation.
—Tu Mu, 803–852

National leaders are not always easy to spot. They should not be confused with demagogues who peddle in promises, ceremonial royalty specializing in photo ops, or kleptocrats whose democratic credentials are bogus window-dressing. Worse of course are the dictators, who share an *apres moi, le deluge* [1] mindset: incorrigible narcissists, history begins and ends with them. To these dregs of our species who, but for history's capricious dice, might have spent their wretched days in chains, *le peuple* is at best an abstraction, usually irrelevant, and too often little more than a nuisance that sometimes needs a bit of, shall we say, pruning (with chemicals as the weapon of choice, preferred by nine out of ten thugs-in-chief).

Leaders may not always be charismatic, although charisma helps. Humility, paradoxically enough, does even more, along with readiness to change course when circumstances require it, rather than sticking to original plans merely for fear of appearing fallible. The best are not driven by raw ambition; they do what they must. Neither afraid nor foolhardy, they are compassionate yet unwavering in their determination to complete the task at hand.

Finally, national leaders have important jobs to do, but if they believe themselves superior to everyone else, the nation is bound to suffer. Though leadership qualities, however various in quality and scope, are not uncommon, the most widely accepted Platonic Idea of a True

Leader envisages Him (almost never Her) as vaguely godlike, a comforting illusion, whose lure reflects the age-long desire for an ersatz Father figure—a powerful, near-omniscient Superman. The terrestrial incarnations of such a mirage, alas, usually turn out to be satanic.

Since no one on this side of paradise, however, is without some limitations, people in leadership position are especially prone to the temptation of becoming overly impressed with their own talents. While insight, intelligence, and experience are vitally important, the one quality that outweighs all the others—patience—happens to be notoriously scarce in overachievers. A national leader should not be unduly swayed by passions, ideology, or ego, yet is often more susceptible to such weaknesses than most ordinary people. He must consciously strive to take the long view, protect his people, and use all the information and tools of statecraft at his disposal, seeking ample advice before settling on a course of action. He must always be leery of war, yet never rule it out. But if pacifists make lousy national leaders, the trigger-happy are arguably lousier. Writes Sun Tzu: "The enlightened ruler is prudent and the good general is warned against rash action. Thus the state is kept secure and the army preserved" (*AoW* VI. 19).

The distinction between rulers and generals, while commonplace to us, was hardly so when those words were written. The momentous bifurcation of the political and military dimensions of strategy into separate functions emerged late in Sun Tzu's lifetime, the Spring and Autumn period of ancient China. Partly the result of major evolutions in warfare that would eventually be completed still later during the Warring States Period, this development constituted an important advance. Already in effect in Sun Tzu's day, the practice of that bifurcation may be assumed to have been familiar. But so was the previous practice of merging the state's political and military functions, which was prevalent during the Spring and Autumn Period's early years, which may explain the grand-strategic design and orientation[2] of *The Art of War*. Sun Tzu understood both.

The division of the two functions has dominated ever since, throughout the world. Today, except for Latin American governments led by military juntas, along with undemocratic regimes that usually emerge in the wake of military coups, civilian leadership and military command are nearly always kept separate—if only because warfare has become far more complex and specialized as weapons and technology have evolved. In the United States, the president is a civilian, although the Constitution prescribes that the office-holder doubles as the nation's commander-in-chief. While several US presidents, such as the iconic George Washington, the populist Andrew Jackson, the underrated (as president, though not as military commander) Ulysses S. Grant, and the savvy Dwight D. Eisenhower, had previously served as generals, they were all retired before being elected, and acted in a civilian capacity.

Although experience offers ample proof that political and military talents are not only dissimilar but often antithetical, their interconnection is demanded by the logic of national conflict. Thus when these functions are held by distinct individuals, the two have to work in tandem, whether they like it or not. The primacy of politics notwithstanding, a winning strategy is impossible unless it conforms to the realities on the ground, and takes into consideration the judgment of astute military commanders. That said, political considerations must prevail in the end—hence the ultimate supremacy conferred upon the (political) head of state.

As already mentioned, Sun Tzu thought intrusive measures, especially lethal action, were to be avoided at almost any cost, not resorted to without weighty forethought, very much as a last resort—a necessary evil. He believed that it is better to refrain from engaging in anything that triggers unanticipated undesirable consequences, which wars are particularly—though by no means exclusively—wont to do. So: if you harbor any doubt whatsoever about intervening in the natural course of events, don't do it. This is not isolationism; it is simple prudence.

Political expedience, Sun Tzu advises the enlightened ruler, dictates that if a certain action "is not in the interests of the state, do not act" (*AoW* VII. 17). Once the ruler finally concludes that acting, rather than not acting, does advance the national interest after all, the next question is, what kind of action to take. War being the most dangerous, unless a guaranteed slam-dunk, it should be ruled out. Warned Sun Tzu: "If you cannot succeed, do not use troops. If you are not in danger, do not fight" (*AoW* VII. 17). (If a reminder were needed, inaction too can lead to consequences that may not be deemed desirable. "Anti-interventionism" is therefore no more morally-free an approach to foreign policy than is any other ideology. Libertarians take note: no one has the luxury of moral abstention merely by doing nothing. Just because an event has been set in motion by someone else, if there is a realistic chance of averting it, one may still be considered responsible, however indirectly, for its having taken place.)

All deliberate human action is potentially subject to rational planning, wise or unwise. And it makes sense that planning is more likely to be wise if no one who might offer important insights is excluded from the conversation without sound reason. Sun Tzu observes: "it is said that enlightened rulers deliberate upon the plans, and good generals execute them" (*AoW* VII. 16). Implicitly rejecting the idea of a divinely inspired, infallible ruler, he notes that even kings do not necessarily come up with those plans themselves, without consultation. After carefully examining the options laid out before him, however, a national ruler must decide on the proper course, based upon political considerations, which the general is then tasked to implement. At the end of the day, it is the king, not the general, who has the last word.

Although the preeminence of politics in warfare had been recognized by Sun Tzu about two millennia before Clausewitz, the latter is nevertheless usually credited with that insight. The Prussian general waxes almost poetic on the subject: "Politics . . . is the womb in which war develops;"[3] "war is only a branch of political activity . . . [and] cannot be divorced from political life;"[4] concluding that "no other possibility exists, then, than to subordinate the military point of view to the political."[5] He too, like Sun Tzu, warned against rushing into war, and for similar reasons; you don't have to be a general to know that war is hell. Moreover, once begun, war is unpredictable in the extreme. The original battle plans, indispensable as they may be, will necessarily have to be adapted, even revamped, in light of evolving circumstances, all the while staying faithful to the strategic interests of the nation as determined and articulated by its supreme political ruler; a very tall order indeed.

Unlike his Chinese predecessor, Clausewitz endows the ideal leader and strategist with extraordinary, almost mystical qualities, needed to prevail amidst the ambiguity and unpredictability of war. While "the play of chance and probability within which the creative spirit is free to roam" might be exciting to creative spirits fond of such games, the uncertainties of war are incalculable and daunting in the extreme. Borrowing a word from engineering, Clausewitz lumps these together as "friction." But friction in the physical world is generally small, amounting mostly to a margin of error. The uncertainties of war, by contrast, are central, usually surpassing and overwhelming that which is known, or rather what is thought to be known yet too often turns out otherwise.

But there is still another complication: besides all the physical and logistical uncertainties that elude ordinary scientific calculation, leaders who forget that "all military action is intertwined with psychological forces and effects" are doomed from the start, for "they consider only unilateral action, whereas war consists of a continuous interaction of opposites."[6] For Clausewitz, however, to describe anything as an "interaction of opposites" would seems to rule out an analysis of war in accordance with Western—even if Hegelian, rather than Aristotelian—logic.[7] And indeed, though he had set out to write a theory of warfare applicable to a variety of circumstances, Clausewitz in the end commendably refrains from oversimplifying strategy, conceding that "it is simply not possible to construct a model for the art of war that can serve as a scaffolding on which the commander can rely for support at any time."[8] So where does this leave the hapless military general? If no cookie-cutter model works in so profoundly uncertain an environment, he has to rely on something else. Maybe what he needs is something almost magical—like, say, innate talent, a *je ne sais quoi* ("I know not what"), an indefinable spiritual quality.

It is Clausewitz's "refusal to make things simpler than they are"[9] that prompts Naval War College professor Daniel Moran to call him a true *realist*. For while uncertainty is everywhere at all times, Clausewitz knew that violence is especially disruptive. It always opens a veritable Pandora's box of unexpected, dire consequences. This Sun Tzu knew too, along with everyone else who has ever experienced war. Also like Sun Tzu, Clausewitz believed that leadership requires personal experience, which even the most astute treatise on warfare can never supplant.

To illustrate that point, Clausewitz's choice of image could not have been more apt: as if subliminally attuned to Sun Tzu, he turns to—what else?—a water metaphor. Noting that a man immersed in water cannot walk the same way as he would on land, Clausewitz likens the purely theoretical strategist to a swimming master who presumes to teach the trainee something that he himself has never done. Theory cannot substitute for experience, and reason cannot play the role of tacit knowledge. A purely rational theorist, then, is like a man seeking to extrapolate from walking on dry ground to walking under water—a nearly absurd task. Nor should one expect the metaphorical water of combat to be shallow, flat, or standing still. He then expands the analogy even further: if war is like "an unexplored sea, full of rocks . . . [indeed] if a contrary wind also springs up, that is, if any great accidental event declares itself adverse to" what had been expected, a great general needs "the most consummate skill, presence of mind, and energy."

Clausewitz calls this skill "genius," [10] leaving it essentially undefined. Moran suggests that genius is "friction's theoretical compliment,"[11] an analogy that captures the shared vagueness of the two terms. Except that while *friction* effects a net negative impact, *genius* refers to the aspect of a commander's innate talent needed to win, and is therefore positive. Otherwise, Clausewitz agrees with Sun Tzu that scientific precision is outright impossible in the real world of warfare; for "whenever he [the General] he has to fall back on his innate talent, he will find himself outside the model and in conflict with it . . . [since][12] talent and genius operate outside the rules, and theory conflicts with practice."[13] If this means that "models" take second place to something "outside the rules," in other words something that is not rational according to traditional scientific standards, so be it. The realist Clausewitz evidently does not shun away from what is in essence an idealist (meaning nonmaterialist) concept.

That Clausewitz used *Geist*—"Spirit"—to refer to the military leader's "genius" is not to imply that he engaged in subversive, antirational, mysticism.[14] But there is no doubt that he was indebted to Hegel, whose *Phänomenologie des Geistes* (*The Phenomenology of Spirit*) was enormously influential in defining Romanticism, a movement that arose in reaction to the previous century's worship of reason. The Romanticism-Enlightenment antagonism is captured perfectly in the pitting of scientific, theoretical precision from the realm of reason, as against genius or "Spirit," which is an inner force. In the end, Clausewitz chose the latter over the former; Sun Tzu, on the other hand, had no problem with the coexistence of opposites. For in the Taoist worldview—which, as we saw in chapter 1, he both shared and influenced—contradiction is not avoided but assumed. That was in essence the *ying-yang* view of change.

Like Clausewitz, Sun Tzu praised personal experience and tacit knowledge: psychological, along with physical, uncertainties are to Sun Tzu the very essence of reality. But ironically, of the two, it is the Prussian officer rather than the Taoist Sun Tzu who turns out to be the more Romantically inclined. Writes Michael Handel: "[T]here is much less room in [Sun Tzu's] theory . . . for uncertainty, friction, and chance," which is, paradoxically (what else?) a reflection of the ubiquitous fluidity of the world. Returning to the water metaphor, Sun Tzu would point out that walking in the water and walking on land are just two ways of walking. In both cases, unanticipated circumstances not only can but must be expected. In both cases, moreover, thorough analysis and experience will help as much as tacit knowledge or instinct, or whatever it is that we learn through repeated experience and personal talent.

Not even walking in the shallow water of simulated exercises can emulate what it's like to walk in the waters of war: the differences are not merely a matter of degree, as Clausewitz's analogy implies, but qualitative. This is not to say that training is irrelevant. Indeed, Sun Tzu would be in agreement with Clausewitz that walking even in shallow water provides an incomparably better simulation exercise for walking in either a river or the sea than is walking on land. The problem with Clausewitz's approach is that if leaders, specifically military leaders, have to possess "genius," they become shrouded in an almost magical aura—a dangerous proposition that threatens to undermine the superiority and primacy of the rational *political* leadership that Clausewitz himself, paradoxically, endorsed.

But Handel believes that the two giants of strategy actually differ less on how they see leadership than on how each sees his own task. While Clausewitz focused almost exclusively on military matters; Sun Tzu's scope is broader. "The diplomatic or economic environment in which war takes place is just not within the scope [of Clausewitz's *On War*]."[15] In contrast, "Sun Tzu, on the other hand, views the political, diplomatic, and logistical preparations for war and the fighting itself as integral parts of the same activity."[16]

As a result, writes Handel, Sun Tzu believes that a true leader must be sure to utilize all the instruments of influence at his disposal, preferably in this order: "the highest realization is to attack the enemy's plans; next is to attack their alliances; next to attack their army; and the worst policy is to attack their cities" (*AoW* III. 4–7). Since the last options are the most violent, drastic, unpredictable, and risky, they should be used only if the others have failed; adequate preparations and savvy, imaginative use of information, effective diplomacy and constant vigilance should provide ample opportunities to prevail. So while Sun Tzu's approach reflects the blend of civil and military leadership that must guide all actions against an enemy, his treatise focuses mainly on the latter. Sun Tzu's advice to all leaders, both military and civilian, is thus broader, extending beyond the battlefield and beyond war itself.

Thus attacking the enemy's plans and alliances—which should come first in a hostile, adversarial situation—can and should also be practiced in peacetime. Yuen, in the spirit of Sun Tzu, blames the Western predilection to militarize war and the "tacticization of 'strategy' that have blinded us from identifying and rediscovering the countless opportunities in the non-military spheres of war."[17] His scope being larger than that of Clausewitz, Sun Tzu encourages forward-looking, preemptive thinking at all times, especially during (relative) peace. He is not particularly fazed by the human, or psychological, component, whose subjective nature does not imply that it cannot be understood and even controlled, at least to some extent, and certainly influenced. (Special "genius" is not needed to intuit another's inner life, although emotional intelligence certainly helps.) That influence may be wielded as much (if not more) by the threat of violence as by violence itself. And, as already mentioned in chapter 2, it often requires "deception."

As discussed before, the ancient Chinese word for "deception" is closer to "nontraditional" (also, "nonorthodox") or "indirect." The pejorative moral connotation of "deception," however, is impossible to avoid in its English equivalent, which usually implies outright lying or cheating. The word comes from the Latin *capere*, meaning "to take," and *decipere*, which refers to taking something from another, stealing, cheating, and ensnaring, with no room for moral ambiguity. This can be misleading; for while China experts Ralph D. Sawyer[18] and Michael Pillsbury[19] acknowledge that modern Chinese strategic theory and behavior can only be described as cynical and devious, it owes more to Mao's version of deceptive "stratagem" viewed through a Marxist lens [20] than to Sun Tzu.

A few considerations, however, are in order. In the first place, it must be remembered that once war is waged, and the contest becomes a matter of life or death, hardly anyone doubts that deception is implicitly justified. On the other hand, lying and cheating have been shunned in most cultures, being deeply subversive of civilized intercourse, which is heavily based on trust. Moreover, deception becomes counterproductive, especially in the long run. Viewed in that light, the use of deception is less anomalous than it may seem to the simplistic eye.

But far from promoting the wide use of outright subterfuge, Sun Tzu in fact puts a very high premium on ethics. The suggestion that Sun Tzu favored a nihilistic, amoral approach to conflict could not be further from the truth. The realistic Sun Tzu, whose aphorisms are often cited out of context in the manner of pithy proverbs embroidered on pillows, counsels respect for the flow of nature. He is not a *realist* in the misleading, unhelpful way defined by political scientists as the pursuit of naked self-interest and engaging in power politics. But more about that later.

Instead, Sun Tzu states that the first—and by implication, most important—of five factors that determine the course of war is moral influence, which he defines as the quality that impels people to follow their leaders, and promotes national harmony among implicitly uncon-strained individuals (a notion antithetical to totalitarian systems, their promotional propaganda notwithstanding). Another very important factor, called "command," as indicated in the previous chapter, refers to a "general's qualities of wisdom, sincerity, humanity, courage, and strictness." All five leadership traits, further elaborated by the ancient Chinese commentator Tu Mu (803–852), have an ethical component:

> If wise, a commander is able to recognize changing circumstances and to act expediently. If sincere, his men will have no doubt of the certainty of rewards and punishments. If humane, he loves mankind, sympathizes with others, and appreciates their industry and toil. If courageous, he gains victory by seizing opportunity without hesita-tion. If strict, his troops are disciplined because they are in awe of him and are afraid of punishment.[21]

The ability to recognize changing circumstances comes first, along with acting without delay—which is not to say without sufficient deliberation and consultation. A true leader is also a good manager, who can be trusted to recognize and respond to both valor and error, impartially yet empathetically, thus gaining the respect and devotion of his subor-dinates. These qualities are central not only to military but to political leaders. Indeed, they are worth including in leadership management textbooks for businesspersons, and even spiritual guides—which explains why the cottage industry of how-to books inspired by *The Art of War* is so spectacularly lucrative.[22]

But if the supreme commander has to master both political and military skills to make the momentous strategic decision of whether or not to go to war, this does not mean that Sun Tzu tacitly accepted the need for a Master Strategist. As Freedman points out, the idea of a Master Strategist is a nonstarter, for no such demigod is even con-ceivable. At the same time, Freedman recognizes that the two spheres are inseparable, the military and the political leaders having to be "in constant dialogue. Political ends could not be discussed without regard for military feasibility."[23] But just as political leaders are not divinely inspired, neither are generals, no matter how much *genius* they might possess.

Sun Tzu certainly does not consider generals to be any more divinely endowed than the political leaders to whom they ultimately have to defer. Rather, he notes that far more important than knowing everything, which is after all humanly impossible, a true leader must be willing to trust those who are in a position to best understand the situation at hand. Having already established that the ultimate source of authority for offensive action is the national sovereign, he then adds a caveat that is nothing short of revolutionary: for in the words of the notable Sun Tzu scholar Marine General Samuel B. Griffith, "this concept is completely inconsistent with traditional thought."[24] Says Sun Tzu: *There are occasions when the commands of the sovereign need not be obeyed.* (*AoW* VIII. 2). Considering the times in which he lived, and especially given the age-honored Chinese reverence for authority—specifically, the authority of the supreme ruler—this admonition seems veritably sacrilegious.

Admittedly, those "occasions" are expected to be few, and even then must be considered very carefully. The book's second-century editor, Ts'ao Ts'ao, clarifies that so extraordinary an event as a mere general's overruling his own supreme sovereign's commands may only take place "when it is expedient in operations"[25]—implying that the supreme sovereign himself would be assumed to wish it, since he would certainly agree to pursue an expedient rather than an inexpedient course of action. It is, after all, simple common sense that only someone thoroughly familiar with conditions on the ground, such as a general undertaking those "operations," can make the specific, tactical decisions that are best suited given the circumstances.

As McChrystal too explains in his inimitable, crystal-clear (no pun intended) manner:

> Being woken to make life-or-death decisions confirmed my role as a leader, and made me feel important and needed—something most managers yearn for. But . . . [a]s much as I would like to think otherwise, I only rarely had some groundbreaking insight. Most of the time I would simply trust the recommendations by those who came to get me, as they knew the most about the issue. My inclusion was a rubber stamp that slowed the process, and sometimes caused us to miss fleeing opportunities.[26]

Like McChrystal, Sun Tzu does not shy away from suggesting that not only political leaders, far from the scene of action, but even generals, are not necessarily the best judges of what should be done at any particular time on the battlefield. Contrasting wise with unwise leaders, Sun Tzu delivers pointed warnings against the latter. Unwise generals are said to possess the following deadly characteristics: recklessness; cowardice; quick temper; lack a sense of humor; and, somewhat surprisingly, excessive show of compassion. How can anyone deny that recklessness causes death, as does a quick temper; cowardice leads to either premature capitulation or capture; the thin-skinned can be lured into reckless behavior out of excessive concern for reputation and honor; and the overly generous are more often ridiculed than admired, ending up endangering rather than helping their subordinates and constituents (*AoW* III. 19–23).

Accordingly, a more open-ended and inclusive interpretation of Sun Tzu's invitation to insubordination, offered by the ancient commentator Chang Yu (who in turn cites King Fu Ch'ai who reigned during the fifth century BC), actually comes closer to the real intent of the original admonition: *When you see the correct course, act; do not wait for orders.*[27] It seems that here "you" refers to anyone in a position to ascertain the "correct course" in a particular situation. In addition to moral qualities, then, a good leader must possess the ability to mobilize his team in accordance with the most accurate possible information, which sometimes requires immediate response—and that implies empowering subordinates. The members of his team must be able to demonstrate initiative when circumstances leave no other choice.

The "correct" course in any situation is determined by its chances of success or failure relative to the ultimate strategic purpose of the operation. Conversely, an "incorrect" action defeats that purpose. Though future contingencies are always a matter of probability, and no mere mortal may be expected to know the future precisely, as a general rule it is always unwise to consider only the favorable and ignore the unfavorable consequences of any action, particularly if the latter are obscured by the relative immediacy of the former. Any action, no matter how beneficial it may seem at first blush, is double-edged—meaning, in the words of Sun Tzu commentator Ho Yen-hsi, "Advantage and disadvantage are mutually reproductive. The enlightened deliberate."[28] For example, it might seem good to take the shortest road to one's destination, but not if it turns out to be booby-trapped or open to ambush. And it might be unwise to occupy a certain territory or facility if defending it turns out to be all but impossible. Similarly, in business, the relative trade-offs between short and long-term considerations constitute a daily dilemma. No matter what the context, short-run but ephemeral advantages should not trump more solid, long-run benefits.

Sun Tzu then explores the contingency that arises when an outright attack against a mortal enemy, though seemingly advisable at first, turns out to be overly risky. Courses of action are still available to the cunning general, notably, what might be called political sabotage or political warfare. It is never wise to assume the best scenario—that the enemy will not attack—*but rather to rely on one's readiness to meet him* (*AoW* VIII. 16). Thus Sun Tzu offers a number of suggestions for undermining the enemy's strength prior to (and even, with a little luck, in the place of) kinetic engagement. Commentator Chia Lin elaborates:

> Plans and projects for harming the enemy are not confined to any one method.
>
> Sometimes entice his wise and virtuous men away so that he has no counsellors.
>
> Or send treacherous people to his country to wreck his administration.
>
> Sometimes use cunning deceptions to alienate his ministers from the sovereign.
>
> Or send skilled craftsmen to encourage his people to exhaust their wealth.
>
> Or present him with licentious musicians and dancers to change his customs.
>
> Or give him beautiful women to bewilder him.[29]

Summarizes Sun Tzu: *He wearies them by keeping them constantly occupied, and makes them rush about by offering them ostensible advantages.* (*AoW* VIII. 15).

We end with the most important quality of a leader, in peace as in war: called "doctrine" in the *Art of War*, Sun Tzu defines it as "organization, control, assignment of supply routes, and the provision of principal items used by the army" (*AoW* I. 8). The true leader must be able to create a system under his control, which is not only disciplined and completely loyal to him but also as decentralized as possible, circumstances permitting. It might be said that he is the team leader of his teams, to quote McChrystal again. Indeed, over the course of the past decade, the complexity of warfare has given rise to a new leadership model: *the adaptive leader*, who must embrace novelty and surprise with creative solutions. According to the Army's *Field Manual 6–22*, adaptive leadership means *being a change agent, helping other members of the organization recognize that an environment is changing and building consensus as change is occurring.*[30]

This brings Sun Tzu right up to us, into the twenty-first century. As Yuen points out, what makes Sun Tzu especially valuable today is his role in inspiring the broader perspective on grand strategy, far beyond the merely military aspect. In other words, his manual is unique in explaining that the Art of War is incomplete without its counterpart, the Art of Peace. Sun Tzu is indeed addressing the general; but he could not fail to simultaneously target the head of state, the political leader of the nation.

Sun Tzu thereby anticipated by about two millennia another celebrated strategist, the versatile and brilliant Niccolo Machiavelli (1469–1527), who similarly perceived the intimate relationship between the political and military components of leadership. Ironically, the only book published during Machiavelli's lifetime, which is far less well known than the much shorter one addressed to the infamous Cosimo de Medici known as *The Prince*, was entitled . . . *The Art of War*. (Freedman observes that, actually, "this might have been the inspiration for the title given to Sun Tzu's work" itself.[31])

Albeit separated by almost two millennia, the great Chinese and Italian strategists have a great deal in common. Just as Sun Tzu's concept of deception has been oversimplified in a mainly pejorative direction, so too "Machiavellian" has come to mean "treacherous," "cynical," "devious," or just plain "immoral." Freedman seeks to correct that impression, noting that

> Machiavelli's approach was actually far more balanced. He understood that the more the prince was perceived to rely on devious methods, the less likely it would be that they succeeded. The wise strategist would seek to develop a foundation for the exercise of power that went beyond false impressions and harsh punishments, but on real accomplishment and general respect.[32]

Sun Tzu could not have agreed more. Both these theorists were true realists: they believed in taking facts as they were and not as we wished them to be; they both understood human nature, and the importance of perceptions; they both expressed a healthy respect for force while recognizing that political vision is indispensable. Both men continue to be rediscovered, their insights recycled to fit new environments, their wisdom persisting beyond the centuries.[33]

The world has changed quite a bit since the time of the Warring States, though states, alas, are still warring. But true leadership continues to require knowledge, experience, and the ability to guide people in complex situations for a common end that transcends any one individual for the safety and good of the whole, with both courage and intelligence. It also requires using all the weapons at one's disposal, the entire spectrum of national power, rather than relying excessively on military might, especially in cases of asymmetric conflict, when opponents possess entirely disproportionate assets.

Today, America has the most powerful military on earth, yet it seems incapable of defeating forces that operate in defiance of international legal norms. By contrast, at its inception, the United States, consisting of merely a dozen or so loosely associated colonies, had the temerity to face off the great British empire with an untrained ragtag army of mostly farmers and other civilians—and prevailed. Sun Tzu would not have been surprised.

Notes

1. "After me, the deluge"- attributed to Louis XVI. http://www.merriam-webster.com/dictionary/apres+moi+le+deluge.
2. Yuen, *Deciphering Sun Tzu*, 59.
3. Clausewitz, *On War*, 149.
4. Ibid., 605.
5. Ibid., 607.
6. Ibid., 136.
7. As explained in chapter 8, Western dialectic, based on the Aristotelian law of contradiction—A and not-A cannot both be true in a rational universe—rules out blending opposites; even Hegel's "synthesis" is less a merger of contradictions than their replacement.
8. Ibid., 152.
9. Daniel Moran, *Strategic Theory and the History of War* (Monterey, CA: Naval Postgraduate School, 2001), 8. https://www.google.com/?gws_rd=ssl#
10. Clausewitz, *On War*, ch. VII.
11. Moran, *Strategic Theory and the History of War*.
12. Ibid.
13. Ibid., 140.
14. Hew Strachan, *Clausewitz's On War: A Biography*, 93.
15. Handel, *Masters of War*, 35.
16. Ibid., 38.
17. Yuen, *Deciphering Sun Tzu*, 109.
18. Ralph D. Sawyer, *The Tao of Deception: Unorthodox Warfare in Historic and Modern* China (New York: Basic Books, 2007).
19. Michael Pillsbury, *The Hundred Year Marathon: China's Secret Strategy to Replace America as the Global Superpower* (New York: Henry Holt and Co., 2015).
20. Consider, for example, the contrast between the Communist leadership of Red China and the advice for national leaders that is found in the Tao Te Ching that while war is clearly the realm of deception, "only righteous and nondeceptive [or orthodox] means should be used when governing the

state" (ch. 57). "Righteous" is not the quite the first adjective that comes to mind to describe the party elite that has anointed itself in Beijing.

21. Griffith, *Sun Tzu - The Art of War.*, 65.
22. Among the most successful are Ching-ning Chu's *The Art of War for Women* (2010), Thomas Huynh's *The Art of War—Spirituality for Conflict* (2008), Gerald Michaelson and Steven Michaelson's *Sun Tzu For Success: How to Use the Art of War to Master Challenges and Accomplish the Important Goals in Your Life* (2003) and the sequel, *Sun Tzu—The Art of War for Managers: 50 Strategic Rules Updated for Today's Business* (2010), Troy J. Doucet's *The Art of War for Lawyers* (2014), the list goes on.
23. Freedman, *Strategy*, 242.
24. Griffith, *Sun Tzu - The Art of War*, 8.
25. Ibid.
26. McChrystal, *Team of Teams*, 202.
27. Ibid.
28. Ibid., 113.
29. Ibid., 113–14.
30. *US Army Field Manual 6–22, Army Leadership* (Washington, DC: Government Printing Office, 2006), 10–8.
31. "Indeed, almost all disquisition on the subject—from that of Raimondo Montecuccoli in the seventeenth century to Maurice de Saze in the eighteenth to Baron de Jomini in the nineteenth—was called *The Art of War.* This was a generic title often covering largely technical matters." Freedman, *Strategy.*, 51.
32. Ibid., 53.
33. Michael A. Ledeen, *Machiavelli on Modern Leadership: Why Machiavelli's Iron Rules Are As Timely And Important Today As Five Centuries Ago* (New York: St. Martin's Press, 2000).

II

The Founders' Art of Peace

It wasn't so long ago that America was David to Great Britain's Goliath, with the added complication that the Mother Country had spawned its recalcitrant offspring's basic political and economic principles, sharing language and culture. For reasons that many even in Britain—notably the eloquent Edmund Burke, the putative father of modern-day conservatism—found entirely reasonable, the colonies had come to the opinion that to be free, they had to become an independent, sovereign nation. The King and Parliament, unsurprisingly disagreed. That obliged the new, barely United, States across the Atlantic to be smart and use all the tools at its disposal to win their freedom. If that meant war, so be it.

Unlikely as it still seems, George Washington was able to adjust his strategy to make use of his ragtag army of brave though untrained militiamen to prevail against the far more professional and well equipped British soldiers and their Hessian allies. Though he did not know it, Washington and his fellow Founders had to engage in grand strategy—and they rose to the challenge with spectacular rapidity, ingenuity, and success. No small part of his success was due to intelligence and strategic communication—information warfare tools that had also been used to cement popular support among the population (deftly orchestrated by Sam Adams) without which so extraordinary a war could never have been waged.

America's secret diplomatic weapon was the scientific genius, entrepreneur, propagandist, and covert arms negotiator Benjamin Franklin. With an almost diametrically different personality but equally devoted to independence and liberty, John Adams too did his part to win support and money from the Netherlands. Adams was convinced that free trade would eventually secure peace on a global level, but in the short run, he conceded that economic warfare seemed necessary. Though the Founders sometimes disagreed about when and against whom to wage it, the limits of that weapon to the infant nation was soon discovered.

Yet still they had trouble accepting the need for a standing army, despite Alexander Hamilton's arguments to the contrary. It did not take long for Hamilton to be proven correct. But neither Hamilton nor his colleagues ever intended for the United States to become a colonial empire. Although devoted to the idea that America had a special place in the world, it was not envisaged as a crusader state. Neither isolationists nor expansionists, the Founders were pragmatic. Their vision was based on universal principles of natural rights to liberty, which they considered necessary for the pursuit of happiness.

5

Sovereignty and Self-Government

It is the true interest of America to steer clear of European contentions.... The cause of America is in a great measure the cause of all mankind.
—Thomas Paine, *Common Sense*, 1776

In politics as in philosophy, my tenets are few and simple. The leading one of which, and indeed that which embraces most others, is to be honest and just ourselves and to exact it from others, meddling as little as possible in their affairs where our own are not involved.
—George Washington to James Anderson, Dec. 24, 1795

If we desire to avoid insult, we must be able to repel it; if we desire to secure peace, one of the most powerful instruments of our rising prosperity, it must be known, that we are at all times ready for War.
—George Washington, Annual Message to Congress, Dec. 3, 1793

If one key element of nationalism is the myth of a Golden Age,[1] our founding period certainly plays that role in the popular imagination. And in a way it was golden, although the nation would struggle for some time, its greatest triumphs still far into the future. But the belief in America's special status as a providentially chosen sanctuary of liberty was arguably never stronger than at the very beginning, when its survival was very far from certain. The leaders of the American Revolution were energized by an entrenched, if not entirely blind, faith in the salutary circumstances of their geography, and above all in the rectitude of their ideas, which solidified their determination to face the daunting task of inventing a new country against near-insuperable odds.

The exceptional role of physical setting is one of the most striking similarities between the Founders' strategic calculus and that of Sun Tzu, whose book starts out with a discussion of "Preliminary Calculations," or "Initial Estimates," giving primacy to "terrain," as well as "ground," which alongside "weather" generally encompass the spectrum of natural conditions. These physical factors reappear throughout the text, notably in his chapter IX, "Marches," which contains many tactical recommendations regarding troop positioning and calculations. Yet Sun Tzu's larger point is strategic: one cannot hope to win a stable peace without the ability to maintain that peace. By implication, if the territory is vulnerable, even if a hostile power is momentarily defeated in one or more battles, the long-term prospects are dim. In chapter X, "Terrain," Sun Tzu goes on to describe different kinds of ground, indicating their relative value. Any ground equally advantageous—or disadvantageous—to the warring parties is considered "indecisive," meaning that it is insecure in the long run. He spells it out in chapter XI, "The Nine Varieties of Ground": "Ground in which the army survives only if it fights with the courage of desperation is called 'death'" (*AoW* XI. 10). That surely concentrates the mind, and it did the minds of the Founders, who were anything but suicidal. Their vision of America was of a sovereign nation whose citizens could till their soil and go about their business safe and secure.

The Founders, who are sometimes referred to as Fathers, sometimes as Brothers, along with the nation's brave if under-recognized Mothers, were uncommonly learned, but also eminently practical: they all had to support themselves and their families. Though many were "visionaries" (Alexander Hamilton's not-so-subtle pejorative), most were hard-headed realists. They were set on launching a new social experiment—the best that reason and virtue could muster under the circumstances, but never lost sight of the obstacles, which they knew to be abundant. For that experiment to have emerged at the end of the eighteenth century, against daunting threats from both within and without, represents a triumph of strategic thinking, remarkable courage on the part of extraordinary individuals at all levels of society, astonishing intellectual leadership, and a hefty dose of luck—much needed to compensate for not a few near-fatal mistakes.

Like every other country on the planet, America considers itself "exceptional." It always did. But the combined effect of ignorance and ideology has led to utter confusion about our relationship to our own nation: we are OK with "patriotism," up to a point, but many distrust "nationalism" because it seems too closely linked to xenophobia, as indeed it often is. Neither are we sure what it stands for, what its goals are. Abroad, should we intervene against injustice, or refrain from meddling? Uncertain yet impulsive, we oscillate from full-speed ahead to reverse, bypassing neutral with whiplashing rapidity. Worse, we alternate from excessive self-confidence to paralyzing insecurity, remorseful over the very success that makes others envy, love, hate, fear, and admire us—often simultaneously. Befuddled and petulant, tired of expectations we didn't elicit or even anticipate, we can't figure out what is best, either for ourselves or for the world.

Looking for guidance, we Americans have sought to learn more about our origins. Eager to oblige, academics, journalists, and ghostwriters have been flooding the market with books, many very good, others more dubious, a few frankly regrettable. Unfortunately, objectivity is almost as scarce as near-infinite patience—the tribute that Clio, the muse of history, stipulates from its supplicants-practitioners. Some authors have relished exposing the Founders' foibles and their inevitable squabbles: Thomas Jefferson's animosity to Alexander Hamilton whom he believed to be a diehard monarchist in part on the basis of the latter's expressing admiration for Julius Caesar at a dinner party; John Adams's allowing his hatred of Hamilton (for what he had—erroneously—assumed to be personal animosity) to affect his policies as president; Benjamin Franklin's alleged womanizing (an impression he cultivated rather too eagerly, at somewhat too advanced an age, to be entirely plausible); and so on.

Of course, no one claims the Founders to have been infallible. Only totalitarian governments embalm ex-rulers, and theocracies alone commit idolatry with their heads of state. The important question is: What vision did they have for America? Indeed, did they have a vision at all? Or were we just the beneficiaries of divine chance, England having lost the Revolutionary War by incompetence and overconfidence. Surely geography worked in our favor; the French navy came to our rescue, did much of the fighting and won the critical battles, with the colonists mostly tagging along. Perhaps all of these, and more. Take your pick among the theories. Still, the prevailing view, whether from left, right, or sideways, is that despite major disagreements and differences, the Founders were a unique sort of team, unlike any before or since.

But were they, in the end, mostly peace-loving, pious loners, who wanted everyone else to leave them be, in exchange for refraining from meddling in other people's business? Or were they rather a militarist bunch, ready to pounce upon any territory they could get their hands on, particularly in the (American) neighborhood? Various combinations of both interpretations have been advanced, with at least some plausibility, though occasionally with a regard for evidence most generously described as cavalier. Too often, history is used, regrettably, to confirm rather than test personal prejudices and predilections.

Carnegie Endowment scholar Robert Kagan, for one, argues that "when [most Americans] think of the nation's relation to the world in the decades before and after the Revolution, the words they tend to conjure are 'isolation,' 'nonentanglement,' 'neutrality.'"[2] Since in his view, this interpretation, though widespread, is thoroughly mistaken, he proceeds to argue the opposite. America, writes Kagan, has always been an expansionist empire, rightly perceived by the rest of the world as "dangerous"—whence the title of his own controversial book, *Dangerous Nation*. He goes on to claim, with characteristic flair, that while "Americans have cherished an image of themselves as by nature inward-looking and aloof, only sporadically and spasmodically venturing forth into the world, usually in response to external attack or perceived threats,"[3] they have deluded themselves.

No wonder the book is controversial. That the Founders had indeed proved themselves splendidly formidable against the British is an accepted fact. But dangerously expansionist? Really? To address that question, we must take a look at the general who led the colonists to victory and later became, however reluctantly, their first president. The facts are unkind to Kagan's thesis.

The eulogy written by Henry Lee for George Washington in 1799 described him as "first in war, first in peace, and first in the hearts of his countrymen."[4] Congress had unanimously chosen Lee for the task since none was better suited. A major general in the Continental Army, member of the Continental Congress, governor of Virginia, Lee had known the first president intimately; both he and his wife had been like family to George and Martha. Few accolades did not apply to Washington, as Lee well knew: humble, pious, just, humane, temperate and sincere, dignified and commanding, the general had been all of this and more. All of which he really had to be, to insure America's birth—a miracle of near-biblical proportions. Washington was first in war because he would be first in peace. At the same time, that peace would never have arrived had he not been the consummate warrior and strategist. Nor would he have been offered the opportunity to exercise his talents had he not been able to gain the affectionate respect of his fellow-countrymen.

Not to detract in any way from the strategic acumen of the incomparable Niccolo Machiavelli, George Washington would not have found the Florentine sage's advice much to his liking. The republican prince of the New World did not mind being feared by his enemies, but definitely not by his constituents. He cherished their good opinion, and even love; though in truth, what the American leader most wanted was to be respected for preserving the safety and peace of the people who had entrusted him with their lives, liberty, and properties. This high goal he manifestly attained, and preserved.

Washington had grasped the fact that a worthy national leader should not inspire the sort of fear that may have been useful and even necessary against jealous rivals in thirteenth century Italy, but would prove anathema to a liberal republic like the United States. That said, a democratic leader might be tempted to court the voters' love by pandering to their prejudices and baser instincts. In the early days, presidential candidates did not campaign but were drafted—in Washington's case, very much against his wishes, especially for a second term. (Even Thomas Jefferson, eager to lead his country in 1800, never openly flaunted that desire lest it be seen as a sign of ambition, a trait thought dangerous in a president. The unseemly ambition so unabashedly paraded on the national stage today would have horrified our well-bred forefathers, and with good reason.)

Unable to afford college, the future first president had always worked exceptionally hard to improve himself, never too proud to learn from the mistakes of others and his own. Knowing when to defer to those who knew more about a particular topic than he did, Washington did not shy away from taking charge or from assuming responsibility when things went wrong. Along with his talented fellow Founders, who together secured America's independence and sovereignty, Washington was instrumental in forging the nation's vision of itself. As we shall see later in this chapter and the next two, that vision—contrary to Kagan's interpretation—did not include the notion of an "American Empire."

The theory that America is at bottom an expansionist, imperialist nation, and that its supposed original isolationism is more myth than reality, nevertheless fits the narrative of many academics and assorted intellectuals. *American Diplomacy* associate editor Michael Hornblow shares Kagan's impression that most Americans prefer to think themselves as originally isolationist, presumably because that is what they had been taught. Praising Kagan's massive tome *Dangerous Nation* as "brilliantly written and carefully researched," he agrees with its conclusion that the much-vaunted self-image of passivity is just plain wrong:

> The book is most noteworthy for debunking a cherished myth about American history, a myth most of us were taught at a young age and have embraced ever since. . . . In school we were taught that George Washington's farewell address restated an isolationist core of American foreign policy, while the Monroe Doctrine reconfirmed our tradition of isolationism, separation and passivity until provoked into action.[5]

Stanford professor David Kennedy, in his *Washington Post* review of Kagan's book, agrees that it "may be read as an effort to make a systematic historical case for just how deeply rooted and stubbornly durable America's international assertiveness has been, thereby suggesting a legitimating pedigree for America's current foreign policies—or perhaps creating a critical instrument for radically revising them."[6] But Kennedy astutely foresees the strangely contradictory reactions Kagan's book was bound to provoke: "Europeans and others wary of America's motives and influence may find that it confirms their deepest dreads; some neoconservatives may wonder if Kagan has decamped to the Chomskyite, America-bashing left." And they would be right to wonder—not so much at Kagan's belief that the Founders promoted a robust, even interventionist foreign policy (an interpretation Kennedy happens to share), but at his description of this perspective as, shockingly, unprincipled.

That is certainly how University of California-San Diego professor William E. Weeks understands it: "Kagan portrays the breakneck expansionism of the pre-1820 period as a yeasty combination of ambition and opportunism."[7] Though noting that only once does Kagan come close to branding America as an "empire" (the Index lists no entry for the term), it is plenty damning: "Each acquisition," charges Kagan, "brought a new horizon and new ambitions. The fulfillment of one desire produced another. Perhaps the most accurate description was that it was an empire attained by determined opportunism."[8] The accusation is powerful. But it is not supported by the evidence.

While they hardly spoke with one voice, one thing the Founders shared was a fierce devotion to principle, to what they all called "liberty," which they defined univocally. Roughly synonymous with *self-determination* (or what is often today described, albeit often inaccurately, as democracy), rooted in reason, the expression of liberty in terms of natural rights was thought universal and God-given, an ideal that kindled the settlers' hearts and inspired them to acts of great courage. Believing themselves perfectly capable of organizing their own affairs, they balked at being ruled—and taxed—from an ocean away.

It helped that many influential voices in the Mother Country agreed, supporting the colonies' independence. Paradoxically, the benign neglect that Britain had shown its colonies, for decades allowing them free reign to govern themselves, had emboldened them. They had proceeded on the assumption that, as Englishmen, they were entitled to organize their society on the same principles of consent they took to be their ancient heritage, having plainly demonstrated that they were capable of organizing their own affairs. Had Britain not suddenly seen fit to change its policies and start enforcing previously benignly overlooked laws, proceeding to levy taxes on its distant subjects, the Americans would have seen no reason to break away—certainly not in 1776.

Yet break they most certainly did. Though long in gestation, the nation's symbolic birth took place on July 4, 1776, just two days after the adoption by Congress of the (heavily edited, yet still breathtakingly eloquent) Declaration of Independence, originally penned by Thomas Jefferson, and endorsed by the best and brightest, certainly the bravest, among the colonists. Although not in unanimous agreement over the wisdom of its timing or its chances of success, these men signed on, mindful that they had just gambled with their lives, conscious of a still highly precarious future. That event marked the official onset of the so-called Revolutionary General War.

Many military historians, notably Dave Richard Palmer, however, argue that "Revolutionary War" is really a misnomer. In the first place, "the very word 'revolution' implies a radical and fractious upending of society, a fundamental break in the political tradition of a people, the violent overthrow of one group or class for another."[9] Moreover, "long accustomed to *de facto*, if not *de jure*, independence, Americans stubbornly resisted Parliament's efforts to impose greater controls on them." So they had thought themselves quasi-independent long ago, and were merely hoping for a continuation of that state. Nor was it a war so much as "a rebellion to retain American government,"[10] although military confrontation obviously did take place.

This is no mere semantics. Political theorist Hannah Arendt implicitly agrees with Palmer, arguing in her seminal work *On Revolution* that revolutions "are not mere changes;" they entail violent destruction amounting to the annihilation of an entire class of people—exhibit A being Paris in 1789. She observes that, contrary to every other modern revolution, only the American "did not devour its own children."[11]

"Radical," from the Latin word for "root" (*radix*), refers to wresting a flower from the soil from the very roots, thereby terminally killing it with no hope of renewal. Revolutions imply an entirely new start, *de nihilo* (from nothing)—the exact opposite of natural evolution, of seasonal transitions, and even of the "appointed recurring cycle into which human affairs are bound by reason of their always being driven to extreme."[12] The idea of regimes in perennial, cyclical rotation, which dates back to Plato (ca. 429–347 BC) and Polybius (ca. 200–ca. 118 BC), could explain ordinary political change; revolution was another matter altogether. Americans would have liked nothing better than to continue to be left alone by their Mother Country rather than fight against it.

This is Arendt's insight into why the American rejection of continued subservience to England would eventually succeed in establishing an independent nation able to stay on its own two feet:

> [T]he course of the American Revolution tells an unforgettable story and is apt to teach a unique lesson; for this revolution did not break out but was made by men in common deliberation and on the strength of mutual pledges. The principle which came to light during those fateful years when the foundations were laid—not by the strength of one architect but by the combined power of the many—was the interconnected principle of mutual promise and common deliberation; and the event itself decided indeed, as Hamilton had insisted, that men 'are really capable ... of establishing good government from reflection and choice,' that they are not 'forever destined to depend for their political constitutions on accident and force.'[13]

The antinomy, or antithesis, of accident is choice, just as consent is the antithesis of force. If violence and accident are irrational expressions of dark forces anathema to civilization, choice and consent are based on reason. And reason is why Alexander Hamilton, speaking for all his fellow-Founders, abhorred war: "When the sword is once drawn," he wrote in *Federalist* 16, "the passions of men observe no bounds of moderation."[14] It is precisely because he hated armed conflict that he advocated being prepared for it.

The often neglected differences between the American "revolution" as opposed to the more appropriately so called conflagrations in both France and Russia are masterfully elucidated by the University of Chicago historian James H. Billington in his seminal study *Fire in the Minds of Men: Origins of the Revolutionary Faith*. There he describes the American version as "a classic contest for political liberty secured by constitutional complexity,"[15] contrasting the rational ideals of our Founders with the visceral impulse of "those seeking the more unlimited gratifications of nationalist fraternity"[16] that lead inexorably to totalitarianism. And as both Arendt and Horowitz[17] have definitively demonstrated, totalitarianisms resort to genocide. Far from intoxicated with overthrowing the prevailing political philosophy as were the Jacobins, not to mention Lenin, Trotsky, and of course Stalin, the American Founders sought to implement it, believing it to be ideally rooted in liberty.

What distinguished the Americans from traditional revolutionaries, for whom bloodshed is a rite of passage, was the former's adoption of essentially traditional, not to say conservative, principles as articulated by English and Scottish philosophers. Those principles, which echoed age-old lessons learned from Greek and Roman sages, were ultimately based on belief in the existence of a benevolent Creator and a deeply ingrained distrust of war and violence. The Americans also grasped, admittedly with varying degrees of clarity, the fact that liberty could not be preserved without a solid constitutional framework based on a realistic assessment of human nature in historical context, with constantly evolving world events. Without that understanding, they might still have won their war, but they assuredly would have lost the peace.

The vision of a new world, extending far and wide, went well beyond theory. There were hard realities to take into account; and who better to provide them, outlined in a deceptively simple scientific paper, than the genius of Philadelphia, Benjamin Franklin. Published in 1751 under the unremarkable title "Observations Concerning the Increase of Mankind," his paper demonstrated by means of careful calculations that population in the British colonies doubled about every two decades. This meant that additional land would be needed soon. The savvy businessman noted also that British merchants would profit from the larger markets, which would likely embroil the Empire in wars with the French and the Indian tribes. It did.

At that early stage, separation from England was the last thing on Franklin's mind. What he worried about was just plain overcrowding. And practically minded as he always was, in 1754 he came up with a possible solution to the predicted demographic crisis: establishing a central colonial administrative body that could both fight the French and address the Indian problem. Though such an idea had little chance of being adopted at that particular time, Franklin was patient, awaiting his opportunity, which came even sooner than he had expected.

Shortly after being appointed Pennsylvania's representative to England, in 1757, he took advantage of his presence in London to convince the British to occupy Canada as well as the land south and west of the Mississippi—and succeeded. It would not be long before the same rationale would logically apply to America's conception of its own size and scope as exceeding the limited territory occupied by the thirteen colonies immediately after winning their war of independence. If the argument that population expansion was intimately connected to the need for security applied to the British, it did so even more to the fledgling United States, whose security was far more precarious.

Franklin's implicit anticipation of a much larger future nation reverberated, if only subliminally, albeit from a very different perspective, in the staunchly Puritan heart of the Bostonian Sam Adams. A Harvard graduate, steeped in Roman history, Adams was a disciple of the English empiricist philosopher John Locke (1632–1704), reputed Father of Classical Liberalism, whose *Second Treatise on Government* (1680) had demonstrated that consent rooted in universal reason legitimized political power. Convinced that Britain was in irreversible decline—in no small part because of the undue power of a wealthy, sclerotic elite—Sam Adams believed its empire not only would fail to expand but expire altogether in the near future for while America was young, Britain was old and feeble, with the size of its military obscuring its fundamental impotence.

Prescient, Adams had felt this as early as 1748, seeing no alternative to a separation between the two realms straddling the ocean. But it would take time for the colonists to contemplate and eventually accept that possibility. The moment came at last after the French and Indian War of 1754–63. Not only had the American troops gained invaluable experience and confidence; they were also struck by the ready availability of great territories. What Franklin had merely calculated, they got to see with their own eyes: there was plenty of room here for the growing and vigorous new nation. Why not take advantage of it?

This sentiment was especially prevalent in Massachusetts, which had contributed a great deal of money and maintained a large army in that war. Small wonder, then, that Parliament's decision to tax the colonies by issuing the infamous Stamp Act, in order to help restock the British treasury, outraged the inhabitants of that worthy colony. A measure that disproportionately hurt the good merchants, printers, lawyers, and other skilled and productive citizens of Massachusetts, the British indifference to their well-being had managed to infuriate the most articulate and influential among them. It fully radicalized Sam Adams, who became the self-appointed leader of a popular movement that galvanized key segments of the population to pursue a break with Great Britain. That movement explains in large part why so many distinguished men were willing to risk signing the momentous Declaration, despite knowing full well that it was treasonous.

By 1776, the Founders had the temerity to seek more than just independence from England. The thirteen colonies that had constituted the original States of America to pursue self-government rooted in ancient ideas about society and the purpose of man aimed higher still. They planned to establish a genuinely secure nation, capable of surviving into the distant future, shielded by ocean waters, preferably on all sides, against intrusion. Without fully understanding that grand vision, which motivated the leadership of the American experiment we call our Revolution, we cannot appreciate the remarkable daring and ingenuity of their strategic approach.

This analysis directly contradicts Henry Kissinger's interpretation of America's original stance, which he takes to have been isolationist. (In this he differs from Kagan, though the two agree that America eventually came to adopt what they both consider a more sensible form of realism, or perhaps *Realpolitik*—to which we will return in chapter 17.) Historical exegesis is not for scholars only: for it matters deeply what the nation originally thought of its mission. It defines who we are. History should never be distorted to boost a particular foreign policy approach. Yet Kissinger seems to do just that. He paraphrases George Washington's admonition to his contemporaries, in his Farewell Address, to refrain from implicating their country "in the ordinary vicissitudes" of European politics, interpreting it as tantamount to an alleged warning "against 'permanent' alliances for any cause whatsoever."[18] Kissinger thus scoffs at what he takes to have been a naïve moralism, which amounted to a "rejection of the truisms of European diplomacy that the balance of power distilled an ultimate harmony out of the competition of selfish interests, and that security considerations overrode the principles of civil law; in other words, that the ends justifies the means."[19]

Never mind that, had the Founders really been so "oblivious" to the workings of European diplomacy, they could scarcely have prevailed in that cauldron. Kissinger is right that the Founders didn't think that the *modus operandi* of European diplomacy, which they considered an "ends-justify-means" pragmatism-cynicism, were "truisms," let alone worth emulating. But Kissinger's claim that, contrary to their rhetoric, "in the early years of the Republic, American foreign policy was in fact a sophisticated reflection of American national interest,"[20] and hence a sign of hypocrisy, is dead wrong. It was not. The Founders saw no contradiction between America's national interest and its repudiation of European power politics. Quite the opposite.

Kissinger next turns to the Monroe Doctrine as the smoking gun that, in his view, proves America's moralism to be, as always, disingenuous: "Under the umbrella of the Monroe Doctrine, America could pursue policies which were not all that different from the dreams of any European king—expanding its commerce and influence, annexing territory—in short, turning itself into a Great Power without being required to practice power politics."[21] Kissinger's misreading of America's original approach to foreign policy might elucidate his own political philosophy, but it ruefully misrepresents his adopted nation's vision. Though American tactics could not fail to adapt to the realities of the day, the same was not true of the principles guiding its leaders' policies, which were very different indeed from "the dreams of any European king." Kissinger got it wrong: The Founders rejected cynicism, and they were not naïve.

In his book *The Way of the Fox: American Strategy in the War for America 1775–1783*, General Palmer explains clearly the complex purpose of the Revolutionary War, which included, besides the obvious one of independence from Britain, a limited territorial expansion beyond the original thirteen colonies. Most Founders thought such an expansion would be required for future survival:

> An aim neither so well known nor so generally accepted as independence, nor ever formally announced, it was nonetheless an acknowledged objective even before hostilities began. The drive to expand preceded the desire for independence. Together they formed a concise statement of the goal of grand strategy in the Revolutionary War: a United States unencumbered by European control and preeminent on the North American continent.[22]

Not until after signing the Declaration did anyone dare hope to fulfill that second aim, and then it was merely whispered, in secret instructions to American diplomats. For that reason, Washington's adaptive strategy included both offensive and defensive components, required by the larger goals that he had been determined to achieve. Writes General Palmer: "[T]he view beyond the horizon of war of the war showed a

United States independent of Europe and dominant in North America.... *Success or failure in winning the peace would depend upon whether patriot aims achieved the dual objective of the revolution.*[23] Inability to appreciate this fact is to miss entirely the very core of this nation's vision of itself and of its place in the world.

The ideas that ultimately became the Monroe Doctrine were actually anticipated four decades earlier, in 1781, by Alexander Hamilton/Publius in *Federalist* 11. "[O]ur situation," observes Hamilton, "invites[,] and our interests prompt us[,] to aim at an ascendant in the system of American affairs"[24]—explaining that the world may be divided into four geopolitical regions, namely Europe, Asia, Africa, and America. The latter, with poignantly deliberate ambiguity, implicitly includes the Western hemisphere as a whole.

Remonstrating Europe for being tempted to "plume itself mistress of the world" on the basis of unwarranted, "great pretensions," Hamilton has the chutzpah to admonish it, adding that it was now America's job to "teach that assuming brother moderation," and obviously resist becoming one more vassal state. The New World would be no meek little sibling; it would erect (and here comes the grand vision) "one great American system superior to the control of all transatlantic force or influence and able to dictate the terms of the connection between the old and the new world!"

Contrary to Kissinger's view, nothing was farther from Hamilton's mind than to create a double standard. Surely he was not castigating European imperialism while defending similar behavior by the United States: Hamilton believed that European colonialism was the natural consequence of condescending elitism and hostility to democracy. His opinions on imperialism had been clearly expressed in defense of recognizing the independence of Vermont against efforts by Hamilton's own state of New York to forcefully annex the Green Mountain state. In his memorable, though now all but forgotten, speech of March 14, 1787, Hamilton denounced coerced seizure of another community as a matter of principle. Writes historian Karl-Friedrich Walling: "Though neglected by Hamilton's partisans and critics alike, his short speech deserves to be considered as one of the classic American discussions of imperialism."[25]

For domestic political reasons, trying not to alienate his opponents more than necessary, Hamilton argued first on practical grounds that Vermonters, who were de facto, even if not de jure, no less independent than New Yorkers, would simply forge an alliance with foreign nations, thereby threatening the entire Union and thus, New York itself.[26] But his philosophical rationale against coercing people to live under occupation, as New York appeared ready to do, was far more comprehensive.

The occasion soon presented itself to express those views when, a few days later, on March 28, New York lawyer Richard Harison explicitly suggested, in a fit of hubris, that New Yorkers emulate the Romans. Hamilton forcefully retorted: "Neither the manners nor the genius of Rome are suited to the republic or age we live in. All her maxims and habits were military, her government was constituted for war. Ours is unfit for it and our situation still less than our constitution, invites us to emulate the conduct of Rome, or to attempt a display of unprofitable heroism."[27] He added that "a scheme of coercion" would be ill-suited to the "disposition of our citizens; the habits of thinking, to which the revolution has given birth, are not adapted to the idea of a contest for dominion over a people not inclined to live under our government."[28]

What Hamilton expressed was a conviction that the idea of self-government was incompatible with imperial designs and imperial behavior. Walling observes that here were "the seeds of the Monroe Doctrine as a vehicle for resisting European imperialism;" and though "there was no possible way for Hamilton to offer prescriptions when the Latin American colonies had not yet won their independence . . . he was not encouraging imperialism in any way."[29] It is quite true, of course, that American ascendance could lead to imperialism—and did so, in the late nineteenth century—but not only was this not inevitable, it was in fact contrary to the Founders' vision. Walling doesn't mince words: "[L]ate-nineteenth century views of imperialism as a positive benefit for peoples subjugated by Americans were as much a corruption of the Founders' thought as were views of slavery as a positive good before the civil war."[30]

It is interesting how closely this approach tracks Sun Tzu and the Taoists. As British scholar John Gittings notes in *The Glorious Art of Peace: From the Iliad to Iraq*, Sun Tzu was deeply skeptical of warfare, as stated bluntly in the first sentence of *The Art of War*. The treatise as a whole is predicated on the notion that defeating an enemy's strategy is far superior to waging battles, further implying that military conflict is at best a necessary evil. Gittings finds that early Chinese strategic thinking parallels ancient Greek approaches to war in that both gradually evolved toward a "more considered view" of war. He shows how the Greeks turned away from glorification of valor in battle, as demonstrated in Homer's *Iliad*, to disillusion accompanied by an increased appreciation for the peaceful virtues, as illustrated later in his *Odyssey*. And so too, finds Gittings, did the Chinese: "There is a shift over time from a single-minded focus on the martial virtues—*wu*—under the Shang dynasty—to viewing these as complementary to the civil virtues—*wen*"[31]

And indeed, as we have seen, Sun Tzu believed that true leadership must be based on moral influence—which is antithetical to force. Moral influence is "that which causes the people to be in harmony with their leaders" (*AoW*, I. 4)—obviously impossible if the leader subjugates them. But perhaps the most important principle of Sun Tzu philosophy that most faithfully applies to the Founders' own credo, is this: *If not in the interests of the state, do not act. If you cannot succeed, do not use troops. If you are not in danger, do not fight.* (*AoW*, XII. 17) Regarding this last sentence, Samuel Griffith comments: "The commentators make it clear that war is to be used only as a last resort."[32] In other words, unless attacked, leave others alone. America's Founders had not sought to fight unless they deemed it indispensable to their survival. Nothing could more clearly express the non-expansionist attitude that our Founders most certainly shared.

Hamilton's views resonated with the young John Quincy Adams, who would later become the real author of the doctrine that came to bear the name of the president who adopted it in 1823. James Monroe having requested the advice of all his cabinet members concerning America's foreign policy, John Quincy responded by expressing his "earnest remonstrance against any interference of the European powers by force with South America, but to disclaim all interference on our part with Europe." He thus submitted a proposal that "the American continents by the free and independent condition which they have assumed, and maintain, are henceforth not to be considered as subject for future colonization by any European power"—words that Monroe included verbatim in his Doctrine, which he would address in Congress to the world. Harlow Giles Unger believes that everyone understood: "[M]ost European leaders realized [that] it would be far less costly to trade with Americans than to try to subjugate them."[33]

Far from morally equivalent to the kingdoms of Europe, the United States' system of government was, to use John Quincy's own words, "essentially extra-European." He wrote to the American representative in Moscow on July 5, 1820: "To stand in firm and cautious independence of all entanglements in the European system has been a cardinal point of their [the U.S.] policy under every administration of their government, from the peace of 1783 to this day."[34] Historian Paul A. Varg notes that "whether one examines the writings of Jefferson, Madison, or John Quincy Adams, one finds repeatedly a symbol of America and another of Europe," but "this moralism did not inhibit a hard-headed pragmatic approach to foreign policy. The founding fathers made the best of all worlds, appeal to justice and energetic defense of national interest."[35] Although Alexander Hamilton was the only one who explicitly underscored the latter, Jefferson and Madison were no less sanguine defenders. Unlike Kissinger, however, Varg refuses to impugn their motives: "This was not a devious employment of rhetoric, but a sincere expression of their honestly held views."[36]

Unfortunately, the all-too American propensity to engage in self-righteous rhetoric eventually came to cloud our own judgment of ourselves, and undermined our ability to recognize that morality and the pursuit of the national interest are not in conflict but can, and should, complement each other. What further obscured our vision was a peculiar reading of our Declaration as implying that since all men (people) are equal, there is a moral imperative to defend the natural rights of everyone. Some go still further, interpreting equality not only as a right to freedom, or a right to noninterference, but a substantive, positive right to equality of outcome, which would include the elimination of income disparity along with most other forms of equality. Both readings, though especially the latter, which sets the Founders' vision completely on its head, ignore the radical contrast between the Lockeian roots of our own conservative liberalism[37] as against the pre-Marxist utopia-fever that afflicted the leadership of the cannibalistic French conflagration of 1789 and, later, the other genocidal totalitarianisms of the twentieth century.

In brief, the Americans knew what their end game was, and were prepared to attain it by all means at their disposal. That said, moral selfishness and disregard for individual rights was farthest from the Founders' mind. Not only did they seek to advance and institute those same individual rights rather than merely, hypocritically, pursue the interests of power politics, they sought to do it with the least bloodshed, and not only because of the colonies' obvious military inferiority. The Founders shared a deeply rooted, even excessive, conviction in the efficacy of instruments of peace. Those included diplomacy, commerce, and propaganda, naturally all bolstered by effective intelligence. Although some of the Founders temporarily succumbed to ideological fervor that clouded their better judgment, for the most part they got it spectacularly right.

Notes

1. See Mary Matossian, 221–22 and John Hutchinson, 123, in John Hutchinson and Anthony D. Smith, eds., *Nationalism* (Oxford: Oxford University Press, 1994).
2. Robert Kagan, *Dangerous Nation* (New York: Alfred Knopff, 2006), 1.
3. Ibid., 5.
4. http://www.mountvernon.org/research-collections/digital-encyclopedia/article/henry-lee-jr/
5. Michael Hornblow, "Not the Quiet City on a Hill," *American Diplomacy*, May 2007. http://www.unc.edu/depts/diplomat/item/2007/0406/book/book_hornblow.html
6. David M. Kennedy, "Rogue State," *Washington Post*, October 29, 2006.
7. Thomas H. Maddox, "Dangerous Nation: Review," in *H-Diplo*, April 29, 2007. http://www.h-net.org/~diplo/roundtables/PDF/DangerousNation-Roundtable.pdf
8. Kagan, *Dangerous Nation*, 137.
9. Dave Richard Palmer, *The Way of the Fox: American Strategy in the War for America 1775–1783* (Westport, CT: Greenwood Press, 1975), xiii.
10. Ibid.
11. Hannah Arendt, *On Revolution* (New York: Penguin Books, 1965), Hannah Arendt, *On Revolution* (New York: Penguin Books, 1965), 44.
12. Ibid., 21.
13. Ibid., 213–14.
14. Alexander Hamilton, James Madison, and John Jay, *The Federalist Papers*, with an introduction by Clinton Rossiter (New York: The New American Library, 1961), 114.
15. James H. Billington, *Fire in the Minds of Men: Origins of the Revolutionary Faith* (New York: Basic Books, 1980), 10. This is the best, most readable account of the Romantic origins of the French and Russian revolutions.
16. Ibid. If Marx called religion "the opium of the people," Billington cleverly suggests that "the new faith might well be called the amphetamine of the intellectuals." (p. 8). I might suggest "cocaine" instead.
17. See Irving Louis Horowitz, ref.
18. Henry Kissinger, *Diplomacy* (New York: Touchstone Books, 1994), 32.
19. Ibid., 33–34.
20. Ibid., 30.
21. Ibid., 36.
22. Palmer, *The Way of the Fox*, 77.
23. Ibid., 92 (Emphasis added).
24. Hamilton, Madison, and Jay, *Federalist* 11, 90.
25. Karl-Friedrich Walling, *Republican Empire: Alexander Hamilton on War and Free Government* (Lawrence: University Press of Kansas, 1999), 85.
26. http://Founders.archives.gov/documents/Hamilton/01-04-02-0056
27. Ibid.
28. Ibid., 87.
29. Ibid., 115.

30. Ibid.
31. Gittings, *The Glorious Art of Peace*, 69–70.
32. Griffith, *Sun Tzu - The Art of War*, 142.
33. Harlow Giles Unger, *John Quincy Adams* (Philadelphia, PA: Da Capo Press, 2012), 219.
34. *Annals of America*, vol. 4, 643.
35. Paul A. Varg, *Foreign Policies of the Founding Fathers* (Baltimore, MD: Penguin Books, 1970), 304.
36. Ibid.
37. For a superb analysis of the Lockeian roots of the American system of government, see Carl. L. Becker, *The Declaration of Independence: A Study in the History of Political Ideas* (New York: Vintage Books, 1942), esp. ch. II.

6

Influencing

*The revolution was in the minds and hearts of the people,
and this was effected from 1760–1775, in the course of
fifteen years, before a drop of blood was shed at Lexington.*
—John Adams to Thomas Jefferson, August 23, 1787

*There is nothing more necessary than good intelligence to frustrate the
enemy, and nothing that requires greater pains to obtain.*
—George Washington to Robert Hunter Morris, January 5, 1766

The extraordinary phenomenon that was the American system of self-government erected upon the shores of the New World could only be understood from the shores of the Old by an equally extraordinary mind. Such a one providentially could be found, applauding from the Mother Country no less. In awe of what these plucky descendants of Englishmen were able to accomplish, and so quickly, the Dublin-born British MP Edmund Burke (1729–1797) told his colleagues in the House of Commons on March 22, 1775: "America is a noble object."[1] But on that occasion, Burke did more than explain why he opposed an armed conflict with the American colonies; ever the measured philosopher, he outlined the various reasons why a peaceful resolution of conflict, whenever possible, is invariably preferable to violent confrontation. His perspective provides the perfect backdrop for analyzing the Art of Peace in its American version.

What Burke proposed was not a complicated and unstable peace process achieved after lengthy negotiations, or after "universal discord" had already, poisonously, penetrated the sinews of the Empire, but merely a "simple peace, sought in its natural course, and in its ordinary haunts." Since evolution in human affairs is exceedingly complex, Burke believed that opposition to a natural course in social change is fraught with peril, for it assumes both excessive trust in the power of human intervention and unwarranted overconfidence in the moral rightness of the interventionists. A contemporary of Adam Smith, Burke fully agreed with the latter's faith in an "invisible hand" guiding nature toward felicitous ends.

Burke's response to the counter-argument—that America was too precious for England to just let go "without a fight"—was to agree sarcastically that yes, "certainly it is, if fighting a people be the best way of gaining them." Regardless of the weapons the Empire chose to resist the budding nation, Burke presumed that England would probably prevail: "I do not look on the direct and immediate power of the colonies to resist our violence as very formidable."[2] The casual aside that followed—"in this, however, I may be mistaken"—only underscores his point that ultimately it did not matter, since a forced, unnatural victory is *no victory* at all. Besides, how can it make sense to wound grievously, let alone destroy, a coveted prize? "It seems to my poor understanding a little preposterous to make them [the colonies] unserviceable in order to keep them obedient."[3] Instead, Burke proposed taking a closer look at the realities on the ground, which seemed to overwhelmingly support the proposition that England would do well to recognize, if not embrace outright, the colonists' astounding success in applying the very lessons learned from their British masters.

Those realities, in Burke's view, all pointed toward accepting the legitimacy of American aspirations to autonomy, based on empirical facts. For one thing, the sheer size of the population and its continued rapid growth rate made it all but impossible to manage from afar, especially by a tiny island such as Britain, no matter how culturally sophisticated. The commercial and economic impact of the new democratic powerhouse across the ocean, moreover, was so massive that, were its value to be diminished as a result of violent confrontation, no one would be better off.

Burke persuasively declared that his "opinion is much more in favor of prudent management than of force; considering force not as an odious but a feeble instrument for preserving a people so numerous, so active, so growing, so spirited as this in a profitable and subordinate connection with us."[4] This argument is first of all pragmatic: considering all the relevant evidence, the use of force alone would simply not work. The remedy would be temporary at best, and force would soon have to be wielded again, which all but defeats the purpose of a war supposedly designed to end calls for independence: a nation cannot be said to be governed when it is "perpetually to be conquered." Yet Burke is also, and more importantly, advancing a moral defense of

American independence: force is not merely a feeble instrument but an *odious* one.

By far the most striking reason why Burke favored allowing the colonists to exercise self-rule is their "temper and character:" Americans are an amazingly *spirited* people. Their most striking trait is an unquenchable love of freedom. Not only are they "devoted to liberty, but to liberty according to English ideas, and on English principles."[5] The colonists are England's own children; far from attacking and destroying them, it should feel proud of their accomplishments and help them along even further, like a doting parent, not a stern foe. Even more remarkable is their demonstrable ability to apply those principles, by organizing provincial legislative assemblies, passing laws, and abiding by the rule of law. Highly educated, especially in law, the colonists are also deeply religious—and Protestants to boot. As if the name itself wasn't self-explanatory, Burke warns that Americans belong disproportionately to just "that kind which is the most adverse to all implicit submission of mind and opinion. . . . a persuasion not only favorable to liberty, but built upon it."[6] Thinking for themselves is who they *are*.

The presumptive father of modern conservatism, Burke stood in awe of the near-miraculous new implant on the continent beyond the Atlantic. Devoted to the great ideals of Western—and specifically British—civilization, Americans proved capable of evolving into a self-sustaining, self-governing civil society, even in the absence of formal democratic rules, yet rooted in popular consent, and all *without resort to violence*. For that above all, Burke's admiration was boundless. "They have formed a government sufficient for its purposes without the bustle of a revolution or the troublesome formality of an election. Evident necessity and tacit consent have done the business in an instant."[7] Burke would have undoubtedly understood the political implications of Sun Tzu's observation: "When torrential water tosses boulders, it is because of its momentum" (*AoW* V. 13). Indeed, the colonists' torrential commitment to self-government and sovereignty would toss boulders at the British military were it to stand athwart the revolutionaries' fierce desire for self-government, its momentum unstoppable.

Perhaps better than anyone in Britain at the time, Burke had grasped what made the new American society unique: dedicated to the universal right to freedom, which encompasses the unhindered exercise of both liberty of conscience and of property; individualistic yet spiritual; energetic and ambitious, yet distrustful of European-style empire building and conquest. Though bordering on the idyllic, this description certainly fits the ideal shared by most of America's key Founders. It provides the necessary background for understanding the roots of the nation's strategic culture.

On one key point, however, Burke had been wrong: to have "done the business" of self-governance, it took far longer than "an instant." Nor was it only a matter of time; the necessity was by no means "evident" to all; and consent was painstakingly forged, long before it became "tacit." It all took enormous amounts of work, undaunted determination, and unmatched talent, on the part of an elite of—what historian Philip Davidson, in his classic *Propaganda and the American Revolution 1763–1783*, has called—"propagandists."

Davidson defines propaganda as "simply an attempt to control the actions of people indirectly by controlling their attitudes."[8] To diffuse its negative connotations, he tries to differentiate the *purpose* of the attempt, which may be unobjectionable, from the *techniques* used to promote it, which could be shady. Even in the unlikely eventuality that this linguistic sleight-of-hand were adopted, however, the negative connotations of the word would still be inescapable. In the first place, even the noblest of causes suffers from crass salesmanship. What is more, by the time Davidson's book was published in 1941, his audience had already experienced the full impact of Nazi propaganda, whose soul-numbing obscenity had terminally sullied the term. Nor did the linguistic garbage of its Communist clone, who embraced "propaganda" with neo-evangelical enthusiasm far exceeding the zeal even of its originators,[9] do the term's reputation any good. Trying to restore its more neutral meaning was no longer an option; Davidson came too late.

But his definition is flawed on another count as well: Attempting to *control* attitudes is very different from seeking to *influence* them. While the former, understandably, is generally thought illegitimate except in rare circumstances, the latter defines all engagement—though it may indeed be more or less deliberate, and more or less successful. Therefore, if "propaganda" is defined simply as "an attempt to influence people's attitudes," it becomes superfluous: *influencing* will do by itself, minus the stigma.

After all, any form of communication seeks to have an effect on attitudes, which implies a desire, however subliminal, to influence the outcome. Ideally at least, every teacher influences (presumably for the better), and every student, at least ideally, expects to be influenced. Mandatory education is predicated on the assumption that those being educated may rightfully demand to be influenced by being taught; it is widely accepted that staying ignorant, except in very rare cases, is a handicap. The survival of a free society especially depends on the widespread availability of information. Davidson is right that "the more democratic a community, the more need for first marshaling opinion."[10] Opinion should be thus marshalled, and shared. Whatever it may be called, Davidson argues that influencing was absolutely "indispensable to those who first promoted resistance to specific British acts and ultimately urged revolution."[11] That said, however, they could not have *controlled* attitudes even if they had wanted to—which, truth be told, they often did. But they didn't have to; their persuasive powers alone proved sufficient.

The colonial revolutionaries, most of them well-to-do, had not originally intended to overthrow anything—quite the contrary: "Instead of attempting to change the existing situation, they tried to maintain it."[12] Lawyers and judges, merchants in the North and planters in the South, the majority of the colonial ruling class had been unprepared for the sudden decision by the British government, starting in 1763, to increase and enforce legislation designed to raise taxes and regulate commerce. Their first reaction was to seek a return to the previous conditions when Parliament had made it easy for colonists to evade most regulations without repercussions. But with the changed circumstances, calls for "independence" increased exponentially, at higher and still higher decibels, notwithstanding the danger.

Admittedly, that word did not necessarily connote total separation from Great Britain.[13] For one thing, advertising such a desire would invite the charge of treason—a potentially suicidal tactic. Instead, the elite American influencers adopted a multilayered, shrewd approach to what would eventually become a full-fledged pursuit of sovereign independence and statehood, consisting of: "[P]rivate efforts to work out a concerted program, public denials that they had anything of the sort in mind, a cautious propaganda campaign subtly suggesting the idea, and, finally, as the thought took hold, an open campaign in favor of it."[14] What this general description, however, fails utterly to capture is the astounding ingenuity and courage, the improvisations and constant calibrations, performed by the authors of this delicate performance that changed the course of history. But even among that amazingly talented elite group of influencers and practitioners of political warfare, one stood out far ahead of the others. His name was Sam Adams.

Adams was a superb pamphleteer, usually writing under a pen name so as to enhance the impression that there were many more voices speaking, his ego subsumed to the service of his mission. Aside from publishing opinions, his own and that of others, Adams engaged in voluminous correspondence with leaders throughout England and the colonies, whose thinking he sought—and was usually able—to affect. He also created a chain of organizations called Committees of Correspondence, which coordinated political action with breathtaking effectiveness, joining a slew of other committees which exchanged information, planned mass rallies and engaged in other forms of popular expression, which all served to nurture the revolution, as his cousin and future president John Adams put it, "in the hearts and minds of the people."

A term that is both more comprehensive than *propaganda* and more relevant to the contemporary scene is *strategic communication*. In the absence of a universally accepted definition, arguably the best has been proposed by RAND Corporation senior social scientist Christopher Paul: "I define strategic communication as **coordinated actions, messages, images, and other forms of signaling or engagement intended to inform, influence, or persuade selected audiences in support of national objectives."**[15] *Coordinated action* became Sam Adams's most stunning instrument, skillfully emulated by others for common objectives that would soon deserve being described as *national*.

There was certainly no World War I–style Bureau of Public Information in colonial times; but given sufficient ingenuity, it was possible to put the existing government (mostly state) agencies to good use. Indeed, the earliest protests against the newly enacted British laws considered palpably unjust by most colonists, far from being instigated by ruffians and rabble rousers, were actually carried out through regularly established official bodies. It helped that the lower houses in the assemblies, along with the colonial courts, the town governments of New England and the county governments of middle and southern colonies, were dominated by pro-republican Whigs rather than pro-British loyalists. Resolutions could be passed, with even the slimmest majority of one sufficient to give an impression of unanimity, which could then be communicated to other colonies with pleas for support. At the outset, this was done principally through Committees of Correspondence. But once the royally appointed governors caught on to this practice and took to dissolving assemblies, tactics changed accordingly: provincial congresses were set up, often in an adjoined room to the assemblies, and business went right on, with new Committees of Correspondence.

Though the complete plan for coordinating the action of colonial assemblies had been the work of Virginians Richard Henry Lee and Thomas Jefferson, there had been no regular system of communication among towns. That did not stop town leaders from stimulating other activities by means of town meetings, which would soon proliferate throughout the colonies. But Sam Adams saw the importance of better central organization, along with establishing regular Committees of Correspondence beyond towns. But ever the realist, as a first step, he needed to know whether "the Sentiments of the Country are different from those of the City [regarding opposition to British laws]. Therefore a free Communication with each Town will serve to ascertain this matter; and when once it appears beyond Contradiction, that we are united in Sentiments there will be a Confidence in each other, & a plan of Opposition will be easily formed, & executed with Spirit."[16]

Information-gathering would certainly help the planners of an effective revolution to assess as accurately as possible the mood of the people. But at least as important, setting up an elaborate relay of communication across a wide territory would send a signal to the enemies who, "should [they] see the flame bursting in different parts of the Country & distant from each other, it might discourage their attempts to damp & quench it."[17] Note that Adams did not presume to *kindle* the flame of opposition but merely to *stoke* it; nor at this stage did he plan to necessarily hurt the enemy, only to deter it.

The committee set up by Sam Adams in Boston on November 2, 1772, was ordered to make a report on the rights of the colony of Massachusetts and document their violation. Next, Adams wrote to friends in other towns, in Massachusetts as well as elsewhere in New England, seeking their support in setting up similar such committees—which they did. The towns proceeded to engage in regular communication, with the result that previously inactive rural towns became energized and mobilized to support opposition actions.

The pivotal point was reached in May, 1774, when a proposal by radicals in Massachusetts to boycott all import and export trade with Great Britain to protest unfair taxation was deemed sufficiently momentous to debate throughout the colonies, and a "continental congress" sent to Philadelphia later in October of that year. By August, the entire country had been covered by the ingenious communication system. Writes Davidson: "The political [influence] machine was complete."[18] He adds: "[T]he system of committees created to unify the protests of the towns and colonies and to arouse the people against British legislation constituted the most important organization for the dissemination of [strategic communication] that was created throughout the entire period."[19]

But the proverbial devil, or in this case, angel, is in the details, whose intricate complexity required masterful leadership; for example, alongside the elite members of the assemblies and town leaders, the consciousness of two more groups was raised to high pitch by British taxation: merchants and mechanics. The former created what today are called chambers of commerce, while the latter established a powerful group that became known as the Sons of Liberty. Made up entirely of working men, the importance of the Sons of Liberty, established in the summer of 1765, almost instantly skyrocketed, so that by November, it "practically directed throughout the colonies the entire movement against the [Stamp] act."[20]

There was a problem, however, with this incredibly influential group. Predictably, its loudest and strongest members were basically mob leaders who specialized in violence. They had to be tempered: Were this detail left to the devil, it could jeopardize the whole enterprise. Fortunately, the sophisticated leadership of the colonists took effective measures to keep the uncouth ruffians in control. Coercive measures against the enemy were not ruled out; but these could not be allowed to flare up without very close strategic oversight and direction.

The savvy influencers' ingenious tactics notwithstanding, no communication relay, no matter how smooth, would have succeeded were not the substance of the message in tune with the people's hearts, and seamlessly argued to conquer their minds. That was indeed the crux of the matter: in addition to a careful reading of popular attitudes, it took a solid classical education, particularly a deep knowledge of the law, to craft the message. Indispensable too were a talent for rhetoric, genuine empathy, and a keen insight into the needs, interests, and aspirations of colonists along a wide stretch of land, in disparate circumstances. To be sure, not all the Founders possessed this entire panoply of qualities, certainly not in equal degree. And then too, personalities inevitably clashed, to the detriment of the common interest; still, the ensuing harmony was sufficient for eventual success.

The torch that effectively lit the revolutionary flame in January 1776 was an anonymous pamphlet titled *Common Sense*, which became an instant bestseller, outdone only by the Bible. The work of master rhetorician Tom Paine, the clarion sermon on a political mount thundered: "The cause of America is in a great measure the cause of all mankind."[21]

The anonymity of their authorship tacitly implied that the nation spoke with one voice, the sentiment of those fine words unanimous. Paine's incendiary publication had arrived at precisely the right time, its popularity providing Congress, by April, the courage to defy British mercantile laws and open American ports to the entire world.[22] By June, Richard Henry Lee would resolve that "these United Colonies are, and of right ought to be, free and independent states," which empowered them to form the "foreign alliances" needed to prevail against their mammoth enemy. Days later, the Declaration of Independence was signed. America was born.

It would take volumes to list the plethora of *influencing* tactics and venues that together, in ways large and small, contributed to galvanizing the population and created the necessary support for the Revolution. Among these were: sermons and newspaper articles; speeches by college presidents and professors; letters to the editor; strategically targeted private correspondence to key opinion leaders; leaked incriminating personal letters by loyalists, variously intercepted, published to embarrass; anti-commemorations, throughout the colonies, of British actions portrayed as, and often believed to have been, egregious; incitements of volatile British soldiers, whose opinions of the colonists were notoriously low and egregiously wrong; morale-building and British-bashing songs, plays, and poems; and many other tactics. Once the war heated up, after the battle of Lexington, the newspapers continued their work, playing up American successes for all their worth (and then some, for good measure), while simultaneously magnifying British losses (with equal panache, and the occasional embellishment). Spin control, though hardly invented by the colonists, was performed with consummate skill.

Having lived through these momentous events himself, Dr. David Ramsay writes with authority in *The History of the American Revolution*, published in 1789, the year of the Constitution: "[I]n establishing American independence, the pen and the press had a merit equal to that of the sword."[23] Nearly two centuries later, historian Arthur M. Schlesinger confirmed that his own research "fully sustains Dr. Ramsay's conclusion . . . that 'the exertions of the army would have been insufficient to effect the revolution, unless the great body of the people had been prepared for it, and also kept in a constant disposition to oppose Great Britain.'"[24] It had been a full-spectrum effort using all the instruments of power.

Sun Tzu would have approved with enthusiasm. For influencing was precisely the point of his famous admonition that success is based on "attacking the enemy's strategy" rather than resorting to battle. Address the conceptual basis for the conflict, including sowing discord among your enemy's supporters—"disrupt his alliances" (*AoW* III. 5)—while obviously building your own, for "he whose ranks are united in purpose will be victorious" (*AoW* III. 27). Much of Sam Adams's influencing involved uniting the ranks of the colonists, then building those ranks, and defining their purpose: How could they fail to be victorious? He would make Sun Tzu proud.

Influence operations, however, had to target not only the American public but also the relevant foreign audiences—both friend and foe. This was particularly true once the fighting started, when the colonists needed every advantage they could possibly garner. If a ragtag bunch of untrained, unpaid, often hungry militiamen attacking the most formidable army in the world sounds like a movie plot, it would have to be a comedy. But unbeknownst to His Majesty's smugly resplendent Goliaths, they were up against some mighty clever Davids, whose fierce commitment to their nation's independence and its righteousness knew no bounds. Yankee Doodle could care less what anyone called the feather in his cap: sartorial splendor wasn't on his agenda. Victory was.

A crucial technique the clever upstarts would soon come to master was, no surprise to Sun Tzu, deception, including the use of double-agents and disinformation. Though espionage is perhaps the world's second oldest profession, its methods have evolved. By the eighteenth century, spycraft had become more sophisticated—as a tall young colonel from Virginia, assigned as aide to British Maj. Gen. Edward Braddock in the French and Indian wars, would learn, and not forget. Astute and diligent, never too proud to learn more, by the time George Washington assumed his position as the Continental Army's chief of intelligence, he was already master of the trade. He came to value intelligence immensely, having apparently "well understood that the greatest British failure in the French and Indian war had been poor basic intelligence."[25]

It should be noted that during the eighteenth century, the concept of intelligence encompassed a far wider field of resources than it does today, as it referred to any new information or news received. In contrast, the current definition is restricted to "information about an adversary usually obtained through secret means."[26] Former CIA officer Kenneth A. Daigler believes that Washington may have been far more impressed by his British superiors' lack of cultural and understanding than by the absence of what we would call "classified" material. Despite his inexperience, what Washington possessed was an appreciation for grasping local conditions, known in contemporary spy-talk as "counterintelligence situational awareness."[27]

The older, broader definition of intelligence may in fact be preferable, and could be experiencing a comeback, as open source information is exploding thanks to the internet, and with the advent of social media. Then as now, truly understanding any environment requires broad appreciation of context, which is gained through a wide variety of sources and methods. Wisely mined, the past contains invaluable, rich troves of wisdom. The most precious of old lessons—if, ironically, least heeded—are learned from errors. Washington knew this, having approached his apprenticeship in the British expedition as an educational and professional experience, rather than merely a means to advancement. Unafraid to recognize his own limitations, Washington "was well aware of the military mistakes he had made, and one of his great strengths of character was his ability to recognize such mistakes and learn from them."[28]

Thus by 1754, when the French and Indian war ended, Washington had mastered the art of spying: "He had demonstrated skills in elicitation, propaganda, deception, and the use of collection agents."[29] He would write to a friend on January 5, 1766: "There is nothing more necessary than good intelligence to frustrate a designing enemy, & nothing that requires greater pains to obtain."[30] Faithful to his own advice, when he later encountered an enemy busy "designing," Washington proved able to outdesign him.

In his appreciation for the indispensable role of reliable intelligence, and relevant information more generally, he followed, however unwittingly, Sun Tzu. The Chinese sage's observation that "the reason the enlightened prince and the wise general conquer an enemy whenever they move and their achievements surpass those of ordinary men is foreknowledge" (*AoW* XIII. 3) applies perfectly to Washington, who functioned simultaneously as wise general and enlightened prince. His achievements clearly surpassed those of ordinary men, and resulted in no small measure from his reliance on just that sort of "foreknowledge."

Washington would also have agreed with Sun Tzu that good intelligence "cannot be elicited from spirits nor from gods, nor by analogy with past events, nor from calculations. It must be obtained from men who know the enemy situation" (*AoW* XIII. 4). In other words: spies. Intelligence, moreover, is always necessary, in war as in peace, on the battleground and elsewhere: "There is no place where espionage is not used" (*AoW* XIII. 14), for vigilance must be maintained at all time to prevent surprise attacks.

Nor is intelligence restricted to gathering information, but extends to undertaking deception operations, including covert action, appropriately used "at appropriate times" (*AoW* XIII. 20). Advises Sun Tzu: "Secret operations are essential in war; upon them the army relies to make its every move" (*AoW* XIII. 23). Though applied during warfare, Sun Tzu is talking about weapons that are not intrinsically lethal. Influencing and intelligence are not only useful in offensive operations but at least as necessary for defensive action, and may help preempt military confrontation or at least minimize casualties.

Washington used such "secret operations" with alacrity. Early in the Revolutionary war, for example, in July 1776, after learning, from a British soldier who had just deserted, that supplies were running low, he surmised that more soldiers might be willing to give up the fight. Immediately, he ordered that both leaflets and oral communication be used to convince British troops that food, health care, and personal freedoms were ready for the taking if they switched sides. Though only the last could actually be guaranteed, and the number of deserters does not appear to have been large, the real impact of the influence operations "was to contribute to low British morale, which in turn led to inactivity on the part of the British command."[31] Mission accomplished.

Covert action was another invaluable tool wielded by American revolutionaries during the early stages of the war, specifically in obtaining military assistance and loans from the French government. The French also provided (again, covertly) military officers with special skills, ships, and—most important—the use of their ports for American naval operations. Benjamin Franklin was key to securing these arrangements: among his most prized accomplishments was setting up a system of American port agents at French harbors to capture British ships, handle naval resupply, refitting, and crew recruitment. The sage of Philadelphia seemed to have had an endless supply of tricks up his sleeve.

Franklin approached diplomacy liberally and creatively, as comfortable with overt as with covert action, provided it worked. Having befriended many distinguished Englishmen while living in London as an envoy for Pennsylvania during the years 1757–62, he corresponded with them after returning to America. As a commissioner in Paris, the letters continued, but with added precautions, notably through the use of "mail drops" at addresses of American sympathizers, and aliases meant to protect the true identifies of the intended recipients. In his correspondence, Franklin suggested political themes that the Whigs who were on the side of the Americans could use in parliamentary and other debates. It is not far-fetched to imagine that he might have inspired, among his political friends and pen pals, the formidable Edmund Burke.

The list of effective influencers during the nation's revolutionary era is long and distinguished. What emerges most strikingly from the Founders' remarkable display of ingenuity and dedication, however, is the delicate blend of strategic central steering with considerable individual autonomy, a feat made possible only by the unwavering dedication that transcended pettiness and ego. Not that egos weren't sizeable—on several occasions, inadvertently coming close to causing great harm to the national interest. But for the most part, the Founders trusted one another and, even more, the principles that guided them all.

Much of the credit is due to the man who literally guided the nation both in war and in peace, the unparalleled George Washington. The secret of Washington's success has been summarized simply by Daigler:

> He learned the business by blending his personal code of conduct with commonsense approaches to dealing with people and establishing organizational structures. These characteristics were most likely also the reason he did well in two other areas where he had no formal training: business management of his plantations and his military planning and leadership. He also had great personal discipline, and this was a key ingredient that made him successful in both his political career and his intelligence work.[32]

As a leader, Washington was no ersatz-king. Though he believed in the central direction and focus of intelligence, for example, he "decentralized implementation of these activities."[33] But the same was true of Sam Adams, and the others. To their credit, the Founders appreciated that the true engine of change, of democracy, and future stability, lies with the population at large. Without a solid consensus, without a dedicated constituency standing solidly behind their leaders who courageously, if not always flawlessly, engaged in advancing the common national interest, the unprecedented birth of America simply could not have happened. It most certainly would not have lasted.

America's birth had truly been a team effort, led by arguably the best Team of all the Teams the nation ever had. Sun Tzu knew the importance of leadership, but also the need for extraordinary team leaders, having observed that "only the enlightened sovereign and the worthy general who are able to use the most intelligent people as agents are certain to achieve great things" (*AoW* XIII. 23). They were all breathtakingly intelligent as well as committed to the common cause, and they did prevail. But one important reason is that the greater team they influenced most effectively was their own brave and independent people.

Notes

1. *Annals of America*, vol. 2, 313.
2. Ibid., 317.
3. Ibid., 318.
4. Ibid., 313.
5. Ibid., 314.
6. Ibid., 315.
7. Ibid., 317.
8. Philip Davidson, *Propaganda and the American Revolution 1763–1783* (Chapel Hill: University of North Carolina Press, 1941), xiii.
9. "The word had been coined in 1622, when Pope Gregory XV, frightened by the global spread of Protestantism, urgently proposed an addition to the Roman curia. The Office for the Propagation of the Faith . . . far from denoting lies, half-truths, selective history or any of the other tricks that we associate with 'propaganda' now, that word meant, at first, the total opposite of such deception." Edward Bernays, *Propaganda* (Brooklyn, NY: Ig Publishing, 1928), 9. Bernays' book is an excellent study of the topic.
10. Ibid.
11. Ibid., xvi.
12. Ibid., 31.
13. Ibid., 38.
14. Ibid., 39.
15. Christopher Paul, *Strategic Communication: Origins, Concepts, and Current Debates* (Santa Barbara, CA: Praeger, 2011), 3 (Italics in the original; bold added.)
16. Davidson, *Propaganda*, 56–57.
17. Ibid.
18. Ibid., 61 (Note: Davidson uses "propaganda.")
19. Ibid., 62 (Note: Davidson uses "propaganda.")
20. Ibid., 65.
21. Thomas Paine, *Common Sense and Other Political Writings* (Indianapolis, IN: Bobbs-Merrill, 1953).
22. Walter LaFeber, "*The American Age: U.S. Foreign Policy At Home and Abroad – 1750 to the Present,*" *The American Age: U.S. Foreign Policy At Home and Abroad - 1750 to the Present,* 2nd ed. (New York: W.W. Norton & Company, 1994), 20.
23. Ibid.
24. Arthur M. Schlesinger, *Prelude to Independence: The Newspaper War on Britain 1764–1776* (New York: Random House, 1965), vii.
25. David A. Clary, *Washington's First War: His Early Military Adventures* (New York: Simon & Schuster, 2011), 144–60.

26. Kenneth A. Daigler, *Spies, Patriots, and Traitors: American Intelligence in the Revolutionary War* (Washington, DC: Georgetown University Press, 2014), xvi.
27. Ibid., 7.
28. Ibid., 11.
29. Ibid., 15.
30. George Washington to Robert Hunter Morris, January 5, 1766, in John Fitzpatrick, ed., *The Writings of George Washington*, vol. 1 (Washington, DC: Government Printing Office, 1931–44), 268.
31. Daigler, *Spies, Patriots, and Traitors*, 59.
32. Ibid., 242.
33. Ibid., 243.

7

Diplomacy and Commerce

Be a craftsman in speech that thou mayest be strong, for the strength of one is the tongue, and speech is mightier than all fighting.
—Ptahhotep, Twenty-fifth cent. BC

Our plan is commerce, and that, well attended to, will secure us the peace and friendship of all Europe.
—Thomas Paine, *Common Sense*, 1776

Among the myriad challenges the new republic faced in the last decade of the eighteenth century, James Madison gave the conduct of diplomacy pride of place. He believed that "the management of foreign relations appears to be the most susceptible of abuse of all the trusts committed to government."[1] Maybe this meant the way to avoid the danger was to refrain from dealing with foreign affairs altogether? It might seem that way, if one considers that the principal reason for changing the name of the "secretary of foreign affairs" to "secretary of state" in the late 1780s was. . . . the nature of his workload. Hard as it may be to believe, the sum total of Thomas Jefferson's responsibilities in that job amounted to little more than guarding the nation's Great Seal, publishing laws, and . . . taking the census![2] But this still does not justify Henry Kissinger's contemptuous assessment of early America's approach to the world: "In a nutshell, the foreign policy of the United States was not to have a foreign policy."[3]

It may not have been what Kissinger would consider a foreign policy, but it was that—even if it wasn't always handled by the person who held the office that Kissinger himself would inherit, two centuries later. Notable among the architects of American international engagement was the Founder whom the renowned historian Forrest MacDonald accurately dubbed "Prime Minister,"[4] since that was indeed his (unofficial) function at the time: Alexander Hamilton. If the foreign policy of early America was not always the wisest, especially when judged through the clairvoyant rear-view mirror of hindsight, it had to adapt to reality. That it adapted splendidly is attested by the nation's astonishing success.

As already mentioned in chapter 5, Kissinger had misread George Washington's admonition in his Farewell Address, delivered on September 17, 1796, not "to implicate ourselves, by artificial ties, in the ordinary vicissitudes of [European] politics," by assuming the president implied unequivocal opposition to all permanent alliances—in Kissinger's words "for any cause whatsoever."[5] Washington, and his ghost-writer/prime-minister Hamilton, went on to add that temporary alliances, at least, would sometimes be eminently prudent, depending on changing circumstances, as circumstances are wont to be. Franz-Friedrich Walling notes the importance of this caveat, which should not have escaped the brilliant Kissinger: "[T]hough the idea of no alliances of any kind quickly became an American dogma that lasted until World War I, Hamilton had deliberately built exceptions into the rule to allow for a significant degree of strategic flexibility."[6] Alliances had never been ruled out; only the "entangling" and permanent kind, that tied us to a European power by endangering our national interest. The Washington-Hamilton admonition would prove prescient sooner than anticipated.

Kissinger is again mistaken when he takes Hamilton's examples, in *Federalist* 6, of republics such as Sparta, Athens, and Rome as being even less peaceful than non-republics to imply that Hamilton regarded republican government with skepticism.[7] Maybe Kissinger had been unduly persuaded by those who accused Hamilton of monarchical tendencies—charges routinely hurled against John Adams as well, with equal frivolity. Whatever skepticism Hamilton may have expressed toward government as such, republican or otherwise—a propensity tacitly shared by all the Founders, devoted students of John Locke—he never wavered from his commitment to the unique constitutional system he had done so much to create and defend. All that Hamilton was trying to show by appealing to ancient history was that republicanism did not *guarantee* the elimination of belligerency. Obviously no government can do that merely through its form and structure.

America's early diplomatic history, notes Paul Varg, reflected the fact that most Founders "distrusted power and particularly military power,"[8] and tended toward (perhaps excessive) moralism. Fortunately, "the determination to approach foreign relations in terms of the ideal rather than in terms of existing realities [which had] predominated during the Revolution, lost much of its hold during the Washington administration, [though it admittedly] regained prominence with the election of Thomas Jefferson."[9] The latter's mistakes afforded an additional source of education, first to James Madison and later to John Quincy Adams, who recognized the pitfalls of underestimating the role of military power. But that original hostility to a strong homegrown military, though hardly an unmitigated advantage, was not without merit: for it did provide an impetus to greater reliance on other instruments of power. And that was all to the good.

It is difficult to underestimate the challenges faced by a barely constituted nation, obliged to navigate international tsunami-sized waves, a mere canoe among destroyers. Though not immune to unwarranted bouts of self-righteousness and overconfidence, exacerbated by idealism at times insufficiently tempered by reason, the Founders knew (long before Trotsky coined the pithy phrase) that "you might not be interested in war, but war is interested in you." Or as Hamilton put it more ornately in *Federalist* 34: "Let us recollected that peace or war will not always be left to our option; that however moderate or unambitious we may be, we cannot count upon the moderation, or hope to extinguish the ambition of others."[10]

Not that America's Founders had ever been unambitious. They had dreamed—at first subliminally, but gradually emboldened—of an expansive territory long before 1776, however improbable that seemed (and was) in those early years. And yes, the dream had become deeply entrenched by 1776, a quarter century after Franklin's demographic calculations demonstrated that the brave inhabitants of this new world would soon need space to accommodate their rapid growth. The inclusion of this concept in the seminal treaty of alliance with France signed that year—thanks to the astute diplomacy of the genial genius from Philadelphia—was thus no accident. That alliance had specified that the United States was to have possession of any territory formerly British conquered on the continent of North America, and also Bermuda. Though mere promises at the time, those treaty provisions expressed real hopes, and reflected a far-reaching strategy.

Conquest was out of the question. The colonial army never envisaged actually invading these territories; they would have to be acquired in a peaceful manner. As Varg, again, points out, "from the beginning of the Revolution the Americans assumed that the [goal of] new nation [was] to win not only independence but to gain additional territory far surpassing the original thirteen colonies." It certainly would not be done by means of hard power. Rather, "they had to place their faith in diplomacy."[11] No one thought it would be easy; Americans may have been visionaries, but they were not delusional. Fortunately, they had been blessed with exceptionally talented diplomats.

Foremost among them was, of course, the inimitable Franklin. Pulitzer-prize winning historian Gordon S. Wood puts it best: "In 1776 Franklin was the most potent weapon the United States possessed with the greatest power on earth." Neither more nor less. For "without his presence in Paris throughout that tumultuous time, the French would never have been as supportive of the American Revolution as they were. And without that French support, the War of Independence might never have been won."[12] The secret to Franklin's success—his "genius, was to understand how the French saw him and to exploit that image on behalf of the American cause."[13]

Equipped with extraordinary insight into human nature, a brilliant writer, and a master of public relations, with a flair for satire and an unfailing sense of reality, Franklin maneuvered with unprecedented skill long after that initial, undoubtedly his greatest, success. Explains Wood:

> Probably only Franklin could have persuaded [French foreign minister] Vergennes to keep on supporting the American cause, and probably only Franklin could have negotiated so many loans from an increasingly impoverished French government. . . . He was the greatest diplomat America has ever had.[14]

He was certainly the busiest.

> In addition to his duties as minister plenipotentiary, which included dealing with countless persons offering advice, seeking favors, and asking for information, he effectively acted as consult general, director of naval affairs, and judge of admiralty. He handled mercantile matters, commissioned privateers, and served as judge in the condemnation and sale of the prizes captured by the privateersmen; at one point he was even called upon to help plan a prospective French invasion of England.[15]

Far less successful in France as America's envoy, future president John Adams, who woefully misunderstood Franklin (and also, for that matter, Hamilton, Jefferson, and a slew of other distinguished colleagues, a favor richly returned) found his element in the Netherlands, where he more than redeemed himself. Though by his own account socially awkward, on that critical assignment Adams compensated for what he lacked in emotional intelligence and worldliness with hard work, tenacity, and commitment. Thanks largely to his diligent effort to understand the Dutch perspective, he eventually secured that government's financial and commercial support for the American cause, on June 11, 1782.

His first hurdle had been to dispel Dutch misconceptions about America. As he wrote with much dismay in a letter to Congress in October, 1780, the population of Holland "has little knowledge of the numbers, wealth, and resources of the United States, and less faith in their finally supporting independence, upon which alone a credit depends. They also have an opinion of the power of England vastly higher than the truth. Measures must be taken with great caution and delicacy to undeceive them."[16] He then proceeded to take those measures, with all the skill he could muster. To help him in that difficult endeavor, he wisely secured the assistance of some fine Dutch friends, whom he described as "people of the first character," who recognized that America's struggle had universal importance. As they knew both the right political targets and the particular arguments that would resonate most effectively among their countrymen, such friends proved indispensable.

Undeterred by repeated setbacks over many months that felt far longer, away from his family, at last Adams prevailed, when on March 28, 1782, the Dutch recognized the new American republic. It was a triumph for the nation, and for Adams personally. At the celebration, the Spanish ambassador generously commended him for having "struck the greatest blow that has been struck in the American cause." Although the much-needed loan of $2 million was a lot less than the hoped-for $10 million, it had been indeed a considerable achievement.

His diplomatic prowess did nothing to diminish Adams's distaste for European power-politics, which he continued to believe was dangerous business, not to be practiced if it could be avoided. He candidly admitted: "It is obvious that all the powers of Europe will be continually maneuvering with us, to work us into their real or imaginary balances of power. . . . I think it ought to be our rule not to meddle, and that of all the powers of Europe not to desire us, or perhaps even to permit us, to interfere, if they can help it."[17] Adams had no illusions that America would be obliged to live in the real world, and could not afford to put its head in the sand. Not meddling is not the same as staying aloof and detached; not succumbing to the desire of European powers that America interfere on their continent did not imply closing our eyes and ears to the world. Take note, Mr. Kissinger.

It emphatically did not mean closing off trade. The Founders were united by an unquestioning enthusiasm for the unhindered intercourse of international commerce, which they believed would promote peace and prosperity more readily than would anything else. Free trade was thought necessary to the unfettered pursuit of happiness that the Declaration had included among the universal rights of all mankind, intertwined with life and liberty. It seemed all but providential for Adam Smith's magnum opus, *An Inquiry into the Nature and Causes of the Wealth of Nations*, to be published in the same year, 1776.

Why couldn't all these clever Europeans figure it out, fretted Adams? He spoke for many, if not indeed most, of his countrymen, when he thundered, in 1780:

> There are at this moment so many politicians piddling about peace general and separate, that I am sick to death of it. Why is there not one soul in Europe capable of seeing the plainest thing in the world? Any one of the neutral powers saying to the rest, 'America is one of us, and we will all share in her commerce. Let us all as one declare it.' These words once pronounced peace is made, or at least soon and easily made.[18]

In truth, though Adam Smith argued in favor of free trade as more efficient than any alternative policy, he did not go so far as to suggest that it guaranteed world peace. That honor belongs to his contemporary, the French philosopher Montesquieu, who declared: "Peace is the natural effect of trade. Two nations who traffic with each other become reciprocally dependent; for if one has an interest in buying, the other has an interest in selling; and thus their union is founded on their mutual necessities."[19] Curiously, however, he did not think this beneficent effect applies equally to individuals, offering by way of example Holland, "where the people move only by the spirit of commerce, they make a traffic of all the humane, all the moral virtues; the most trifling things, those which humanity would demand, are there done, or there given, only for money."[20] Forget sheer compassion. Smith does not contest this, but finds that a pacific outcome is an aggregate that transcends its dissonant, disparate components.

It may be the faithful observance of that philosophy that rendered Americans so ready to translate the theory's economic superiority into a veritable political panacea. Varg underscores that "the roots of these anti-mercantilist and anti-balance of power views extended to the very depths of the American experience . . . [and] in these views lay in large part the force behind American diplomacy."[21] These ideas, which may be traced back to John Locke, as mentioned in chapter 5, underlay the social and political philosophy of Classical Liberalism. Like no other society, Americans, from the earliest decades, appear to have endowed commercial-fiduciary considerations with almost supernatural status. Unfortunately, a kind of economic determinism which presumes that human behavior is disproportionately affected, or worse, by material factors has since prevailed among both leftward-oriented and some laissez-faire economists in the United States (though not Austrian economists in the venerable tradition of Ludwig von Misses).

Overconfidence in the salutary political power of the unfettered Invisible Hand, further popularized by Paine's *Common Sense*, pervaded the country. A typical opinion was expressed by a writer for the *Pennsylvania Journal:* "it never will be in the interest of any nation to disturb our trade while we trade freely with it, and it will ever be our interest to trade freely with all nations."[22] So too, the three American commissioners in Paris, Arthur Lee, Silas Deane, and even Benjamin Franklin for a time, shared the hope that the French, presumably like all rational nations, would recognize the palpable advantages of "uninterrupted commerce." The same argument would be reiterated by American envoys to the Netherlands, Prussia, Tuscany, and Spain, with predictably disappointing results. To the Americans' disappointment and surprise, it seemed not everyone was equally convinced of the near-automatic pacific effects of Nature's and Reason's Invisible Hand. Americans would have to learn that lesson the hard way: The world, alas, tended to have less regard for principle, no matter how reasonable, than for short-term advantage.

This exaggerated trust in the power of free trade to advance simultaneously the cause of American independence and world peace was so deeply entrenched, however, that it required repeated encounters with reality to diminish. That encounter came soon enough, and hit hard when it did. First to flout it was the Mother Country itself, any potential remnant of maternal affection having evaporated in the aftermath of the war, as parliament decreed that US ships could not trade with the British West Indies. So too, adding insult as well as additional injury to injury already inflicted, certain goods could thenceforth be carried only on British ships, and Canadian-US trade would be severely limited.

All of this seriously hurt the United States, which bought three times as many goods from the British as they sold back. The only sensible solution seemed to be to suspend buying anything from them until the barriers had been lifted—an impossibility under the Articles of Federation then-in effect, immediately after the War. The need for a unified, strong government capable of making policy for all the American states, in the interest of their common security, was becoming increasingly obvious. It provided additional impetus to the establishment of a federal Constitution, whose urgency grew with each passing day. Evidently, America's worthy commitment to free trade would unfortunately not protect the newborn nation. Others weren't yet ready to emulate us; meanwhile, our job was to survive.

No one grasped from the outset as clearly as did the consistently realistic Alexander Hamilton the naivety of trusting economic interests to trump the hunger for conquest and glory. In *Federalist 6*, he had dismissed the silly illusions of those "visionary or designing men who stand ready to advocate the paradox of perpetual peace between the States" on the ground that "the genius of republics (they say) is pacific; the spirit of commerce has a tendency to soften the manners of men, and to extinguish those inflammable humors which have so often kindled into wars." The rhetorical question asked by Hamilton/Publius contains its own response: "Is not the love of wealth as domineering a passion as that of power or glory?"[23] Reason plays a barely supporting role in this drama.

Although no less a disciple of free trade than his fellow Founders, Hamilton sensibly argued in *Federalist 8* that "safety from external danger is the most powerful director of national conduct. Even the ardent love of liberty will, after a time, give way to its dictates." Surely external danger, military attack, was what the fledgling United States had to worry about most. Security will always come first; liberty and happiness cannot very well be pursued without life. But overemphasis on security can obviously undermine liberty. Warned Hamilton: "The violent destruction of life and property incident to war, the continual effort and alarm attendant on a state of continual danger, will compel nations the most attached to liberty to resort for repose and security to institutions which have a tendency to destroy their civil and political rights."[24]

It is precisely to avoid having to resort to such institutions that Hamilton argued in favor of a standing army and building a navy. Noting that thanks to America's salutary geographic situation, "extensive military establishments cannot be necessary to our security,"[25] these should not be feared unduly. He warned instead against another threat, all the more insidious for being underestimated: the short-sighted, vicious squabbles within, which could sabotage our very existence. By declaring, in *Federalist 9*, that "a firm Union will be of the utmost moment to the peace and liberty of the States as a barrier against domestic faction and insurrection,"[26] he prepared the stage for the tour-de-force that became James Madison's most important contribution to political theory: the philosophical justification of federalism, superbly argued in *Federalist* 10.

The federalist republican system brilliantly conceived by Madison and eventually adopted by the delegates at the Constitutional Convention, while reserving considerable power to the states, wisely conferred upon the central government the all-important role of defending the collective security of all the American people. In the aftermath of the Revolutionary war, most (though not all) Founders quickly recognized that providing for the common defense, which involved a number of related functions, could only be performed by a firm Union that needed to be established with the greatest urgency. To that end, the Constitution created a single-person executive as well as an agency to conduct foreign policy. It also tasked Congress, rather than the states, to "regulate Commerce with foreign Nations, and among the several States, and with the Indian Tribes," and conferred upon it also the power to lay and collect taxes, duties, imposts, and excises.

The Federalist Papers were published in 1787 and 1788 to garner support for the new Constitution. Their and the Constitution's basic premise, writes historian Walter LaFeber, was that Americans "could survive as a people only if they could effectively fight the other great world empires. The United States has never been isolated or outside the world's political struggles. It was born in the middle of those conflicts, and its great problem was—and has always been—how to survive those struggles while maintaining individual liberty at home."[27] Even if it had wanted to be "isolated," America had no choice but to engage.

Realistically, this mandated the establishment of a strong executive. Though Jefferson and Madison, along with other Republicans, had always dreaded a creeping quasi-monarchy almost as much as—or maybe even more than—they feared foreign powers, no one doubted that the president of the new nation had to be empowered to make decisions in the national interest. It helped that the first president would be George Washington, the eminently practical general who had no monarchical ambitions, and whose strategic acumen had been amply demonstrated during the Revolutionary War as he nimbly adapted to the changing circumstances on the ground.

Palmer commends Washington's uncanny ability to calibrate his tactics to all four distinct phases of the war, especially during the final two years, when "the war was fought mainly in theaters other than the United States, including the negotiating arenas in Europe."[28] Audacity being needed at the outset, Washington was audacious; when, next, serious setbacks required caution, he proved cautious; as decisive victory became possible, he turned decisive; and after the critical victory at Yorktown, when steadfastness was key, "he became the nation's solid anchor."[29] Malleable as circumstances demanded, he nevertheless did not lose sight of the ultimate goal: "From first to last, he never added or subtracted from the vision of a United States free of Europe and supreme in North America."[30]

No one could fail to trust such a man to pursue the national interest with acumen and pragmatism. Fully aware of its daunting challenge, the job held no great charm for him. Though grateful for the universal heartfelt support of his people, Washington assumed his office with trepidation, leery of the hugely complex dangers threatening the fledgling nation. He knew that he was walking in uncharted territory. Though the Constitution's framers had finally agreed to endow the central government with sufficient powers to act in the common interest, the question still remained how to wield it effectively. True, the commander-in-chief had the authority to act; now all he needed was the wisdom to know when, where, and how. The international storms, meanwhile, were gathering; indeed, there had hardly been a cloudless moment all along.

Some policies were adopted by default. Given the nation's military unpreparedness, for instance, Congress seemed to have little choice but to start engaging in some form of economic warfare—which it promptly did, rather too precipitously. Among the first moves by the newly established US Congress was to temporarily forget about Adam Smith and indulge in protectionism—passing bills levying tonnage duties eight times higher on foreign vessels than on US ships in American ports, as well as levying taxes on foreign goods entering the country. Notes Walter LaFeber: "Americans wanted freer trade, but they were prepared to play rough mercantilist trading games if necessary."[31]

As Alexander Hamilton soberly pointed out, however, before Americans could properly engage in economic warfare (or economic diplomacy, if you will), they had to put the nation's own fiscal house in order. The financial genius thus proceeded to put together a program that promised to do just that, including a plan to pay the quite sizeable national debt, without which credit to borrow from other nations would not be forthcoming, along with a national bank. Unsurprisingly, this—or for that matter, any other—plan was heavily dependent on British funds. Unfortunately, the influential Thomas Jefferson, along with James Madison, opposed this approach. The Republicans were all viscerally hostile to the British, and sympathetic to the French, who had, after all, helped the colonies during the war of independence. Those sympathies not only continued after the collapse of the French monarchy on July 14, 1789; they escalated, as the American Francophiles assumed a philosophical kinship with the Parisian mob. The question was: How to reconcile both the need for British credit and waging economic war against the Mother Island?

Washington soon felt overwhelmed. Though prepared to do whatever his country required of him, the task was herculean. Hardest was figuring out how to respond to the increasingly belligerent developments in 1792 and 1793, as France, Britain, and Spain scrambled for advantage and territory. Unsure of what course to take, Washington sought advice from[32] his cabinet members. His Secretary of State Thomas Jefferson and Treasury Secretary Alexander Hamilton, unsurprisingly, offered divergent views. Responding with characteristic intemperance, Jefferson responded bluntly that were Britain to send troops to Canada against the French, and/or attack the Spanish in New Orleans, the United States should declare war against the British Empire.

What Jefferson, in his zeal, neglected to indicate, however, was just what sort of preparations, exactly, should be made for such an eventuality. Indeed, far from recognizing, at last, that the United States would profit from having a robust military capability, Jefferson paradoxically continued to decry, as he always had, the absence from the Constitution of an outright prohibition against standing armies. (In the words of Professor Forrest MacDonald, "Jefferson inverted Theodore Roosevelt's maxim: he spoke loudly and self-righteously and carried no stick at all."[33]) So how **could** war be declared against Britain? It sounded bizarre. Washington realized that this was worse than "no foreign policy," to use Kissinger's words; it was just plain bad policy. So Jefferson failed to prevail, at least for the moment.

Hamilton, by contrast, offered his commander-in-chief practical reasons why belligerence might be unwise. Not only was it strategically inadvisable to have a powerful and hostile neighbor, he argued, but Great Britain was the primary market for American exports. That said, he suggested that if Washington decided, for whatever reason, to choose to play hardball, loud talk wouldn't suffice: In the event that the President saw any prospect of fighting, he had to be prepared to support his stand "if necessary by sword." In addition to obtaining effective—and plentiful—swords, added Hamilton, it would behoove Washington to call a special session of Congress, so as to insure popular support. In other words, he intimated that declaring war on Britain would be sheer madness. The times called for nuance.

Washington got the message. With the President's tacit approval, Hamilton then proceeded to speak informally with the young British minister to the United States, George Hammond, and suggested that Britain evacuate military posts it continued to have in the United States (in violation of the treaty that had promised their removal), while handling the ongoing problem of outstanding British as well as American debts through private courts. Observes McDonald: "None of these conversations amounted to negotiations, but they were sophisticated diplomacy all the same."[34] It would not be the first time that Hamilton would be on roughly the same wavelength with Washington. The next occasion would soon present itself, as France declared war against Spain, Great Britain, and Holland, only eleven days after beheading the hapless Louis XVI on January 21, 1793. Washington readily agreed with Hamilton: siding with France at this point would be nothing short of suicidal.

The thorny question, from the perspective of international law, was what the United States should do about the Franco-American treaties it had signed during the dire days of the Revolution, to avoid going to war in support of France without seeming to have reneged on its commitments. All of Washington's cabinet agreed that Congress should proclaim neutrality; the treaties, after all, had been signed under completely different circumstances, negotiated with a regime that had since been deposed. Still, Jefferson and Madison continued to favor a pro-French policy, arguing in favor of a mercantilist policy designed to force American trade away from Britain and toward France. In the end, only the audaciously clumsy behavior of France's envoy to America, "Citizen" Jean Genet, along with revelations of shady wheeling and dealing on the part of French diplomats (in what became known as the X, Y, Z Affair) were finally able to turn the American public decisively against any alliance with France. The French had obligingly shot themselves in the foot, much to Hamilton's—and Washington's—great relief.

The debate over neutrality, which centered on what became known as the Jay Treaty of 1793, provided America the opportunity to articulate its position on a number of important principles of foreign policy. Once again the job fell to Hamilton, who explained that since the

Franco-American alliance established during the Revolutionary War conditioned American support on France being attacked by a foreign power, no such obligation existed if France herself was the attacker. Clarifying the distinction between aggressive and defensive war in his May 2, 1793, memorandum to President Washington, Hamilton concluded that, on the basis of available evidence, "France, it is certain, was the first to declare war against every one of the Powers with which she is at War. Whether she had good cause or not therefore in each instance, the War is completely offensive on her part."[35]

In the same letter, Hamilton went further, singling out the one measure by the new French government that was especially disturbing: an invitation and encouragement to all nations to engage in revolution and insurrection. As stated in the *Decree* of 15 December, 1793: "The French Nation declares—That it will treat as enemies of the People, who refusing or renouncing Liberty and Equality, are desirous of preserving their Prince and privileged casts, or of entering into an accommodation with them." Hamilton interprets this as "an outrage, little short of a declaration of war, against every Government of Europe, and as a violent attack upon the freedom of opinion of all Mankind." He continues that such a policy should give "just cause of umbrage and alarm to neutral Nations in general"—as indeed, to every other. Hamilton's denunciation of imperialism could not be more thundering: "The pretext of propagating liberty can make no difference. Every Nation has a right to carve out its own happiness in its own way, and it is the height of presumption in another, to attempt to fashion its political creed."[36]

It may seem odd that Jefferson and Madison expressed enthusiasm for the French Revolution even long after its abuses had become hard to ignore. But this sentiment was rooted in a firm conviction that America's example should and would strike a sympathetic chord throughout the globe: France was only the first of an expected set of dominos. It was almost a kind of pre-Hegelian progressivism. Hamilton exhibited no such ideology. While he too believed that a republican government was best, he exhibited a conservative respect for context and circumstance, and for allowing each society to choose for itself the specific manner in which it exercises self-government. He saw no precipitous following in the offing.

But his did not imply any lesser enthusiasm on Hamilton's part for self-government as a philosophical and practical ideal; only the specific, practical means of attaining that ideal could not be settled a priori, and the timing of political evolution differed from case to case.

The institutions best suited for a particular society at any one time depended on their history and culture; for like individuals, so each nation had the right to pursue "its own happiness in its own way"—a lesson well worth heeding to this day, as the United States seeks to assist failed states and those seeking to rebuild after wars and regime change. Imposing our system, especially when done in a roughshod, heavy-handed manner, not only cannot work but, as Hamilton put it, is "the height of presumption." Eventually everyone would finally realize how badly mistaken the American supporters of the French Revolution had turned out to be.

Their differences notwithstanding, the Founders were all convinced that America's principles were the best the world had so far encountered. Most too preferred diplomacy rather than war to resolve disputes, and believed that free trade was inherently peaceful, even if insufficient without a strong military in case of attack. Diplomacy, of course, required understanding the target audience, as well as working diligently, through local allies, to convince foreign powers to side with the United States. The benefits of free trade were on some level self-evident as well, but the Founders were not so naïve as to deny that other, noncommercial, factors influence human conduct. Though economic warfare had its benefits, it could not be wielded successfully without a strong domestic economy and a clear-headed, practical assessment of the relative impact on all the relevant states. Imposing sanctions on the basis of sentimental attachments, without a thorough and candid assessment of the probable impact, was recognized to be ultimately unwise. Eventually, even the Republicans came to recognize that a viable defense would be impossible without a credible military deterrent. As it grew in size and importance, America found that it had to project not only prosperity and freedom but power and resolve.

Notes

1. James Madison to Thomas Jefferson, May 13, 1798. http://www.loc.gov/item/mjm013484
2. LaFeber, *The American Age*, 41.
3. Kissinger, *Diplomacy*, 36.
4. Forrest McDonald, *Alexander Hamilton: A Biography* (New York: W. W. Norton, 1982), ch. XIII, "Prime Minister," 285 ff.
5. Kissinger, *Diplomacy*, 32.
6. Walling, *Republican Empire*, 235.
7. It is interesting that Kissinger thinks this skepticism represented a view of "a tiny minority." If so, not only was Hamilton not among them; neither was Washington. Kissinger, *Diplomacy*, 33.

8. Varg, *Foreign Policies of the Founding Fathers*, 1.
9. Ibid., 4.
10. Hamilton, Madison, and Jay, *Federalist* 34, 208.
11. Varg, *Foreign Policies of the Founding Fathers*, 38–39.
12. Gordon S. Wood, *The Americanization of Benjamin Franklin* (New York: Penguin Press, 2004), 171.
13. Ibid., 180.
14. Wood, *The Americanization of Benjamin Franklin*, 196.
15. Ibid., 196–7.
16. David McCullough, *John Adams* (New York: Simon & Schuster, 2001), 249.
17. Ibid., 281.
18. Varg, *Foreign Policies of the Founding Fathers*, 38 – see reference.
19. *The Spirit of Laws*, Book 20, Ch. 1. From Philip B. Kurkland and Ralph Lerner, eds., *The Founders' Constitution* (Chicago, IL: University of Chicago Press and the Liberty Fund, 1987). http://press-pubs.uchicago.edu/founders/documents/v1ch4s2.html
20. Ibid.
21. Varg, *Foreign Policies of the Founding* Fathers.
22. Ibid., 28 – see ref.
23. Hamilton, Madison, and Jay, *Federalist* 6, 56–57.
24. Hamilton, Madison, and Jay, *Federalist* 8, 67.
25. Ibid., 71.
26. Ibid., 71.
27. LaFeber, *The American Age*, 35.
28. Palmer, *The Way of the Fox*, 202.
29. Ibid.
30. Ibid., 203. Palmer cites Marcus Conliff to compare Washington's consistent, if flexible, approach with the intrinsically flawed policy of the British: "Victory was the goal he kept in sight; unlike the British commanders, he never hopelessly confused the secondary advantage with the primary aim."
31. Walter LaFeber, *The American Age*, 45.
32. McDonald, *Alexander Hamilton*, 267. Hamilton to Washington, September 15, 1790
33. Ibid., 269.
34. Ibid., 270.
35. http://Founders.archives.gov/documents/Hamilton/01-14-02-0265
36. Ibid.

8

A Brave New World

By what means this great and important alteration in the religious,
moral, political, and social character of the people of thirteen
colonies, all distinct, unconnected, and independent of each other,
was begun, pursued, and accomplished, it is surely interesting
to humanity to investigate, and perpetuate into posterity.
—John Adams, letter to Hezekiah Niles, Feb. 13, 1818

When Puritan lawyer John Winthrop warned in 1630 that America had been destined to become a "shining city on a hill," he wasn't idly gloating. Rather, he meant that the eyes of the world were now upon us, whether we liked it or not. Far from implying that the new inhabitants were better than everyone else, the metaphorical hill was a mixed blessing: while admittedly providing a place of relative safety, the elevation was also a platform, the stage-lights focused on the performance. Seemingly divinely chosen to attempt a new start, the settlers were on display. The dice had been cast, without assurance of success. Fellow creatures would be watching to see whether the self-transplanted Americans could rise to the challenge. If not, the world would know about it. If, on the other hand, we proved equal to the task, we had a chance to serve as an inspiration to all.

Winthrop predicted nothing; but he did capture the feeling of many colonists that they had been presented with a unique opportunity, theirs to seize or squander. Though often cited, invariably out of context, as proof of that infamous American hubris later denigrated as a smugly solipsistic, and crassly nationalistic, exceptionalism, Winthrop's remark at the time was meant to remind the colonists that "if we deal falsely with our God in his work we have undertaken, . . . we shall shame the faces of many of God's worthy servants and cause their prayers to be turned into curses upon us."[1] That infamous unpolished Yankee cockiness, so mercilessly (if justly) ridiculed by Mark Twain, was still in the future.

Even the flamboyant Thomas Paine, whose phrase "the cause of America is in a great measure the cause of all mankind" did so much to inspire his fellow Revolutionaries, had not meant to suggest that America should be fighting on behalf of the oppressed all over the world. That crusading interpretation would have been unthinkable when the nation itself had yet to be born. Continued Paine: "Many circumstances have and will arise which are not local but universal, and through which the principles of all lovers of mankind are affected and in the event of which their affections are interested."[2] In other words, America's cause is deemed "universal" inasmuch as it shared the aspirations of all other freedom-seeking people. The master marketer of the Revolution had simply managed to capture, with flair worthy of Madison Avenue, that America's cause was far more than a local rebellion. Indeed, the very universality of its relevance made it exemplary rather than exceptional. So then, where did that pesky, crusading "exceptionalism" come from?

Credit for coinage is sometimes given to the insightful and sympathetic French observer of American culture Alexis de Tocqueville (1805–1859), who noted, in 1840, that the "situation of the Americans is . . . entirely exceptional, and it is to be believed that no democratic people will ever be placed in it."[3] But that too is a strain. The passage mainly points to the fortuitous combination of circumstances that conspired to create an unusually fertile ground for the blossoming of a special breed of people who turned out to be, paradoxically, both highly practical and deeply religious. In other words, he directly contradicts Paine's claim that America is typical. Tocqueville argues that, quite the opposite, these are highly unusual circumstances, which is to say, unique. He thus advises against viewing "all democratic nations under the example of the American people, and attempt [instead] to survey them at length with their own features"—a proposition thoroughly unremarkable, if not trivial.

Somewhat more plausible is the suggestion that American exceptionalism was first practiced, if not actually defined, by President Woodrow Wilson, who sought to justify America's entrance into the Great War of 1914 by claiming that the venture "enlisted the spirit of the human race," which he believed "is the only distinction that America has."[4] ("Only" should raise eyebrows, but let's let that pass.) The clumsy rhetoric was amply matched by the clumsiness of his performance as a very ill, and ill-advised, commander-in-chief. "Wilsonianism" as the presumed expression of a messianic, crusading American exceptionalism has since become synonymous with idealistic, meaning quixotic, "expansionism," whose result is inevitable ruin, fruitless killing, all in the name of some hazily defined form of American-style virtuous "democracy."

Among these disparate interpretations, it is the image of America as a "shining city on a hill" that comes closest to what Robert Kagan, in *A Dangerous Nation,* considers "a vivid symbol of what are widely seen as dominant isolationist and 'exceptionalist' tendencies in American foreign policy."[5] Kagan insists that the settlers thought themselves as missionaries destined to spread "European civilization" to the New World. As he puts it: "Along with the idea of destiny came a belief in the right of conquest of backward peoples in the name of this civilization."[6]

As already mentioned in chapter 5, however, no conquest of backward peoples was envisaged by the Founders. Many, particularly Sam Adams, felt that so-called "European civilization," far from worthy of transplantation, was in decline, and patently decadent. Instead, the colonists were hoping to settle pristine lands which they had planned to improve through their labor, in order to go on living and worshiping as they pleased. Attitudes toward the natives varied, and the latter reciprocated: some tribes were definitely hostile, but many were friendly, and others indifferent though willing to engage in trade.[7] To call this multifaceted interaction a form of "conquest" *tout court* is belied by the evidence.

Similarly, while Kagan's assertion that "the colonists found nothing objectionable in the idea of empire" is technically correct, it is also highly misleading. It is not only that the word "did not connote to them despotic and arbitrary rule by a superior power"[8] over a weaker one. Indeed, it did not connote that to *anyone* in the eighteenth century: to *have empire* over something meant to *rule* over it.[9] This is not simply an obscure scholarly quibble about colonial word usage; it is crucial to understanding the mindset of the Founders, which lies at the foundations of this country's vision of itself.

Kagan's first chapter of *A Dangerous Nation* is titled "The First Imperialists." But were they? To be sure, sensibly enough, "Anglo-Americans would not have sought to implant civilization in the wilderness had they not been motivated by more self-interested motives, chiefly the desire for land" and of course for all the other benefits, including spiritual, that came with it. Did that make them imperialists? Hardly. While many of the colonists, by the mid-eighteenth century, "were becoming convinced that they were destined for greatness—greatness as part of the British empire but also, perhaps, as an empire on their own,"[10] the ambiguity of the homonym "empire" is at best unhelpful.[11] At worst, it might even appear disingenuous, however unwittingly.

Tellingly, Kagan's view of the Founders' alleged desire for empire leads him astray in his portrayal of President Jefferson's intervention against the Barbary states of northern Africa in 1801 as an example of expansionism. Kagan notes, ironically, that while a nation desirous of remaining aloof from foreign adventures "might have simply withdrawn from further involvement in the Mediterranean," the young United States—"an ambitious nation zealously committed to overseas trade" and eager to defend its "honor"—decided to go on the attack. He points out that Jefferson had argued as far back as 1784 that the most economical way to deal with pirates was to build a naval squadron, in addition to creating an international league for policing the sea. Once elected president, Jefferson finally went to war in 1801, when he "returned to his earlier dreams of using the new American navy against the Barbary powers and uphold the principles of international law.[12] Kagan cites the incident approvingly. For while admitting that the war, which lasted four long years, "did not end piracy in the Mediterranean," he concludes that "Jefferson's naval campaign was largely successful."[13]

Most historians see it very differently.[14] The warships sent by Jefferson in 1801 met with disaster: one ship ran aground, and the crew was seized. Four years later, the Americans could hardly claim victory: Historian Frederick Marks III chides Kagan for "lead[ing] the reader to believe that Jefferson's war against the Barbary pirates was successful when in fact, it was an embarrassing failure. Four hundred American sailors were taken prisoner — the equivalent in today's terms of forty thousand—and in the end, Jefferson had to eat humble pie, resuming annual tribute to the pirates and paying a hefty ransom for the return of captives"[15] in the amount of $60,000 in return for the promise not to capture US ships. That promise held only until 1812, when President Madison once again had to dispatch a small fleet that forced them to retreat. Although the veterans of the earlier naval engagement had learned a great deal, in the end it took a combined Anglo-Dutch naval force to defeat the Barbary states, whereupon peace finally prevailed. Hardly an encouraging portent, Jefferson's attempt to intimidate the pirates was a clumsy, under-resourced response to criminal attacks on American property and its citizens, which mainly served to demonstrate the nation's military weakness at that time.

Kagan is not alone in shining a positive light on Jefferson's hapless war: journalist Joseph Wheelan goes as far as to credit Jefferson with having ended Mediterranean piracy. While conceding that it didn't really happen until 1816, and only at the conclusion of the war that, by the way, Madison had had to fight because the armistice negotiated by Jefferson had soon fallen apart, Wheelan, still maintains that it had been "Jefferson and his fighting sailors and Marines [who] had freed America and Europe from the Terror."[16] Wheelan's skewed view of history appears to be motivated by his desire, undoubtedly commendable, to apply its lessons to current challenges, and to an equally commendable admiration for Jefferson's idealism. He writes: "While the Barbary War resembles today's war on terror, both tactically and strategically, it resonates most deeply in its assertion of free trade, human rights, and freedom from tyranny and terror."[17] Were it so.

In the same vein, Wheelan commends Jefferson for being "willing to go to war with a people whose customs, history, and religion were alien to the early American experience"[18]—seeming to imply that it took courage to not let those customs stand in the way of defending the nation. That Jefferson was standing up to people whose customs and religion were different was not the point—those were pirates, pure and simple, and they were stealing American goods and endangering American lives. Case closed. In no way can Jefferson's war against the Barbary pirates be considered America's first attempt at enforced cultural hegemony, whether the claim is made sympathetically or not.

Wheelan also applauds President Jefferson's decision to send American forces to fight on foreign soil in order to make "a statement of national character: the American belief that nations as well as people had a right to freedom from tyranny"[19] How he arrives at that conclusion, however, is a mystery. It doesn't help that the statement itself is inscrutable. Nations have a right to freedom only in so far as their people do, and vice versa. So "as well as" should be changed to "which is to say." Whether or not Jefferson believed that people of other nations had a right to freedom, and that Americans should assist them in the security of it, is another question altogether, to which we have no answer. Certainly his reason for engaging the Barbary pirates militarily was to defend American lives, honor, and property. In that he differed little from his predecessors; the difference lay in the calculation of relative cost vs. benefit.

While in agreement with Kagan, who sees Jefferson as the first expansionist president who embraced the use of military means to advance American power, Wheelan goes further, to commend the learned Virginian's idealism and devotion to human rights. Unfortunately, in their zeal to prove his exceptionalist credentials, what both

Kagan and Wheelan fail to acknowledge is that Jefferson's tactical calculation turned out to have been just plain wrong; in 1801, America did not yet possess the military might to deter piracy on the high seas. Ransom still had to be paid, and in addition, American lives had been lost. Though Wheelan is not wrong in his assertion that the eventual defeat of Mediterranean pirates "happened sooner rather than later because of Thomas Jefferson,"[20] the statement is trivial: obviously, lessons were learned during the war, but the event itself was a failure. More to the point, there is no reason to think that Jefferson had intended to expand American power; success would have meant only that pirates would no longer prey upon our ships. That amounts to little more than enforcing the nation's sovereignty while also preventing the disruption of free international commerce. No mean feat, to be sure, but that's the extent of it.

Another clue to the reason for Wheelan's skewed view of Jefferson as an early exponent of a Reaganesque "peace through strength" may be found in his citation from a letter sent to John Adams in which Jefferson had admitted that "I very early thought it would be best to effect a peace through the medium of war."[21] But the statement is quoted out of context. Written on July 11, 1786, it was a response to a letter that John Adams, then in England, had sent Jefferson a week earlier, seeking advice about the best way to deal with the pirates at that time. Adams was concerned that "at present we are Sacrificing a Million annually to Save one Gift of two hundred Thousand Pounds. This is not good OEconomy [sic]."[22] Would Jefferson advise to "fight them, though it Should cost Us a great Sum to carry on the war, and although at the End of it we should have more Money to pay as presents"? Financial hurdles aside, the political odds against war seemed higher still: if "you can persuade the Southern States into it, I dare answer that all from Pennsylvania inclusively northward would not object." But the latter couldn't do it alone. Adams then adds, almost as an aside: "It would be a good occasion to begin a Navy."[23] (You'd think.)

In his response letter, Jefferson starts by listing the reasons he would prefer waging war to paying ransom: "1. Justice is in favor of this opinion. 2. Honor favors it. 3. It will procure us respect in Europe, and respect is a safe-guard to interest. 4. It will arm the federal head with the safest of all the instruments of coercion over their delinquent members and prevent them from using what would be less safe. I think that so far you go with me."[24] But then comes the disagreement between the two great Founders.

Jefferson is less worried about the cost, stating (without supporting evidence): "5. I think it least expensive." On pragmatic grounds, it's a toss-up: "6. Equally effectual." (Again, no evidence.) Painting on a larger canvas, he believes that the colonies would not fight alone, as other nations would make common cause with the Americans: "Naples will join us," since their naval minister prefers peace, and "every principle of reason tells us Portugal will join us." (There's rationale at least, though arguable overconfidence in Reason.) This eventuality leads Jefferson to "suppose then that a Convention might be formed between Portugal, Naples and the U.S. by which the burthen of the war might be quotaed [sic] on them according to their respective wealth, and the term of it should be when Algiers should subscribe to a peace with all three on equal terms."[25]

But as to Adams's reference to political opposition from Southern colonies, Jefferson readily and candidly admits: "With respect to the dispositions of the states *I am utterly uninformed.* I cannot help thinking however that on a view of all circumstances, they might be united in either of the plans."[26] So vague a hope, based on so little supporting data, could not possibly convince the pragmatic Adams. Though both agreed that continuing to pay ransom was dishonorable, waging war by colonies loosely united through the weak Articles of Confederation, three long years before the Constitution was even contemplated, in the vain hope that a Convention *might* be formed with Naples and Portugal, would have been nothing short of disastrous. Seen in the proper light, therefore, Jefferson's putatively principled position was not commendable but, on the contrary, dangerously impractical. Or, as Hamilton would say, visionary.

On still another occasion, only a few years later in 1794, the Americans were once again weighing war against economic sanctions. But this time, the enemy were British, busily engaged in jumping American vessels on the high seas and impressing alleged British deserters who, all too often, were nothing of the sort. There was widespread outrage among the American people, who rightly, saw England's blatant violation of neutrality as an insult to their new nation. Once again considerations of honor and of cost came to the fore. One of the options being considered was negotiations that would address, among other matters, piracy in the Mediterranean, to be pursued while simultaneously starting to build a navy. The other was a temporary embargo against British goods, which had the advantage of satisfying the desire to punish the offending Empire—though, unfortunately, it would end up being far more damaging to American merchants instead.

Hamilton had proposed the former option, along with a recommendation to bolster military forces, while Republicans preferred sanctions alone. Their reason, according to Karl-Friedrich Walling, was that "though they hated England, they seemed to have feared both Hamilton and military preparations more than the combined military threat from England, France, and Spain."[27] In the end, the Republicans prevailed, and sanctions were instituted—with the predictable negative consequences to the Americans rather than Britain. While Congress did order the construction of six frigates, it was only "partly as a result of this crisis . . . but mainly for protection against Algerian pirates."[28] In fact, that decision went against the advice of Jefferson's fellow Republican James Madison, who had suggested that bribing the pirates would be cheaper and safer. It is not a little ironic that the war which ultimately ended the piracy would be carried out by Madison—two decades later. And yes, the navy proved indispensable, as Adams had surmised and his fellow-Federalist Hamilton never doubted.

Hamilton was no less staunch a defender of national honor than were his Republican colleagues. He believed that although "it should always be the policy of our Government to cultivate peace," the best way to guarantee peace in a warring world was to be prepared to fight and to negotiate from strength to avoid the necessity of fighting.[29] But he categorically opposed engaging in war without sufficient resources. If Jefferson's trust in America's ability to prevail in a war with the Barbary pirates was unwarranted in 1801, in 1786 it had been preposterous. Hamilton was right that "'tis as great an error for a nation to overrate as to underrate itself. Presumption is as great a fault as timidity."[30] The Founders were all principled, and all patriots; but they were not equally realistic.

Both Wheelan and Kagan misread the Barbary wars and the true nature of American exceptionalism, even if the Founders, like most Americans, did indeed think themselves special, perhaps outright "exceptional," even if they didn't say so. In the very first paragraph of *Federalist 1*, for example, Hamilton speaks for them all when he notes: "It has been frequently remarked that it seems to have been reserved to the people of this country, by their conduct and example, to decide the important question, whether they are forever destined to depend for their political constitutions on accident and force." Should the verdict turn out to be failure, that tragic outcome would "deserve to be considered as the general misfortune of mankind."[31] No one doubted that the success or failure of America the Shining City, perched on its metaphorical hill across the Atlantic, represented, at a deeper level, the success or failure of humanity itself. If this constituted "exceptionalism," it was not exactly boasting, at least not yet: the jury was still very much out whether Americans would prove equal to the challenge, and the Founders knew it better than anyone.

That, however, was essentially the extent of the Founders' belief in their role as history's unique experiment. To extrapolate from this sense of specialness to any one foreign policy mindset—whether expansionist or isolationist—is unwarranted. University of Virginia professor of politics James Ceaser is right to disagree with "attempts by some historians to connect the founders' idea [of a special mission with global relevance] to a particular kind of policy, whether exemplary or by use of more forceful means. . . . [because that] serves only to confuse the meaning of the mission."[32] The Founders did not fit any of the ideologies that later political theorists would try to pin on American foreign policy. That in itself actually constituted a notably underestimated strength.

Ceaser cites Walter McDougall, Pulitzer Prize-winning professor of international relations,[33] as a prime example of a historian who links the Founders' alleged view, "which he then defines as exceptionalism—to a foreign policy of restraint, contrasting it to the views found in the politics of manifest destiny and imperialism."[34] When idealistic internationalists like Wheelan, "realist" expansionists like Kagan, and isolationists like McDougall, can all claim justification for their preferred theory by tracing it to America's early years, something is decidedly wrong.

What is wrong is the temptation to rewrite history to buttress political preferences, a seemingly irresistible affliction to which an antidote has yet to be discovered. The reality, to the extent that documents allow us to glimpse it, is rather less dramatic, though actually more profound: notwithstanding the Founders commitment to the ideal of freedom, most of them were pragmatists, in foreign as well as domestic matters. No doubt, Americans believed that they had a mission, which inspired and energized them. But Ceaser is right that it was meant in a political rather than a messianic and religious sense. This was especially true of the Federalists, who "appeal[ed] to Americans' reason and understanding of the situation," which requires prudence and factual evidence; accordingly "by the nature of the case, prudential judgments cannot be fixed in advance but must be determined by considering America's power and resources and the conditions prevailing in the world."[35]

In other words, America could not afford to ignore how the world works. Had the Founders not been as well educated, principled, yet strategically versatile and capable of recalibrating in the face of changing circumstances, astutely securing support from all the nations and individuals willing to help for whatever motive, America would never have gained independence, let alone keep it and attain the highest level of prosperity and power in the world. It is a notion worth heeding.

Both those who argue that the Founders were really, deep down, expansionists, whether or not they admitted it even to themselves, along with those who, on the contrary, interpret outgoing President George Washington's warning against "entangling alliances" as a sure sign of what would later be called isolationism, are equally mistaken. Obviously, as a fledgling nation that was creating itself while busy fighting for its birth, the United States could ill afford to do more than survive as best it could, by its wits and strategic acumen, bolstered by every tool at its disposal and every friend it could find, while fending off foes. From the outset, however, the aim was for the nation to become strong enough to seek peace on its own terms: in the words of George Washington's Farewell Address, looking forward to a time "when we may choose peace or war, as our interest guided by justice shall Counsel."

In his excellent essay on the foreign policy of America's founders, Hillsdale College professor Matthew Spalding writes that theirs

> was a worldview that was both principled and practical, where the preeminent virtue of statesmanship was prudence: the practical wisdom and ability to relate universal principles to particular circumstances. By implication, the Founders rejected modern approaches in American foreign policy represented in what today is called power politics, isolationism, and crusading internationalism. Instead, they designed a truly American foreign policy—fundamentally shaped by our principles but neither driven by nor ignorant of the place of necessity in international relations.[36]

Tracing this interpretation to historian Samuel Flagg Bemis, who called this approach "strategic independence,"[37] Spalding prefers the term "self-sufficiency," but is careful to distinguish this from the unduly narrow, self-interested aka selfish, power-politics (which some call *Realpolitik*) version. Writes Spalding:

> In order to command our own fortunes in the world, we must first provide for the nation's security and serve its interests, but our actions must always be enlightened by the fundamental and universal principles that are at the heart of our national identity.[38]

Those universal principles included promoting the cause of liberty abroad.

They did not, of course, imply advancing it by expansion and conquest. Although he was referring to France, writing on July 3, 1793, Alexander Hamilton had opposed promoting regime change no matter what the purpose of such action. While justified to "afford assistance" to a nation that has been oppressed, argued Hamilton, a nation should not even encourage insurrection and revolution, let alone undertake it itself.

> When a nation has actually come to a resolution to throw off a yoke, under which it may have groaned, and to assert its liberties, it is justifiable and meritorious in another, to afford assistance to the one which has been oppressed, and is in the act of liberating itself; but it is not warrantable for any nation beforehand, to hold out a general invitation to insurrection and revolution, by promising to assist every people who may wish to recover their liberty, and to defend those citizens, of every country.[39]

Implicit in the last statement is that "promising to assist every people who may wish to recover their liberty" is not only unjustified but patently absurd. That said, there was nothing wrong with offering assistance to one that has been oppressed. The United States was a deeply principled nation—and proud of it.

Important as the articulation of principles and vision may be, however, it cannot ring true unless supported by action. Among the first demonstrations of American commitment to repair at least some of the damage to its moral standing caused by the lingering presence of slavery in the nation's founding documents came after Congress outlawed the importation of slaves in 1807, during the presidency of Thomas Jefferson. As analyst Marion Smith points out in his fine study of early American grand strategy:

> In the following decades, the U.S. military sought to enforce U.S. restrictions on the slave trade, increasingly understood to be an immoral feature of the international system, although it did not threaten the country's immediate security or commercial interests. the U.S. Navy, in cooperation with Britain, which had already abolished the slave trade, conducted operations in the Caribbean to enforce the abolition upon pirates and slave traders (1814–1825); with the Navy's African Slave trade patrol in the waters of West Africa, the Caribbean, and South America (1820–1823); and Commodore Matthew Perry's patrol off the Ivory Coast (1843–1845).[40]

Notwithstanding the risk and the cost, America also used ships of its Mediterranean Squadron (which had been established by President Jefferson in 1801 and indefinitely stationed in the Mediterranean by President James Madison in 1815) and deployed them to Palestine in 1858 to help an American missionary and his family who had come under attack by local thugs. Observes Smith: "While the U.S. military was not constitutionally obligated to protect American citizens and property abroad, the Founders and early U.S. statesmen understood that doing so was desirable and benefitted overall U.S. foreign policy."[41]

From the outset, moreover, the United States saw the defense of unfettered maritime commerce not only a prerequisite to the well-being of its own citizens but to everyone else's as well. This principle by implication required a global presence, which the nation was prepared to assert, with the express intent of policing the seas. Far from belligerent, the intent was to enhance international concord, by allowing every trading partner to transport goods without fear of seizure or molestation.

It would be the fate of the little boy who had watched with horror, along with his mother, the bloody battle taking place at Bunker Hill in 1775, where their beloved family doctor lost his life, to formulate the principles of American leadership regarding the two American continents and hence, implicitly, the world at large. "It is only when our rights are invaded or seriously menaced that we resent injuries or make preparation for our defense,"[42] wrote John Quincy Adams, words that would be included by then-President James Monroe in his annual address to Congress on December 2, 1823. The United States had no plans to interfere in the business of distant nations that did not encroach upon its interests. But "[w]ith the movements in this hemisphere we are of necessity more immediately connected, and by causes which must be obvious to all enlightened and impartial observers."

Given the amicable relations existing between the United States and its European allies, therefore, he deemed it only appropriate to declare candidly

> that we should consider any attempt on their part to extend their system to any portion of this hemisphere as dangerous to our peace and safety. With the existing colonies or dependencies of any European power we have not interfered and shall not interfere. But with the Governments who have declared their independence and maintain

it, and whose independence we have, on great consideration and on just principles, acknowledged, we could not view any interposition for the purpose of oppressing them, or controlling in any other manner their destiny, by any European power in any other light than as the manifestation of an unfriendly disposition toward the United States.[43]

While this is the gist of what would become the so-called "Monroe Doctrine," far more important a statement of general principle was expressed in a different part of the same speech, which touched on a nation that was nowhere nearby:

> A strong hope has been long entertained, founded on the heroic struggle of the Greeks that they would succeed in their contest and resume their equal station among the nations of the earth. It is believed that the whole civilized world take a deep interest in their welfare. *Although no power has declared in their favor,* yet none according to our information, has taken part against them. . . . The ordinary calculations of interest and of acquisition with a view to aggrandizement, which mingles so much in the transactions of nations, seem to have had no effect in regard to them. From the facts which have come to our knowledge there is good cause to believe that their enemy has lost forever all dominion over them; that Greece will become again an independent nation. That she may obtain that rank is the object of our most ardent wishes.

It would fall to the incomparable orator Daniel Webster to spell out the implications of this unprecedented statement of support for the Greeks in their quest to regain their independence, when no other power "has declared in their favor," simply on the basis of principle. In a speech delivered to the House of Representatives a month later, in support of a resolution that stated simply that provisions should be made by law for providing resources toward appointing an ambassador ("Agent or Commissioner") to Greece whenever the President might deem it expedient, Webster took pains to spell out that this should not be read as in any way belligerent or intrusive. He underscored "that the just policy of this country is, in the first place, a peaceful policy. No nation ever had less to expect from forcible aggrandizement. The mighty agents which are working out our greatness are time, industry, and the arts. Our augmentation is by growth, not by acquisition; by internal development, not by external accession."[44]

But though we do not seek to impose the same system on others, surely we have a duty to express our sympathy with those who already share them. The case of Greece was not simply one nation fighting another, but a clash between two forms of government. Webster described the situation clearly:

> The substance of the controversy is whether society shall have any part in its own government. Whether the form of government shall be that of limited monarchy, with more or less mixture of hereditary power, or wholly elective or representative, may perhaps be considered as subordinate. The main controversy is between that absolute rule, which, while it promises to govern well, means, nevertheless, to govern without control, and that constitutional system which restrains sovereign discretion, and asserts that society may claim as matter of right some effective power in the establishment of the laws which are to regulate it.[45]

He does not use the word "democracy," preferring instead "constitutional system which restrains sovereign discretion"—all the better to avoid semantic confusion. The phrase compensates in clarity for what it lacks in elegance. If only we could adopt it; but the centuries have retired it into obsolescence. Twitter-friendly it manifestly is not. Alas.

Why should it matter to a United States still in its infancy to stand athwart the incomparably more powerful empires, on behalf of Greece, asks Webster, and provides the ready response: "Our system, the great increase which has taken place in the intercourse among civilized and commercial states, have necessarily connected us with other nations, and given us a high concern in the preservation of those salutary principles upon which that intercourse is founded." Since America is founded on the principle of free trade, we cannot but be concerned about the rest of the world. Webster turns the tables on the question of why we should be interested in faraway regions by retorting—*why should we not be*? "What do *we* not owe to the cause of civil and religious liberty? to the principle of lawful resistance? To the principle that society has a right to partake in its own government? As the leading republic of the world, living and breathing in these principles, and advanced, by their operation, with unequalled rapidity in our career, shall we give **our** consent to bring them into disrepute and disgrace?"

The Founders had no use for vain utopias; they fully appreciated the real-world limits on what could and could not be done. The Constitution did not provide for "foreign aid"—on the contrary, the enumerated powers of Congress barely justified a modicum of taxation, and the general hostility even to establishing a standing army underscored the deep distrust of a peacetime military. But there was never a question of what America stood for, and what message it was to send to the world. In a letter to his friend Samuel Cooper on May 1, 1777, Benjamin Franklin had reported from France that "all Europe is on our side of the Question [of independence], as far as Applause and good Wishes can carry them. Those who live under arbitrary Power do never the less approve of Liberty, and wish for it. They almost despair of recovering it in Europe . . .," adding that "'Tis a Common Observation here that our Cause is the Cause of all Mankind; and that we are fighting for their Liberty in defending our own. 'Tis a glorious Task assign'd us by Providence; which has I trust given us Spirit and Virtue equal to it, and will at last crown it with Success."[46]

To belabor the obvious, Franklin was no fire-and-brimstone preacher.[47] But the notion that all people desire to have their destiny decided by no one other than themselves and their freely selected representatives was at the time considered a truism. America alone, almost miraculously, had built its system of government on that premise. Its leadership consisted in living up to it, but it had to be within the limits of the possible. Its ambitious foundational ideals notwithstanding, tactical or operational means of promoting those ideals were another matter. Not even the loftiest of ideals justify botched tactics—as illustrated by the disastrous Bay of Pigs invasion, to mention but the most notorious.

Daniel Webster was careful to avoid giving the wrong impression—especially at a time when the United States' military capabilities were minimal—by seeming to imply armed support for the Greek freedom fighters. So then, "what can *we* do? Are we to go to war? Are we to interfere in the Greek cause, or any other European cause? Are we to endanger our pacific relations? No, certainly not. What, then, the question recurs, remains for us? If we will not endanger our own peace, if we will neither furnish armies nor navies to the cause which we think the just one, what is there within our power?" His response expresses the moral aspect of the American position without suggesting that we can do the impossible. The House resolution to provide for an ambassador merely reinforces President Monroe's earlier statement expressing America's hope that Greece will retain its independence. Webster also mentions "the correspondence between the Secretary of State and the Greek Agent in London, already made public, in which similar wishes are expressed, and a continuance of the correspondence apparently invited."

But he does not thereby retract the principles he just articulated. For he hastens to remind his audience of the overwhelming support for the Greek independence movement among the general population throughout the United States, of "the unexampled burst of feeling which this cause has called forth from all classes of society, and the notorious fact of pecuniary contributions made throughout the country for its aid and advancement." That, along with the official statements and resolutions, was what America most certainly could offer: moral support, which it did with greater alacrity than any other nation at that time. And it was no small matter. Declared Webster: "The time has been, indeed, when fleets, and armies, and subsidies, were the principal reliances [sic] even in the best cause. But, happily for mankind, a great change has taken place in this respect." There is no question about it; the world would never be the same.

No less lofty a sentiment had been just as eloquently expressed by John Quincy Adams, five years to the day before the near-simultaneous deaths of his father and of Jefferson, when he addressed Congress, on July 4, 1821, with these words: "*Wherever the standard of freedom has been or shall be unfurled, there will be her [America's] heart, her benedictions and her prayers be.*" At the same time, he categorically denies any wish to invade or engage in armed regime change; for "*she goes not abroad in search of monsters to destroy. She is the well-wisher to the freedom and independence of all. She is the champion and vindicator only of her own. She will recommend the general cause, by the countenance of her voice, and the benignant sympathy of her example.*"[48]

If the "benignant sympathy of her example" might justify branding John Quincy a proto-isolationist, the promise to "recommend the general cause" of freedom in particular cases is proof of his sober yet unequivocal idealism. Indeed, in the same speech, he goes on to encourage others to follow America's example:

> My countrymen, fellow-citizens, and friends; could that Spirit, which dictated the Declaration we have this day read, that Spirit, which 'prefers before all temples the upright heart and pure,' at this moment descend from his habitation in the skies, and within this hall, in language audible to mortal ears, address each one of us, here assembled, our beloved country, Britannia ruler of the waves, and every individual among the sceptred lords of humankind; his words would be, 'Go thou and do likewise!'

Far from thereby contradicting Hamilton's admonition, articulated in *Pacificus* 2, not to hold out an unwitting global invitation to resurrection and revolution, John Quincy's carefully crafted speech contains simply a personal speculation as to what the Higher Spirit that inspired the Americans might say. If this be thought an invitation, it is a very subtle and indirect one. It certainly implies no promise of material assistance, though it is definitely a strong and unequivocal expression of moral support. In years to come, that more than anything else would be America's unequalled weapon for waging peace, as no other country would rival its reputation for keeping its word.

How far America might be prepared to go to support fellow freedom-lovers abroad, even before it had become rich and powerful, was not merely a question of principle but of realistic calculation, without which ideals are mere words. That said, words are hardly ever mere. When Daniel Webster invoked the cause of Greek revolutionaries who had risen against their Turkish occupiers, he commended them for looking to "the great Republic of the earth—and they ask us by our common faith, whether we can forget that they are struggling, as we once struggled, for what we now so happily enjoy?"[49] While the question did not imply a request for either military or economic assistance, this did not leave America without any means of support. As befits one of the greatest American orators of all time, Webster proclaimed that his nation had inaugurated a new approach to the Art of Peace: yes, it is true that previously "there was no making an impression on a nation but by bay-onets and subsidies, by fleets and armies: but the age has undergone a change; **there is a force in public opinion, which, in the long run, will outweigh all the physical force that can be brought to oppose it**.[50]

Webster's words were echoed by President James Monroe, who expressed "the nation's 'most ardent wishes' that Greece should 'gain its independence.'" Yet powerful as all these words were, America's assistance in fact did go beyond diplomacy: the president had spoken not merely for his government but for his people. Monroe had implicitly adopted a whole-of-society perspective. As Marion Smith points out, the private sector was effectively engaged, constituting a tacit national mobilization to promote the nation's ideals. It was all the more powerful for lacking any element of coercion. Writes Smith:

> [T]he U.S. government signaled approval of its citizens' material support for Greek independence. Many Americans, animated by their commitment to the cause of liberty and emboldened by American dip-lomatic support for the Greeks, donated funds and supplies to aid the Greeks' fight for independence. Even former president John Adams[51] sent a donation and a letter to the Greek Committee in New York expressing that his heart 'beat in unison' with their cause.[52]

147

Offering additional examples of private American assistance to free-dom-fighters in faraway lands, notably to Hungarians in 1848, which invited the ire of Austria, Smith concludes:

> One vital and truly exceptional element of American diplomacy was the activity of private U.S. citizens abroad. The U.S. government was often able either to facilitate or to build upon the private endeavors of American citizens who were engaged in religious, charitable, commercial, or political activities around the world. These unoffi-cial ambassadors of American society played an important role in extending the reach of American ideas and interests to the far corners of the globe.[53]

In truth, it is the American people, not the government, who are the ultimate engine of peace or war. It is American society that lights the beacon of freedom; its government can help or hinder the process. What makes America truly exceptional is the devotion to its ideals along with the courage to face facts. If it loses that ability, no amount of hardware or software can make any difference. John Adams understood that at bottom, the problem is human nature itself. Though as ardently devoted to the American idea as any of his fellow Founders, he harbored deep doubts about the prospects for democratic self-rule, given human foibles. In a private letter to his friend John Taylor written in 1814 but published only posthumously, Adams reflected sorrowfully that

> democracy never lasts long. It soon wastes, exhausts, and murders itself. There never was a democracy yet that did not commit suicide. Those passions are the same in all men, under all forms of simple government, and when unchecked, produce the same effects of fraud, violence, and cruelty. When clear prospects are opened before vanity, pride, avarice, or ambition, for their easy gratification, it is hard for the most considerate philosophers and the most conscientious moralists to resist the temptation. Individuals have conquered themselves. Nations and large bodies of men, never.[54]

At least so far, the American people have proven our curmudgeonly second president wrong. But the inability of this republican democracy to learn from its mistakes and to reform its national security apparatus to adapt to new challenges, rebalancing toward a more effective use of all the instruments of power at its disposal, cannot be explained easily. Whether from bureaucratic inertia, undue influence from a variety of pressure groups and special interests, or inability to think beyond short-term goals, the nation is short-changing itself. We do not suffer from a deficit of bravery, as our men and women in uniform have proven time and again. But we do seem to lack what it takes to take on the status quo in civilian governance. In part, it's an imagination deficit.

We need to shed old categories and recalibrate our mind to picture the world before acronyms, taskforces, subcommittees, and crowd sourcing. Rewind two and a half millennia to the other side of the globe to rediscover Sun Tzu, and open our minds: it cannot fail to be invigorating.

Notes

1. John Winthrop, "A Model of Christian Charity," in *Annals of America*, vol. 1, 115.
2. Thomas Paine, *Common Sense and Other Political Writings* (Indianapolis, IN: Bobbs-Merrill, 1953), 3.
3. Alexis de Tocqueville, *Democracy in America* (New York: Signet Classics, 2010), 160.
4. Woodrow Wilson, Annapolis Commencement Address, June 5, 1914. http://www.presidency.ucsb.edu/ws/?pid=65380
5. Kagan, *Dangerous Nation*, 7.
6. Ibid., 13.
7. For an excellent description of the complex relationship between early English settlers and native Indian tribes, see Nathaniel Philbrick's *Mayflower: A Story of Courage, Community, and War* (New York: Penguin Books, 2007).
8. Ibid., 19.
9. Walling, *Republican Empire*, 106.
10. Kagan, *Dangerous Nation*, 34.
11. William E. Weeks writes in *"Dangerous Nation* Roundtable:" "Notwithstanding the effusion of texts from across the political spectrum that use the term American Empire it remains an ideological hot button and Dr. Kagan resists pushing it. Yet can anyone read the *Dangerous Nation*'s narrative of relentless territorial, commercial, and above all, ideological expansion and not think of the United States as an empire, albeit one unlike any other in history?" *H-Diplo*, April 29, 2007, 11.
12. Kagan, *Dangerous Nation*, 99.
13. Ibid., 100.
14. To put the event in context, the pirates from the Barbary Coast of Africa had become a serious nuisance to Americans after 1794, when Britain, in order to lure the Portuguese on their side against France, negotiated and subsidized a truce between the pirates and Portugal (which had been battling the pirates for many years). The result was to release the pirates into the Atlantic, incidentally freeing them to prey upon the Americans. Though Hamilton at the time had proposed building a navy to protect American shipping, the Republican Madison, who was leery of the military, recommended bribing them as a cheaper and safer alternative. George Washington decided to side with Madison and pay the bribe—a tactic continued by John Adams, Washington's successor as president—though Congress nevertheless agreed to finance the construction of six frigates. Those came in handy once Jefferson

became president, when he decided to risk nonpayment of the ransom the Barbary pirates were demanding in exchange for seized ships and brutalized sailors.

15. Frederick Marks III, *"Dangerous Nation,"* Roundtable, 16.
16. Wheelan, *Jefferson's War: America's First War on Terror 1801–1805* (New York: Carrroll & Graf Publishers, 2003), 367.
17. Ibid., xxvi.
18. Ibid.
19. Ibid., 366.
20. Ibid., 367.
21. Ibid.
22. http://Founders.archives.gov/documents/Jefferson/01-10-02-0025
23. Ibid.
24. http://Founders.archives.gov/documents/Jefferson/01-10-02-0058
25. Ibid.
26. Ibid. Emphasis added.
27. Walling, *Republican Empire*, 219.
28. Ibid., 218.
29. McDonald, *Alexander Hamilton*, 344.
30. Walling, *Republican Empire*, 218.
31. Hamilton, Madison, and Jay, *Federalist* 1, 33.
32. Ceaser "The Origins and Character of American Exceptionalism," *American Political Thought: A Journal of Ideas, Institutions, and Culture*, 14.
33. See Walter McDougall, *Promised Land, Crusader State* (Boston, MA: Houghton Mifflin, 1997).
34. Ceaser, ibid.
35. Ibid.
36. Matthew Spalding, "America's Founders and the Principles of Foreign Policy: Sovereign Independence, National Interests, and the Cause of Liberty in the World," The Heritage Foundation, First Principles Series Report #33 on Political Thought, October 15, 2010. http://www.heritage.org/research/reports/2010/10/americas-Founders-and-the-principles-of-foreign-policy-sovereign-independence
37. Much of the best work of Samuel Flagg Bemis on the founding era is collected in *American Foreign Policy and the Blessings of Liberty: and Other Essays* (New Haven, CT: Yale University Press, 1962).
38. Ibid., 7.
39. *Pacificus* 2. *The Pacificus-Helvidius Debates of 1793–1794: Toward the Completion of the American Founding* [1793]. http://oll.libertyfund.org/titles/1910
40. Marion Smith, *The Myth of American Isolationism: Commerce, Diplomacy, and Military Affairs in the Early Republic*, The Heritage Foundation Special Report from The Kenneth B. Simon Center for Principles and Politics, No. 134, September 9, 2013, 37.
41. Ibid., 41.
42. http://www.ourdocuments.gov/doc.php?doc=23&page=transcript
43. James Monroe: "Seventh Annual Message," December 2, 1823. Online by Gerhard Peters and John T. Woolley, *The American Presidency Project*. http://www.presidency.ucsb.edu/ws/?pid=29465

44. Edwin P. Whipple, The Great Speeches and Orations of Daniel Webster (1923) June 13, 2004. eBook #12606, http://www.gutenberg.org/files/12606/12606-8.txt. Speech delivered in the HOUSE, Jan. 19, 1824. (Emphasis added.)

45. Ibid.

46. http://founders.archives.gov/documents/Franklin/01-24-02-0004

47. Writing to Ezra Stiles written on March 9, 1790, shortly before his death, Franklin had expressed "Doubts as to [Jesus's] Divinity: tho' it is a Question I do not dogmatise upon, having never studied it, and think it needless to busy myself with it now, when I expect soon an Opportunity of knowing the Truth with less Trouble." http://www.beliefnet.com/resourcelib/docs/44/Letter_from_Benjamin_Franklin_to_Ezra_Stiles_1.html

48. John Quincy Adams, "Address to Congress," July 4, 1821, in Hezekiah Niles ed., Niles' Weekly Register, Vol. 20 (Baltimore, MD: 1821): 331.

49. Daniel Webster, Speech Delivered to the U.S. House of Representatives, January 19, 1824, in Niles, ibid., 348.

50. Ibid., 346. Emphasis added.

51. John Adams to the Greek Committee in New York, December 29, 1823, quoted in Edward Mead Earle, "American Interest in the Greek Cause, 1821–1827," The American Historical Review 33, no. 1 (1927): 49.

52. Smith, The Myth of American Isolationism, 20.

53. Ibid., 21.

54. John Adams, The Works of John Adams, Second President of the United States: with a Life of the Author, Notes and Illustrations, by his Grandson Charles Francis Adams (Boston, MA: Little, Brown and Co., 1856). 10 volumes. Vol. 6. 9/11/2015. http://oll.libertyfund.org/titles/2104#Adams_1431-06_1197

III

Strategic Deficit Disorder

While the electorate turns to the military to solve international conflicts, nonlethal weapons become less relevant, even as their importance rises in a complex world where non-state actors turn to nontraditional forms of attack. The notions of peace and war are unclear, as the two concepts are pitted against one another in a Manichean dialectical divide, one good the other bad. The human condition, however, can never completely obliterate conflict, unless the peace we seek destroys our humanity in the process. But do we even know what kind of peace is worth pursuing? We seem incapable of articulating a sensible and effective national security strategy. Do we remember America's basic principles? The Founders knew what they were fighting for; our politically correct generation, not so much.

A major problem is that we do not have a clear enough idea how to tell our friends from our enemies—as evidenced most vividly in Afghanistan. We do not take threats from nonstate actors sufficiently seriously early enough. We underestimated Al Qaeda in the mid-nineties and Daesh[1] two decades later; in both cases, we had to relearn counterinsurgency doctrine, having promptly decided to forget it after Vietnam. In both Afghanistan and Iraq, we did not know the culture. Our intelligence operations put a premium on signals and technology at the expense of human sources, and classified secrets instead of open sources, even though the latter form the bulk of the needed information.

If only there were some clarity about the nature of nonmilitary power, which is a major component of national power. But unfortunately, the term "soft power," coined by Professor Joseph Nye, refers to a country's power of "attraction" in a distinctly nonstrategic sense. No wonder the United States wields it in a nonstrategic manner. Neither is the term "smart power," meant to capture a blend of hard (military) and soft power, much of an improvement; rather, it obviates the need for a holistic grand-strategic approach that is sorely lacking at present. We are in semantic free-fall.

An important component of the strategy against our enemies which also serves to solidify and articulate the ties binding us to our allies involves fighting a war of ideas—or, to put it in less belligerent terms, engaging in an effective dialogue about our values, defending truth against lies and distortions. At the moment, Americans are doing a spectacularly miserable job of it.

9

American Self-Ignorance

*A nation of well-informed men who have been taught to know and
prize the rights which God has given them cannot be enslaved.
It is in the region of ignorance that tyranny begins.*
—Henry Steuber, *The Works of Dr. Benjamin Franklin*, 1825

Experience teaches only the teachable.
—Aldous Huxley

Marine General Jim Mattis, the much admired top commander of
the US Central Command (CENTCOM), announced his unexpected
retirement in 2012 with this candid explanation: after watching years
fly, too many of them spent in meetings, he confessed, "one day you look
up and you're sixty, still sitting in these goddamn meetings."[2] Though
never hesitant to speak his mind, retirement has allowed him to vent
to his heart's content. Addressing the Senate Armed Services Committee on January 27, 2015, Mattis called it like he saw it: "We have lived
too long now in a strategy-free mode."[3] The statement reverberated
through the media.

By June, even President Obama conceded that "we don't yet have a
complete strategy."[4] Though referring specifically to Daesh, given the
preeminence of that threat to global security, the admission revealed
the hollow core of the administration's foreign policy as a whole. It
was stunning at least for its candor, if not its substance. To be fair,
the previous administration had been no less flummoxed by threats it
hadn't seen coming, similarly caught without a compass. The mighty
United States was—is still—suffering from acute strategic deficit syndrome (SDS). The first symptom of that insidiously festering malady
is that you don't know you have it. And just like alcoholism, step one
to recovery is admitting you have a problem. But then—and here's the
rub—you have to go to step two, which takes faith. By comparison, the
next ten[5] are a cakewalk.

We had come close to an admission after World War II, but stopped short, thinking we could talk our way out of the problem—the self-delusional technique of choice. Thus in 1947, Congress passed the National Security Act, which was designed "to provide for the establishment of integrated policies and procedures for the departments, agencies, and functions of the Government relating to the national security.[6] That proved woefully insufficient, as the Vietnam War demonstrated in spades. So we went to what we thought was step two: in 1986, the Goldwater-Nichols Reorganization Act upped the ante by an inch and required the executive branch to regularly produce a single document purporting to encompass the nation's strategy.[7] We now have such a document, *habem documentum*, appropriately called The National Security Strategy of the United States of America (NSS). It hasn't done much good. It couldn't have: it was just the next logical step in the charade known as "denial by paperwork."

In the real world, where things are supposed to get done, the United States does not have a single strategy: it has many; too many. Unsurprisingly, the political process inevitably involved in crafting such documents undermines their multiple and sometimes conflicting purposes. The NSS itself is just one, and the least specific at that, among the countless "strategic" reviews and guidance documents that inform the work of a myriad agencies, bureaus, task forces, and such. Issued in the president's name, the NSS has nevertheless been considered "the pinnacle of the national security architecture, and as such, it's the closest we get to what is sometimes loftily known as 'grand strategy.'"[8]

Closest perhaps; but the NSS has been neither especially grand, nor strategic. The latest installment, which the Obama administration posted in early February 2015, dismayed even the Council on Foreign Relations (CFR), an organization not known as a hotbed of anti-establishmentarianism. Speaking on a panel held upon the NSS's release, CFR Senior Fellow Robert D. Blackwill did not hold back:

> If strategy can be defined as the means that we use to get others to do what we want, if we do this, it will maximize the likelihood that *they will do that,* **this national security strategy contains virtually no strategy,** no connecting means to ends. Rather, it is essentially an administration vision statement, if I can put it like that, a wish list, disassociated from what is actually happening in the world, and how to achieve U.S. foreign policy objectives.[9]

That Blackwill's scathing criticism made no headlines seems to have surprised no one. After all, he really had not said anything particularly newsworthy: it has become all but a commonplace, albeit unspoken, that the United States doesn't really "do" strategy—at least, not anymore. Actually, it is not so much unspoken as spoken off the record. Colin Gray reports, not without dismay:

> Several senior American military professionals, whose names must be withheld in order to protect the guilty, have confided to this theorist an astrategic, bordering on an antistrategic, proposition. They have suggested that when a country is so potent in the quantity and tactical effectiveness of its armed forces that it should always win the warfare, it has scant need for strategy. Rephrased: perform well enough tactically and perhaps operationally, and strategy, as the necessary strategic effect, will take care of itself.[10]

He is talking here about military strategy, as do most experts when using the word "strategy" without any qualifiers. The implication, unfortunately well founded, is that when it comes to national security, there isn't any other kind.

The latest National Military Strategy evidently does not to break that mold. Released almost stealthily on July 2, 2015, as most people were mainly focused on picnic plans for the Independence Day weekend (a fact not lost on reporters), its impact, or more precisely nonimpact, was summarized by Aaron Mehta, writing for the journal *Defense News*: "[A]nalysts warn that the document talks too much in generalities to provide much in the way of hard guidance for how the Pentagon should go forward on the major issues of the day."[11]

In still plainer English, a serious strategy this is anything but. Speaking for many, former Defense official Andy Hoehn told Mehta that one would expect a strategy to indicate how to use resources to obtain certain objectives; yet this document "never really gets to that." It had fallen with an embarrassing thud, like an undetonated firework—except no one had been expecting a bang anyway.

An excellent attempt to spell out at least one important aspect of strategic planning, which encompasses military land power, came in the study released on January 16, 2013, jointly by the US Army, the US Marine Corps, and the US Special Operations Command, entitled *Strategic Landpower: Winning the Clash of Wills*. The study recognizes the primacy of peacetime thinking: "Preventing conflict is always difficult, but it remains a far better option than reacting after fighting has erupted. Success at maintaining the peace however carries its own paradoxical risk. Forward deployed, actively engaged forces have proven essential to contributing to peace by reassuring our friends and deterring our enemies." But the paper does not confine itself only to the job of military forces; it outlines as well what the job of a National Security Strategy should be, at least in principle:

> The National Security Strategy of the United States outlines how the U.S. pursues comprehensive engagement with nations, institutions, and peoples around the world to protect and advance its national interests. It does this with a whole of government approach that includes defense, diplomacy, development, and other tools of American power. This nation takes action in the international arena aimed at influencing human activity and the environments in which that activity occurs. It could not be otherwise, as all institutions—states, corporations, NGOs [nongovernmental organizations] etc.—are populated, controlled, and directed by people. Influencing these people—be they heads of state, tribal elders, militaries and their leaders or even an entire population—remains essential to securing U.S. interests. All elements of national power have an important role in these interactions with other nations and peoples.[12]

What a fine vision that would be—though a daunting one, to put it mildly.

The *Landpower Strategy* was soon followed by the U. S. Army's Operational Doctrine, which spells out the service's Operating Concept, ambitiously, almost presumptuously, entitled *Win in a Complex World 2020–2040.* In the preface to that document, Commanding General David G. Perkins echoes the idea already spelled out in the *Landpower Strategy* that "win" does not refer to wars alone:

> 'Win' occurs at the strategic level and involves more than just firepower. It involves the application of all elements of National Power. Complex is defined as an environment that is not only unknown, but unknowable and constantly changing.[13]

Which is, of course, what grand strategy is all about: the application of ALL elements of national power.

But is it any wonder that the military, with its enormous resources and superbly trained leaders, "gets it"? Conversely, is it fair to keep asking the civilian leadership to keep trying to write a comprehensive national strategy, considering how much trouble it has had so far coming up with anything resembling it? Is one reason why we haven't really had a strategy worth the name at least since the end of the Cold War the fact that we have assigned the responsibility to the politicians and their staff?

According to William C. Martel, whether we can even do it anymore is very much an open question. He doubts it, for at least two reasons. First, because

> the United States has become unmoored from the traditions in its grand strategy, and thus is struggling to define core principles to guide its foreign and domestic policies. Second, the absence of guiding principles has led to policies that lurch from one priority to another, often based primarily upon urgent, short-term concerns rather than on a coherent, long-term strategy of what best serves the nation's overall interests.[14]

It may well be that long-term thinking goes against the grain of all democracies. But that does not let us off the hook; we have to face the fact that no other nation is as indispensable to global peace and stability. Much as some academics might wish to dispense with the unquestionably irksome exercise of formulating strategy,[15] the alternative leaves America in a purely reactive mode, which is a highly dangerous proposition. General Jim Mattis was right when he told Congress on January 27, 2015. "America needs a refreshed national strategy."[16] That refreshment, which entails both a conceptual and practical recalibration, is overdue by decades. Without an urgent reboot, we are operating in altogether unsafe mode—in fact, about as unsafe as it can possibly be, short of meltdown.

The price of failing to strategize for peace is exceptionally high. In the two recent wars in Afghanistan and Iraq, some seven thousand American soldiers have been killed and over 50,000 wounded in battle, to say nothing of far more non-Americans. Meanwhile, the price tag to US taxpayers has been estimated to have ranged from $4-6 trillion, making this combined military campaign the most expensive in history.[17] Of that, over 60 billion dollars were spent on "stabilization and reconstruction," with results ranging from dubious to counterproductive to outright against the US national interests. And yet neither of these military entanglements can be considered to have been "won." No easy answer is possible to the question of what went wrong when it is even harder to know what did not, since we never quite defined what exactly we meant to accomplish in the first place. That's what happens when you don't have a strategy that looks at the full context of the military engagement and at all instruments of power. Failure doesn't come cheap.

One thing is fairly clear: we have neglected both history and tradition. General H. M. McMaster certainly thinks so: "Many of the recent difficulties we encountered in strategic decision-making, operational planning, and force development have stemmed, at least in part, from the neglect of history and continuities in the nature of war, especially war's political and human dimensions."[18] History would have inspired a far more holistic approach to national security, which in turn requires close-knit cooperation between the military and nonmilitary sectors of our society. A holistic approach recognizes the gradualist nature of warfare, predicated on a deeper appreciation of the continuities between waging war and waging peace. If we fail to adapt, we will continue to win battles and lose wars—by losing the peace.

It's the nonmilitary sector that limps far behind, though it has made a few attempts to help articulate a grand strategic vision. A recent step in that direction was launched in July, 2009, after then-Secretary of State Hillary Clinton initiated a process modeled after the Pentagon's long-standing and statutorily required Quadrennial Defense Review (QDR). The Quadrennial Diplomacy and Development Review (QDDR) was released soon thereafter, in December, 2010, to great anticipation, since it had been designed to elevate diplomacy and development to the level of military power in order to meet US foreign policy goals in the twenty-first century.

Loftily entitled "Leading through Civilian Power," the first QDDR was long and ambitious. In her foreword, Secretary Clinton promised that "we will build up our civilian power: the combined forces of civilians across the U.S. government to practice diplomacy, carry out development projects, and prevent and respond to crises. . . . [And t]he State Department and USAID [the U.S. Agency for International Development] will take a lead role in making that happen. We will provide the strategic framework and oversight. . . ."[19] Unfortunately, as cynics had predicted, these turned out to be mostly nice but empty words.

The disappointment of hopeful experts and the NGO community was nearly instantaneous, and quickly spread through the media.[20] Especially devastating was the assessment of Anthony H. Cordesman of the Center for Strategic and International Studies (CSIS), whose report, *The QDDR: Concepts Are Not Enough*, starts out ominously enough: "There are times to be polite about a dismal bureaucratic failure. Wartime is not one of them." It gets worse:

> The Quadrennial Diplomacy and Development Review (QDDR) has many useful ideas but it fails to address the legacy of nearly a decade of failure on the part of the State Department, USAID, and the civil departments of the US government to come to grips with the need to provide effective civilian partners in the wars in Iraq and Afghanistan.... Nor does it discuss that aid programs: emphasized spending without fiscal controls regardless of effectiveness; failed to effectively coordinate the civil side of the US country team in either war; and proved unable to support the US military with solid, real world civil inputs to a joint campaign plan. It grossly understates or ignores the lack of contracting skills and controls, and the fact that both State and USAID are still floundering in seeking meaningful metrics and reporting on their efforts in both wars after nearly a decade of experience.[21]

As he and others had anticipated, the QDDR proved basically irrelevant. Although several initiatives were soon introduced in the US Congress during the one-hundred-and-eleventh session, in the end none passed. Congressional Research Service's Susan Epstein, in her analysis released on February 17, 2011, acknowledged that "possible passage of legislation by the 112th Congress requiring a national strategy and putting in statue an ongoing four-year review could provide clarity on the value of diplomacy and development."[22] Maybe it could have; but it didn't. And for the moment, no such clarity is anywhere in sight. It hasn't helped that Congress has so far received precious little guidance from an administration which has repeatedly emphasized that its priorities are domestic rather than foreign affairs.

Admittedly, a second QDDR was initiated in July of 2014, but this time around there is no anticipation even among State's and USAID's most sanguine supporters—not if this report ends up being anything like its predecessor. Former USAID official Gerald Hyman shoots straight:

> The last one in 2010 was devoid of strategy; produced mostly a collection of wish lists from the various constituent bureaus and agencies; negotiated among a committee of interested parties to a common denominator that ensured no serious protests among the constituents but denied little real policy guidance to any of them; remained at a most general level; created few if any priorities, and designed nothing even remotely strategic.[23]

Continues Hyman: "Worse, perhaps because it was so general and generous, it was dead on arrival at the Office of Management and

Budget, at the Oval Office, and on Capitol Hill. It was orphaned even by its parents." One reason may well be that its parents weren't sure they really wanted this baby, but abortion was not an option: legislation mandated the pretense that it had been conceived, so a procedural gestation would have to be initiated at least *in vitro*.

Yet some might argue that the baby really had been born, and was now dead—or so it has been half-whimsically suggested by *War on the Rocks* contributor Adam Elkus. And yes, he muses on, we killed it:

> We killed American strategy because we simply weren't willing to deal with the intellectual challenge of strategy as it really is, not what we wanted it to be. Unless we come to grips with the flaws, risks, and dangers inevitable in the very expectation that we can use violence to accomplish political objectives, we will be stuck forever watching reruns of this particular episode. Can we learn from our mistakes and do better? [24]

The short answer should be—must be—yes. But addressing SDD (strategic deficit disorder) will require taking some serious steps beyond admission of diagnosis. And where else to begin if not with a soul-searching expedition within, and a recognition that the main reason for this chronic, severely debilitating, potentially terminal condition is very close to home. We don't know who we are as a people. But we cannot afford not to.

One obvious problem is the steep increase in political polarization among the electorate, which has been stoked, even if not caused, by the remarkably monolithic ideological orientation of the country's intellectual elite. Pitting the military against the civilian sector in an epic duel, blood-thirsty warmongers as against peace-loving doves, is not enhancing the legitimate conversation we should be having regarding the best means of deterring our avowed adversaries from harming the United States. If only the highest levels of our government would pitch in. Actually they do, but not always helpfully.

In a speech delivered at American University on August 4, 2015, for example, President Obama confirmed that the task he had set himself when he first campaigned for the office had been to end what he calls the "mindset" that had led to the war in Iraq:

> It was a mindset characterized by a preference for military action over diplomacy, a mindset that put a premium on unilateral U.S. action over the painstaking work of building international consensus, a mindset that exaggerated threats beyond what the intelligence supported. . . .

> It's a mindset out of step with the traditions of American foreign pol-
> icy where we exhaust diplomacy before the war and debate matters
> of war and peace in the cold light of truth.[25]

No doubt. But the president then goes on to say that what he means
by "diplomacy [is] hard, painstaking diplomacy, not saber rattling, not
tough talk, that ratcheted up the pressure on Iran."

But foreign-policy actions demand careful consideration of alternative courses of action in the face of huge unknowns, not least being
the motives of the opposing side. Though certain tactical approaches
may be painted with a broad brush—such as hard vs. soft, "sticks" vs.
"carrots"—which option is most appropriate in any particular case
should not be selected on the basis of personal or political preferences.
Decisions affecting the nation's survival, like all prudential considerations, should not be prejudiced in favor of one over the other except
on the basis of facts and informed judgment. What matters above all
is respect for the most reliable evidence available, to figure out what
actions would best protect the nation, and no reasonable alternative
tactics should be dismissed with contempt. 'Saber rattling' can sometimes come in handy.

To be sure, mindsets, or ideologies, are not without some use, even
in foreign policy: they help cut through a flood of facts that the ordinary
voter is expected to master in making responsible choices at the ballot
box. But given their deeply emotional content, they are bound to be
misleading. While feelings are an important factor in any decision, great
care has to be taken not to allow them to obscure realities that all too
often defy desires and expectations. At the time then-Senator Obama ran
for president, for example, the nation was tired of lingering wars whose
purpose had never been clarified, engagements that had lasted far longer,
and cost considerably more than promised and anticipated. A "peace"
candidate like Barack Obama had the clear advantage: hard power did not
seem to be working—the Iraq surge, for one, had only begun. Manifestly,
large swaths of the public believed that the time had come for change
they "could believe in." Candidate Obama's promise had the advantage
of vacuity: it meant whatever the audience wanted it to mean, filling in
the blank with whatever they believed in. The technique worked—as
sophists from time immemorial knew it usually does. Ordinary people
wanted relief by whatever name—"change" would do just fine.

Politics and campaign promises will always play a huge role in the
conduct of foreign policy. It is why the Founders originally eschewed

a contested presidency, until forced to accept it as a necessary evil, but an evil nonetheless. Ideology is impossible to avoid altogether, since facts must be organized into systems where facts become intertwined with values and emotions. Then again, too, generalizations grab the audience and reinforce their most deeply held prejudices. Savvy politicians specialize in feeding on just those impulses, and always did—as Plato reminded his students in *The Republic*. But the masses, as a rule, don't read Plato.

Rhetoric that inflames popular passions is good for voter turnout, but rather less suited for sober deliberation. Though traditionally inherent in the democratic *agora*—the (literal) marketplace where differing views are exchanged freely, and thus wildly—polarization has recently grown to alarming proportions. According to a survey released by the Pew Research Center on June 12, 2014, "[i]n each party, the share with a highly negative view of the opposing party has more than doubled since 1994. Most of these intense partisans believe the opposing party's policies 'are so misguided that they threaten the nation's well-being.'"[26] Thus not only are Republicans and Democrats more ideologically apart than ever—they do not trust one another's motives: "Among all Democrats, 27% say the GOP is a threat to the well-being of the country. That figure is even higher among Republicans, 36% of whom think Democratic policies threaten the nation."[27]

The intensity of the ideological partisanship, moreover, has been exacerbated rather than mitigated by the communication revolution, which makes it easier than ever to access only the sources of information that conform with one's prejudices. In fact, increasingly, "A Wired Nation Tunes Out the News" altogether, as David T.Z. Minidich's aptly titled article points out.[28] Similarly paradoxical, and counterintuitive, is the finding that college education tends to *reduce* rather than increase one's exposure to contrary views, as a result of the "expectation of confirmation" culture that institutions of higher learning have been fostering. This might be taken as refutation of the Founders' supreme trust in education as the path to wisdom, were it not for the fact that "education" not only isn't equivalent with time spent in school, the two are, increasingly, inversely proportional.

Having turned into bastions of political correctness, colleges today encourage the tendency to cluster ourselves in self-affirming cliques as a kind of mini-tribalism.[29] But the result is not only that a public trusted to make decisions through the ballot box is under-informed, indeed misinformed; worse, the citizenry is blissfully unconcerned about its own dangerous ignorance. In their introduction to a well-documented, depressing new anthology, *The State of the American Mind*, Mark Bauerlein and Adam Bellow find that "[i]nstead of acquiring a richer and fuller knowledge of U.S. history and civics, American students and grown-ups display astounding ignorance of them, and their blindness is matched by their indifference to the problem."[30]

It is this indifference that should worry us most. The fact that we seem oblivious to our tradition, to the sacrifices and ideals of those who came before us and bequeathed us civil institutions designed to secure rights and liberties more effectively than anywhere else on earth, is troubling. But allowing ourselves to be lulled into stupidity by elites that, however well-meaning, seek to undermine if not destroy those institutions, is unconscionable.

Stupidity is not monolithic: it comes in at least two flavors. One is just plain lack of knowledge (as in, "who won the Civil War? Ehhr. . . America?"[31]); another, even more dangerous, is misinformation. That's when you think you know but in fact you've been deliberately misled to believe something false. This last, in turn, is further divisible into (a) myths designed to bolster patriotism, such as the fairy-tales surrounding George Washington, and (b) ideologically-motivated distortions designed to show that Americans are not only at least as bad as everyone else but worse. It is this last subcategory that is most pernicious. But in the end, ignorance about America's past—as it was, warts and all—obscures the truly special qualities of the nation we call home. In a democracy, such ignorance is especially corrosive. One might expect the educational establishment to fully agree, but that is hardly the case.

To remedy this problem, professors Amy and Leon Kass along with Diana Schaub thought it necessary to pull together some of our cultural masterpieces in order to nourish and protect the idea of America. Both a book and a website, *What So Proudly We Hail: The American Soul in Story, Speech, and Song* is about American identity, American character, and American citizenship, designed "to make Americans more appreciatively aware of who they are as citizens," to produce "thoughtful patriots and engaged citizens."[32] Nonpartisan, the patriotism it seeks to encourage is "deep, not superficial; reflective, not reflexive; and above all, thoughtful." The authors ask, rhetorically: "How do we identify ourselves, as individuals and as a people? What do we look up to and revere? To what larger community and ideals are we attached and devoted?" Understanding the nation's Founders, their hopes and fears, the ideals they sought to advance, can only help in articulating a more coherent vision in foreign no less than in domestic affairs. But we certainly have a ways to go.

"Don't know much about history"... So goes the oldie-but-goodie Sam Cooke song, popular in the 1950s, but equally appropriate now. The infamous Jay Leno walk-among-your-fellow-dumb-Americans-and-cringe videos have been entertaining viewers for years with appallingly bone-headed answers, from even the college educated among us, to the most elementary questions about US history and politics. Leno's observations are, unhappily, confirmed by plenty of scientific samplings.

Surveys of adults nation-wide, such as the one conducted by the Annenberg Public Policy Center in 2014, supply some distressing statistics:

- While little more than a third of respondents (36 percent) could name all three branches of the U.S. government, just as many (35 percent) could not name a single one.
- Just over a quarter of Americans (27 percent) know it takes a two-thirds vote of the House and Senate to override a presidential veto.
- One in five Americans (21 percent) incorrectly thinks that a 5–4 Supreme Court decision is sent back to Congress for reconsideration.[33]

Similar results were obtained through a test administered by the American Revolution Center in 2010: more than a third did not know the century in which the American Revolution took place, and half of respondents believed that either the Civil War, the Emancipation Proclamation, or the War of 1812, occurred *before* the American Revolution. But here's the bigger surprise: when respondents were asked, prior to taking the test, whether they thought they would pass it, 89 percent expressed confidence they would; it turns out that 83 percent went on to fail.[34] Not only are too many people stupid—they don't even know *how* stupid.

If adults don't know much about American (or any other) history, neither does the next generation. The latest quadrennial survey conducted by the Education Department's National Assessment of Educational Progress, *The Nation's Report Card: U.S. History 2010*, for example, found that no fewer than 80 percent of fourth graders, 83 percent of eighth graders and a whopping *88 percent* of high school seniors flunked the minimum proficiency rating.[35] A 2013 White Paper by the Pioneer Institute, which expresses alarm at the findings, predicts that

> poor performance in history and civics portends a decay of the knowledge, skills, and dispositions needed for a lifetime of active, engaged citizenship. The reasons for this decline are many: the amount of time

devoted to history in K-12 education has demonstrably shrunk over time; demands to make curriculum more inclusive have led schools and teachers to dwell on social history, race, and gender in ways that distort the nation's historical narrative.[36]

These latter reasons are especially troubling, because they are at bottom ideological. And since their effect is to distort the facts, ignorance is compounded by dangerous error.

Historian Wilfred M. McClay attributes the decline in literacy to the demise of historical scholarship and the increasing loss of self-confidence among its practitioners. Fueled by "a fear that the study of the past may no longer be something valuable or important," historians are now worried that their discipline "is likely to be seen as a relativistic funhouse, in which all narratives are arbitrary and all interpretations are equally valid."[37] McClay agrees with fellow historian Daniel T. Rodgers that we live in a querulous "age of fracture," in which all narratives are contested.[38]

Nor is this "just a feature of academic life, but seems to be an emerging feature of American life more broadly."[39] It is reflected not only in a deterioration of historical knowledge but in what McClay describes as "our startling incapacity to design and construct public monuments and memorials," since the whole idea of such edifices is undermined by the intellectual elite who are enamored of a new discipline known as "memory" studies. The debunking of historical memory is ideologically based, reflecting a relativist historicism rooted in the materialist determinism familiar to all readers of Marx. In other words, after dispensing with jargon: if what people know and remember (or, more precisely, *think* they know and remember) is conditioned by their economic and social status, what's *truth* got to do with it (to paraphrase Tina Turner)? In the words of historian John Gillis, memory has "no existence beyond our politics, our social relations, and our histories," a materialist explanation that leads irrevocably to a new cultural reality: "We have no alternative," for such is the power of ideological, neo-Marxist determinism, "but to construct new memories as well as new identities better suited to the complexities of a post-national era."[40]

How stunningly candid. Gillis has just admitted that relativism is basically a means to an end, promoted to dismantle tradition while serving a specific agenda. That agenda leaves the conscientious (neo-Marxist) historian "no alternative"—so don't bother blaming him for what is preordained—other than "constructing new memories," aligned with the radical, "post-national" agenda of its proponents. And yes, the oxymoron is deliberate: for those "memories" are supposed to be "new"—and hence not exactly real (if you'll pardon the word) but "constructed." Thus falsely touted as history, the past is redrawn in the interest of forging a better, post-national world. McClay is right that "the audacity of this agenda could not be clearer. It is nothing less than a drive to expel the nation-state," which "would mean a complete rupture with the past, and with all admired things that formerly associated themselves with the idea of the nation, including the sacrifices of former generations."[41] Say it isn't so.

A post-national era might seem ideal to some, but nothing that falsifies reality can come to much good. In the end, what we lose along with the past is nearly everything. The Founders would be rendered speechless: they may have prevailed against the formidable British Empire with a ragtag army, but would never have anticipated their Experiment in republican self-rule to be sabotaged from inside the nation's own academy. This modern-day confrontation is all the more dangerous for being deeply insidious. Adding insult to injury, moreover, the victims pay for their own miseducation at inflated prices that condemns them to crippling debt before they've even seen their first (usually meager) paycheck.

Yet this is the same radical agenda driving the effort to change the framework for teaching American history, outlined in the Advanced Placement examination revisions by the College Board (CB), started in 2014. A private New York-based organization, the CB administers the exam to high school students, traditionally reflecting the typical college introductory survey course in American history. Those courses having gradually been discontinued, the CB has changed focus. Its revised purpose is to test students' ability to examine "how various identities, cultures, and values have been preserved or changed in different contexts of U.S. history, with special attention given to the formation of gender, class, racial, and ethnic identities." In a word, the new framework represents a shift from national identity to subcultural identities, underscoring the divisions rather than sources of national unity and cohesion. Summarizes McClay: "Instead of combating fracture, it embraces it."[42]

Our national dentity is thus sabotaged from below; one nation under God becomes many subcultural identities under one federal behemoth that tracks them relentlessly, come what may. Notwithstanding the purportedly good intentions, racism returns in the guise of paternalism—and we all lose in the process. Treating people as members of groups rather than as individuals thus paradoxically undermines the values of the larger community: as Americans, we are all different, yet united by that very difference, which cannot and should not be reduced to facile labels.

Knowledge is indeed often difficult to attain—it takes time-consuming reading and research, critical thinking, and hard experience. But ignorance, especially regarding oneself—both individually and as a coherent community—is a recipe for trouble. The Founders all appreciated the importance of education and self-knowledge as prerequisites to understanding the complicated world around us, absent which the notion of self-governance is just a theoretical conceit.

As Thomas Jefferson wrote to his friend Littleton Waller Tazewell on January 5, 1805:

> Convinced that the people are the only safe depositories of their own liberty, and that they are not safe unless enlightened to a certain degree, I have looked on our present state of liberty as a short-lived possession unless the mass of the people could be informed to a certain degree.[43]

It was not an unrealistic expectation: the electorate did not need to become enlightened beyond "a certain degree." To have demanded more would have doomed the republican experiment from the outset.

But that "degree" had to include at least a basic appreciation of the nation's principles, and at least a modicum of information regarding its early years. Jefferson would undoubtedly have sympathized with the lament of Professor Paul Hollander that the ignorance of Americans, particularly about their own tradition, is profoundly corrosive, if not outright dangerous to the future of the nation. The conspiratorially inclined may want to blame it all on subversion.

It was that, in part, as we shall soon see. But it turns out that what Hollander calls "domestic anti-Americanism" was to a very large extent homegrown, "a product of knowing little history and of the world outside the United States."[44] Far more than a slick bumper-sticker cliché like "pinheadism" (as in Jim O'Reilly's of Fox News strident "pinheads vs. patriots"), anti-Americanism is a potentially cancerous affliction, not to be taken lightly. Hollander identifies three different types, distinguishing foreign from domestic strains of the insidious virus. Aware of these nuances, he writes:

> Understanding anti-Americanism requires not merely a renewed effort to grasp the deep and widespread ambivalence evoked by the costs and benefits of modernity, but more generally an understanding of the irreconcilability of many human values and desires that becomes more apparent with the progress of modernization.[45]

This inevitable paradox of the human condition, however idiosyncratic its current manifestations, is especially irksome to utopians, who refuse to acknowledge the complexity of our stubborn nature, which has always eluded idealist expectations, and in all likelihood always will.

Ambivalence toward material amenities made widely available through advancing technology certainly contributes to elite dissatisfaction with American culture, who find it coarse and soul-numbing. Their reaction is understandable, even justified; but it can be carried too far. Novelist and filmmaker Susan Sontag, for example, condemned America in 1969 as "a cancerous society with a runaway rate of productivity that inundates the country with increasingly unnecessary commodities, services, gadgets, images, information."[46] Yes, we are guilty of committing modernity; but this hardly excuses indulging in a foreign policy of self-loathing.

To her, it does. Unflinchingly, she goes on to draw far-reaching conclusions about the very legitimacy of America's involvement abroad, particularly in Indochina. To the likes of Sontag, "Vietnam offered the key to a systematic criticism of America."[47] The war provided the perfect means to get back at the nation she had actually started to detest much earlier, as had many of her class. Sontag well knew that she spoke for a whole generation of antiwar protestors, many of whom would soon join the academy. They shared her undisguised animosity, imbued with raging anger: "America has become a criminal, sinister country—swollen with priggishness, numbed by affluence, bemused by the monstrous concern that it has the mandate to dispose of the destiny of the world."[48]

Cultural critic Roger Kimball describes in fascinating detail the evolution of leftism from essentially a curmudgeonly distaste for consumerism to something far more sinister (note that in Latin, *sinister* means "left"). Kimball illustrates how liberals' disillusionment with the Soviet Union, once they "finally understood that Stalinism was the natural fulfillment, the outcome of revolutionary Marxism," rather than a mere aberration, morphed into "a kind of metaphysics of anti-Americanism."[49] Among the best known of those early metaphysicians was liberal essayist Jason Epstein, who claimed that America had "fallen into a frenzy of self-destruction, tearing its cities apart, fouling its landscapes . . . not for any substantial human happiness . . . but for higher profits . . ."[50]

Which brings us to *Das Capital*. The impact of the Communist Party USA (CPUSA) and its so-called "fellow-travelers" in the media and the academy, meticulously documented in numerous studies by historians of the left Harvey Klehr and John Earl Haynes, cannot be dismissed as the mere rantings of the lunatic right.[51] Klehr and Haynes point out that "Communism's incompatibility with American values became especially intense and apparent once the Cold War began after World War II [, for that] war was not only a military confrontation and a geopolitical context but also a global ideological war."[52] Not only American Communists but many of their leftwing friends aligned themselves with America's enemies, "an allegiance that contributed to, as well as reflected, their homegrown anti-American disposition."[53]

Unfortunately, the excesses of the McCarthy hearings that took place in the mid-1950s were so ludicrous that they seemed almost designed to sabotage investigations into the Communist infiltration of the media and the highest levels of the US government, turning them into a veritable circus. Only recently was the true extent of that infiltration fully and incontrovertibly documented, after previously classified cables and other data became publicly available.[54] Although the predominantly left-leaning ideology of the intelligentsia today is by no means a direct consequence of those activities, they cannot be dismissed as entirely irrelevant either.

Politicians, especially in a democracy, cannot ignore public sentiment: to go against it is impractical if you want to get elected.

No wonder the American people tell pollsters they distrust politicians of all stripes—and journalists too, for good measure. Meanwhile, as veterans return to their homes, many grievously injured, their sacrifices speak for themselves. Surveys consistently show that when it comes to national security, Americans prefer to place their faith, along with a large bulk of the national budget spent on foreign affairs and defense, in the nation's military. It is not that we don't believe in diplomacy. It's that we are hard-headed pragmatists, skeptical of both diplomacy and development assistance being able to deliver, to end conflicts so we can go back to our lives.

When the stakes are high, a matter of life and death, Americans want results—and as fast as possible, as efficiently as possible. In a word, they want their money's worth. They want to help others, of course, but the price must be worth the sacrifice, and something must be achieved at the end of the day. Most Americans might describe themselves as realists. That said, they are not now, and never have been, isolationists. They believe in engaging the world, no matter how complex. But when, how, and why should we engage, and with whom? Just what exactly is our vital national interest and what is only marginal? It used to be so much easier when the United States led the Free as against the Unfree—Totalitarian Communist—world. Now there are shades of gray, with apparently no discernable white and black lines on either side of the multicultural spectrum. Conservatives insist that America is as pure as any nation can expect to be, while the more left-leaning among our fellow-citizens detect a far darker side, which especially gladdens our enemies' hearts—though nothing so much as the disagreement itself. Not that we have an especially good idea of who our enemies are—or our friends, for that matter. Stupid we are not; but smart is a stretch. "Intelligence-challenged" comes close.

Notes

1. In this book, I will be using Daesh rather than either ISIS or ISIL to refer to the Islamic State of Iraq and the Levant, also known as the Islamic State of Iraq and Syria.
2. "CENTCOM Commander 'Mad Dog' General James Mattis Set to Retire," *DuffelBlog*, April 27, 2012. http://www.duffelblog.com/2012/04/centcom-commander-general-mad-dog-mattis-set-to-retire/
3. Reprinted as "A New American Grand Strategy," by General Jim Mattis, in *Defining Ideas—A Hoover Institution Journal*, February 26, 2015. http://www.hoover.org/research/new-american-grand-strategy
4. Jordan Fabian, "Obama: 'We don't yet have a complete strategy' against ISIS," *The Hill*, June 8, 2015. http://thehill.com/policy/defense/244272-obama-we-dont-yet-have-a-compete-strategy-against-isis
5. A reference to the famous Alcoholics Anonymous 12-step program.
6. The National Security Act of 1947—July 26, 1947, Public Law 253, 80th Congress; Chapter 343, 1st Session; S. 758, http://global.oup.com/us/companion.websites/9780195385168/resources/chapter10/nsa/nsa.pdf
7. For a good overview of the context, see Matthew Baldwin, "In Search of U.S. Grand Strategy: National Security Strategy since Goldwater-Nichols," Duke University Thesis, 2003. http://www.comw.org/qdr/fulltext/03baldwin.pdf
8. Catherine Dale, *National Security Strategy: Mandates, Execution to Date, and Issues for Congress*, Congressional Research Service Report for Congress, Aug. 6, 2013, p. 1. https://www.fas.org/sgp/crs/natsec/R43174.pdf

9.   Robert D. Blackwill, "Media Call: The 2015 National Security Strategy," February 10, 2015 (emphasis added). http://www.cfr.org/grand-strategy/media-call-2015-national-security-strategy/p36117

10.   Colin S. Gray, "The Strategist as Hero," *Joint Forces Quarterly*, Issue 62, 3d quarter 2011, 43.

11.   Aaron Mehta, "Mixed Reaction to US National Military Strategy," *Defense News*, July 12, 2015. http://www.defensenews.com/story/defense/policy-budget/2015/07/12/national-military-strategy-mixed-reaction/29968861/

12.   United States Army, United States Marine Corps and the United States Special Operations Command, *Strategic Landpower: Winning the Clash of Wills*, January 16, 2013. http://www.tradoc.army.mil/FrontPageContent/Docs/Strategic%20Landpower%20White%20Paper.pdf

13.   *The U.S. Army Operating Concept: Win in a Complex World—2020–2040*, TRADOC Pamphlet 523-3-1, Oct. 7, 2014, iii.

14.   William C. Martel, *Grand Strategy in Theory and Practice*, 344.

15.   See David M. Edelson and Ronald R. Krebs, "Delusions of Grand Strategy: The Problem with Washington's Planning Obsession," *Foreign Affairs*, November/December 2015, 109–16. The authors claim that "a pragmatic approach would consider threats on their own terms rather than as part of a larger strategic worldview" (116). But that begs the question, since threats are never on "their own" terms but as part of a worldview which defines them as threats.

16.   Mattis, "A New American Strategy."

17.   Sara Thannhauser and Christoff Luehrs, "The Human and Financial Costs of Operations in Afghanistan and Iraq," in *Lessons Encountered: Learning from the Long War*, eds. Richard D. Hooker, Jr., and Joseph J. Collins (Washington, DC: National Defense University, September 2015), 421–40.

18.   H. R. McMaster, "Discussing the Continuities of War and the Future of Warfare: The Defense Entrepreneurs Forum," *Small Wars Journal*, October 14, 2014. http://smallwarsjournal.com/jrnl/art/discussing-the-continuities-of-war-and-the-future-of-warfare-the-defense-entrepreneurs-foru

19.   "Leading through Civilian Power—The First Quadrennial Diplomacy and Development Review," 2010, 6.

20.   An overview of reactions may be found on the website of Inter-Action, the large and influential alliance of nearly 200 globally acting nongovernmental organizations, at http://www.interaction.org/qddr

21.   Anthony H. Cordesman, "The QDDR: Concepts Are Not Enough," CSIS, December 21, 2010, 2.

22.   Susan B. Epstein, *Foreign Aid Reform, National Strategy, and the Quadrennial Review*, CRS R41173, Feb. 15, 2011, 23. https://www.fas.org/sgp/crs/row/R41173.pdf

23.   Gerald Hyman, "Lessons for the 2014 QDDR," Sept. 23, 2014, Center for Strategic & International Studies, http://csis.org/publication/lessons-2014-qddr

24.   Adam Elkus, "CSI: Pentagon—Who Killed American Strategy?" *War on the Rocks*, October 12, 2015. http://warontherocks.com/2015/10/csi-pentagon-who-killed-american-strategy/?utm_source=WOTR+Newsletter&utm_campaign=570e052d46-WOTR_Newsletter_8_17_158_15_2015&utm_medium=email&utm_term=0_8375be81e9-570e052d46-60136989

25. *The Washington Post*, Aug. 5, 2015. http://www.washingtonpost.com/news/post-politics/wp/2015/08/05/text-obama-gives-a-speech-about-the-iran-nuclear-deal/
26. http://www.people-press.org/2014/06/12/political-polarization-in-the-american-public/
27. Ibid.
28. Mark Bauerlein and Adam Bellow, eds., *The State of the American Mind* (West Conshohoken, PA: Templeton Press, 2015), 97–109.
29. Greg Lukianoff, "How Colleges Create the Expectation of Confirmation," in *The State of the American Mind*, 212.
30. Bauerlein and Bellow, *The State of the American Mind*, xii.
31. Neely Low, "American College Students Don't Know Who Won the Civil War," August 16, 2015, https://www.youtube.com/watch?v=2A8OBYmpMpw
32. Amy A. Kass, Leon R. Kass, and Diana Schaub, eds., *What So Proudly We Hail: The American Soul in Story, Speech, and Song* (Wilmington, DE: ISI Books, 2011), xi. The book is featured at a wonderful website, a "one-stop source for free, literary-based curricula to aid in the classroom instruction of American history, civics, social studies, and language arts." http://www.whatsoproudlywehail.org/about_general
33. http://www.annenbergpublicpolicycenter.org/americans-know-surprisingly-little-about-their-government-survey-finds/
34. Max Fisher, "Americans vs. Basic Historical Knowledge," *The Wire*, June 4, 2010. http://www.thewire.com/politics/2010/06/americans-vs-basic-historical-knowledge/19596/
35. http://nces.ed.gov/nationsreportcard/pdf/main2010/2011468.pdf
36. Robert Pondiscio, Gilbert T. Sewall, and Sandra Stotsky, "Shortchanging the Future: The Crisis of History and Civics in American Schools," A Pioneer Institute White Paper, No. 100, April 2013
37. Wilfred M. McClay, "History, American Democracy, and the AP Test Controversy," *Imprimis*, July/August 2015, Volume 44, Number 7/8.
38. Daniel T. Rodgers, *The Age of Fracture* (Cambridge, MA: Harvard University's Belknap Press, 2012).
39. Ibid.
40. John R. Gillis, *Commemorations: The Politics of National Identity* (Princeton, NJ: Princeton University Press, 1994), 20.
41. McClay, "History, American Democracy, and the AP Test Controversy."
42. Ibid.
43. http://www.let.rug.nl/usa/presidents/thomas-jefferson/letters-of-thomas-jefferson/jefl166.php
44. Paul Hollander, ed., *Understanding Anti-Americanism: Its Origins and Impact at Home and Abroad* (Chicago, IL: Ivan Dee, 2004), 35–6.
45. Ibid., 37.
46. Susan Sontag, "Some Thoughts on the Right Way (for us) to Love the Cuban Revolution," *Ramparts*, April 1969, 6–19.
47. Ibid.
48. Cited by Roger Kimball, "Susan Sontag: a Prediction," *The New Criterion*, December 28, 2004.
49. Roger Kimball, "Anti-Americanism Then and Now," in *Understanding Anti-Americanism*, 246.

50.   Jason Epstein, "The CIA and the Intellectuals," The New York Review, April 20, 1967. http://www.nybooks.com/articles/archives/1967/apr/20/the-cia-and-the-intellectuals/

51.   John Earl Haynes, who during the 1970s served as a legislative assistant to Democratic senator Wendell Anderson, later worked as a specialist in 20th century political history in the Manuscript Division of the Library of Congress. Harvey Klehr is the Andrew W. Mellon Professor of Politics and History at Emory University.

52.   Harvey Klehr and John Earl Haynes, "The Rejection of American Society by the Communist Left," in *Understanding Anti-Americanism*, 274.

53.   Ibid.

54.   See M. Stanton Evans and Herbert Romerstein, *Stalin's Secret Agents: The Subversion of Roosevelt's Government* (New York: Threshold Editions, 2013) and Herbert Romerstein and Eric Breindel, *The Venona Secrets: The Definitive Exposé of Soviet Espionage in America (Cold War Classics)* (Washington, DC: Regnery History, 2014).

10

Intelligence Deficit

The haft of the arrow had been feathered with one of the eagle's own plumes. We often give our enemies the means of our own destruction.
—Aesop, Sixth century BC

For the enemy to be recognized and feared, he has to be in your home or on your doorstep.
—Umberto Eco, *The Prague Cemetery*, 2010

The best-equipped army in the world can still lose a war if it doesn't understand the people it's fighting.
—Gen. Ray Odierno, Apr. 22, 2012

The first book of the Old Testament reveals the shocking fact that the first murder in history was committed by the first son born of human parents. Still worse, the victim was his own hapless brother. Cain had become enraged at God's seeming preference for young Abel's offering. Yet despite God's urging Cain to master himself, and not allow sin to "crouch at his door," adding that the young man had nothing to worry about so long as he did the "right thing," Cain was unable to back down. He couldn't stop himself: luring the unsuspecting Abel to a field, Cain attacked and slew him, with no sign of hesitation or remorse. (*Genesis* 4, 1–8)

When God confronts him after discovering the crime, Cain responds insolently: "Am I my brother's keeper?" Though God, incensed, banishes the unrepentant murderer, and curses him to become a fugitive and a poor vagabond to whom the earth will yield nothing, He is ultimately merciful: not only does God let Cain live, He places a sign on Cain's forehead indicative of divine protection. If this seems contradictory, it need not be. Leon Kass explains "Cain may at this moment glimpse the difference between a god to whom one sacrifices vegetables and the God who takes notice of, and who is outraged by bloodshed (and who, at least for now, provides even for murderers)."[1]

This story, like all biblical narratives, is remarkable on many levels. Consider for instance that Abel is murdered despite having done nothing deliberately to anger his brother; nor, in retrospect, could he have possibly done anything to avoid the circumstances that led to his brother's envy and rage. Too often we think that others' enmity can be avoided if only we do what is right and try not to upset anyone; unfortunately, it doesn't always work. Never mind being "kept" by one's brother; blood ties may fail to prevent even being murdered by him, if his hatred is too overwhelming, whatever its cause. It surely seems odd that, while the biblical God is supposedly merciful to all His children, He could not—or anyway did not—prevent Cain from murdering Abel. True, the biblical Cain, though initially insolent, is said later to have been humbled and learned his lesson: he ends up dedicating himself to his family and children, and even builds a city. Yet that city, observes Kass, is "founded in fear of violent death, but first, in fratricide. This taint, one must believe, is from the Bible's point of view, inherent in civilization as such."[2] God, it appears, had meant to warn his children from the outset. This is tough love, but love nonetheless— and worth heeding.

Civilization entails complexity—ethnic, religious, racial, economic, and social. These divisions in turn channel the inherent human passions of envy, resentment, and fear through nationalism, Islamism, and a whole slew of other ideologies, whose conceptual veneer barely disguises their visceral core. The advance of technology exacerbates these clashes, as communication becomes more widespread yet also more vulnerable to manipulation. Misunderstandings become more dangerous. And as weapons increase in lethality, perceived injustices which lead to murderous rage have more devastating consequences, and brothers turn against one another, as they always have, for reasons both real and imagined. Even if most people are peace-loving and generous, it does not take a lot of enemies to cause havoc, if they are vicious enough.

As Sun Tzu might have put it, the *ying* and *yang*, or the push and pull, the ambiguity that defines all life continues unabated, changing only in the details, the specifics, and the severity of each cycle. However powerful, America is very much part of the world, hardly immune to the envy and rage of its brothers abroad who feel slighted by destiny, and like Cain, are wont to vent their spleen. Some convince themselves that America is to blame, a comfortable substitute for more plausible but politically less palatable sins and errors. In any event, guilty or not, given its economic, political, and economic strength, the United States stands at the center of the storm; self-deceptive earplugs might make the thunder go away, but not the lightning, nor the flood of ire. Human nature has stayed remarkably constant through history, however different each individual is and will always be from every other, like a snowflake or a tear. Cain is still with us, and not about to leave anytime soon. We may be stronger than ever, but still quite vulnerable.

The world certainly isn't getting any safer, which makes President Obama's policy of "keeping international affairs at bay"[3] while he focuses on domestic issues almost as baffling as his overconfidence in his personal strategic abilities. We have it straight from *New Yorker* editor David Remnick, who reported on January 27, 2014: "Obama told me that what he needs isn't any new grand strategy—'I don't even need George Kennan right now.'"[4] This is surprising even for Mr. Obama. For surely any president can use the help of someone like Kennan, who offered expert advice on how to deal with a complex and duplicitous foreign power by relying on personal observations and experience in that country.

Is the president overconfident, or so under-informed that he isn't even aware of what he doesn't know? Many people are taken aback by the President's approach to a number of regimes that have long been considered enemies of the United States, treating them with excessive leniency and trust. Technically known as *appeasement*, the tactic has long been discredited, its practitioners all but guaranteed a place in history's Hall of Shame. It seems to have done less than nothing to deter dictators who support anti-Western terrorists, who consistently engage in brazen anti-American disinformation, conduct cyber warfare, and openly threaten Americans and allies. No wonder some people are tempted to wonder whether the president really knows what he is doing.

George Mason University professor Colin Dueck describes the president's approach as follows: "By all appearances Obama sincerely believes, and has said repeatedly over the years, that the United States should be more accommodating toward potential adversaries and rivals overseas . . . [who thus] can be turned, if not into friends, then at least into something other than adversaries."[5] Dueck has concluded that the president's underlying world-view, or mindset, is fundamentally pacifist: "At heart, . . . Obama *does not really believe that conflict is at the essence of world politics*. On the contrary, he believes that genuine and overarching international cooperation is possible, if apparent adversaries can learn to listen to and accommodate one another."[6] (We might call this "the Abel Syndrome," defined by the notion that we can be safe from attack if we don't hurt someone else; although this is obviously unfair to poor Abel, who had never even considered alternatives to a threat he couldn't possibly have fathomed.)

The belief that conflict will diminish if we act meekly and turn the other cheek has notoriously little basis in experience. Instead, history indicates that highly authoritarian regimes seldom respond generously to enemies' signs of benevolence—on the contrary, they take it as a sign of weakness. Former chess champion and anti-Putin activist Gary Kasparov, who knows what such regimes are like from hard personal experience, concludes ironically that now is the best time in history to be an enemy of the US. Exasperated, he exclaims: "It's delusional to think you can make peace with an unrepentant state sponsor of terror like Iran or a Russian regime that is sending tanks across a European border and adopting fascist propaganda."[7] Continues Kasparov: "These terrible deals with Cuba, Russia, and Iran—it's like the old joke about the businessman who sells each unit at a loss but says he'll make it up in volume."

From a businessman's perspective, however, temporary losses may indeed be worth future gains, if volume brings with it brand recognition that may translate into future profits. But in international affairs, if you consistently sell at a loss, you will soon find yourself alone, as everyone wonders what's wrong with you. America is ill-advised to hope that generosity will be rewarded in kind; that approach might impress ourselves and perhaps some of our good friends, if we are lucky. Assuming we have any friends at all.

Lord Palmerston (1764–1865) may or may not have been the original author of the adage that "nations have no permanent friends or allies, they only have permanent interests," but far from original, it's common sense. In human affairs, permanence is a mirage: like individuals, nations too change throughout their lifetime, sometimes unrecognizably. The nineteenth-century French theoretician Ernest Renan (1823–1892) even went so far as to claim that "a nation is a *daily* plebiscite," the strength of its own members' allegiance requiring constant nurturing. How much greater is the challenge of keeping the trust of its friends. To be sure, friends, like enemies, need not be perpetual to deserve the title. What is more, feelings are treacherous: undue affection can blind us to someone's worst traits while, conversely, hatred can lead to hurting those who genuinely try to help us.

Thus our first president, George Washington, in his Farewell Speech of September 19, 1796, had warned that "history and experience prove that foreign influence is one of the most baneful foes of Republican Government. . . . Excessive partiality for one foreign nation and excessive dislike of another, cause those whom they actuate to see danger only on one side, and serve to veil and even second the arts of influence on the other. The Great rule of conduct for us, in regard to foreign Nations is in extending our comercial [sic] relations to have with them as little political connection as possible."[8] Though consistently applauded by those who disdain all alliances and would have the United States act (or, preferably, not act) alone, recognizing neither friend nor foe except as commercial interests dictate, Washington added an important qualifier: "So far as we have already formed engagements let them be fulfilled," What Washington had really warned against, then, was "excessive partiality;" he urged keeping a detached, objective evaluation of the national interest as the ultimate goal of any alliance. It should be obvious that he could not have opposed all alliances as such, for without them the United States would never have been created in the first place.

Our ancestors took great pains to understand, and whenever possible cultivate, their native-born neighbors as well as the nations of faraway Europe. Though this is often forgotten, not all the Indian tribes had been hostile to the uninvited newcomers; and most colonists did a commendable job of enlisting some Native Americans—notably in Massachusetts[9]—to help them survive in the harsh environment of the New World. So too, the Revolutionary War had been conducted against fellow Englishmen, even as many colonists were more sympathetic to their former compatriots than to their own neighbors who had taken up arms in what they saw as an illegal rebellion—which meant that the revolutionaries needed to be extra vigilant with their own brothers, sometimes quite literally.

Benjamin Franklin's son was by far the most prominent example of an adversary within the colonial family: a staunch loyalist, devoted to Britain, his father would never forgive him for his treachery. Similarly, Dr. Benjamin Church, member of Boston's elite group of revolutionaries and grandson of the revered early colonist with the same name who had secured the help of key Indians, betrayed his revolutionary brethren in Boston and turned British spy, to the consternation of all who had trusted him as one of their own. The Founders were not only facing a formidable military adversary; they were also obliged to tiptoe around human minefields in their very midst. Occasional lapses notwithstanding, they did so with spectacular agility and success.

The threats from without were just as daunting. It took a great deal of discipline, sophistication, and understanding for the young United States to navigate the rough waters of international conflict, both before and after winning independence, lest it fail to survive. But the nimble little David-America had figured out how the European Goliaths played their games, and for the most part kept its head cool, mindful that it could ill afford to lose it. Keeping a cool head, of course, doesn't mean closing your eyes and ears. Soon David would grow, and his European neighbors would age, some friends becoming enemies, while others became distracted elsewhere. As lethal weapons outpaced human abilities to adjust their strategies, the world became more dangerous than anyone could have predicted.

If *Homo sapiens* have been evolving, they have done so imperceptibly at best. To this day, wounded pride continues to be a major reason to react violently, and often in a self-defeating manner. We are all Cain's descendants, in that each of us is susceptible to lashing out upon being slighted for what may seem to others (and even to ourselves, in calmer moments) negligible reasons. For that matter, we are also like Abel, oblivious to enemies who want us dead even though we merely go about our own business, not intending to hurt them. But unlike Abel, most of our current enemies give us plenty of warning.

It is small comfort that Cain was subsequently vilified while Abel was mourned by all, becoming the first martyr—many Christians considering him a precursor of Jesus.[10] Martyrdom, of dubious value even to individuals whose candidacy for sainthood is otherwise at best remote, can never be an option for nations. Responsible leadership entails demonstrating steadfast, realistic vigilance based on accurate intelligence, predicated on the presumption that anyone can become an enemy, even if unprovoked. Steadfastness should minimize the propensity for rage. Though it might provide temporary relief from immediate pain, overreaction usually solves nothing. Worse, precipitous action gives rise to new and often more serious dangers. Any drastic action, especially if it involves hard power, should only be taken after very careful analysis based on accurate information and as thorough an understanding of the human environment as possible. Leaders should never volunteer their nations' suicide.

Such understanding, however, involves long-term engagement and must incorporate insights from trusted members of the local populations.

Sun Tzu had warned against a sovereign raising an army simply because he is enraged, and against a general fighting because he is resentful: "For while an angered man may again be happy, and a resentful man again be pleased, a state that has perished cannot be restored, nor can the dead be brought to life. Therefore, the enlightened ruler is prudent and the good general is warned against rash action" (*AoW* XII. 18–19). In a democracy, the admonition has to be conveyed to the population and, in turn, to its elected representatives, who often do its bidding reflexively, pandering to volatile voters instead of exercising leadership. In order to avoid overreacting when surprised, we should avoid being surprised, especially when better intelligence is within our reach.

But we keep being surprised. One reason is that we don't do well with lesson learning. Perhaps nothing illustrates this better than our experience in Vietnam: America's defeat there half a century ago should have resulted in a major reassessment of goals and tactics, but it didn't. The dismal failure to understand Vietnam's political environment led to disastrously ill-advised actions that doomed our efforts, predicated as they were on woefully insufficient cultural knowledge. As William L. Stearman, who had been deeply involved in that quagmire, for example, points out in a post-mortem titled "Lessons Learned from Vietnam," "Our most fundamental mistake of the war was encouraging the overthrow of [South Vietnam's leader] Ngo Dinh Diem in 1963."[11] For while Diem's administration was not especially popular, it was far less corrupt than its Northern counterpart, whose profoundly ideological nature and extensive Communist training and equipment, were also discounted by the United States. The incursion had been doomed from the outset: our inability to properly assess the strengths and weaknesses of the Viet Cong, along with overconfidence in our own superior military prowess, all but guaranteed our undoing.

Steadman is convinced that the Vietnam debacle need not have happened; indeed, he thinks it would have been wiser never to have escalated the ground war in the first place. He argues that one of the major mistakes was not beginning the Vietnamization process earlier: "As soon as the situation had stabilized in 1966, we should have devoted considerable resources to training officers and noncoms and to upgrading the weapons and other equipment of South Vietnamese forces . . . [Unfortunately, a]t the time, the condescending attitude of most who served in Vietnam was 'stand aside, you little guys, and let us experts do the job.' I must confess that I was among those who felt that way."[12] But did we learn anything? Apparently not.

Instead of taking to heart the lesson that American intelligence had to become more astute and culturally attuned, the experience in Vietnam served principally to erode America's faith in its ability to engage militarily outside its comfort zone of conventional warfare. The lesson that we took away was to cease tinkering with human terrains, where we were obviously out of our league. "No more Vietnams!" became the mantra. Get better at understanding it? Nah. Just stay away from such wars, and hope that they'll stay away from you. We saw how well that worked.

But there was one other wrong takeaway from that ill-starred war. As strategy expert Robert R. Tomes points out, after Vietnam the nation's and specifically the military's "aversion to military interventions went much deeper than avoiding another small war. . . . *Post-Vietnam, national security decision-making imperatives reversed the learning curve for American intelligence agencies when it came to human dynamics.*"[13] The United States, not as slowly as surely, "shifted to technical collection methods," with the result that what Tomes calls "socio-cultural intelligence" atrophied to nonexistence.

Aside from not anticipating the 9/11 attacks, the most notorious, and tragic, intelligence failure of recent times is the erroneous analysis of data concerning Saddam's alleged weapons of mass destruction (WMDs). In March 2005, the Commission on the Intelligence Capabilities of the United States Regarding WMDs (the WMD Commission) concluded that the inability to discern crucial aspects of Iraq's weapons program stemmed from failures to understand "the context of Iraq's overall political dynamics of Saddam Hussein's Iraq."[14] The United States went into Iraq knowing precious little not only about WMDs; far more troubling, it knew next to nothing about its people and their circumstances. Context is everything. So are the details that make all the difference.

Take the Ba'athists. What were we to make of them? Though our prime enemy had been Saddam Hussein and his sons, what about his supporters? Did that include everyone in the Ba'ath party or not? One would think that a thoughtful answer to that question, which should have involved the most thorough possible consultation with everyone who could offer the decision-makers relevant information, would have produced a better response than the bone-headed decision to disband the Iraqi army and everyone who had ever been a Ba'athist. Widely blamed for that decision, L. Paul Bremer, the first presidential envoy to Iraq, defended it in the *New York Times* on September 6, 2007, stating that "the policy was carefully considered by top civilian and military members of the American government."[15] Perhaps so—and it seems that he was indeed correct. But then he added: "And it was the right decision,"[16] thereby confirming that he should never have been trusted with such a job.

It manifestly had not been the right decision. Predictably, before long, the same former Ba'athists who had been so cavalierly given pink slips would become enraged, and a sectarian civil war nearly tore the country apart. It would be left to General David Petraeus to organize the famous surge, ordered by President Bush despite his advisors' reticence and lack of public support, that eventually led to the eventual (if later squandered) military success. The cost of the original mistake had been staggering, but once again the adage that Americans would always do the right thing after trying everything else was proven correct. Eventually, George Bush made the right call: within a remarkably short period of time, Iraq became sufficiently stable to allow the United States to leave. And left it did, with characteristic, albeit inexcusable, abruptness. Again predictably, the violence returned. Peace had never quite come to Iraq—at least, not for long. It might have; but in the end, it didn't.

Though top deciders are easy targets for criticism, however, they are not the only ones to blame. The problem is far more profound, as we seem incapable of appreciating social complexity and what it takes to influence it effectively. Tomes explains:

> When there is a national security crisis or war, socio-cultural intelligence efforts are funded, social scientists are mobilized, and policymakers have access to key insights into foreign populations. Lacking the imperative for such support or direct intervention by senior leaders, however, funding for sociocultural intelligence activities atrophy. Too often the available resources for socio-cultural intelligence collection and analysis fall between the traditional intelligence organizations or, because they are deemed unclassified or "open source" activities, are relegated to lower priority. This paradigm must change.[17]

Yes. But can it?

Recent history is not encouraging. While citing the errors of the Iraq war is now fashionable, some of the same problems plagued the intrusion into Afghanistan, which even President Obama has called "The Good War." In adopting the term for the title of his new book, however, award-winning journalist Jack Fairweather intends that description ironically. The clue is in its subtitle, *Why We Couldn't Win the War or the Peace in Afghanistan*: obviously, no war can be called good if it cannot be won. Fairweather's use of "couldn't" rather than "didn't" underscores the inevitability of the failure which, as he amply demonstrates, was caused by massive intelligence deficit. That should have come as no surprise, considering that whatever contacts the United States still had, and they were few and far between, dated from the Soviet army's defeat in the early 1990s.

To begin with, our exit had not been especially gracious. In typical "mission-accomplished" style, as soon as the USSR retreated after being roundly defeated, Washington packed up and left. In an astonishingly short-sighted move, Congress immediately proceeded to terminate any assistance to the people who had made the seminal victory possible, leaving the warlords to do what they did best: fight among themselves. In that they excelled, at the same time managing to reduce the country to a state of gruesome terror and chaos. The (hardly benign) neglect of the beleaguered Afghan population by the United States under George H. W. Bush was continued by the Clinton administrations.

Small wonder that almost any security, as opposed to none, would resonate with ordinary Afghans. But the Taliban turned out to be their worst nightmare. Soon sturdy poppies that yielded rapid, high revenues replaced the traditional agricultural crops, which had gradually become abandoned in the midst of all the fighting. Between 1981 and 1994, opium production grew fourteen-fold, amounting to about half of world opium and heroin production.[18]

When the Taliban took over in 1996 to introduce their unique, draconian brand of order, the production of poppies escalated even more rapidly, as did taxes on opium. Soon, the entire ecology of Afghanistan and the region would change radically, destabilizing the region—and the world. Historian Alfred McCoy spells out the chilling magnitude of the effects: "During the 1990s, Afghanistan's soaring opium harvest fueled an international smuggling trade that tied Central Asia, Russia, and Europe into a vast illicit market of arms, drugs, and money-laundering. It also helped fuel an eruption of ethnic insurgency across a 3,000-mile swath of land from Uzbekistan in Central Asia to Bosnia in the Balkans."[19] America, meanwhile, was busy celebrating the end of history.

And then, in 2000, Taliban's leader Mullah Omar suddenly did something odd: he ordered a ban on all opium cultivation. Many saw it as a desperate attempt to achieve some sort of international recognition—that, of course, he did not achieve, but he did manage to devastate a wretched population, which by now had become completely dependent on poppy production. So by the time the United States decided to topple the Taliban, "the regime was already a hollow shell and essentially imploded at the bursting of the first American bombs."[20] If greatly oversimplified, as it leaves out the enormous sacrifice and courage of the Special Forces and other national security personnel who had been fighting under incredibly difficult circumstances, the bottom line is that the Taliban crumbled fast. But, again to quote the great sage Yogi Berra, it ain't over till it's over. And over it still ain't.

It surely wasn't in 2003. Much as President Bush, his advisors, and the American people—to say nothing of the benighted Afghans—would have liked to put it all behind them, some loose ends were all too obvious. For one thing, Osama Bin Laden was still at large. For another, though the administration had done its best to not acknowledge it, whatever war had been waged—whether against the Taliban regime or Al Qaeda or both—nothing that had emerged either walked, talked, or squawked like peace. The people's duck (or was it goose?) had been cooked—and it smelled burned. No matter how little interest George W. Bush may have had in what he had deprecatingly called "nation-building" in his second presidential debate against Vice President Al Gore on October 11, 2000,[21] the pile of rubble and misery, which maps identified as "Afghanistan," was anything but a nation when we prematurely imagined that we had won.

What candidate George W. Bush said in 2000 about the US intervention in Somalia, which had been launched by his father a decade earlier, provides some insight into his thinking and the quality of the intelligence to which he was privy, which led to the wrong conclusions about the way to handle threats before they become enormous:

> [Somalia had] started off as a humanitarian mission and it changed into a nation-building mission, and that's where the mission went wrong. The mission was changed. And as a result, our nation paid a price. And so I don't think our troops ought to be used for what's called nation-building. I think our troops ought to be used to fight and win war. I think our troops ought to be used to help overthrow the dictator when it's in our best interests. But in this case it was a nation-building exercise, and same with Haiti. I wouldn't have supported either.

What had gone wrong in both Somalia and Haiti, in fact, was that we had harbored the illusion that any situation other than perhaps a natural disaster, if that, can ever be considered merely as a "humanitarian" problem. To think otherwise is at best naïve, if not self-deceptive. Somalis were certainly suffering from hunger, but the issues they were facing were deeply and dangerously political. As it happens, the enemies of the poor people of that benighted country struggling to be a state were also our enemies, even if we didn't want to hear it.

They told us, too, plainly enough. Though it is true that Washington appeared not to be even aware of Al Qaeda[22] when Bush Senior came to the Somalis' help, by 2000 there was no longer any doubt of its role there. In his 1997 interview with journalist Peter Arnett,[23] for example, Osama Bin Laden boasted that his Arab holy warriors had banded with Somali Muslims in October 1993 to kill US soldiers in a bloody battle on the streets of Mogadishu. Al Qaeda's firsts attack against the United States had been carried out on December 29, 1992, in Aden, Yemen. That very evening, a bomb went off at the Gold Mohur hotel, where US troops had been staying on their way to Somalia, though the troops had already left when the bomb exploded. The bombers targeted a second hotel, the Aden Movenpick, where they believed American troops might also be staying. This bomb detonated prematurely in the hotel car park, around the same time as the other bomb explosion, killing two Australian tourists.

In his 1997 interview with Arnett, Bin Laden had called the United States "unjust, criminal, and tyrannical"—a year after having issued a declaration of jihad against "the Americans."[24] By 2000, Bin Laden should have been taken far more seriously by both political parties. It had been President Bill Clinton, after all, who brought the Marines home from Somalia in 1993. George H. W. Bush's stated rationale for sending Marines to Mogadishu in 1992 had been a desire to help the Somali people, who could not receive food aid "because relief workers cannot run the gauntlet of armed gangs roving the city."[25] Obviously those "armed gangs" were no mere criminals. Though in both countries people suffered, Haiti and Somalia constituted very different national security threats.

Haiti at least was not being threatened by Al Qaeda. Though criticizing the incompetent way the United States was operating in Haiti is fully justified, East Africa was on another plane. Well-informed leadership should have known—and should have helped the public understand—in what ways the "armed gangs" in Somalia were also America's enemies. (So too, it would have been nice had someone explained what "nation-building" is and is not, but we'll turn to that in chapter 16.) It certainly would have been useful for George W. Bush to know something about the region and its culture. Though in a pinch, a little common sense would have gone a long way—as would listening more closely to what our enemies were actually telling us, loud and clear.

This is how Bin Laden described the Marines' landing in Mogadishu:

> The U.S. government went there with great pride and stayed there for some time with a strong media presence wanting to frighten people that it is the greatest power on earth. It went there with pride and with over 28,000 soldiers, to a poor unarmed people in Somalia. The goal of this was to scare the Muslim world and the whole world saying that it is able to do whatever it desires. As soon as the troops reached the Mogadishu beaches, they found no one but children. The CNN and other media cameras started photographing them (the soldiers) with their camouflage and heavy arms, entering with a parade crawling (on the ground) and showing themselves to the world as the "greatest power on earth". Resistance started against the American invasion, because Muslims do not believe the U.S. allegations that they came to save the Somalis.[26]

Note Bin Laden's helpful hint about how CNN and other media could be put to good use through clever public diplomacy. But are we listening?

Without much by way of explanation, President Clinton withdrew what he considered his predecessor's ill-advised incursion, mission seemingly left unaccomplished, while the Somali people continued to suffer, and Al Qaeda would declare that it had vanquished the mighty American military forces. It looked as if we had not realized what we were getting ourselves into. A decade later, Americans would once again be sent into a complex environment, this time in response to an attack on the homeland. And once again, the nation's national security structure and the lack of strategic compass would fail. Just as we had nearly no understanding of Somalia, both Afghanistan and Iraq were virtually unknown. Most Americans could barely find these places on the map; the political leadership proved not much better.

A major problem facing the United States as it prepared to attack Afghanistan after 9/11 was that tactical considerations ended up dictating strategy. Since the public wanted a quick victory, its leaders sought to provide it; so a key question was what would work in the least amount of time. To do the job swiftly, the President decided to enlist the CIA. The agency, in turn, did what it could: it turned to the warlords with whom it had worked during and after the war against the Soviet army. That, however, had been over a decade earlier; and once the Soviets were gone, we had immediately left the Afghans to fend for themselves—hardly the friendliest thing to do to an ally. Worse, we had dumped a boat-load of ammunition on the place, which we tried unsuccessfully to retrieve, but to no avail. That only served to transform the nation into a lawless hell, which also could hardly have gone unnoticed by the population. If we had been fickle friends, however, the warlords would soon have their comeuppance, proving to far surpass us in the art of duplicity.

To be sure, they seemed perfectly happy to help their erstwhile allies when we returned, in 2001: after all, they had never welcomed the Taliban taking away all their drug money, for its own use. But beyond driving out the Taliban, the warlords' utility was dubious at best. Writes Jack Fairweather:

> The only quality the Americans could count on from these men was their own self-interest and petty rivalry. . . . When the warlords' men did venture up the valley to al-Qaeda positions, they were just as likely to end up pointing their guns to each other as at the presumed mutual enemy.[27]

Our new BFFs were certainly not "best friends forever"—they were merely "best *found* friends," or at any rate, the best that we could find under the circumstances. Not that we had looked very hard. Fairweather, citing the findings of a 2012 study released by the Center for Naval Analyses (CNA), notes that "the Americans had little knowledge of the country, and often relied on their Afghan proxies to tell them whom to target. Warlords like Gul Agha Sherzai in Kandahar readily exploited such ignorance to pursue their own vendettas against rival clans."[28] The study concludes that "the policy of working with warlords from certain tribes resulted in the exclusion of other tribes." The consequences were predictable: "the Taliban won over the allegiance of these marginalized tribes as well as other marginalized groups." In short, it turned into a fiasco.

But behind the antiseptic studies and statistics, there are countless heart-wrenching individual stories of ordinary Afghans caught in a net of intrigue and misunderstanding, while the well-meaning but clueless Americans did the bidding of men they should never have trusted. It is impossible to read the personal account of journalist Anand Gopal, *No Good Men Among the Living*, which describes some of these tragic stories, and not be deeply moved. The title refers to a Pashtu aphorism which, like all (and, apparently, especially Pashtu) aphorisms, has many shades of meaning. But for "an Afghan who had lived through decades of war," writes Gopal, what it now "means is that there were no heroes, no saviors, in his world. The categories of the American war on terror—terrorists and non-terrorists, fundamentalists and democrats—mattered little, not when his abiding goal, like that of so many caught in the conflict, was simply to finish each day alive."[29] Those simple dichotomies, Manichean[30] black-and-white antitheses better suited for describing conventional conflicts among national armies, turned out disastrously for us and for the Afghans we had sought to help. It wasn't the military's—nor the CIA's—fault; it was America's.

The implications for real people on the ground, soldiers and civilians alike, of the blurred or at least not easily discernible difference between friend and foe, however, are existential. This is how SEAL Team 10 member Marcus Luttrell, lone survivor of Operation Redwing, saw it:

> these terrorist/insurgents know the rules as well as they did in Iraq. They're not their rules. . . . every terrorist knows how to manipulate them in their own favor. Otherwise the camel drivers would be carrying guns. But they don't. Because they know we are probably scared to shoot them, because we might get charged with murder, which I actually know they consider to be on the hysterical side of laughable. . . . The truth is, in this kind of terrorist/insurgent warfare, no one can tell who's a civilian and who's not.[31]

In what has to be one of the most dramatic episodes of military history ever recorded, Luttrell describes what happened when he and his three fellow SEALs, on their way to locating a high level Taliban target, encounter some one hundred goats, an old man and a boy, in that order—all unarmed, especially the goats. And yet, obviously, "if these Afghans blew the whistle on us, we might all be killed, right out here on this rocky, burning-hot promontory, thousands of miles from home, light-years from help. . . . To let these guys go on their way was military suicide."[32] But unable to reach anyone by radio to give them guidance, the trapped SEALs put it to a vote among the four of them, and Luttrell cast the deciding ballot in favor of letting the two go. He immediately regretted it as "the stupidest, most southern-fried, lamebrained decision I ever made in my life. I must have been out of my mind."[33]

The old man and the boy had been Taliban informers. For the next two hundred pages, Luttrell describes in harrowing detail how each of his brave buddies behaved with almost superhuman courage, giving more than everything they had, all but defying the laws of nature.

Immediately after it was published in 2007, the book, *Lone Survivor*, became number one on the *New York Times* bestseller list.

Tragically, just as American soldiers were forced to decide who was an enemy and who was not, with their own lives on the line, so too their compatriots on the ground, both military and civilian, in both Afghanistan and Iraq, were unsure whom to trust and how to differentiate between friend and foe. Calling this environment "complex" was the mother of all understatements. Slowly, too slowly, it was beginning to dawn on the leadership in Washington that none of its "operations" would be quick. Neatly excising the tumor and then sewing the patient back up was not an option.

The cancer had spread, malignant cells nearly impossible to differentiate from those still relatively healthy. Saving the patient required destroying the cancer not only with laser-like precision by external means but boosting the healthy cells' ability to survive. In other words, the United States had stumbled into just the sort of situation it had hoped to avoid when it decided to throw out the old counterinsurgency (COIN) materials that had been collecting dust at Special Forces headquarters in Fort Bragg, North Carolina.[34]

It was Vietnam 2.0—*déjà vu* all over again, as guru Yogi Berra said. But we had vowed not to repeat Vietnam, we had tried and succeeded to forget whatever little we had learned there. As a result, the "peace building" part of the engagements in both Afghanistan and Iraq turned out to be unsurprisingly messy, ill-conceived and worse managed. Our friends and allies, both from the government and private—including certainly the nonprofit—sectors, were often more of a hindrance than a help. Cultural divides occur not only among enemies. Commenting on just one small aspect of that divide, journalist Rajif Chandrasekaran, speculates in his book *Little America: The War Within the War for Afghanistan*: "Had the British not torpedoed their relationship with the Marines through unseemly deals and a nineteenth-century attitude toward the Afghans, and had the Marines not always equated British restraint with appeasement, the two militaries could have been true allies."[35] That was but one small example; there were countless more.

This is how Fairweather describes NATO headquarters in Kabul: "a medley of nations, competing national prerogatives, cavalier egos, and political calculations, with only a cursory knowledge of one another's military systems, and in the case of some Italian officers roped in, not even a shared language."[36] With friends like this, who needs enemies? It is not that the leaderships of our allies were ill-intended; it is rather that coordinating such a wide variety of interests is exceedingly difficult and requires a far more effective system than is currently available. To have underestimated that challenge was the United States's fault; once again we had barged in with insufficient knowledge of the circumstances.

Though knowledge of the circumstances (or "terrain," to use Sun Tzu's terminology, which echoes the Army's "human terrain," a term that leaves most ordinary civilians understandably puzzled) has always been critical, the most radical recent change in conceptualizing the notion of an "enemy" has been the rise of terrorist cells and insurgent networks. No longer could we count on a clear delineation between combatants, members of a professional military properly attired and observing the rules of war, on the one hand, and noncombatants on the other. As a result, traditional bureaucratic and logistical boundaries would be strained. Yet what has been called the "iWar paradigm"—referring to Identity, Information, and Individualization—requires obtaining accurate *information* regarding the *identity* of *individuals*. We cannot depend on aggregate data; it has been replaced by "network-based targeting," which is far more personalized.[37]

Naturally, this implies that the nature of these novel, nontraditional security threats "makes it virtually impossible to draw neat lines between war and peace, foreign and domestic, emergency and normality."[38] Welcome to the end of dialectics and the beginning of complexity: as dualisms become overrated, opposites detract. But while enemies and friends become harder to tell apart, we must resist the temptation to oversimplify the social terrain as is our default mode, imagining that all we need to do now is rely on technology to identify networks, then surgically and euphemistically "remove" them. Mission accomplished? Far from it. As Army intelligence officer Col. Glenn J. Voeltz points out, "the doctrinal and technical innovations of iWar dealt with a very specific operational challenge of identifying, screening and targeting network-based adversaries and individual combatants. However, it has very little to offer in terms of dealing with the underlying causes of instability and political violence. For this reason, the methods of iWar must be applied with circumspection and in a manner that does not conflate targeting with strategy."[39]

The task of understanding our fellow human beings is no less daunting now than it has ever been. And technological advances notwithstanding, the best way to approach it is still the old fashioned one of personal interaction—cautious yet empathetic engagement sustained over time. Friends can turn into enemies and enemies into friends, but common sense is still the best compass—certainly far superior to gadgets and numbers. Those have their place, and we couldn't do without them, but that place should not be overrated.

The importance of good, timely, but also contextual and above all human intelligence, grows with the complexity of the environment. Unfortunately, so does the quantity of data, and with it the appetite for more and more information, even as its value decreases almost proportionately to its volume. Though civil libertarians rose en masse in outrage at the revelation of the National Security Agency's practice of gathering reams of telephone conversation data—as it happens, all quite legal—fewer wondered about the effectiveness of the technique itself. Bulk data, crowd sourcing, and other forms of mass collection seem to be all the rage. Should they be?

How satisfying it is to hear none other than the dean of American intelligence education, Mark M. Lowenthal, rail against the newest idol of the technocrats:

> The Intelligence Community should stop chasing intellectual fads that have little substantive basis and are of little relevance to the business of intelligence analysis. "Crowds" do not produce wisdom; they produce riots. We look at "white swans" in part because there are more of them and they are more often the source of our problems. "Black swans" may be important but they are rare and therefore only of passing interest. And so on. In a moment of whimsy, I bundled several of the recent intellectual fads into a single sentence: "I saw a crowd of wise black swans blinking at the tipping point."
>
> The most dangerous and prevalent fad is "big data." What is big data and what do you do with it? Big data advocates tend to be IT folks, not intelligence analysts. They are selling their wares, not even analytical tools. Big data suffers from what I call the X Files fallacy: "The truth is out there." The big data advocates are certain that, if you play with the data long enough, something good will emerge. Most likely, more data, but big data will not get at the questions that most bedevil policymakers and analysts—**intentions**. No amount of big data, or small data, will tell us what Kim Jung Un will do next or what Vladimir Putin is planning. Moreover, policymakers will tell you that they do not want data; they want knowledge and expertise. Hence, we circle back to knowledge building.[40]

How utterly delicious to the ear of one such as this author, educated in the now-nearly extinct humanities. Indeed, crowds do not produce wisdom; but tell that to the crowd-sourcing-sycophants and the number-crunchers. Oh yes, knowledge of human motivation: let's agree that it's important. But won't that mean letting in that old canard, pesky subjectivity? Intentions cannot be quantified, or even photographed. As for expertise, doesn't that, too, mean having to rely on *personal* experience? Won't we have to worry about—dare we even utter the word—*bias*? Isn't intelligence meant to be untainted as possible by unwelcome prejudice or subconscious preconceptions?

Obviously, yes. But just as obviously, no. For while every person perceives the world in light of idiosyncratic early experiences and, yes, preconceived ideas, it is not entirely impossible to sort out subjective and erroneous impressions from what we may consider to be objectively true. Most ordinary Americans understand that; not so much members of the academy, especially in the social sciences and the humanities, where relativism seems to have gained considerable traction in the past couple of decades.

Equally unfortunate is a marked hostility among many in the media, and the intellectual establishment generally, to the national security community generally, a hostility that has grown exponentially since Vietnam. And while incipient anti-Americanism can be traced to the infancy of the Republic,[41] its contemporary version is as important a factor in formulating foreign policy today as it was during Vietnam. Foremost among the aftereffects of that war is what former Secretary of State Condoleezza Rice described as a national "allergy to intelligence."

Although not the principal culprit, it was this attitude that Secretary Rice blamed, at least in part, for the lack of preparedness on 9/11. "The terrorist threat to our nation did not emerge on September 11, 2001," she told a Congressional hearing on May 13, 2004. "Long before that day, radical, freedom-hating terrorists declared war on America and on the civilized world. The attack on the Marine barracks in Lebanon in 1983, the hijacking of the Achille Lauro in 1985, the rise of al Qaeda and the bombing of the World Trade Center in 1993, the attacks on American installations in Saudi Arabia in 1995 and 1996, the East Africa embassy bombings of 1998, the attack on the USS Cole in 2000, these and other atrocities were part of a sustained, systematic campaign to spread devastation and chaos and to murder innocent Americans."[42] She spoke these words a decade ago; but there is little evidence that things are any better today.

Having lived in relative isolation from the rest of the globe for most of its history, now that the United States has been thrust into the limelight as sole Superpower, it has shown itself both philosophically and emotionally underprepared for the challenge. We seem unable to accept that we might be unpopular with people who either completely misunderstand or willfully misrepresent our intentions. It doesn't help that some of our own homegrown skeptics, who blame America for being hated by the "less fortunate" whom it allegedly "exploits," hold positions of authority at our best universities and throughout the government. America's civil-military divide represents nothing less than a cultural, ideological, and demographic rift, which is reflected in the way we characterize ourselves and our enemies.

There was a brief respite after the beginning of the end of the Cold War in 1989, when it seemed for a few moments that we had no more enemies left. Though Saddam Hussein invaded Kuwait in 1991, the US military put an end to that almost instantaneously, seemingly having demonstrated to the world or rather, more dangerously, to ourselves, that we were all but invincible in the battlefield. We were eager to reap the fruits of hegemony, which we took to be a license, as hippies liked to sing in the sixties, to "study war no more."

After the Soviet Union left Afghanistan in 1989, and the United States picked up and left, human intelligence (HUMINT) was steadily losing its *cache* everywhere as spycraft, already deep in the throes of signals intelligence (SIGINT), caught the cyber bug. In less than no time, as messy pesky humans were becoming more expendable, "information superiority"—referring mainly to super gadgetry—became fashionable in intel circles, as in most of the rest of society. That left decision-makers woefully underinformed, with dire consequences for the conduct of US foreign policy.

Though foreign policy is determined by government leaders who decide what actions should be taken on the basis of all available intelligence, adequate knowledge is key to all sectors of society as people seek to determine how best to defend America's key interests and the cause of peace. A major, if not the main, aspect of that intelligence, however, is accurate knowledge concerning our own relative strengths and weaknesses. This is of course Sun Tzu's principal lesson, which marketing expert Mark McNeilly interprets as follows: to know oneself, one must "know the strengths and weaknesses of one's nation. To pit one's strengths against the enemy's weakness and avoid getting surprised by their attacks, it is critical to realize both where one is strong and where one is weak."[43] And one of our main weaknesses is that we have failed repeatedly to detect domestic spying and leaking of classified information until it was far too late to prevent massive damage.

Congressman Mac Thornberry, chairman of the House Armed Services Committee, stated the painfully obvious on September 20, 2015, when he complained that we are our own worst enemy: "Whether it was Wikileaks or Snowden or now the Hillary [Clinton] emails, we have done more to hurt ourselves than the Russians, the Chinese, the terrorists, or anybody else that you want to name.... The damage to the country is just enormous when you put these compromises together."[44] He was talking about the present; had he added the previous two decades, he could have mentioned the infamous CIA spies Aldrich Ames[45] and Edward Lee Howard, as well as FBI spy Robert Hanssen.[46] Former CIA operative Henry Crumpton, noting the incalculable damage that these men have caused to the nation, is worried that the American public has a very poor understanding of the role of intelligence, about which our "society holds variant expectations and ambivalent views." Specifically, "respect, romanticism, ignorance, suspicion, fear, and loathing are jumbled together in our national psyche when we think about spies."[47]

Crumpton explains that the title of his book, *The Art of Intelligence: Lessons from a Life in the CIA's Clandestine Service*, was meant in part as a tribute to Sun Tzu and partly to the CIA's first director, Allan Dulles, who had cited Sun Tzu in the first sentence of his own book, *The Craft of Intelligence.* Crumpton specifically references Sun Tzu's admonition to "know your enemy and know yourself"—adding that "what was true in ancient China holds true today. Increasingly war and intelligence are vital not only to the state but also to nonstate actors and citizens—because we are entering a new era of conflict with its own unique characteristics and requirements."[48]

It is no secret that the intelligence community is plagued by huge problems. Perhaps the highest concern is the threat of infiltration and sabotage, demonstrated by the recent case of Lebanese-born Nada Nadim Prouty, a Hezbollah mole who managed to fool both the FBI and the CIA for almost two decades.[49] Add to that embarrassingly flawed counterintelligence, as evidenced by Secretary of State Colin Powell's testimony at the U.N., whose supposedly incontestable proof to all the world that Saddam had weapons of mass destruction had been based on the dubious fabrications of a highly unreliable source whose ironically appropriate nickname was Curveball.[50]

Worst of all, however, is treating innovation and reform with retribution. Here is how *Foreign Policy*'s Sean D. Naylor describes what happened to Army Lt. Gen. (Ret.) Michael Flynn, the former director of the Defense Intelligence Agency (DIA):

> He ruffled feathers in the organization by trying to reshape it for the wars of the 21st century, while also incurring the wrath of the Obama administration for making public statements that had not been fully vetted, according to a Defense Department official who works closely with the DIA and the Office of the Director of National Intelligence. The official pointed in particular to Flynn's presentation of the DIA's 'annual threat assessment' to the Senate Armed Services Committee in February 2014 that predicted the Islamic State would probably 'attempt to take territory in Iraq and Syria to exhibit its strength in 2014, as demonstrated recently in Ramadi and Fallujah, and [by] the group's ability to concurrently maintain safe havens in Syria.' This forecast would, of course, prove true, but it clashed noticeably with Obama's description the previous month of the Islamic State as 'a jayvee team.' [51]

Fast forward to September 9, 2015, as *The Daily Beast* posts this "Exclusive: 50 Spies Say ISIS Intelligence Was Cooked." The headline elaborates: "It's being called a 'revolt' by intelligence pros who are paid to give their honest assessment of the ISIS war—but are instead seeing their reports turned into happy talk."[52] Is this "politicization" of intelligence? That could mean distorting evidence to bolster a particular course of action preferred by political actors, as alleged by the article (a suspicion that, however probable, has yet to be confirmed). It might, however, refer merely to what Mark Lowenthal has called "the thin line separating policy and intelligence," which is "best thought of as a semipermeable membrane."[53] But while that membrane is sometimes crossed by analysts deliberately, it can also be crossed unconsciously—and in that regard it may resemble other types of biases known as "cognitive," which are the result of the way we perceive the world.[54] The latter, though morally far less reprehensible, are almost as dangerous. Knowing oneself also requires knowing our physical and psychological limitations.

Skepticism regarding intelligence is one thing—outright hostility to intelligence quite another. The irrational "allergy" deplored by Condoleezza Rice is certainly a self-defeating attitude. So is the old pseudo-panacea of more restructuring and centralization. Writes Peter Mattis of the Jamestown Foundation:

> Americans always seem want to approach 'intelligence reform' as an organizational problem and one that can be solved changing authorities and shifting the lines-and-boxes of authority. Yet, intelligence is a very human profession, requiring flexibility and intangibles not readily foreseen by clarifying and solidifying lines of authority.[55]

It is precisely the human element of intelligence (HUMINT) that has suffered most in recent years, to the point of near extinction. Yet the human element is what matters most. As Robert David Steele, founder of the Marine Corps Intelligence Center, who served in three of the four Directorates of the CIA, wrote in an insightful 2010 study for the Strategic Studies Institute,

> HUMINT has spent the last quarter-century being displaced by the technical collection disciplines in every sense of the word but one: results. One good HUMINT asset, whether overt or covert, is worth more and costs less than any constellation of complex technologies whose product cannot be processed in a timely fashion, and that requires tens of thousands of human beings to create, maintain, and exploit.[56]

Restructuring ends up costing a great deal and often exacerbates rather than ameliorates human interaction, creating new frictions and adding layers of bureaucracy.

Right up there with restructuring is the next worst nonsolution to the problem of flawed intelligence: throwing more money at it, especially at the CIA, generally known as "the Agency." Coming on the heels of drastic cuts during the Clinton years, when the CIA's reputation had hit rock bottom and "its budgets had been slashed, its stations closed, its agents and their prized assets mothballed,"[57] this was a very bad idea: after all, assets cannot be reinstated overnight nor new agents instantly trained. One cannot turn on intelligence like a spigot. Spiking its budget was a bit like gorging after a long fast: bad indigestion, with taxpayers doing both the feeding and the subsequent holding of the figurative throw-up bag.

Former CIA agent Ishmael Jones (a pseudonym) reports that in the aftermath of 9/11, "the Agency was given virtually unlimited billions of dollars by Congress, and it had to figure out ways to spend it. It was difficult to deploy case officers oversees, so the Agency began deploying them to assignments within the United States."[58] And as more officers accumulated at home, the CIA didn't know what to do with them. It didn't want to send them overseas—that was too much trouble, they required training which took time, and few wanted to go anyway. So the problem was solved by creating more offices, funded by money that Congress had intended for non-State Department programs. Inconveniently, these were to be *overseas* programs; but, given the secrecy of the appropriations, the CIA managed to get away with it.

Referring to them as "Potemkin offices," Jones describes them as reminiscent of a newsroom, especially since their main feature consisted of a television set with a huge screen. He cites a colleague who had been put in charge of setting up one of these offices as having been given $40,000 to buy TV sets: "I told them I didn't want any, but they said I had no choice."[59]

Far more serious than mere waste of money, however, is that what we get for all those dollars is not worth much. Steele puts it bluntly:

> Today it can reasonably be argued that only the U.S. President receives decision support (mediocre at best) from a $75 billion a year U.S. Intelligence Community (USIC), while cabinet officials and congressional committees receive none at all. Defense officials receive 4 percent, at best, of what they need to know from secret sources and methods, little of that useful to the Quadrennial Defense Review (QDR) or other whole of government planning.[60]

An inability to approach intelligence holistically, embracing all the relevant information from the environment during both peacetime and war, the compartmentalization of "intelligence" and unwarranted divinization of secret, especially clandestinely obtained, data, is seriously debilitating. When selecting particular targets that seem to "cause" a conflict and focus on them too much or even exclusively, we are in danger of ignoring the greater context. General Flynn's devastating conclusion should be a wake-up call:

> Eight years into the war in Afghanistan, the U.S. intelligence community is only marginally relevant to the overall strategy. Having focused the overwhelming majority of its collection efforts and analytical brainpower on insurgent groups, the vast intelligence apparatus is unable to answer fundamental questions about the environment in which U.S. and allied forces operate and the people they seek to persuade. Ignorant of local economics and landowners, hazy about who the powerbrokers are and how they might be influenced, incurious about the correlations between various development projects and the levels of cooperation among villagers, and disengaged from people in the best position to find answers—whether aid workers or Afghan soldiers—U.S. intelligence officers and analysts can do little but shrug in response to high level decision-makers seeking the knowledge, analysis, and information they need to wage a successful counterinsurgency.[61]

It was indeed a wake-up call, as it turns out, but the wrong one. Not long after publishing this, General Flynn was forced to retire. This is no way to win the peace.

Notes

1. Leon Kass, *The Beginning of Wisdom: Reading Genesis* (Chicago, IL: University of Chicago Press, 2003), 145.
2. Ibid., 145.
3. Eric Edelman, "Response: The Obama Doctrine," *Mosaic Magazine*, February 16, 2015. http://mosaicmagazine.com/response/2015/02/the-obama-doctrine-constraining-american-power/
4. David Remnick, "Going the Distance," *The New Yorker*, January 27, 2014. http://www.newyorker.com/magazine/2014/01/27/going-the-distance-david-remnick
5. Colin Dueck, *The Obama Doctrine: America's Grand Strategy Today* (Oxford: Oxford University Press, 2015), 35.
6. Ibid. Emphasis added.
7. Gary Kasparov, "Springtime for America's Enemies," *The Daily Beast*, July 22, 2015. http://www.thedailybeast.com/articles/2015/07/22/springtime-for-america-s-enemies.html
8. http://gwpapers.virginia.edu/documents_gw/farewell/transcript.html#p25
9. See for example Nathaniel Philbrick's *Mayflower: A Story of Courage, Community, and War* (New York: Penguin, 2007).
10. "Although his appearance in Genesis was brief and tragic, the subsequent incarnations given to him in interpretive traditions made him into an ideal figure. The fact that he was the first to offer an acceptable sacrifice in a post-Edenic world made him the first righteous individual." John Byron, *Cain and Abel in Text and Tradition: Jewish and Christian Interpretations of the First Sibling Rivalry* (Themes in Biblical Narrative) (Leiden and Boston, MA: Brill Academic Publishing, 2011), 204.
11. William L. Stearman, "Lessons Learned from Vietnam," *Military Review* March–April 2010, 111.
12. Ibid., 115.
13. Robert R. Tomes, "Toward a Smarter Military: Socio-Cultural Intelligence and National Security," *Parameters* 45, no. 2 (Summer 2015): 64. Emphasis added.
14. *The Commission on the Intelligence Capabilities of the United States Regarding Weapons of Mass Destruction, Report to the President of the United States*. Unclassified (Washington, DC: US Government Printing Office, 2005), 173–4.
15. It does seem that President Bush raised no objection when Bremer disbanded the Iraqi army despite contravening decisions, which the National Security Council had approved unanimously, with Bush present. As Fred Kaplan writes in *The Insurgents: David Petraeus and the Plot to Change the American Way of War* (New York: Simon & Schuster, 2013): "The decision-making machinery was broken when it came to national security matters." 196.
16. http://www.nytimes.com/2007/09/06/opinion/06bremer.html?_r=0
17. Tomes, "Toward a Smarter Military," 62.
18. Alfred McCoy alleges that the United States was complicit in the tragedy that befell Afghanistan, since "in the history of the three Afghan wars in which Washington has been involved over the past 30 years—the CIA covert warfare of the 1980s, the civil war of the 1990s (fueled at its start by $900 million in CIA funding), and since 2001, the US invasion, occupation,

and counterinsurgency campaigns." Alfred W. McCoy, "Can Anyone Pacify the World's Number One Narco-State? The Opium Wars in Afghanistan" *TomDispatch*, March 30, 2010, http://www.tomdispatch.com/blog/175225/ alfred_mccoy_afghanistan_as_a_drug_war

19. After taking power in 1996, the Taliban regime encouraged a nationwide expansion of opium cultivation, doubling production to four thousand six hundred tons, then equivalent to 75 percent of the world's heroin supply. Signaling its support for drug production, the Taliban regime began collecting a 20 percent tax from the yearly opium harvest, earning an estimated $100 million in revenues." McCoy, "Can Anyone Pacify the World's Number One Narco-State?"

20. Ibid.

21. *The Second Gore-Bush Presidential Debate*, October 11, 2000. http://www. debates.org/?page=october-11-2000-debate-transcript

22. "With the benefit of hindsight, we know that the spiritual leader of international Islamists and head of the Afghan Service Bureau Front, Abdullah Azzam, conceptualized *al-Qaeda* in 1987 and wrote its founding document in 1988. Osama bin Laden was Azzam's deputy. For purposes of understanding US counterterrorism policy, it is essential to remember that Washington was not aware of the existence of *al-Qaeda* until about five years later. In 1992, there was an attack on a hotel in Yemen which *al-Qaeda* thought was being used by US soldiers en route to Somalia. There were no US personnel in the hotel. At the time, Washington had no idea the perpetrator was *al-Qaeda* and only determined this later." David H. Shinn, "Al-Qaeda in East Africa and the Horn," *The Journal of Conflict Studies*, Vol 27, no. 1 (2007). https://journals.lib.unb.ca/index.php/JCS/ article/view/5655/6658

23. "Transcript of Osama Bin Ladin interview by Peter Arnett." http://www. anusha.com/osamaint.htm

24. http://www.cnn.com/2011/WORLD/asiapcf/05/02/osama.timeline/

25. George H. W. Bush, "Address on Somalia," December 4, 1992. http://miller-center.org/president/bush/speeches/speech-3984

26. Bin Ladin interview with Arnett, http://www.anusha.com/osamaint.htm.

27. Jack Fairweather, *The Good War: Why We Couldn't Win the War or the Peace in Afghanistan* (New York: Basic Books, 2014), 49.

28. https://publicintelligence.net/cna-war-in-southern-afghanistan/

29. Anand Gopal, *No Good Men among the Living: America, the Taliban, and the War Through Afghan Eyes* (New York: Henry Holt and Co., 2015).

30. "Manichean: an adherent of the dualistic religious system of Manes, a combination of Gnostic Christianity, Buddhism, Zoroastrianism, and various other elements, with a basic doctrine of a conflict between light and dark, matter being regarded as dark and evil." http://dictionary.reference.com/ browse/manichean

31. Marcus Lutrell with Patrick Robinson, *Lone Survivor: The Eyewitness Account of Operation Redwing and the Lost Heroes of SEAL Team 10* (New York: Back Bay Books, 2007), 168–9.

32. Ibid., 203.

33. Ibid., 206.

34. Kaplan, *The Insurgents*, 134.

35. Ibid., 216.

36. Ibid., 134–5.

37. Glenn J. Voelz, *The Rise of iWar: Identity, Information, and the Individualization of Modern Warfare*, (Washington, DC: Strategic Studies Institute and U.S. Army War College Press, Oct. 2015), 17.

38. Ibid., 125, cites Rosa Brooks, There's No Such Thing as Peacetime, *Foreign Policy* March 13, 2015. http://foreignpolicy.com/2015/03/13/theres-no-such-thing-as-peacetime-forever-war-terror-civil-liberties/

39. Ibid., 126.

40. Dr. Mark M. Lowenthal, "Intelligence Education: Quo Vadimus?," 10 (Emphasis added.)

41. Notably by James W. Ceaser in his superb *Reconstructing America: The Symbol of America in Modern Thought* (New Haven, CT and London: Yale University Press, 1997).

42. http://www.cnn.com/2004/ALLPOLITICS/04/08/rice.transcript/

43. Mark McNeilly, *Sun Tzu and the Art of Modern Warfare* (Oxford: Oxford University Press, 2001), 86.

44. Bill Gertz, "House Armed Services Chief: Intel Losses, Including Clinton Emails, Caused Serious Damage" *Washington Free Beacon* September 10, 2015. http://freebeacon.com/national-security/house-armed-services-chief-intel-losses-including-clinton-emails-caused-serious-damage/

45. See Sandra Grimes and Jeanne Vertefeuille, *Circle of Treason: A CIA Account of Traitor Aldrich Ames and the Men He Betrayed* (Annapolis, MD: Naval Institute Press, 2014).

46. See David Wise, *Spy: The Inside Story of How the FBI's Robert Hanssen Betrayed America* (New York: Random House, 2003).

47. Henry A. Crumpton, *The Art of Intelligence: Lessons from a Life in the CIA's Clandestine Service* (New York and London: Penguin, 2012), 14.

48. Ibid.

49. Bill Gertz, *The Failure Factory* (New York: Random House, 2008), 81–92.

50. Ibid., 92–4.

51. Sean D. Naylor, "Out of Uniform and Into the Political Fray," *FP* June 19, 2015. http://foreignpolicy.com/2015/06/19/out-of-uniform-and-into-the-political-fray/

52. "Exclusive: 50 Spies Say ISIS Intelligence Was Cooked," *The Daily Beast*, September 9, 2015. http://www.thedailybeast.com/articles/2015/09/09/exclusive-50-spies-say-isis-intelligence-was-cooked.html These are not merely to anonymous grumblings but formal complaints sent to the Pentagon's inspector general, convincing him that "there are deep-rooted, systemic problems in how the U.S. military command" handles intelligence related to ISIS, worthy of a deeper investigation, which has now commenced. The article goes on to cite one (obviously anonymous) defense official who charges that "the cancer was within the senior level of the intelligence command." Some analysts have accused the director himself, along with his deputy, of having changed their reports "in order to be more in line with the Obama administration's public contention that the fight against ISIS and al Qaeda is making progress."

53. Mark Lowenthal, *Intelligence: From Secrets to Policy*, 5th ed. (Washington DC: CQ Press, College, 2011).

54. Peter Tomes outlines the distinction in his excellent "On the Politicization of Intelligence," *War on the Rocks*, September 29, 2015. http://warontherocks.com/2015/09/on-the-politicization-of-intelligence/?utm_source=WOTR+Newsletter&utm_campaign=4b2eddf0d4-WOTR_Newsletter_8_17_158_15_2015&utm_medium=email&utm_term=0_8375be81e9-4b2eddf0d4-60136989

55. Peter Mattis, "4 U.S. Intelligence Assumptions That Need to Go," *The National Interest*, February 2, 2015. http://nationalinterest.org/feature/4-us-intelligence-assumptions-need-go-12165?page=show

56. Robert David Steele, "Human Intelligence (HUMINT): All Humans, All Minds, All the Time" (Strategic Studies Institute, May 2010), 53.

57. Jack Fairweather, *The Good War: Why We Couldn't Win the War or the Peace in Afghanistan* (New York: Basic Books, 2014), 7.

58. Ishmael Jones, *The Human Factor: Inside the CIA's Dysfunctional Intelligence Culture* (New York: Encounter Books, 2010), 252.

59. Ibid., 271.

60. Steele, "Human Intelligence (HUMINT)," 1.

61. Flynn, "Fixing Intel," 7.

11

Soft Power for Softies

The fundamental concept in social science is power in the sense in which energy is the fundamental concept in physics. Like energy, power has many forms, such as wealth, armaments, and influence on opinion. No one of these can be regarded as subordinate to any other.
—Bertrand Russell, *Power: A New Social Analysis*, 1938

The new circumstances in which we are placed call for new words, new phrases, and for the transfer of old words to new objects.
—Thomas Jefferson to John Waldo, Aug. 6, 1813

Mount Olympus did not include among its residents a God of Power. It didn't have to; all the gods were considered mighty. That said, none, not even Zeus, won every time. Weakness and strength being notoriously relative, the immortals took turns prevailing over one another through a wide variety of schemes, subterfuges, and the odd plain luck. Hedging their bets, then, lowly humans generally offered sacrifices and libations to several deities at once. Some gods were known to have specific preferences, such as Athena toward her namesake city, and could be counted on to go the extra mile for their constituents and favorites, sexual or otherwise. With the advent of monotheism, divine assistance would be sought from only one Supreme Power, so ritual and libations were duly simplified. Noticed too was the Power's seemingly disproportionate helpfulness to those who helped themselves.

Power may be measurable, but is distinctly context-dependent. We say that an adult is weak if he cannot lift a twenty-pound weight, and strong if he can lift as many as 100 pounds, but this doesn't mean that "being able to lift 20 pounds" defines being weak, any more than lifting 100 pounds is the essence of strength. That said, if one compares two adults of roughly similar age, one able to lift 5 pounds and the other 100, it is legitimate to consider the former (comparatively) weak, and the other clearly stronger (all of which could change in the event of an accident, or using a tool, etc.)

This is common sense, if too often forgotten, as evidenced by the fact that most insurgencies and guerilla-style wars succeed against nations and even empires with vastly superior experience, skills, and various resources. Even before Afghanistan and Iraq, the United States recognized that its armed forces would be called upon to exert leverage in nontraditional forms of conflict,[1] yet failed to adjust and anticipate the new challenges. The blunders committed in the course of those operations exposed America's vulnerability and lack of preparedness. The result has been a slow, uneven, and highly confused effort at reconceptualizing warfare.

The theoretical exercise actually started long before these recent engagements. It was first prompted by the onset of the "post industrial" age—a term coined by sociologist Daniel Bell in 1973.[2] Yet it was primarily after the onset of the information-technology (IT) revolution that the need for a radical reconsideration of the notion of power became obvious. After the initial euphoria over the new connectedness through the worldwide web, which was expected to bring mankind closer together, the danger from cyberattacks became obvious. Even if they did not cause physical destruction, these attacks offered a terrifying glimpse into the horrifying devastation they could inflict upon the political and economic structures of entire nations, jeopardizing the livelihoods and lives of untold numbers of people.

The advent of cyber made it harder to ignore the increasingly obvious fact that *national power* could not continue to be defined in terms of crassly simplistic objectively measurable variables. These had always been primarily quantitative: size of population; gross national product (GNP), which mainly reflects the quantity of goods produced, along with the availability of services, in a nation-state; the size of a nation's military; geographic location and extent; demographics; and other such tangible items. Left aside, meanwhile, were a whole host of other, less obvious yet key indicators of national power such as creativity, trust, and personal freedoms. Even technological innovation and applications have not been adequately factored in, which explains in part the largely cavalier attitude toward the transfer of militarily-sensitive technology to China and, before that, to the USSR.[3]

The traditional approach to national power had been flawed from the get-go. For starters, it would never have predicted America's success in gaining its independence as a sovereign nation in the late eighteenth century. Nor did it anticipate, explain, or even recognize the enormous impact of Soviet disinformation during the Cold War. The principle that "if it can't be measured, it don't exist" was always flawed; but the internet explosion has made it all but impossible to continue ignoring such admittedly ethereal and elusive, yet indispensable tools as access to information and ability to communicate electronically. Information has always constituted a critical, if not indeed *the* critical factor determining the outcome of a confrontation, whether either or both adversaries have been state or non-state actors. Today, its preeminence is undisputed.

At the dawn of what would become the field of International Relations as a subset of political science, in the apocalyptic year 1939, British political thinker Edward Hallett Carr advanced a concept of political power that became especially influential across the Atlantic. Power, he said, consists of three elements: military, economic, or power over opinion; but all are based on personal (meaning, class) interests, consistent with his Marxist perspective.[4] As military and economic power "become concentrated in fewer and fewer hands," (think materialist dialectics) the "inevitable" (think determinism) result was "the centralized control of opinion," aka "the mass-production of opinion," or in plain English, "propaganda."[5] But can propaganda produced by a class on its way to extinction, as Marxist ideology dictates, "influence" in any meaningful sense? In a determinist context, "influence" is incoherent, which makes that definitional path a nonstarter.

It would be left to Carr's most illustrious student, though hardly a disciple, Hans Morgenthau, to articulate a far more useful approach. In his classic *Politics Among the Nations: The Struggle for Power and Peace*, first published in 1948, while conceding that traditional measures of force will always matter, he zeroes in on the growing importance of the "information edge." He points out, however, that unfortunately, "information power is . . . hard to categorize because it cuts across all other military, economic, social, and political power resources, in some cases diminishing their strength, in others multiplying it."[6] That is exactly what makes it exceedingly unwise—not to mention all but impossible—to overlook.

Carr's taxonomy, however flawed, at least put "the power over opinion" on the theoretical map.[7] That said, it was Morgenthau who helped shape America's post-World War II foreign affairs policies. His belief in the importance of wielding some influence over world opinion was shared by President Dwight Eisenhower, who established the US Information Agency (USIA) in 1953. USIA's mission was "to understand, inform and influence foreign publics in promotion of the national interest, and to broaden the dialogue between Americans and U.S. institutions, and their counterparts abroad."[8] That settled it: if information had its very own agency, it had to be something real. As goes the official government soliloquy, to be is to be a line-item in an appropriation bill.

USIA's principal function, insofar as it could be defined, was "public diplomacy." The term had been coined in 1856, when it was merely a synonym for civility, soon to include engaging the public in matters of international action,[9] and was first used in its modern sense in 1965 by diplomat Edmund Gullion to denote the influence of public attitudes on the formation and execution of foreign policies.[10] The State Department (DOS) often insists that it alone and no other agency—especially not the Defense Department (DOD)—has this mission. Indeed, the US Code of Law assigns the conduct of public diplomacy (PD) to DOS under Title 22, whereas military budgets and conduct are regulated under Title 10. Defense and State, wouldn't you know, are under separate budgetary authorities. Hence the funding for public diplomacy-related missions is determined separately, even if the missions overlap in practical application.[11] No one said that to be, in governmental terms, means to have to make sense.

USIA's life span turned out to be brief—especially for a bureaucracy. Abolished in 1999, its function was essentially (more or less) absorbed into the State Department. There were no obituaries—at least, not at the time. The end of the cold war was taken to have signaled the triumph of Western ideas and the end of "history" as ideological warfare, so why continue paying for a separate agency to engage in a dialogue that no longer needed to be broadened?[12] But in the absence of an agency tasked with disseminating information abroad, the notion became even harder to define, and certainly to locate.[13] Opinions varied as to whether everybody or nobody was doing it, though it was hard to tell the difference given the relative nonimpact.

"Information operations" (IO) became a catch-all term that combined, confusingly, three different components, best explained by National Defense University's Daniel Kuehl. There is first, the *physical dimension*, which consists of "the stuff that we see and use every day," like phones and computers; then second, the *content* carried by those technologies; and finally, there is the *cognitive dimension*, which is "where the content that is delivered by the connectivity impacts human beings and how we think, decide, etc."[14] Noting that "far too often anything related to Information Operations is seen through the single-focus lens of technology," Kuehl warns that "in fact the issue is much more complex," underscoring the critical importance of the *cognitive* effect of IO. But that is also the most slippery, and hardest to measure.

As he puts in *The Case for a National Information Strategy*, which Kuehl co-authored with Retired US Army Col. Dennis Murphy,

> cognitive impact . . . is where the human mind applies meaning to the information it has received, where beauty is appreciated, persuasion is accomplished, loss is mourned, and decisions are made. However, this dimension of the information environment is the most difficult to influence because it is rarely quantitatively calculable, and therefore it is difficult to manipulate or even predict. Audiences will respond to information content in ways shaped by cultures, backgrounds, experiences, emotions, and myriad other factors.[15]

But if you can't measure it, does it exist?

Such radically different dimensions of a capability, ranging from the highly technical to the politically sensitive and culturally esoteric, obviously require very different skill sets and approaches. This is no easy task, especially given the size of the federal bureaucracy leviathan. But if Kuehl is right, and he is, that "information, as an element of power and a field for military operations and warfare, is critical to our military capability and future national security strategy,"[16] it does not appear to have been taken as seriously as it deserves to be.

Not that the DOD has not tried. It did its best to come to grips with the complexity of national power by focusing on the Diplomatic, Informational, Military, and Economic elements, which led to the catchy acronym DIME. It was soon followed by the equally catchy MIDLIFE— Military, Informational, Diplomatic, Law enforcement, Intelligence, Financial, and Economic. Still others, similar if mostly longer, formulas were proposed and used in various contexts, but unfortunately, catchy or not, none is especially clear. Though strategist D. Robert Worley observes that "MIDLIFE conveys more of a mechanistic or tool mindset," so do the others. This is hardly surprising, since the mechanistic and quantitative part of IO is simpler and obviously more palatable to the military mindset. But as a result, the military component continues to far outweigh the others in importance, funding, use, and force development. "No such emphasis," laments Worley, "is apparent for the other instruments of power."[17]

Absent the overbearing "M," the remaining acronyms provide unintended yet ominous puns as both DIE and the vaguely Freudian ID-LIFE, conceptually orphaned without hard power, connote the end of human, or at least civilized existence. And while "information" is duly mentioned, its meaning still eludes us—especially if we try to find a definition that transcends any particular agency. There isn't one.

That said, DOD should certainly be commended for trying to achieve at least some measure of clarity regarding that component of national power which applies to its own domain of IO, and even more for admitting how difficult it is. For example, Kevin P. Chilton, then-commander of STRATCOM,[18] admitted in 2009: "You ask ten different people what IO is, and you'll get ten completely different answers. We have a lot of doctrinal work to do here."[19] And to be fair, much has been done. In the Winter 2014 issue of *IOSphere*, an article on "Redefining Information Operations (IO): Applying Rand Corporation's Analysis of Army IO to Joint IO" explains the rationale for the Army's updated definitions.

Interestingly, the authors note that "IO is often described as 'soft-power' . . . [which is deemed] accurate when describing inform and influence activities . . . [but] decidedly false when applied to technical operations such as CO (cyberspace operations) and EW (electronic warfare)."[20] This explains why two definitions, at least in this case, are better than one. The first captures IO:

> Inform and influence activities are the integration of designated information-related capabilities in order to synchronize themes, messages, and actions with operations to inform United States and global audiences, influence foreign audiences, and affect adversary and enemy decisionmaking [sic].[21]

The second deals with all cyber electromagnetic activities, including CO as well as EW and SMO, and is altogether too complicated, and hence confusing.[22]

Unfortunately, the attempt to differentiate between activities designed to inform and influence, on the one hand, and cyber electromagnetic activities, on the other, will only get us so far. For in the first place, it perpetuates what the authors of the article themselves admit is a highly compartmentalized community, where IO and EW practitioners have limited understanding of the others' work: "While the Army EW career field has grown rapidly, Service-level IO does not integrate EW."[23] The two communities "have very little technical overlap with each other and their knowledge of other information capabilities is limited." And that's just in the "I" component of DIME; never mind the other elements of national power. Yet compartmentalization is precisely what we don't want when seeking to synchronize all those elements.

Another serious obstacle to capturing the true nature of national power, besides the perennial quandary over "information," lies in the difficulty of estimating what might be called *vulnerability*, which also cannot be measured in any simple way. Yet especially in the area of information, the vulnerabilities are in almost direct proportion to strengths. This is acknowledged upfront in the Executive Summary of the revised JP 3-13 *Information Operations*: "The ability to share information in near real time, anonymously and/or securely, is a capability that is both an asset and a potential vulnerability to us, our allies, and our adversaries."[24] Does all this mean that we cannot really measure national power at all? Not exactly. But it does mean that it's harder than one might have hoped.

The main obstacle to understanding the power of information is that it is really not a thing that can be delivered. Even diplomacy, though considerably more ethereal than money, wheat, or tanks, produces treaties and other agreements, which are tangible enough, if not necessarily respected. It is quite another matter when it comes to the "information" component of national strategy. As Leigh Armistead and his collaborators wrote in *Information Operations: Warfare and the Reality of Soft Power*, for America to prevail after 9/11, it will have to use everything it has; and "the force that binds these elements of national power together is information."[25] Hans Morgenthau lives!

This is not an easy picture to grasp: information is indeed a component of national power, but it also transcends all the others. Not just more important than the others, it is the glue the absence of which would render them all irrelevant. That is what makes it a paradoxically double-edged sword, blessing or curse depending on its use, misuse, or inability to use at all. But that message is difficult to convey, especially in a culture that feels more at home with products than with ideas, that puts a higher premium on gadgets than on concepts. As soon as we leave the hard-nosed world of hardware, we are flummoxed. We then tend to lump the whole business together, and the scramble leaves us, well, scrambling. So, now, let's see: what's not-hard power? Hmm. . . . what's left? Maybe "soft" power?

Conceived in 1990, the expression "soft power" became the title of a book released, not coincidentally, at the very moment that the Iron Curtain collapsed of its own weight, without a Western shot being fired.

The quite literal crumbling of the Berlin Wall seemed to validate the image of hardness defeating itself. All the West had to do was emanate democracy and prosperity for the regimented proletariat to overthrow its Communist dictators. Hardly a handful of insiders even knew of the herculean efforts, behind the scenes, of a Brian Crozier coordinating British and American covert actions that went on for half a century;[26] and few fully recognized the providential synchronicity of the three great leaders of the era—Pope John Paul II, Prime Minister Margaret Thatcher, and President Ronald Reagan.[27] Never mind all that. The West had been waiting for a long time to bask in victory, and this was its moment.

The book's author, Harvard professor Joseph A. Nye, was ready with the conceptual marching band. Cheerleading for his neologism, he defines "soft power" in opposition to the nasty, hard stuff:

> A country may obtain the outcomes it wants in world politics because other countries—admiring its values, emulating its example, aspiring to its level of prosperity and openness—want to follow it. In this sense, it is also important to set the agenda and attract others in world politics, and not only to force them to change by threatening military force or economic sanctions. This soft power—getting others to want the outcomes that you want—co-opts people rather than coerces them.[28]

So then, it couldn't be clearer: soft power is "not-hard-power." The point is for a nation to eschew violence, to seek becoming a beacon onto others, "a shining city on a hill," by adopting values that others will admire and want to emulate. If this sounds like American exceptionalism, actually it is not. In Nye's version, it is neither American nor particularly exceptional, for he thinks *any* nation can attract another—and there is nothing special about ours. He certainly disagrees with the version of American exceptionalism, generally adopted by conservative internationalists (some of whom, especially if they are Jewish, have come to be labeled, usually derisively, as "neoconservatives"), that considers success at home to carry with it a certain responsibility to help others reach it as well, specifically, though not necessarily, through military intervention against their oppressors.

In Nye's formulation, what soft power absolutely excludes is *threatening* someone—whether with military force, or economic sanctions, or any other kind of hardball tactics. Soft power is getting others to want what you want, just by being admirable. It is the power that a nation exudes by sheer example, by nothing more than attraction, by its commendable reputation for "prosperity and openness," as Nye puts it. The idea that prosperity may be considered a symptom of decadent materialism, or that openness is seen in some cultures as extending *carte blanche* to heresy and to behaving in deliberately offensive ways, meant to subvert opposing religious teachings, never appears to have crossed Nye's mind. This oversight could be forgiven in 1990, but not today. Still less explicable, or at any rate justifiable, is his seeming lack of appreciation for the omnipresent evidence suggesting that in all ages, and across virtually all societies, success is far more likely to generate envy than love. Cain could have reminded him of that.

Equally puzzling is his surprise that some states, especially the most autocratic, turn out to be more effective at manipulating public perception, cleverer at wielding soft power, and more agile in adapting to changing circumstances than are democracies. Rather embarrassingly, Nye complains today, a quarter century later: "[W]ho would have expected that someday the term [soft power] would be used by the likes of Hu Jintao or Vladimir Putin?"[29] With all due respect, professor, who would have expected anything *else*?

Nye often substitutes for "soft power" the only slightly longer, not to mention redundant, expression "the soft power of attraction," which serves to underscore its essential passivity: attraction is something that one emanates whether intentionally to or not, which actually contributes to its charm. Soft power is exerted by its possessor simply being attractive—like an irresistibly gorgeous young thing (though plastic surgery and an expensive haircut are permissible, definitionally speaking). A maximally attractive country is the earthly equivalent of Eden. Who would want to harm such a place? Who wouldn't want to live there, or replicate everything about it in his own land? Nye advises all heads of state to increase their nation's soft power because by adding it "to your toolkit, you can economize on carrots and sticks." The implication is that soft power is not only cheaper but equally or at least no less effective than "carrots and sticks." Did you make a note of that, Presidents Bashir, Mugabe, and Kim Jong-un?

Except, come to think of it, what exactly are "carrots"? Obviously, "sticks" refers to power of varying hardness, and includes economic sanctions, because they too are coercive rather than attractive. But since "carrots" connotes something positive and desired (though maybe not to uncompromising carnivores), and hence might be taken to imply a lack of coercion, why are they excluded from the category of "soft power" tools? Maybe it is because "carrots" are designed to influence deliberately, through incentives; and that very intentional quality, the conscious targeting, is seen as running counter to the angelic *passivity* that Nye finds so appealing about pristine soft power. As he defines it, the soft-hard dichotomy is mutually exclusive, morally speaking: instruments of power are either coercive—lethal or not—or they are passive, and the latter alone are truly legitimate. As a result, far from exploring the various "carrots" that might be used in a potentially dangerous situation, he advises against them, alongside instruments of hard power, in favor of his preferred "soft power of attraction." Carrots are hereby left to fall into a semantic, and hence strategic, black hole. The ensuing compost is predictably a conceptual quagmire.

Nye's semantics reflects—one gathers, not unconsciously—a world-view that recoils from American assertive engagement in world affairs to protect the national interest. On first blush, his passionate advocacy of "soft power" is highly commendable, for coercive methods indeed do tend to wreak havoc, especially when wielded clumsily. As a rule, violence is greatly to be deplored, and all efforts should be expended on seeking its avoidance, whenever possible. For most Americans, this is a no-brainer. From its founding, America has defined its main mission as promoting individual rights (even if it hasn't always lived up to its highest ideals) rather than intervening in other nations' affairs. But that attractive goal is most effectively attained when using *all* the tools in the kit of statecraft, and tools that are neither military or lethal, nor unconsciously attractive, are yet highly significant. By leaving them essentially uncategorized, and implicitly underestimated, Nye expressly—and unfairly—neglects them.

To recapitulate, the fatal flaw of the "attractive soft power" concept consists in its unduly limited range, since it leaves out a huge range of nonlethal weapons that certainly cannot be considered "hard." But another problem is the concept's hopeless circularity: soft power attracts because it is attractive. This is like saying that paper is flammable because it lights up when exposed to a match. (Or, as the medieval philosopher would put it, it is due to the Attribute of Flammability. QED.)

Nye tries to explain what he means by soft power by describing it as a kind of aura, more or less like a magnetic field, produced by a combination of the nation's three resources: "its culture (in places where it is attractive to others), its political values (when it lives up to them at home and abroad), and its foreign policies (when they are seen as legitimate and having moral authority)." Except that if foreign policies constitute soft power only when they are *seen* as legitimate, it follows inexorably that soft power is attractive only when it is *seen* as attractive. But nations cannot, strictly speaking, control others' perception (by Nye's own admission, that would be considered coercive—that just *is* what "control" means). Moreover, what might be very attractive to one group of people might not be seen that way by another.

Suppose our adversaries seek values that are foreign, perhaps even anathema, to us, as adversaries are wont to do. Imagine too that their goals have nothing to do with those that Nye considers self-evidently attractive, but everything to do with their opposite? For example, what if frugality and antimaterialism, driven by unquestioning piety, are admired, as are female "circumcision" and keeping women illiterate? And instead of openness, which is seen as heretical, what if these people's highest ambition is achieving total consensus of opinion and zero democracy? Moreover, what if those adversaries will stop at nothing, including their own suicide, to oppose our values and destroy everyone who disagrees with theirs? In such circumstances, America's "soft power" boomerangs: we cut our own throats, with no benefit of virgins to boot.

Colin Gray has articulated better than anyone why Nye's concept of soft power has limited, if any, use as a conceptual tool in national security strategy:

> Provided the different natures of hard and soft power are understood— the critical distinguishing factor being coercion versus attraction—it is appropriate to regard the two kinds of power as mutual enablers. However, theirs is an unequal relationship. The greater attractiveness of soft power is more than offset in political utility by *its inherent unsuitability for policy direction and control.*[30]

Having been defined as immune to control, soft power in Nye's sense is virtually ruled out as a potential instrument of national policy, given that, as Gray points out, "it utterly depends upon the un-coerced choices of foreigners." That utter dependence implies immunity from national control; or to put it differently, the degree of soft power in our arsenal is not up to us. This appears to leave only one kind of tool, by sheer process of elimination. For given Nye's Manichean dichotomy, Gray's conclusion is hard to contest: "Soft power cannot sensibly be regarded as a substantial alternative to hard military power."[31]

Put perhaps a tad less elegantly, the concept is worse than useless. For here's the rub: "Familiarity with the concept alone encourages the fallacy that hard and soft power have roughly equivalent weight and utility. An illusion of broad policy choice is thus fostered, when in fact effective choices are severely constrained."[32] The problem, in other words, is twofold: (a) the relative values of soft and hard power do not, even though they seem to, mirror the linguistic parallelism; and (b) circumstances might favor one over the other—an asymmetry masked by the simplistic dichotomy. But even that is only half the story. As already noted, many highly effective choices cannot be described as either "hard" or "soft" (in the sense dictated by Nye), and thus remain unexplored, because unacknowledged in the first place.

The problem is not merely semantic; it goes to the heart of modern American culture, which has traditionally placed far too much importance on its ability to attract, and woefully failed to understand other cultures. Americans thereby engage in what logicians call "mirror imaging," defined as the assumption that others are, simply put, "just like us." Writes Gray:

> Ironically, the empirical truth behind the attractive concept [of soft power] is just sufficient to mislead policymakers and grand strategists. Not only do Americans want to believe that the soft power of their civilization and culture is truly potent, we are all but programmed by our enculturation to assume that the American story and its values do and should have what amounts to missionary merit that ought to be universal. American culture is so powerful a programmer that it can be difficult for Americans to empathize with, or even understand, the somewhat different values and their implications held deeply abroad.

Like most widely held beliefs, unfortunately, this one contains enough truth to be dangerous. Continues Gray:

> American values, broadly speaking 'the American way,' to hazard a large project in reductionism, are indeed attractive beyond America's frontiers and have some utility for U.S. policy. But there are serious limitations to the worth of the concept of soft power, especially as it might be thought of as an instrument of policy. To date, the idea of soft power has not been subjected to a sufficiently critical forensic examination.[33]

Given these two choices, Gray chooses hard power as the only realistic instrument of warfare, as he well should under the circumstances. He bluntly states that sometimes there is no choice but to wage war. And warfare means, in his view, "military force, which means violence that causes damage, injury, and death."[34] He sees no way of avoiding the nastiness of it all. When faced with a very serious threat, war is the only answer.

Gray is correct that war cannot be prevented even by an angelic, sinless America (which it manifestly is not); mankind has learned repeatedly, and at great cost, that there is no substitute for military strength against irreconcilable, or even seemingly irreconcilable, foes. Nye's simplistic dialectic seems to have perpetuated an old, very common, error called an informal fallacy known as "the false dichotomy." The choice should not rest between coercion and a charm offensive. Waging peace involves far subtler forms of engagement.

If we adopt Nye's definition of soft power, mostly unchallenged since its introduction, left unlabeled—and thus ignored—are a plethora of preventive measures and varying types of influence, strategically deployed, which can shape the international environment so as to render it as safe as possible for nations under threat from hostile forces, both state and non-state, to pursue their interests without unnecessary destruction. These are still often referred to as forms of soft power for lack of another term; as a result, they are infected by the un-strategic connotations of Nye's definition.

Not entirely oblivious to his term's limitations, in 2003 Nye came up with another, which seeks to combine "hard" and "soft" elements of power: *smart power*, defined as the ability to combine hard and soft power depending on the situation.[35] Unfortunately, not everyone seems to have gotten the memo; Clinton-era diplomat Suzanne Nossel, writing at around the same time, argues that "smart power means knowing that the United States' own hand is not always its best tool"[36] but should rather enlist the help of other nations. These definitions are quite distinct. Besides, the question inevitably arises: is there such a thing as stupid power? Any tool, of course, can be used well or badly, together with other tools or alone. That doesn't make it inherently "stupid;" what is stupid is its use, or more precisely, its user.

A 2007 report by the Center for Strategic and International Studies' (CSIS) Commission on Smart Power, chaired by Joseph Nye and CSIS Trustee Richard L. Armitage, tried again to define smart power, this time as "an approach that underscores the necessity of a strong military, but also invests heavily in alliances, partnerships, and institutions of all levels to expand American influence and establish legitimacy of American action."[37] In other words, what makes power "smart" is an approach rather than a tool. It refers to knowing *when* to use hard power—which is mainly military strength—and when to involve "institutions at all levels" to expand American influence. So then "soft power" includes "institutions at all levels"? Does that leave *anything* out? If having "smart power" is knowing when to use what tool, we are back to the agent being smart or dumb. Not much of a semantic improvement here.

Former State Department official Christian Whiton, in his recent book *Smart Power: Between Diplomacy and War*, argues that "smart power should be thought of as progressing toward the foreign *political* outcome vital for American security and prosperity,"[38] thus deftly evading defining the term. Instead, he describes what it does: make life difficult for America's enemies, helping our friends (or at least, at times, our enemies' enemies), espionage-related practices, and similar activities. In brief, he trusts that most people "understand smart power intuitively . . . It is their government and their foreign policy establishment in Washington that have forgotten."[39] Appealing to common sense and forgetting about technical language altogether may indeed be the best way to approach the Art of Peace. But we have to try to explain at least what a word does *not* mean, and use words as unambiguously as possible. For without a clear and succinct vocabulary, we simply cannot communicate—not even to ourselves. And we certainly cannot formulate policy.

Council on Foreign Relations (CFR) fellows Max Boot and Michael Doran (who is now at the Hudson Institute) agree. In a CFR Policy Innovation Memorandum released in June 2013,[40] they blame the absence of words to describe the multifaceted Art of Peace on the fact that no government agency views the use of nonmilitary instruments as "a core mission." Not dignifying "soft power" even with a mention, they opt for "political warfare," as defined in a State Department memorandum written on May 4, 1948, by the policy-planning staff under the direction of George Kennan. Touted as the logical application of "Clausewitz's doctrine in time of peace," Kennan's memo defined political warfare in its broadest sense as "the employment of all the means at a nation's command, short of war, to achieve its national objectives."[41] Boot and Doran concede that "'political warfare' may be an alien-sounding concept in 2013, but that is precisely the problem."[42]

Precisely, yes. And *that* problem they identify as political correctness in national security lingo, which in turn reflects an undercurrent of self-doubt about America's role in the world. Both "political" and "warfare" are rhetorically radioactive terms, not unlike "terrorism," "war on terror," "Islamism," "psychological operations," and a score of other words that have been floated in an attempt to define our adversaries and means of influencing or engaging with them without actually daring to say so. Although on March 10, 2015, the Special Operation Command issued a Special Forces Support for Political Warfare White Paper, which essentially adopts the CFR report's use of the term to encompass a whole-of-government approach, the chances that it will resonate with the nonmilitary agencies are not high.

It is not merely a question of allaying the concerns of most Americans, who prefer more soothing language than "political warfare," with its nefarious connotations of covert action and scary-nasty propaganda. It's that we seem to have a problem with the very idea of influencing. That, at bottom, is a major reason why "propaganda" has been rendered useless, as the negative connotations overwhelmed its originally positive meaning, and why "psychological operations" (PSYOP) has been replaced by the Army with a politically more palatable equivalent, "military information support operations" (MISO). But why this squeamishness? Since all power, ultimately, is largely a matter of perception, it is important to take seriously the fact that perceptions can be damaging, and there is nothing wrong with seeking to alleviate that damage—especially by perfectly legitimate means. There is nothing wrong with influencing as such.

Thus in his classic 1997 book *Arts of Power: Statecraft and Diplomacy*, Ambassador Chas. W. Freeman, Jr., notes that "the power of states is measured by their ability to alter and channel the behavior of other states [and] rests on their will to apply their national strength and potential in contests with others," which in turn depends on a state's own estimate of its power as well as the degree to which its population is willing to sustain it. In the end, "power itself lies, in the first instance, however, in the mind of opponents."[43] This statement underscores the enormous importance of strategic communication. For it is the balance of *perceived power* between states that decides the outcome of struggles short of war.[44] Even military might will prove insufficient if enemies believe that (a) it will not be used, (b) it will not be "relevant" to the battle-space (as is the case in many asymmetric conflicts), or (c) determination to sustain the effort is lacking. Thus national power is not only a matter of all hands clapping, and doing so effectively, but being perceived as such.

After the spectacular success of the Revolutionary era, when the Founders' influencing talents excelled beyond imagining, the road has been for the most part rocky. Public diplomacy is not our strong suit.[45]

Public affairs officials argue that they should do all the "PR" for the US government—there is no need for any additional "spin doctors." It is no accident that after the dissolution of USIA, the State Department created a new post, the Under Secretary for Public Diplomacy and Public Affairs, which oversees these functions together, with notable lack of success. Hardly a day goes by when the sorry state of US foreign communication is not bemoaned on the website of the Public Diplomacy Council or similar venues, and with good reason.

Without adequate communication even with its own people, the leadership in Washington is caught in a dilemma: should it take chances by taking actions that seem to go against the wishes of a largely ignorant public, or should it seek to inform the people, only to be excoriated for trying to influence them? If a specific initiative is unpopular, a true leader will try to explain why it is needed and even buck the mindset of an electorate inclined to disagree. But how difficult that can be is illustrated by this revelation from former Defense Secretary Robert Gates's recent memoir:

> In strongly supporting a surge in Afghanistan, Hillary told the president that her opposition to the surge in Iraq had been political because she was facing him in the Iowa primary. She went on to say, 'The Iraq surge worked.' The president conceded vaguely that opposition to the Iraq surge had been political. To hear the two of them making these admissions, and in front of me, was as surprising as it was dismaying.[46]

Gates's dismay (one cannot but notice) was yet insufficiently strong for him to immediately resign. He had been long enough in government to know that politicians make such calculations all the time, though admittedly they are usually more circumspect about it.

In truth, it was particularly hard to defend an unpopular change of course to the Iraq war when the Bush administration had been so inept at communicating its policies all along. Why that was, no one quite seems to understand, not even those who served in it. Doug Feith, for example, reports that Defense Secretary Donald Rumsfeld had long "wanted Defense and other departments to coordinate with the White House in a professional, systematic effort to explain our Iraq policy to the Congress, news media, and the public."[47] The President fully agreed, having "commented continually that the Administration should improve its strategic communication. But no effort was ever organized that satisfied the President, Rumsfeld, or the other top officials." In the end, the bureaucratic infighting quashed the initiative. The mind is boggled.

The challenge for a behemoth such as the US government not only to coordinate its "soft-power" assets but to give the impression of unity, resolve, and efficiency, cannot be understated. Scattered and operating in stovepipe-fashion, with each department, agency, and office more insular and risk-averse than the next, these "soft" assets get lost inside the ever-expanding Behemoth of state power. As British writer C. K. Chesterton once quipped, "Large organization is loose organization. Nay, it would be almost as true to say that organization is always disorganization."[48] He should have added that large *government* organization is practically an oxymoron.

Counterinsurgency is predicated on the centrality of political power, with support for the people as "the center of gravity." It was no accident that the first step in adopting that approach would be made in Iraq, by the indomitable General H. R. McMaster, in July 2006. McMaster worked with town leaders and tribal elders, and had his soldiers sleep alongside the people rather than isolated barracks, to earn the locals' trust. Journalist Fred Kaplan describes it as: "the first classic multistaged counterinsurgency in total independence from headquarters (as was every operation across the country, good, bad, or otherwise). And it was a model success, at least for the year that McMaster's regiment remained."[49] What McMaster understood before many others was the fact that if you want to understand, let alone, influence the local population, you have to interact with the people.

Being able to sort out enemies from friends, cultivating those friends, and understand the enemy strategy, are elementary prerequisites for preserving national security and keeping the peace. But according to the new *Army Counterinsurgency Field Manual* (*FM 3–24*), as Colonel David S. Maxwell points out with approval, "counterinsurgency is not a substitute for strategy." For there is "a broad range of insurgencies and revolutions) and it can be said with near certainty that no two are the same," notes Maxwell. Explicitly echoing Sun Tzu, he fully agrees however that "countering insurgencies [is] surely an important form of warfare and therefore attacking the enemy's strategy is the best path to success"—or rather, "more correctly stated, we must be able to advise and assist our friends, partners, and allies to understand and attack their enemies' insurgent and revolutionary strategies."[50] But Maxwell is not sanguine about the prospects of that happening. "I believe," he writes, "that the culture of the US military remains hard pressed to let go of the reins of control nor has the patience to allow another government and its security forces to be in the lead when countering insurgencies in their countries."[51] Letting go is hard to do.

> A decade and a half have passed since 9/11 yet the war on terror, by whatever name, isn't over. True, Osama bin Laden is no more. But our collective psyche is once again being sorely tested by the phenomenon of Daesh, also known as ISIS, ISIL, IS, etc., which has expanded upon and upgraded the al Qaeda business model. Books are being published, and our elected officials are scrambling to figure out what to do. The president has recognized that part of the danger lies in something uncomfortably intangible: the group's ideology. A review that appeared in the August 13, 2015, issue of *The New York Review of Books* (written by an unnamed "former official of a NATO country") accuses us all for having failed to anticipate the rise of this satanic group, and, now, failing to understand it:
>
> "None of our analysts, soldiers, diplomats, intelligence officers, politicians, or journalists has yet produced an explanation rich enough—even in hindsight—to have predicted the movement's rise. We hide this from ourselves with theories and concepts that do not bear deep examination. And we will not remedy this simply through the accumulation of more facts. It is not clear whether our culture can ever develop sufficient knowledge, rigor, imagination, and humility to grasp the phenomenon of ISIS. But for now, we should admit that we are not only horrified but baffled."[52]

Part of the problem, the anonymous writer concedes, is that Western audiences "are rarely forced to focus on ISIS's bewildering ideological appeal." Ideology is cerebral, verbal, cognitive; Daesh's (ISIS's) appeal is far more visceral and its operatives highly pragmatic. What we need is not merely to accumulate more facts but "sufficient knowledge"— which is multifaceted, and not easily measurable. "Rigor," moreover, obviously does not imply rigidity—quite the contrary. For as Sun Tzu explained, water must take the shape of its terrain to be able to then have the force of boulders: water is not rigid, which is why it can be devastatingly strong. Imagination is exactly what Sun Tzu's approach enhances: don't simply verbalize the context—picture it, feel it, see analogous situations. But above all, be humble. Do not assume you have the answers. Keep testing and questioning. It's all so simple, yet impossibly hard.

Notes

1.   Violent interstate and intrastate conflicts since 1945 have been documented on such websites as the UCDP/PRIO Armed Conflict Dataset—the Uppsala Conflict Data Program at the Department of Peace and Conflict Research in

Uppsala Sweden. https://www.prio.org/Data/Armed-Conflict/UCDP-PRIO/ These identify a large number of armed conflicts that may be described as small, or irregular wars.

2. Daniel Bell, *The Coming of Post Industrial Society: A Venture in Social Forecasting* (New York: Basic Books, 1973), 20.

3. A splendid exception is the new study by Stephen D. Bryen, *Technology, Security, and National Power: Winners and Losers* (Piscataway, NJ: Transaction Publishers, 2015)

4. Edward Hallett Carr, *The Twenty-Years' Crisis 1919–1939: Introduction to the Study of International Relations* (New York: Palgrave, 2001), with an Introduction by Michael Cox, xxiv.

5. Ibid., 122.

6. Hans Morgenthau, *Politics Among Nations: The Struggle for Power and Peace* (New York: Alfred A. Knopf, 1967), xviii.

7. For another useful discussion of Carr, see D. Robert Worley's *Orchestrating the Instruments of Power: A Critical Examination of the U.S. National Security System* (Lincoln, NE: Potomac Books, 2015)

8. "USIA—An Overview," http://dosfan.lib.uic.edu/usia/usiahome/oldoview. htm#overview

9. For an excellent history of the term, see "'Public Diplomacy' Before Gullion: The Evolution of a Phrase," CPD Blog, April 18, 2006. http://uscpublicdiplomacy.org/blog/060418_public_diplomacy_before_gullion_the_evolution_of_a_phrase

10. http://fletcher.tufts.edu/Murrow/Diplomacy/Definitions

11. See Rachel Greenspan, "Public Diplomacy in Uniform: The Role of the US Department of Defense in Supporting Modern-Day Public Diplomacy," *American Diplomacy: Foreign Service Dispatches and Periodic Reports on US Foreign Policy*, March 2011. http://www.unc.edu/depts/diplomat/item/2011/0104/comm/greensapn_pduniform.html

12. See Nicholas Cull and Juliana Geran Pilon, "The Crisis in U.S. Public Diplomacy," in *Project on National Security Reform—Case Studies Working Group Report*, Vol. II, ed. Richard Weitz (Washington, DC: US Army War College Strategic Studies Institute, 2012), 543–642.

13. For excellent overviews of organizational and conceptual changes in executive management of information operations, see Leigh Armistead, ed., *Information Operations: Warfare and the Hard Reality of Soft Power* (Washington, DC: Potomac Books, 2004) as well as his *Information Warfare: Separating Hype from Reality* (Washington, DC: Potomac Books, 2007).

14. Ibid., 2.

15. Col. Dennis Murphy, US Army, Retired and Lt. Col. Daniel Kuehl, PhD, US Air Force, Retired, "The Case for a National Information Strategy," *Military Review*, September–October 2015, 71.

16. Ibid., 3.

17. Ibid.

18. US Strategic Communications Command located near Omaha, Nebraska.

19. Cited in Sparling, Lt. Col. Bryan, Joint Advance Warfare School (National Defense University) thesis *Coming of Age: Information Operations and the American Way of War* (Norfolk: JAWS, 2010), 7.

20. Maj. Jonathan Sirard, Lt. Col. Steve Walden LTC, Joseph El Hachem, "Redefining Information Operations (IO): Applying Rand Corporation's Analysis of Army IO to Joint IO," *IOSphere*, Winter 2014, 13.

21. US Army, *Field Manual 3–13*, Inform and Influence Activities, January 2013.

22. "Cyber electromagnetic activities are activities leveraged to seize, retain, and exploit an advantage over adversaries and enemies in both cyberspace and the electromagnetic spectrum, while simultaneously denying and degrading adversary and enemy use of the same and protecting the mission command system. CEMA consist of cyberspace operations (CO), EW, and Spectrum Management Operations (SMO)." US Army, *Field Manual 3–38*, Cyber Electromagnetic Activities, February 2014.

23. Sirard et al., "Redefining Information Operations (IO)."

24. JP 3–13, *Information Operations*, November 20, 2014, ix.

25. JP 3–13, 6.

26. Brian Crozier, *Free Agent: The Unseen War, 1941–1991* (New York: HarperCollins, 1993).

27. John Sullivan, *The President, the Pope, and the Prime Minister: Three Who Changed the World* (Washington, DC: Regnery Publishing, Inc., 2006).

28. Joseph S. Nye. *Soft Power: The Means to Success in World Politics* (New York: Public Affairs, 2004), x.

29. Joseph S. Nye, "What China and Russia Don't Get About Soft Power," *Foreign Affairs*, April 29, 2013.

30. Colin S. Gray, *Hard Power and Soft Power: The Utility of Military Force as an Instrument of Policy in the 21st Century*, Strategic Studies Institute, April 2011, ix (emphasis added).

31. Ibid. (emphasis added).

32. Ibid., viii.

33. Ibid., vi.

34. Ibid., viii.

35. "'Smart power' is a term I developed in 2003 to counter the misperception that soft power alone can produce effective foreign policy." Joseph S. Nye Jr., "Get Smart: Combining Hard and Soft Power," *Foreign Affairs*, July/August 2009. https://www.foreignaffairs.com/articles/2009-07-01/get-smart

36. Suzanne Nossel, "Smart Power," *Foreign Affairs* March/April 2004.

37. Richard L. Armitage and Joseph S. Nye, co-chairs, *CSIS Commission on Smart Power: A Smarter, More Secure America* (Washington, DC: Center for Strategic & International Studies, 2007).

38. Ibid., xxi.

39. Ibid., xxiii.

40. Max Boot and Michael Doran, "Political Warfare," Policy Innovation Memorandum #33, Council on Foreign Relations, June, 2013

41. Ibid.

42. Ibid.

43. Amb. Chas. K. Freeman, Jr., *Arts of Power: Statecraft and Diplomacy* (Washington, DC: US Institute of Peace, 1997), 15.

44. Ibid., 20.

45. Juliana Geran Pilon, *Why America Is Such a Hard Sell : Beyond Pride and Prejudice* (Lanham, MD: Rowman & Littlefield, 2007).

46. Robert Gates, *Duty: Memoirs of a Secretary at War* (New York: Vintage, 2015), 376.

47. Douglas J. Feith, *War and Decision* (New York: HarperCollins, 2008), 317.

48. C. K. Chesterton, "The Bluff of the Big Shops," *The Collected Works of G.K. Chesterton*, Vol. 5 (San Francisco, CA: Ignatius Press, 1987), 85.

49. Ibid., 173.

50. David S. Maxwell, "Counterinsurgency is Not a Substitute for Strategy," *Small Wars Journal*, May 6, 2014. http://smallwarsjournal.com/jrnl/art/%E2%80%9Ccounterinsurgency-is-not-a-substitute-for-strategy%E2%80%9D

51. Ibid.

52. Anonymous, "The Mystery of ISIS," *New York Review of Books*, August 15, 2015.

12

One-Hand Clapping

Clapping with one hand only will not produce a noise.
—Malay Proverb

When we take the serious decision to fight, we must bring to bear all our nation's resources. [We] should question how the diplomatic and development efforts will be employed to build momentum for victory and our nation's strategy needs that integration
—Gen. James N. Mattis, Jan. 27, 2015

However ill-equipped the military may have been for the wars they had been asked to fight in 2003, however slow in recalibrating and reluctant to coordinate, the civilian participants were in even worse shape. What is more, their contribution to national security tends to be underappreciated, particularly since most nonmilitary activities fall under the category of foreign relations or foreign affairs—a distinction reflected in the congressional committee structure of both House and Senate. Pulling collectively a common effort that brings everyone together is therefore an especially daunting task, given the size and complexity of the leviathan US government.

There have been efforts—countless, in fact—but they haven't gotten very far. By way of illustration, a conference organized by the Defense Department (DOD) and the State Department (DOS) in September 2007, the Interagency Counterinsurgency Initiative was designed to create some kind of synergy among the many players who were all in some way involved in national security. The conference had been attended by over one hundred officials from seventeen federal departments and agencies, and many words were exchanged. The initiative seemed to recognize that counterinsurgency assessments required a whole-of-government approach—though, as RAND Corporation senior international policy analyst Ben Connable points out in his book *Embracing the Fog of War: Assessment and Metrics in Counterinsurgency,* such efforts have not been typically successful.[1] Informative as it undoubtedly was, the conference ended with little if any follow-up. Participants from Justice, Agriculture, Commerce, and other agencies continued as before, caught inside their separate little worlds.

The conference did little to change what everyone had suspected: in day-to-day activities, civilians from disparate agencies and departments hardly ever cooperate with one another, let alone with the military. This is most unfortunate, since each of them possesses powerful tools of power and influence, and engages in various activities that could, at least in principle, enhance the greater effort. Though intended to facilitate interagency cooperation on counterinsurgency, writes Fred Kaplan, the event only confirmed the reality that "these activities followed their own logic: their managers wanted nothing to do with counterinsurgency; any formal ties to the military would hinder their effectiveness."[2] Such an attitude, alas, is a nonstarter, and the military is left with little reason to keep trying to cooperate. But pinning blame on either side is ultimately futile, since the resulting dysfunction benefits no one—certainly not the nation.

Besides the ever-present albatross of interagency squabbling, short-sighted bureaucratic "stovepiping" (where every department goes its own way with blinders on each side) and the perennial civil-military divide, there is another virus sabotaging successful engagement, which takes the form of a condescending paternalism. Especially damaging in Vietnam, where William Stearman described it as "stand aside, you little guys, and let us experts do the job," the virus is actually spread across the board. That attitude is a direct consequence of our ignorance about the human terrain, and continues unabated, seemingly impervious to repeated experience.

If we did not know or trust the local population in Vietnam, in Afghanistan we did worse: we trusted randomly. Rajif Chandrasekaran describes in *Little America* how one of the United States's most trusted Afghans killed in a car bombing in June 2010 turned out to have been skimming US funds for reconstruction projects in his district and residents had grown angry when they didn't receive a cut. He cites a USAID official: "It was a mob hit. We saw him as a white knight, but we were getting played the whole time." There was little choice, writes Chandrasekaran: "Unable to tell friend from foe, the Americans opted to do more of the governing themselves."[3] It was back to condescending paternalism.

Actually, our own bureaucracies and the international aid community at large had managed to inadvertently hijack the peace effort even earlier, in fact from the outset, in January 2002, at the Tokyo conference. The humanitarian intervention business ended up siphoning off huge funds to pay for expensive consultants, both foreign and Afghan, for projects whose value was determined with no input from the people most affected. As Jack Fairweather points out, "just as the debate about the role of peacekeeping troops had largely taken place in western capitals, far from the reality in Afghanistan, so too did the discussion of reconstruction largely take place without input from Afghans."[4]

A few experienced Western reconstruction experts, notably British lawyer Clare Lockhart, who has long collaborated with Dr. Ashraf Ghani, then Afghanistan's de facto finance minister, now the nation's president since September 2014, understood the significance of relying on the invaluable knowledge of the local population. She also knew the importance of not spending too much money too early. The Americans, alas, ended up proving to behave like the ignorant foreigners they were. Either unwilling or unable to heed her warnings, the liberators, however well-intentioned and well-resourced, squandered their advantage. Afghanistan lost too.

A great deal has gone wrong, but during the course of the last three decades, many lessons have also been learned, at least in the short term. The predilection for cookie-cutter models has given way to a more country-specific, culturally attuned approach. Writes Tom Carothers of the Carnegie Endowment: "Decades ago, such strategic differentiation was rare. Assuming that transitions toward democracy would unfold in much the same way across diverse countries, aid providers favored a standard menu that entailed distributing aid somewhat evenly across all the types of programming included in the three-part framework."[5] It was also noticed that democracy aid was not qualitatively different from other forms of engagement, as Carothers further points out: "The first generation of democracy-aid practitioners often wanted to stay apart from the world of socioeconomic aid. Their mission, they felt, was fundamentally different—not poverty reduction or economic growth, but political transformation." The feeling was mutual: aid providers thought themselves altruistic humanitarians, in contrast to the arrogant, if benevolent, neo-colonialists bent on bringing large-scale changes to countries they knew little about.

But gradually, the two sides approached, however grudgingly at times, as they have come to appreciate the links between economic performance and political reforms. That said, there is still a long way to go. With the uncommonly characteristic candor that has cemented his reputation,

Carothers frankly identifies the core problem as arising "from the basic political economy of the aid industry . . . [, which is that m]any aid organizations are designed and operate more for the interests of aid providers than recipients." The pathology of the "aid industry" (a term they would never use) also obviously undermines effectiveness. Accordingly, while some groups, especially smaller ones, are trying to think out of the box and be responsive to changing circumstances and culture,

> [y]et others, especially some of the larger organizations for which democracy work is only a small part of their overall portfolio, still sometimes operate on strategic autopilot, carrying out many types of programs in any one setting with little careful thought about which among them offer the most fruitful avenues for change. These auto-pilot approaches not only produce poorly conceived programs that fail to pinpoint key issues in troubled transitions, they also undercut the efforts of those actors that are trying to be more strategic.[6]

The challenges faced by the democracy assistance community (as it usually refers to itself) are considerable, especially—though to be sure, not exclusively—in the United States, in no small part because of unrealistically high expectations of quick results. It has not helped that public perception tends to associate it with other types of engagement, such as nation-building and regime change—all vague concepts that no administration, Republican or Democrat, has done much to clarify. Though occasionally paying it lip service, Obama administration has little use for most engagements abroad, preferring "nation-building at home."[7] Writes Carothers: "Although some advisors around President Obama insist that he is strongly committed to democracy promotion, contrary evidence is more persuasive and shows a US hesitation to push hard for democratization in many places."

The numbers support this conclusion. For "even though the overall spending worldwide on democracy aid is generally holding steady (despite drops at some major institutions such as USAID, where spending on democracy programs has shrunk significantly over the past five years), the aid is less grounded in policy frameworks that support the overall endeavor of advancing democracy." In other words, the alleged "strategic" commitment to "democracy and human rights," which supposedly constitutes one of the five goals of the development and diplomacy strategic plan for 2011–17,[8] is little more than words, which is considerably worse than nothing, since it raises expectations and the (legitimate) charge of hypocrisy.

The words themselves are a big part of the problem. Is it really *democracy* that should be promoted, or, rather, *governance*? The latter is indeed vital if we are going to be involved in peace fare, since chaos and lack of governance self-evidently breed terror. As Condoleezza Rice writes in her memoir, *No Higher Honor: A Memoir of My Years in Washington* "After 9/11 it was very clear that weak and failing states were a grave security threat to the United States. They could not control their borders and risked becoming safe havens for terrorists."[9] The implication that it had not been "very clear" before 9/11 is correct, and deplorable. That "everything changed" after that horrible day is not an understatement but a worn-out cliché.

Unfortunately, it was very far from everything: what didn't change is the notion that we can punish our enemies by destroying them militarily. Former CIA operative Kevin McCarty hopes that we might "drive our strategic thinking with a new concept based on creating a durable political victory rather than the unconditional tactical defeat of a threat."[10] But unconditional tactical defeat is what we know best. What words should we use for something as elusive as "durable political victory"? How do you know when you've got it?

Though seemingly theoretical, the question is momentous: words do matter—and continue to plague our national security discourse. A few alternatives are worth considering. "Governance assistance" is less tainted than "democracy promotion," as is "state building." These labels sound less crusading, and hence arguably more palatable, but also more accurate: ultimately, most "democracy promotion" aims to bolster the necessary *means* to empower people to effectively implement their long-ignored aspirations, through viable institutions of their own choosing. For if governance—reasonably free of corruption—is able to take place in a relatively, and increasingly, secure environment, the business of fostering a national spirit, along with enhancing the basic democratic values of respect for individual liberty and compassion for others, must ultimately be left to the people themselves. No one either can or should do it for them. "Peace-building," however awkward, is another plausible semantic option, as we will see in chapter 16.

One other hard-earned lesson from the past three decades is that rebuilding failing states "was a monumental task, one for which the U.S. had inadequate institutions to integrate the military and civilian capabilities as such missions required."[11] That task, which came to be known as "Stabilization and Reconstruction," would turn out to be little short of a fiasco, despite tremendous efforts by courageous and innovative people, military and civilians, called upon to do what they could. As the Special Inspector General for Iraq Reconstruction (SIGIR) Stuart W. Bowen, Jr., writes in his report "Reforming the Management of Stabilization and Reconstruction Operations":

> The 8-year, $62-billion U.S. reconstruction effort in Iraq revealed that the U.S. Government's system for executing SROs is neither coherent nor integrated. From the program's abbreviated preparatory stage in early 2003 to the earlier-than-expected transfer of sovereignty to the Interim Iraqi Government in mid-2004, temporary organizations, expediently created in response to urgent requirements, planned and managed the coalition's variegated rebuilding initiatives. This ever-shifting adhocracy lacked the expertise and capacity necessary to implement the coalition's ambitious reconstruction agenda. It was like a thousand untrained plate-spinners trying to perform during an earthquake, with expected results: lots of broken china.[12]

The image of broken china may be overly benign, but "untrained plate-spinners" is apt. Where were the trained ones, if any?

Stabilization and reconstruction, usually (though not always) used together and referred to as S&R, is roughly what happens after combat has ravaged a country. Stabilization is generally defined as halting additional decline by rebuilding infrastructure, supporting civil society institutions, and boosting sustainable development,[13] while reconstruction can refer to rebuilding an economy either after military conflict or after a major natural disaster. But don't look for standard definitions: as a major report by the United States Institute of Peace (USIP) put it, "[t]he multiple [national and international] institutions working side by side in S&R missions do not share"[14] common definitions or understandings for how different stakeholder view S&R differently.[15]

In most cases, these activities are performed by the military—and in that sense, they are simply reincarnations of that old canard, "nation-building." Ambassador James Dobbins offers at least one approach: "We at the RAND Corporation define nation-building as 'the use of armed force in the aftermath of a crisis to promote a transition to democracy."[16] Even if the transition to democracy is no longer considered to be part of S&R, that doesn't mean it isn't implied, which only adds to the confusion. The term clearly deserves closer analysis.

Foreign policy experts Gary T. Dempsey and Roger W. Fontaine argue that nation-building first became a fashionable topic of analysis among political scientists during the 1960s, when it "focused on cultivating a sense of national identity in the newly independent colonies rather than on the formation of the countries themselves."[17] This politicized the concept, diverting attention from the painstaking process of developmental assistance to shattered communities. Dempsey and Fontaine then proceed to offer their own, quite expansive definition of nation-building as "the massive foreign regulation of the policymaking of another country"—which they correctly observe would be "perhaps the most intrusive form of foreign intervention."[18] Indeed it would be.

So all-encompassing a definition, however, is of dubious utility. Among the US government's "nation-building organs," for example, Dempsey and Fontaine identify "the United States Institute of Peace, a federally funded institution that was created during the Reagan era to 'strengthen the nation's capacity to promote the peaceful resolution of international conflict.'"[19] But whatever one might say about the quality and impact of this admittedly lavish think tank sitting on prize real estate next to the State Department, it is not clear how USIP's conflict resolution mandate could facilitate "massive foreign regulation" of another state. If anything, American so-called nation-building has been less imperial than flaccid.

For many reasons, then, the ambiguous concept of "nation-building" is mostly confusing. The main culprit is "nation"—a highly charged, ambiguous, Western term, as controversial as "democracy," if not more. Far more palatable, it seems to me, is "peace-building," which not only connotes providing technical expertise in institutional governance, it decidedly does *not* imply intrusive and unwanted "foreign regulation." What it does convey is the centrality of solid and sustainable, and hence constituency-backed, stability, which may safely be called "peace." As to freedom, even though it is not explicitly stated as a necessary ingredient, it need not be: for even if, on the way to more permanent peace, semi-authoritarian periods may be required, those would be expected to soon be superseded by more genuine self-government. Some may wish to call that "democracy," others may prefer "self-determination"—either works, so long as the substance remains. But in any event, from a practical perspective, American engagement in peace-building must involve "whole-of-government" operations that include DOD along with many of the civilian agencies as well as coalition partners. Whatever it ends up being called, with S&R or nation-building or something still different, there is no escaping the practical implications.

It took a while before we realized that this needed to happen. Secretary Rice reveals that it was not until late 2002—a year after George W. Bush decided to attack Afghanistan—that the United States finally developed "a new model to help bring together the different pieces of the puzzle."[20] One model that was soon to be tried, known as Provincial Reconstruction Teams (PRTs), was designed to couple the military's protective forces with civilian personnel who were experts in development and reconstruction. A number of PRTs were set up in collaboration with coalition partners, deploying them to all parts of the country. This model would also be used in Iraq, but there was little time to address what would emerge as a serious problem, which undermined their usefulness.

In a literature review of several studies on lessons learned from PRTs, conducted by National Defense University's Center for Complex Operations, researcher Christoff Luehrs finds widespread confusion about such basic questions as

> how PRTs should be organized, how they should conduct operations, or what specifically they should accomplish. At the same time, no endstate has been defined at which the PRTs would be replaced by "regular development" teams, making it more difficult for personnel on the ground to balance the desire for rapid results with sustainable development and capacity-building; all too often, this results in the pursuit of "feel-good projects." Predictably, a lack of clarity on the objectives that PRTs should pursue translates into a similar state of affairs with regard to strategy. Thus, virtually all documents under review lament the lack of an overarching strategy and put forward a range of "strategic fixes" from civilianizing the PRTs across the board, to limiting their role, to "buying time" for kinetic military efforts and "development proper," to setting up in-country interagency coordinating bodies with a mandate to fit PRT efforts into broader U.S. foreign policy objectives.[21]

USAID evidently had little choice but to work hand-in-hand with the military. But it did not come easily. For as Rice points out, the cultures of even the State Department and USAID were "very different," to say nothing of both as against the DOD, with USAID outright "eschewing the idea that it was involved in 'U.S. foreign policy'"[22] at all. She adds: "that attitude, I was sure, would have come as a shock to taxpayers," noting: "I saw—and still see—nothing wrong with the proposition that development assistance ought to support broader U.S. foreign policy objectives."[23] Nothing wrong, indeed.

Rice's observation is no anomaly. In a recent book about US efforts to regain influence in the Middle East through peacebuilding efforts, journalist David Rohde recounts one USAID employee telling an aide to Ambassador Richard Holbrooke: "We joined AID to do good development work in Latin America and Africa. We don't want to be part of your dirty war on terrorism."[24] This candid outburst, which will surprise no one with even a limited acquaintance with the development community's mindset, speaks volumes about the difficulty of reconciling two radically different orientations to global engagement.

The American Anthropology Association (AAA) is typical of the academic community's pervasive hostility to the military that came to affect the recent reconstruction efforts of the US government. As Naval Postgraduate School professor George Lucas demonstrates in his excellent study of ethics and the military, the AAA, while not outright prohibiting, "strongly disapproves" of its members' engaging with the military. Nor is this restricted to the AAA. Far from involving just one profession, Lucas admits, "I discovered that this tendency toward indiscriminate conflation of these vastly disparate and morally distinctive activities could be traced to a widespread underlying ideological antipathy toward the military itself, manifest in the opposition of academics and scholars toward engagement at any level with the military."[25]

Lessons we might have learned from Iraq went essentially unheeded by all the agencies engaged in the process. Congress kept appropriating the money, and the agencies kept contracting it out as fast as it could, with insufficient oversight. As noted above, SIGIR Bowen concluded the United States had wasted billions. Even a cursory look at the public record betrays overwhelming mismanagement. Upon the publication of the SIGIR final report in March 2013, Iraqi Justice Minister Hassan al-Shimari's observed that "the Americans built goodwill by bankrolling small projects near their bases, but few were self-sustaining. 'If I were a government minister in 2004, I would have given the Americans a vision,' Shimari said. 'That's what was missing. Because there was no mission, there were no priorities.'"[26] Journalist Ernesto Londono added that "several Americans interviewed for the [SIGIR] report acknowledged the lack of coordination. Senator Claire McCaskill (D-MO), a critic of Iraq war policy, said that interagency cooperation was an 'utter, abject failure' and that government divisions worked at cross-purposes, forming a 'circular firing squad.'"[27]

USAID did not bear the brunt of the blame. A reluctant and unprepared DOD, having been put in charge of the entire war effort at the outset by President George W. Bush, was doling out most of the money. Oversight seemed but an afterthought, apparently lost in the shuffle. And no wonder: DOD hadn't done this sort of thing, on such a scale, before. The sums involved were huge: average US expenditures for Iraqi reconstruction in 2005 alone, for example, were more than $25 million a day. Yet when Bowen's auditors went looking for documents supporting billions of dollars of fund transfers to the Iraqi government in that period, they discovered the paperwork was "largely missing." The SIGIR report concludes that contracting abuses and mismanagement resulted in at least $8 billion wasted by Washington on Iraq's post-war recovery under what it called "nation (re)building by adhocracy."[28]

Findings of the Special Inspector General for Afghanistan Reconstruction (SIGAR) mirror those of his colleague's office: even more billions wasted. As late as January 2015, following major fraud and bribery charges against former employees of two prominent USAID contractors, International Relief and Development (IRD) and the Louis Berger Group, Inc. (LBG), the Senate was asking the Obama administration to explain why, despite previous track records of not just poor performance but outright criminal abuse, IRD and LBG continued to be among the top recipients of US taxpayer dollars for reconstruction in Afghanistan. The former CEO of LBG,[29] after all, had pleaded guilty for defrauding American taxpayers of tens of millions of dollars over two decades, while a former employee of IRD had been indicted for bribery in connection with securing US government contracts.[30]

On December 17, 2015, the NGO ProPublica released a report based on more than 200 audits, special projects and inspections done by SIGAR since 2009. Having set up a database to add up the total cost of failed reconstruction projects, the report reveals a grim picture of the overall reconstruction effort and a repeated cycle of mistakes. In just six years, the IG has tallied at least $17 billion in questionable spending, including $3.6 billion in outright waste, projects teetering on the brink of waste, or projects that can't—or won't—be sustained by the Afghans, as well as an additional $13.5 billion that could be considered wasteful.

Often the programs' goals were reportedly "out of whack with the reality of life in Afghanistan. After the invasion, the United States rushed forward with bold plans to create a democratic, fiscally secure, ethical government and society—out of whole cloth. It was the same country-building bravado that had earlier tripped up the United States in Iraq when it dismissed the local culture and ignored corruption. None of the programs was required to prove it had even limited success. Officials tracked dollars spent, not impact. For instance, no one evaluated whether Afghan security forces actually learned to read and write after going through a $200 million literacy program."[31]

Though not everyone is equally sanguine about the Special Inspector General's reporting, the principal objection is to the methodology rather than the bottom line—namely, that mistakes were made, and they are inadmissible. For example, in a thoughtful critique of SIGAR's approach, Jeff Goodson, chief of staff at USAID in Afghanistan, noted that focusing on dollars alone doesn't really get to the heart of the problems unmasked. Thus in one case, SIGAR focused on the cost of building a fueling station rather than why the US government was so slow getting the project started in the first place. Similarly, in evaluating education, SIGAR failed to ask why there aren't more primary schools in the east and south to divert boys away from Pakistani-funded madrassas, and so forth. Writes Goodson:

> More broadly, SIGAR hasn't asked how USAID performed its national security responsibilities as the lead development agency for Afghan counterinsurgency operations. Nor has it asked what USAID's de facto abdication of those responsibilities, as described in its June 2015 policy statement on future cooperation with the Defense Department, portends. This issue has profound implications for how the United States will conduct future irregular warfare campaigns, including who will do the strategic development work and what it will cost.[32]

Goodson is exactly right to point out that just as it isn't sufficient to highlight waste in dollar amounts, so it won't suffice to reorganize on paper, set up nominal responsibility, or mandate cooperation. Far more important is making sure that a strategy is set, that people know what they are supposed to do, and that they are properly equipped and qualified to do it. Well-meaning efforts at executive coordination have been attempted through the years, yet they all seem Sisyphean, almost doomed from the start. Sadly, the reconstruction effort in both Iraq and Afghanistan has been a rather dismal—and dismally expensive—failure.

The lack of coordination inside the US government both reflects and contributes to the lack of grand strategy. A Congressional Research Service study, conducted in 2011, that looked at all the different interagency collaborative arrangements indicated that, typically, notwithstanding their rapid increase in recent years, such arrangements tend to be of "highly limited" value, especially because "there is no lead officer or agency in charge . . . [with the result] that some members might not participate adequately or at all."[33] Similarly,

Colonel Bob Ulin writes in the September 2010 issue of *Interagency* that "interagency cooperation" is in reality little more than an empty slogan: "What is needed are interagency doctrine, based upon a realistic examination and analysis of past lessons, and interagency education . . ."[34] The latter is virtually nonexistent outside the military; yet without either adequate evaluations, lessons learned, and interagency education, the effort is doomed. The former is a presidential responsibility. But not even a modern equivalent of a knight in shining armor is likely to solve the root problem of our culture, which is an eroded sense of purpose.

Symptomatic of that erosion is what has come to be known as the "civil-military" divide, characterized by a fairly widespread impression that the military is from Mars (or Ares[35]) and the civilians from elsewhere in the American constellation, with interplanetary travel still in the planning stages. Nearly two decades of war that saw considerable interaction between civilians and warriors at many levels have hardly erased that impression. Even the current commander-in-chief, Barack Obama, has made no secret of his discomfort with military culture and the "hard power" it represents—as indicated by the glaring absence of the defense community from the high-level negotiations with Iran on its nuclear program. The symbolism was lost on no one. Former Pentagon official Stephen Bryen complains that "whether the Pentagon raised any objections to the deal, or tried to take part in the process, remains unknown,"[36] implying that they should have spoken up. But the more startling fact is that they were not even asked to be part of the process.

The civil-military divide in this country, which often looks more like a gorge, is both cause and effect to the confusion that plagues a nation in want of a strategic vision. America seems not to know what it stands for anymore, its pluralist culture turning against itself while the majority of its elite wallow in civilizational self-doubt. Pluralism is what liberty is all about, to be sure. But we must find sufficient common ground to be able to work together. For at the end of the day, favoring one-hand clapping over another for ideological reasons will guarantee that the other side will applaud our defeat.

Notes

1. Ben Connable, *Embracing the Fog of War: Assessment and Metrics in Counterinsurgency* (Washington, DC: RAND Corporation, 2012), 216.
2. Kaplan, *The Insurgents*, 288.

3. Rajif Chandrasekaran, *Imperial Life in the Emerald City: Inside Iraq's Green Zone* (New York: Alfred A. Knopf, 2012), 169.
4. Fairweather, *The Good War*, 63.
5. Thomas Carothers, Democracy Aid at 25: Time to Choose," *Journal of Democracy* 26, no. 1 (January 2015): 59–73. http://carnegieendowment.org/2015/01/13/democracy-aid-at-25-time-to-choose/hzao
6. Ibid.
7. Stephen Sestanovich, "Obama's Focus Is on Nation-Building at Home," *The New York Times*, March 11, 2014.
8. http://www.state.gov/documents/organization/223997.pdf
9. Condoleezza Rice, *No Higher Honor: A Memoir of My Years in Washington* (New York: Crown Publishers, 2011), 109.
10. Kevin McCarty, "Can Kennan Shake Us Out of Our Strategic Groundhog Day?" War on the Rocks, November 9, 2015. http://warontherocks.com/2015/11/can-kennan-shake-us-out-of-our-strategic-groundhog-day/?utm_source=WOTR+Newsletter&utm_campaign=c364fa2052-WOTR_News-letter_8_17_158_15_2015&utm_medium=email&utm_term=0_8375be81e9-c364fa2052-60136989
11. Ibid.
12. Stuart W. Bowen, Jr., "No More Adhocracies: Reforming the Management of Stabilization and Reconstruction Operations," *Prism* 3, no. 2 (2012): 4–5.
13. According to DOD Instruction 3000.05, September 16, 2009, "stability operations is defined as an overarching term encompassing various military missions, tasks, and activities conducted outside the United States in coordination with other instruments of national power to maintain or reestablish a safe and secure environment, provide essential governmental services, emergency infrastructure reconstruction, and humanitarian relief." For a concise overview, See Dave Dilegge, "Stability Operations: DOD Instruction 3000.05," *Small Wars Journal*, Sept. 17, 2009. http://smallwarsjournal.com/blog/stability-operations-dod-instruction-300005
14. *Guiding Principles for Stabilization and Reconstruction* (Washington, DC: USIP Press, Sept. 2013), Introduction 1–5.
15. "[A] number of different terms are used by different organisations, including stabilisation, stability operations, early recovery and reconstruction, are often conflated in S&R." Rainer Gonzalez Palau, Stefanie Nijssen & Steven A. Zyck, "Stabilisation & Reconstruction: Definitions, Civilian Contribution & Lessons Learnt," Civil-Military Fusion Center, September 2011, 2. https://www.pksoi.org/document_repository/doc_lib/CFC_RFI_Stabilisation_Lessons_Learnt_Sep2011.pdf
16. James Dobbins, "Nation-Building: UN Surpasses U.S. on Learning Curve," *RAND Review*, Spring 2005. http://www.rand.org/pubs/periodicals/rand-review/issues/spring2005/nation.html
17. Gary T. Dempsey and Roger W. Fontaine, *Fool's Errands: America's Recent Encounters with Nation Building* (Washington, DC: Cato Institute, 2001), 3.
18. Ibid., 2.
19. Ibid., 15.
20. Rice, *No Higher Honor*, 109–10.
21. Christoff Luehrs, "Provincial Reconstruction Teams: A Literature Review," *Prism* 1, no. 1 (Washington, DC: National Defense University), 97.

22. Rice, *No Higher Honor*, 427.
23. Ibid.
24. David Rohde, *Beyond War: Reimagining American Influence in a New Middle East* (New York: Viking Press, 2013), 86.
25. See George Lucas's *Anthropologists in Arms: The Ethics of Military Anthropology* (Lanham, MD: AltaMira Press, 2009), ch. 5, 131 ff. Also, review by this author in *International Journal of Intelligence Ethics*, Spring 2010, Volume 1, Number 1.
26. Ernesto Londono, "Report: Iraq Reconstruction Failed to Result in Lasting, Positive Changes." Washington Post, March 5, 2013, https://www.washingtonpost.com/world/national-security/report-iraq-reconstruction-failed-to-result-in-lasting-positive-changes/2013/03/05/aa7e6948-85d9-11e2-98a3-b3db6b9ac586_story.html
27. Ibid.
28. *Learning from Iraq*, A Final Report from the Special Inspector General for Iraq Reconstruction, March 2013. pp. 37ff. file:///C:/Users/Owner/Documents/Soft%20weapons/Foreign%20Assistance/sigir-learning-from-iraq.pdf
29. Letter from SIGAR to USAID, June 25, 2015. https://www.sigar.mil/pdf/special%20projects/SIGAR-15-67-SP.pdf
30. Prior to these latest criminal indictments, LBG and IRD were exposed for mismanagement and waste that harmed US reconstruction efforts in both Afghanistan and Iraq. In one notable case, LBG paid millions of dollars in criminal and civil fines for overbilling the government. See "Corker Seeks Review of USAID Contracting Practices after Prominent Firms Implicated in Major Fraud and Corruption Charges," Senate Committee on Foreign Relations Press Release, January 16, 2015. http://www.foreign.senate.gov/press/chair/release/corker-seeks-review-of-usaid-contracting-practices-after-prominent-firms-implicated-in-major-fraud-and-corruption-charges
31. "If this accounting wasn't bad enough, consider this: SIGAR has only examined a small percentage of the $110 billion effort to rebuild and remodel Afghanistan. The waste totals are likely much higher." Megan McCloskey, Tobin Asher, Lena Groeger, Sisi Wei, and Christine Lee, "We Blew $17 Billion in Afghanistan. How Would You Have Spent It?" ProPublica, December 17, 2015. https://projects.propublica.org/graphics/afghan?utm_source=Sailthru&utm_medium=email&utm_campaign=New%20Campaign&utm_term=%2ASituation%20Report#afghan-DR
32. Jeff Goodson, "The Myth of the $43-Million Gas Station in Afghanistan," *War on the Rocks*, November 18, 2015. http://warontherocks.com/2015/11/the-myth-of-the-43-million-gas-station-in-afghanistan/?utm_source=WOTR+Newsletter&utm_campaign=ea51dd82e3-WOTR_Newsletter_8_17_158_15_2015&utm_medium=email&utm_term=0_8375be81e9-ea51dd82e3-60136989
33. Frederick M. Kaiser, "Interagency Collaborative Arrangements and Activities: Types, Rationales, Considerations," Congressional Research Service, May 31, 2011, 6.

34. Bob Ulin, "About Interagency Cooperation," *Interagency*, No. 10-01, September 2010.
35. Mars is the Roman equivalent of Ares, whom the Greeks considered the God of War.
36. Stephen Bryen, "No High Level Military Participation in Iran Deal," *Technology and Security Blog*, July 29, 2015. https://technologysecurity.wordpress.com/2015/07/29/no-high-level-military-participation-in-iran-deal/?utm_source=No+High+Level+Military+Participation+in+Iran+Deal*&utm_campaign=No+High+level+military+Participation+in+Iran+deal&utm_medium=email

13

Communication-Challenged

Esse est percipi. (To be is to be perceived.)
—Bishop Berkley

*Falsehood flies, and the Truth comes limping after it;
so that when Men come to be undeceived, it is too
late; the Jest is over, and the Tale has had its Effect.*
—Jonathan Swift, Nov. 9, 1710

The adage that action "speaks louder than words," as indeed does inaction, doesn't mean that decibels enhance clarity. The same event may, and usually does, mean different things to different people, depending on context. No less than actions, and more insidiously, words can topple regimes or build morale, create ideals or discredit them, and inspire millions to build or to kill. America's Founders knew this, having done everything humanly possible to open and protect lines of communication with their fellow countrymen and with their friends abroad, conveying what needed to be said and done. Since the battlefield was everywhere, communication remained a priority at all times before, during, and after the Revolutionary War. Carefully thought-out actions orchestrated, calibrated, and then publicized by savvy strategic propagandists like Sam Adams, were implemented by everyone they could mobilize. Others were inspired to do the same without additional prompting. What contributed most to the Founders' concerted efforts' becoming so effective was a tacit unity of purpose, eloquently articulated and smartly cultivated.

But that was then. Much was unlearned as two centuries passed, to the point that one could safely say we are below square one. By the mid-1960s, everything had already changed. Despite—or, rather, because of—America's enormous strength, a Goliath-syndrome had gradually set in: we thought we could compensate with military might what we lacked in ability to engage and communicate, both with one another and with the rest of the world. We forgot that might is never everything. We were shocked when Vietnam/David, whose strategic acumen we grossly underestimated, taught America a bitter lesson. The incursion whose name became synonymous with no-win-warfare became the first military escalation to be lost as a direct result of misperception and a fatally eroded political will.

The media bears much, even if certainly not all of the blame, for having grossly misrepresented events on the ground at that time. William Stearman reports his own experiences:

> While I was "in-country" I generally found that what our correspondents were reporting back to the United States bore little resemblance to what I was actually experiencing on the ground. I have had several correspondents tell me that their editors wanted only negative reporting and when they tried to report any positive event or development their material inevitably landed in a waste paper basket or on the floor of a TV cutting room. So they gave up trying.[1]

That said, the political leadership in Washington, having repeatedly miscalculated, did a miserable job of handling the media. The main lesson to be learned from Vietnam, concludes Sherman, is that "public support for any military enterprise abroad is essential . . . [though] our government unfortunately did a very poor job of explaining the Vietnam War to its people and of countering negative media reporting about it."[2] Though easy to blame the media since it flaunted its antiwar bias blatantly and brazenly, Washington's incompetence in getting out its message is at least as disconcerting.

There were mitigating circumstances, to be sure. The war had been started by the young and fiery president John F. Kennedy, but it fell to the more domestically inclined, butter-over-guns Lyndon Johnson to oversee its escalation, his advisors mostly at a loss to figure out what to do as events on the ground kept defying their predictions. If even the commander-in-chief was loath to engage in military action, no wonder he had trouble mobilizing popular support. It did not help that unduly optimistic official reports were often belied by facts on the ground. A skeptical media, coming to distrust even legitimate and accurate information, became increasingly hostile, proving to be a liability that would soon take on a momentum of its own.

Obviously the answer is hardly censorship—the First Amendment sees to that. We learned the perils of ignoring it, early in our history in 1798, when President John Adams reacted to the vicious partisan disagreements tearing at the nation's fragile fabric by signing into law the Alien and Sedition Acts, which included a provision to restrict speech critical of the government.[3] That move proved disastrous[4]—the right to free speech and a free press continues to be inalienable, and so it must remain. No future president would dare forget that lesson.

All the more reason for the US government to do its utmost to communicate clearly to its citizens and the world, without any encroachments on the commercial media. Government press releases are not sufficient to explain intentions and goals in ways that resonate with multiple audiences. We no longer have the luxury of compartmentalized messaging in the age of the World Wide Web. That said, there are still many venues to engage with specific audiences by researching what they watch or listen to, and then seeking to access those sources, preferably in a credible format and in language that is actually understood. If Q & A is an option, take it.

The bottom line is that messaging matters. It matters a great deal. The Vietnam War should have been a wake-up call; it wasn't. During most of the past half-century, the leadership in Washington (except for Ronald "the Great Communicator" Reagan[5]) has failed to take advantage of its privileged platform, even as means of communication rapidly proliferated, consistently underestimating the importance of conveying to the American people what it does and why, as candidly and clearly as possible.

Things may arguably have now sunk even further south since "the Internet and social media have made everyone a player in the use of information as an element of power. A single person, group, or collective can impact the 'I' portion of the DIME (diplomatic, *information*, military, and economics) power model with effects on par with those previously seen by well-crafted strategic communication messages from state governments," laments Navy Commander Bryan Leese, writing in the August, 2015, issue of the *US Naval Institute Proceedings*.[6] In the new information climate, of course, there is no way that official propaganda can command the stage. But that doesn't mean dispensing with it altogether, especially so long as the United States maintains a reputation for telling it like it is, no matter how assiduously its opponents will scoff at it and, too often successfully, seek to undermine it.

Yet that is more or less where we are: in communication free-fall, with the result is that not even our own soldiers know what kind of peace they are supposed to be seeking in the hell-holes where they see their buddies dying or being maimed for life. Navy Seal Marcus Luttrell's exasperated *cri de coeur* could not be a clearer indictment:

> [N]o one seems clear on what we should be called in Afghanistan. Are we a peace-keeping force? Are we fighting a war against insurgents on behalf of the Afghan government, or are we fighting it on behalf of the USA? Are we trying to hunt down the master terrorist bin Laden, or are we just trying to prevent the Taliban from regaining control of the country, because they were protectors of bin Laden and all who fought for him? Search me. But everything's cool with us. Tell us what you want, and we'll do it. We're loyal servants of the US government.[7]

Luttrell's three fearless fellow-warriors died in harrowing circumstances without knowing the answer to those questions. But then again, neither did anyone else. How are we supposed to win a peace we cannot even describe to those we send in harm's way to secure it?

While the commercial media has gained in strength immeasurably, the government's communication skills have atrophied. Luttrell speaks for many servicemen when he decries the media's power and "their unfortunate effect on American politicians. We all harbor fears about untrained, half-educated journalists who only want a good story to justify their salaries and expense accounts. . . . When the media gets involved, in the United States, that's a war you've got a damned good chance of losing, because the restrictions on us are immediately amplified, and that's sensationally good news for our enemy."[8] To be sure, one reason the media seems, and often is, unconcerned about what might help the enemy is that it doesn't have the luxury of time. The outright explosion of information means that if you don't publish something immediately, someone else will beat you to it. In an age of instant communication, waiting around to check out a story is very bad business. But again, none of this lets the US government off the hook. It especially does not do so in case of war, no matter how supportive the population may be "to do something," as it certainly was after the horrors of 9/11. It is the government's job to say why it plans to use the tools of national power, and to what end.

The failure of George W. Bush's administration to do just that has been confirmed by its top officials, notably by Under Secretary of Defense Doug Feith, who describes that one of the first challenges for the administration after 9/11 was to explain the threat of Islam to a nation that had been all but oblivious to it. It was a problem not only for DOD but for everyone:

> how the U.S. government should organize for the battle of ideas. The ideological element of the struggle was essential, but no office in the U.S. government was well suited to handle it; and no official was appointed to take the lead. Both [Secretary of Defense] Rumsfeld and [General Richard G.] Myers wanted the Defense Department to make an effort on this front, hoping it would complement a vigorous, government-wide strategic communications campaign headed by State or the White House. Yet my attempt to fill the gap within the gap would backfire resoundingly, and the Bush administration never put together a comprehensive strategy to counter ideological support for Islamist extremism.[9]

The abortive attempt to which Feith is referring was to be called the Office of Strategic Influence, whose function would be to "promote initiatives to fight jihadist ideology." Notwithstanding its admittedly politically radioactive name, however, this would basically involve "programs to improve other countries' schools, or increasing the audience for moderate Muslim leaders"[10]—hardly alarming. But after the *New York Times* published a story—widely believed to have been planted by DOD's own head of Public Affairs Torie Clarke—alleging that the Office was designed to plant false stories in the media, not only did the initiative die but so did its function. Truth be told, reports Feith, "many officials simply had no interest in ideological warfare. They considered it impractical to try to influence the way millions of people thought."[11] (Or was it *billions?* But who's counting.)

The State Department didn't do much better in its efforts to communicate beyond the borders, especially, though not exclusively, to the Muslim world. While immediately after 9/11 public diplomacy became all the rage, with everyone asking how we could do better to deliver "our message," it was all for naught. And no wonder: to begin with, the wrong people were being consulted. Comments former State Department official Walter Douglas:

> In fact, public diplomacy officers with experience in Muslim countries were largely left out. This was reflected in the recommendations, where the vast majority were Washington related. . . . Real improvements in public diplomacy will only come about through insights culled from decades of experience in the field from officers who understand what works in Muslim countries and what does not.[12]

But public diplomacy, and more generally strategic communication, continued not to be a real priority for the administration. USIA having been abolished in 1999, no one quite knew how to reinvigorate it—especially since it hadn't been doing a great job in the first place. After an embarrassingly bad performance by Wall Street advertisement executive Charlotte Beers as Under Secretary of State for Public Affairs and Public Diplomacy, the post was left vacant for two years, until President Bush finally filled it with his communications advisor and close friend Karen Hughes. But she wasn't much of an improvement, having no foreign affairs experience, a fact that she readily admitted, and which soon became embarrassingly evident.

Though State was now basically in charge of the battle-of-ideas portfolio, it continued engaging in old-style feel-good public diplomacy consisting of cultural exchanges and a smattering of anemic educational activities with negligible impact. Concludes Feith: "The need for a broader strategy remained unaddressed."[13]

It still is. The Obama administration having abandoned "war on terror," "war on terrorism," along with other similarly vague umbrella terms for what had never been adequately explained by his predecessor, we have now lost even that modicum of insight into what or whom we are fighting, let alone what we are trying to achieve.

It also doesn't help that we hamstring ourselves as we continue to operate with antiquated laws. Former Defense Advanced Research Projects Agency (DARPA) program manager Rand Waltzman writes:

> For example, US Law 50 US Code § 3093(f) effectively prohibits our intelligence community from action "intended to influence United States political processes, public opinion, policies, or media." With social media and the Internet, there is no way to guarantee that no US person will be inadvertently exposed to information operations that are not intended for them, and this rule is broadly applied as a basis for banning any type of useful action. While this made sense in the days when influence operations were confined to print, radio, and TV, it does not make any sense in today's global instantaneous information world.[14]

He then provides a graphic example:

> In March of 2006, a battalion of US Special Forces Soldiers engaged a Jaish al-Mahdi death squad (better known as Mahdi Army). The U.S. soldiers killed 16 or 17, captured 17, destroyed a weapons cache and rescued a badly beaten hostage. This sounds like a successful operation,

except for the fact that in the time it took for the soldiers to get back to their base—less than one hour—the death squad soldiers had returned to the scene, cleaned up the mess, and rearranged the bodies of their fallen comrades to make it look like they were unarmed in the middle of prayer when they were murdered by American soldiers. They put out pictures and press releases in Arabic and English showing the alleged atrocity. The U.S. unit filmed its entire action and could prove this is not what happened. And yet it took almost three days before the U.S. military attempted to tell its side of the story in the media. By then it was too late—the desired damage had been done. What is worse, the Army was forced to launch an investigation that lasted 30 days during which time the battalion was out of commission.[15]

It is not enough to prevail on the ground if the world doesn't know about it. The enemy is playing by different rules, which we ignore at our peril; we don't need Sun Tzu or any other sage to tell us. Peace will be lost if the perpetrators of war get to tell what happens, seizing the initiative. Ambassador Freeman had noted that perception is power. Or, as Bishop Berkeley, author of *esse est percipi* (to be is to be perceived) might have declared from his pulpit, in Latin for added ecclesiastic resonance, *percipi est potentia:* "to be perceived is power." Our enemies need no reminder: they've written the book on it. Literally. In Islamist ideology, deception is not only permitted but ordained: the end more than justifies the end—it dictates it.[16]

Public opinion, admittedly, generally does not condone deception. For that reason, some otherwise truth-averse states pay at least a modicum of lip service to it, mainly for the benefit of outsiders though also to a large extent, if rather less convincingly, for domestic purposes. Russia, China, Iran, and North Korea fit that mold, though they are hardly alone. The monolithic leadership of these (risibly) nominal democracies still resorts to censorship, subterfuge, and, especially (though, again, not exclusively) for foreign consumption, disinformation. Censorship continues, with particular effectiveness in North Korea, the most (deliberately) isolated society on earth. Information warfare is used routinely by all these regimes to target not merely foreign but domestic audiences, and for good reason, since their illegitimacy implicitly forces them into a perpetual state of war.

Disinformation is not just lying, nor mere spin, let alone the sort of propaganda that every government (including our own) routinely produces to make itself look good. Former State Department advisor on Soviet Affairs Paul Goble, referring mainly to Russia, describes it as "always a conscious policy and part of a larger policy agenda,"[17] which blends (mostly) truth and useful falsehood for as long as it is effective. Then once the brew reaches maximum toxicity to the point of incredulity, it is modified or even abandoned, but it will have already served its purpose. Russian president, Vladimir Putin, for one, is using it with great skill, remarkable even for a former KGB agent, and not only to raise his popularity at home, for "it has been even more successful beyond that country's borders,"[18] according to Goble. Putin has proved spectacularly adept at using everything he has to make himself powerful, and raise his country's global profile despite its disastrous economic and demographic situation. He blends ruthless suppression of dissenters, especially in the media and the political opposition, through beatings and murder, with false messaging that promotes the regime's narrative on key issues. Even considering his luck in encountering no opposition from a flat-footed United States, Putin's performance is impressive. By contrast, the Western response is impressively dismal.

Russian journalist, now London-based TV producer, Peter Pomerantsev, an expert on Russian disinformation, cites what to us, though obviously not to everyone, are outright preposterous stories, perpetrated by the Kremlin about Ukraine and now Syria. Pomerantsev concludes that here in the West "we have little understanding of the Kremlin's 'weaponization of information.'"[19] This entails a skillful synchronization between lethality and mendacity, brazenly used in the occupation of Crimea and the invasion of Donetsk, the downing of a Malaysian airliner, and the massive bombing of Syrian territory, ostensibly against Daesh, but in fact against anyone opposed to Syrian president Bashir al-Assad.

The United States has all but ignored Russian media manipulation, despite its widely being seen as an intrinsic element of Putin's method of "hybrid warfare."[20] At first, the inattention was largely due to arrogance: why indeed should the United States pay any attention to pronouncements of a leader whose people die at an earlier average age than in Bangladesh? But once the erstwhile superpower now in rags and still smarting from the insult of losing its status, if not its missiles, attacked Georgia, and soon thereafter invaded and annexed Crimea, followed by fanning the flames of war in Western Ukraine, the attitude changed to abhorrence of stooping to nasty political "warfare." This ungentlemanly tactic was apparently anathema to some political appointees at the State Department, to say nothing of career FSO's (Foreign Service Officers) whose jobs could be jeopardized if they said something that might cause controversy.

The limited attempt by a handful of first-rate specialists to address Russian disinformation was thus soon quashed, despite having wasted over a year of time, energy, and money, to say nothing of the unmeasurable cost of doing nothing about the problem. This incredible move was ignored by the media except for one lone journalist, John P. Schindler, who wrote in *The Observer News* on November 5, 2015:

> Nearly a year ago, the State Department created a Counter-Disinformation Team, inside its Bureau of International Information Programs, as a small, start-up effort to resist Russian disinformation. Consisting of only a handful of staffers, it was supposed to expose the most laughable Moscow lies about America and the West that are disseminated regularly via RT and other outlets. They created a beta website and prepared to wage the struggle for truth online. Alas, their website never went live. Recently the State Department shut down the tiny Counter-Disinformation Team and any efforts by the Obama administration to resist Putin's propaganda can now be considered dead before birth. Intelligence Community sources tell me that it was closed out of a deep desire inside the White House "not to upset the Russians."[21]

The official in charge of that department was Rick Stengel, the Under Secretary for Public Diplomacy and Public Affairs, a veteran journalist who was brought into State two years ago, leaving his job as *TIME's* editor. Comments Schindler: "What role, if any, Stengel played in shutting down the State Department's tiny effort to resist Kremlin lies is unclear. A lot about what happened here is murky and Congress may want to ask a few questions about this sorry tale of governmental dysfunction."[22] Congress, take heed: hearings are very much in order.[23]

Europeans, by contrast, are taking the Russian disinformation campaign very seriously. There is growing concern that Russia is preparing the informational environment in Europe for possibly imminent invasion of such countries as the Baltics and other former regions of the now-defunct USSR. Not known for hyperbolic rhetoric, NATO's Supreme Allied Commander General Philip Breedlove has accused Russia of engaging in "the most amazing information warfare blitzkrieg we have ever seen in the history of information warfare."[24] In response, NATO has just established a Strategic Communication Center of Excellence, which hosted a Public Diplomacy Forum in August, 2015, where NATO Deputy Secretary General Ambassador Alexander Vershbow charged that "Russia has torn up the international rule book." The Ambassador then called for a firm and robust response, acknowledging

that "we have become used to Russian propaganda: an endlessly changing storyline designed to obfuscate and confuse."[25]

But he did not stop there: Vershbow set Russia alongside Al Qaeda
and Daesh, noting that during the past year, the Western alliance has
seen the new threats develop

> a significant new dimension. Whether we look to the East or the
> South, they include sophisticated propaganda and disinformation.
> Rarely have we had to deal with such well-financed, well-orchestrated,
> slick and unrelenting information and media campaigns. These
> campaigns use our open societies to try to undermine our values, to
> confuse and demoralize us. Fed by social media, the internet and the
> proliferation of new media outlets, propaganda is part and parcel of
> what we call hybrid warfare.[26]

While Russia's sophistication is the result of longstanding experience,
newcomers Al Qaeda and now Daesh, along with its ever-growing list
of affiliates, are also incredibly effective at gaining converts—a point
no longer contested even by those who seek (however unsuccessfully)
to minimize their relative global danger. The radical Islamists' communication weapon of choice is social media, with grisly videos that
demonstrate the jihadists' prowess to impress sympathizers while
simultaneously intimidating enemies. "This is a struggle for hearts and
minds, an effort to divide us, to pit one radical version of Islam against
all other faiths, and to undermine trust and confidence in our values
and our democracies,"[27] declares Vershbow.

How to respond? Not with "more propaganda, but only with the truth
and facts," he argues; for "credibility is our biggest asset to counter hybrid
communications." Pomerantsev, however, disagrees; while certainly
not opposed to truthful reporting, nor in favor of crass propaganda, he
scoffs at the "residual, 20th-century belief that Russian propaganda can
be countered by delivering 'real information' to audiences,"[28] as was—
and still is—the approach of Radio Free Europe/Radio Liberty. After
all, what good is it to offer "truth" to targets of Russian disinformation
whose sense of "truth" has already been cauterized? Instead, he argues
for giving them "the analytical tools to understand how they are being
psychologically manipulated by Kremlin media. Is there a media version
of Penn and Teller out there—a program that could debunk propaganda
the way the duo demystifies magic tricks?"[29] A splendid idea. Any takers?

The same may be said of many who become targets of messaging
produced by jihadists, who take full advantage of the news-cacophony

produced by the revolution in electronic communication. Yet Vershbow's juxtaposition of Russian and jihadist means of conducting information warfare obscures one fundamental difference: while the Russians are more interested in sowing confusion and attacking the notion of objectivity altogether, the jihadists' main goals are recruitment and intimidation in the name of Allah's Truth, all the while playing fast and loose with the actual facts. (Actually, it's Allah's Truth as seen by the particular jihadist sect releasing the specific message, whether by video, tweet, email, or some other medium.) That said, their ultimate aim is essentially the same as the Kremlin's: to undermine Western, and especially American, values and influence—in brief, to thwart the chances of success for a peace that has room for us all.

But if the State Department cancels a perfectly fine program of combating Russian disinformation that is ready to go live, after spending two years preparing it, for no discernible reason, can we expect it to competently engage Jihadist disinformation? Anthony H. Cordesman certainly hopes so:

> Far too often, the US seems to deal with conspiracy theories by trying to ignore them and hoping they will go away. No one who actually works with even well-educated Arabs can believe this works. The US needs to aggressively refute conspiracy efforts by publicizing the facts and doing so repeatedly.[30]

But in order to engage the jihadists in a dialogue of ideas we have to listen carefully, and then address their claims patiently. Better still, "we" may not be the right interlocutors at all, so much as the facilitators of such a dialogue which needs to take place, after all, within the Muslim community itself.[31] In any case, before saying, or doing, anything on the global scene, the most important thing that we have to do is to listen. And that takes humility.

Former Voice of America director Robert R. Reilly has it right:

> The State Department's new Undersecretary for Public Diplomacy, Rick Stengel, said in a recent speech that, "there is no battle of ideas with ISIL. ISIL is bereft of ideas, they're bankrupt of ideas. It's not an organization that is animated by ideas. It's a criminal, savage, barbaric organization." This is hugely mistaken. It's giving up while sounding tough. As one Islamic State fighter in Syria said,
>
> Before you defeat your enemy you must understand it. This is the first rule in combat and these idiots missed it. It is not enough for the West

to call these people barbarians. Recall that Adolph Hitler exclaimed, "We are barbarians. We want to be barbarians. It is an honorable title."

Calling Hitler a barbarian was useless. In the Nazi case, it was the ideology making barbarism honorable that had to be attacked in a war of ideas. With ISIS, we must object not only to their barbaric acts but to the Quranic principles that inspire and justify them.[32]

Engaging your enemy seriously means taking the time to understand both what he considers to be true and why he acts as he does. It also means figuring out what tactics work to minimize if not eliminate the source of his power over those who are yet to be convinced. Sheer name-calling is among the least effective tactics.

In an excellent article detailing how the United States should tackle Daesh, political warfare specialist J. Michael Waller recommends concentrating "less on the information aspect of the conflict (narrative) and more on the psychological aspect (changes in thought processes and behavior)." And what that entails, among other things, is "knowledge and understanding of the ideology or ideologies that motivate individuals, groups, and organizations to act as an enemy."[33] To do that, "first, the US must follow Sun Tzu's principle of knowing the enemy. [But unfortunately,] 'we do not understand the movement, and until we do, we are not going to defeat it,' Major General Michael K. Nagata reportedly said in confidential minutes leaked to the *New York Times*. 'We have not defeated the idea. We do not even understand the idea.'"[34] To understand, you have to listen, in every sense of that word. And that takes humility.

Humility was the one virtue that Benjamin Franklin had found hardest to conquer. To his credit, he eventually admitted failure— hence paradoxically managing to prove himself wrong. If he and his fellow Founders excelled in one thing, it was the constant awareness of the disparate ratio between their own abilities and the daunting challenges that confronted them and their fledgling nation. Living in those momentous times, humility to them was no mere catechism but an existential requirement. Overestimating either their personal capabilities or their resources risked placing themselves and their countrymen at risk of potentially irreversible defeat.

Being humble, however, is not only a personal attitude—a feeling of not being superior to other people—it is above all a recognition that one's judgments might be flawed because we cannot be omniscient, and yet that decisions must be taken, some of which affect other people.

Humility therefore has a profound moral dimension. But its basis is cognitive: for since everyone's perceptions are necessarily incomplete, affected by personal perspective and idiosyncrasies of character, no one is exempt from what intelligence analysts call *cognitive bias*.[35] One important way to avoid intelligence errors caused by unconscious self-deception is by trying to put oneself into someone else's psychological and circumstantial "shoes"—in short, by listening.

Strangely, that is something we Americans tend to find rather difficult—and not necessarily, or at least not only, because we think we are better than everyone else. Rather, we tend to assume that whatever works for us will also work for others, so why not save everybody a lot of trouble and lead straight to the finish line. How else to explain the mindset leading to the Iraq war which assumed that once the country was free of its dictator, all it had to do was write a new constitution, get on with the business of democracy, and have a nice day.

In truth, the ad hoc approach to postwar stabilization and reconstruction is nothing particularly new. According to Colonel Walter Hudson, after 1945, the army acted not only as a postwar diplomatic corps, but actually engaged in every aspect of governance, including managing refugees, disarming combatants to do public works, secure public safety, organize cultural affairs, not to mention economic and business activities, to say nothing of spying. While these efforts were for the most part successful, they were essentially improvised.[36]

And then, we did what we do best: put all that unpleasantness behind us. As soon as the engagement ended, the Americans went home and proceeded promptly to hope they would never have to do such a thing again—affectionately, with no more than a mere tinge of contempt, known as the Ostrich Policy.[37] Is it any wonder that Vietnam caught us unprepared? Today, after the equally ad hoc, unsuccessful military-led governance activities we reluctantly undertook, there is a very good chance that once again the reaction will be placing our heads in the proverbial sand. Writes James J. Carafano, the Heritage Foundation's head of foreign policy studies: "There is a danger in that rejecting the messiness of Iraq and Afghanistan, too many will argue—as we did after almost every armed conflict—the answer is 'just never do that again.' That thinking is a prescription for unpreparedness and repeating the mistakes of the past."[38] Once again, we don't need Sun Tzu to tell us as much. But the danger is everpresent.

The current strategic retrenchment indicates that the same Vietnam-era mindset has taken hold. And it is one more example of self-deception, exacerbated by an inability to listen. The self-described Islamic State may not have landed on American shores, but can we fail *not* to listen to its rhetoric, and recognize its similarities to that of Al Qaeda and other Islamist jihadist ideologies? Did President Obama really listen before deciding to leave Iraq abruptly in 2011? As New York University professor Stuart Gottlieb writes in the *National Interest*,

> While Obama was celebrating America's withdrawal as evidence that he "ended the Iraq war" with America's 'head held high,' radical Islamist movements were comparing it to the Soviet defeat in Afghanistan in 1989; the American defeat in Somalia in 1993; and even to America's defeat in Vietnam.[39]

Listening takes more than just hearing—though that's a good start. It should lead to insights into the nature of the communication, the context, and thus offer at least a hint of probable reactions to the response. That did not happen; for however determined the president may have been to signal America's peaceful intentions, he seems only to have emboldened the murderous jihadists. Continues Gottlieb:

> None of this is to imply that the United States should be on a permanent war footing, fighting every jihadi group, large and small, all over the world. Nor is it to imply that the United States can simply throw up its hands, say the world is too complicated, and take its global leadership ball and go home (even that would not save the United States from being in the "far enemy" category). It is, however, to remind us that the most important maxim in fighting a war is to know one's enemy. After years insisting that "Al Qaeda is on the path to defeat," the Obama administration now recognizes that despite the death of bin Laden, "bin Ladenism" is alive and well, and expanding.

Were the president to truly listen to and thus understand the message of that "bin Ladenism" he dares not name, he might notice that the United States is certainly in the "far enemy" category that would warrant listening to Sun Tzu's maxim that knowing one's enemy must come first. What comes second is understanding his strategy so that it may be undermined. Not listening to it will make it impossible to undermine and deflect the danger.

Aside from failing to defeat enemies, listening also helps secure friends. For listening indicates that you consider it worthwhile to give someone the attention and care to communicate properly and effectively. The most tried-and-true method of losing friends unnecessarily is by showing a lack of respect. We are pretty good at that, especially since we often don't realize we're doing it. Lack of respect manifests itself in many ways, but failing to listen is one of the most insidious. Unaware of our own self-righteousness bordering on condescension, we sometimes end up behaving like haughty colonizers even if we consciously abhor the practice. For it seems that whenever we intervene beyond our borders, whether we call it foreign aid or nation-building or whatever else, partly not to waste time but also to get on with results, we fail to do what it takes to incorporate local practices, allow traditional ways to adapt to new ideas, and give the population a sense of pride and ownership. In too big a hurry to pursue what we are convinced is the best solution, before giving the matter even a second thought, we fail to remember the old truth that teaching someone to fish is not only the gift of a lifetime but acknowledges another's sense of dignity. It might take longer than catching the thing itself, but the extra bit of time will preclude the potential need to come back to catch him another—to say nothing of preventing resentment that results from wounded pride.

If that last point again sounds like common sense, it's because it is. So is almost everything else that has to happen for America to rebalance its approach to winning the peace—at least in theory. The tough part will be to overcome conceptual and bureaucratic inertia, along with bucking long-entrenched interests that are too comfortable with the status quo. But since the alternative to doing nothing is unacceptable, it's worth a try to at least indicate the way to go. Or should we say, the *tao*.

Notes

1. Stearman, "Lessons Learned from Vietnam," 113. The best description of the perverse role played by US media can be found in what I consider to be the best of all books on the Vietnam War, *Vietnam at War, The History 1946–1975*, by Lieutenant General Phillip B. Davidson, US Army (Retired) (New York and Oxford: Oxford University Press, 1988).
2. Ibid., 116.
3. http://www.loc.gov/rr/program/bib/ourdocs/Alien.html
4. Adams may well have regretted signing it. John P. Diggins, in *John Adams: The American Presidents Series: The 2nd President, 1797–1801* (New York: MacMillan Press, 2003), notes that some historians believe he had "no complicity in framing the acts," while others point to his complaints that attacks on the presidency were "libelous." pp. 110–1.
5. "That was already the conventional wisdom in 1976, according to a column that year by Russell Baker in *The New York Times*." Geoffrey Nunberg, "And, Yes, He Was a Great Communicator," *The New York Times*, June 13, 2004.

http://www.nytimes.com/2004/06/13/weekinreview/and-yes-he-was-a-great-communicator.html

6. Citation by the Public Diplomacy Council. http://www.publicdiplomacycouncil.org/commentaries/09-29-15/quotable-bryan-leese-%E2%80%9Ceveryone-player%E2%80%9D-information-element-power (Emphasis added).

7. Luttrell, *Lone Survivo*, 169.

8. Ibid., 170–1.

9. Feith, *War and Decision*, 139–40.

10. Ibid., 171.

11. Ibid.

12. Walter Douglas, "Public Diplomacy for a New Era," in Craig Cohen and Josiane Gabel, eds., *2012 Global Forecast—Risk, Opportunity, and the Next Administration*, 86.

13. Ibid., 177.

14. Rand Waltzman, "The U.S. Is Losing the Social Media War," *Time*, October 12, 2015. http://time.com/4064698/social-media-propaganda/

15. Ibid.

16. For an excellent, concise overview of Islamist uses of disinformation, see Raymond Ibrahim's "Islam's Doctrines of Deception," *Middle East Forum*, October 2008. http://www.meforum.org/2095/islams-doctrines-of-deception

17. Paul Goble, "Lies, Damned Lies and Russian Disinformation," *Jamestown Foundation.org*, August 13, 2014. http://www.jamestown.org/single/?tx_ttnews%5Btt_news%5D=42745#.Vg3JSnpViko

18. Ibid.

19. Peter Pomerantsev, "Inside Putin's Information War," *Politico*, January 4, 2015. http://www.politico.com/magazine/story/2015/01/putin-russia-tv-113960_Page3.html#ixzz3nMcNr2Hy

20. "Many in the West use the term hybrid to describe Russian actions, noting that hybrid actions use hard and soft tactics. The Russian military does not use the term to describe its own actions." Timothy Thomas, "Russia's Military Strategy and Ukraine: Indirect, Asymmetric—and Putin-Led," *Journal of Slavic Military Studies*, 28, 2015, p. 454.

21. John R. Schindler, "Obama Fails to Fight Putin's Propaganda Machine," *Observer*, November 5, 2015.

22. Ibid.

23. Progress, *mirabile dictu*, appears to be in the offing. An amendment to Rules Committee Print 114-51, introduced on May 17, 2016, by Cong. Mac Thornberry, provides for the establishment of a Global Engagement Center, one of whose principal functions would be "countering foreign propaganda and misinformation that threatens United States national security." http://amendments-rules.house.gov/amendments/GECv3517161723182318.pdf

24. John Vandiver, "SACEUR: Allies must prepare for Russia 'hybrid war,'" *Stars and Stripes*, September 4, 2014. http://www.stripes.com/news/saceur-allies-must-prepare-for-russia-hybrid-war-1.301464

25. "Meeting the Strategic Communications Challenge," Remarks by NATO Deputy Secretary General Ambassador Alexander Vershbow at the Public Diplomacy Forum 2015. http://www.nato.int/cps/en/natohq/opinions_117556.htm?selectedLocale=en

26. He adds: "Russia devotes an estimated 100 million Euros a year to media operations. According to some accounts, it employs no fewer than 12 advertising agencies. It has established new state-controlled media, such as Russia Today and the new news agency Sputnik, available in Europe, North America and around the world. These outlets broadcast in English, French, German and other NATO languages." Ibid.

27. Ibid.

28. Pomerantsev, "Inside Putin's Information War."

29. Ibid.

30. Anthony H. Cordesman, "The Islamic State war: Strategic Communications Require a Strategy," in *The Islamic State and Information Warfare: Defeating ISIS and the Broader Global Jihadist Movement* (Washington, DC: The Threat Knowledge Group, Jan. 2015), 25. http://thegorkabriefing.com/report-the-islamic-state-and-information-warfare-defeating-isis-and-the-broader-global-jihadist-movement/

31. See Fareed Zakharia, *The Future of Freedom: Illiberal Democracy at Home and Abroad* (New York: W. W. Norton, 2007), esp. ch. 4 "The Islamic Exception," 119 ff.

32. Robert R. Reilly, "Measuring Success in the War of Ideas," in *The Islamic State and Information Warfare*, 5.

33. J. Michael Waller, "Designing Information Warfare Campaign against the Global Jihadi Movement," in *The Islamic State and Information Warfare*, 38.

34. Eric Schmitt, "In Battle to Defeating ISIS, U.S. Targets Its Psychology," *New York Times*, December 28, 2014.

35. "A cognitive bias does not result from any emotional or intellectual predisposition toward a certain judgment, but rather from subconscious mental procedures for processing information." Richard Heuer, *Psychology of Intelligence Analysis* (Washington, DC: CIA, 2007), ch. 9. https://www.cia.gov/library/center-for-the-study-of-intelligence/csi-publications/books-and-monographs/psychology-of-intelligence-analysis/art12.html

36. Col. Walter Hudson, *Army Diplomacy: American Military Occupation and Foreign Policy after World War II* (Lexington: University Press of Kentucky, 2015).

37. Jan Klabbers, *Treaty Conflict and the European Union* (Cambridge: Cambridge University Press, 2009), 219.

38. James J. Carafano, "Here's a Blueprint for Not Wasting the Win," *Army Magazine*, October 19, 2015. http://www.armymagazine.org/2015/10/19/november-2015-book-reviews/

39. Stuart Gottlieb, "Four Reasons ISIS Is a Threat to the American Homeland," *The National Interest*, September 20, 2014. http://nationalinterest.org/print/feature/four-reasons-isis-threat-the-american-homeland-11317?page=2

IV

Rebalancing to Win the Peace

In order to either prevent or prevail in a conflict, Sun Tzu tells us, you must know your enemy and yourself. For that, you need good intelligence as well as the ability to act on it, to interact in productive ways, influencing and engaging in culturally disparate environments. Since the principal governmental organization in charge of diplomacy, the State Department and its junior partner, USAID, are both in a shambles and seemingly incapable to learn from their mistakes, these civilian agencies must be radically reformed. We must learn to listen better and engage effectively, based on truthful information, vigorously combating disinformation and lies, while conducting productive strategically targeted conversations that resonate culturally.

The intelligence community, having suffered many setbacks, must become less disdainful of open-source information, while simultaneously increasing the analytical skills of its operators and set much higher priority on human contacts. Sun Tzu and Washington knew this; it's common sense. Networking is key; to that end, the private sector and other government agencies have the potential to add enormously to the common understanding and connectivity across the globe. Strategic goals can be attained far more efficiently by a whole-of-society approach than by top-down, compartmentalized command-style management.

Strategic peace-building is not a form of charity; the role of government is to protect its people and keep the peace while seeking to advance peace elsewhere, but not without specific and clear objectives. Humanitarian assistance can and does have strategic significance, though it is best left to the private sector, with government serving primarily to facilitate strategy and coordination. The doomed terminology of "democracy-building" and "nation building" might be replaced by peace-building, which cannot be successful without strong local buy-in, properly monitored to guard against corruption. Though people can be influenced, we fool ourselves if we think we can force them to want something when they don't. America's Founders showed the world how true that is.

Peace-building is not colonialism, nor imperialism. We are not occupiers; if anything, we Americans have preferred to govern ourselves, and be left alone to pursue happiness as we saw fit. But American global disengagement was never an option; it became increasingly less so. To be sure, engagement can be done well or badly; above all, it must be realistic—meaning, based on reality. Wishful thinking that opposes military engagement on principle, assuming that peace will break out if we don't bother anyone, is equally as unrealistic as is the notion that since overwhelming force can win wars, it is bound to win the peace too. Not so.

Realism is predicated on pursuing the national interest. But Americans have always been committed to freedom and self-government: it's who we are. We happen to believe that such ideals are eminently rational and practical, leading to the greatest prosperity and security. It's the kind of peace worth fighting for. If this be idealism, it is exceptionally realistic and effective: like water flowing downward, it can move boulders.

14

Strategic Dialogue

The wound of words is worse than the wound of swords.
—Arabian proverb

*That totalitarians will seek to seize control of the language of
politics is obvious; that our own foreign affairs establishment
should remain blind to what is happening is dangerous.*
—Senator Daniel Patrick Moynihan, "Further
Thoughts on Words and Foreign Policy," 1979

*[P]ublic relations was invented in the United States, yet we are miser-
able at communicating to the rest of the world what we are about as a
society and a culture, about freedom and democracy, about our policies and our goals. It is just plain embarrassing that al-Qaeda is better
at communicating its message on the internet than America.*
—Robert R. Gates, Landon Lecture, November 26, 2007

Sun Tzu's dictum that the most skillful way to defeat an enemy is to
undermine his strategy implies that all instruments of power should be
used, seeking to avoid bloodshed. Foremost among those instruments
is communication. And while Sun Tzu spends far more time in his book
on actions rather than language, it goes without saying that actions,
too, communicate. In fact, they do so at least as effectively as words,
and may be steered strategically to achieve desired effects. Not to put
too fine a point on it, speech *is itself* a form of action, and an especially
potent kind at that. (The Arabian proverb "*The wound of words is worse
than the wound of swords*" is not merely figurative.)

Sun Tzu recommends that if you wish to stultify and confuse your
enemy, you should do whatever works best, which, as we saw in chapter 1,
entails resorting to opposites: "When capable, feign incapacity; when
active, inactivity" (*AoW* I. 18). "Feigning" is a form of deception, but
as the saying goes, in love and war all bets are off. If we in the West
hesitate to engage in outright deception, our enemies aren't. This is

263

not to say that we should resort to similar tactics, especially given how easily they can backfire. But it does suggest that in a robust engagement, particularly when it takes place in the realm of ideas, the rule is: may the best minds win.

No "Machiavellian" anything-goes end-justifies-the-means strategist, Sun Tzu in no way advocates short-sighted ruthlessness—especially since, for him, "the end" of warfare is never a photo op: there is always life after the last battle, commonly known as peace, which must be worth winning to be lasting and to earn the support of its constituents, which doesn't happen in a flash. Earning support takes trust, and trust takes time. It also takes having the qualities deserving of trust. In the absence of such qualities, any victory is likely to prove ephemeral. For that reason, Sun Tzu lists among the initial estimates of what it takes to evaluate any specific situation, along with geographic and other objective considerations, as important are moral influence and "command," which refer to a leader's humanity and compassion.

These issues, which all must be addressed, relate to the moral fiber of the opponent as much as one's own. To undermine an enemy's strategy even before it has been implemented, it helps to understand the weaknesses of his command. Conversely, to succeed in a confrontation, one has to consolidate one's own morale, solidifying one's own constituency to strengthen its resolve and dedication. Hence Sun Tzu implicitly favored confusing the enemy—for "a confused army leads to another's victory" (*AoW* III. 23)—while simultaneously insuring that one's own army does not itself fall prey to confusion, a victim to the same principle.

What Sun Tzu calls "confusion" of the enemy is commonly produced by effective strategic communication, predicated on a profound understanding of human nature. Sun Tzu commentator Tu Mu, citing Duke Li Ching of Wei, explains that if one is destined to be victorious, "its victories [are won] before seeking battle" (*AoW* IV. 14) by using non-hard power. The Duke, like Sun Tzu, believed the "supreme requirements" of leadership include not only "clear perception" but "a profound strategy coupled with far-reaching plans, an understanding of the seasons and an ability to examine the human factors."[1] That examination must then be put to good use. The far-reaching plans of a "profound strategy" must encompass all aspects of strategic communication—which cannot be in the form of a one-way monologue that falls on deaf ears, but must be able to influence. And no one can influence without first listening. All effective communication is thus ultimately a form of genuine dialogue.

The second step of a "profound strategy" is disrupting an enemy's alliances. As ninth-century Sun Tzu commentator Tu Yu puts it: "Do not allow your enemies to get together."[2] In the realm of ideas, this can mean taking advantage of ideological and religious schisms to pit enemies against one another, thereby deflecting their ire away from oneself, toward each other. More generally, however, the management of alliances, both those of the enemy and of one's own, is a matter for diplomacy, which was obviously very high on Sun Tzu's priorities among the instruments of statecraft.

Considering how well our Founders understood such relatively simple, straightforward ideas even without any exposure to Sun Tzu, it is not a little depressing to contemplate how much we have unlearned. True, the world is far more complex now; but on the other hand think of how much better resources we have now than before. Perhaps our biggest problem is that we think ourselves too high and mighty: our sole-superpower status has gone to our heads. Worse, we are now carrying a heavy baggage of entrenched bureaucratic habits of behavior and thought we had been mercifully spared at the outset. It is hard to think out of the box when you've been inside it too long; it begins to feel like home. We might start by redefining things—like war and peace, hard and soft power, information and intelligence, etc.—take a deep breath, clear our heads, and go back the basics.

Understandably, in the immediate aftermath of 9/11, semantics was the last thing on the minds of America's leadership. Ambassador Richard Holbrooke wrote on October 28, 2001: "Call it public diplomacy, or public affairs, or psychological warfare, or—if you really want to be blunt—propaganda. But whatever it is called, defining what this war is really about in the minds of the one billion Muslims in the world will be of decisive and historic importance."[3] He was right about the last point; but he grossly underestimated the importance of semantics—and specifically the need to be clear about the functions of government agencies whose job it is to engage in dialogue with the rest of the world. So far, the results have been appallingly dismal.

Not that policy experts haven't tried to do something. Countless reports have been written, most highly informative and thoughtful, on the topic of reforming the government's now mainly nonexistent efforts in what Christopher Paul calls "strategic communication"—which, as we saw in chapter 6, he defines "as coordinated actions, messages, images, and other forms of signaling or engagement intended to inform, **influence**, or persuade selected audiences in support of national objectives."[4] Paul reports that one-third of those reports "advocate the development of a clearly defined overall strategy. Such calls range from the very general ('this country should identify what it stands for and communicate this message clearly')[5] to the specific. Multiple GAO [General Accountability Office] reports . . . [for example, ask] how DOS intends to implement public diplomacy in the Muslim world,"[6] etc. But so long as our goals are unclear, the specifics will not and cannot be forthcoming. And so long as the organization whose principal job it is to engage in the global conversation, the DOS, is not radically reformed, reports will sit on shelves, no matter how brilliant their recommendations.

Recall at this point Sun Tzu's concept of constant change, of fluidity, in every environment, not only on the battlefield or in a conflict situation—which demands especially nimble adaptation—but at all times. The imperatives to recalibrate, reassess plans and tactics, apply lessons learned, and go with the evolving flow are key to his approach. Unfortunately, this is hard to do in the unwieldy and bureaucratic morass that is the US government. What is more, Sun Tzu regarded constantly evaluating performance to be absolutely critical: taking stock of what works and what doesn't, above all, *why*, should be routine prior to, and throughout the course of, any endeavor. This is common sense managerial practice. Why wouldn't one try to learn from past mistakes, that of others no less than one's own, and prevent repeating the same blunders? And yet, there you have it; one may safely say it's the default mode of all bureaucracy, in direct proportion to its size.

There are many reasons why evaluation is hard. In the first place, problems must be assessed honestly and clearly, which implies recognizing that they exist. This is hard not only because human beings are loath to admit mistakes; it is also genuinely difficult to avoid self-delusion when one isn't aware of it. (That's what makes self-delusion delusional, or at any rate, deceptive.) Add to that the propensity to cover up and sweep under the rug; bureaucracies have raised that to an art. Then too, the problem has to be evaluated as objectively as possible—that is, the assessor should not stand to gain in any way from one set of results over another. In many instances, this is nearly impossible, as evaluators tend to also be competitors, have pet theories to defend, or are not disinterested for some other reason, like having a relationship to the organization being evaluated, in what is a relatively small field. In addition, the right assessment must be tested for professionalism and accuracy; yet too often the evaluators lack the requisite knowledge and experience. What is more, they may not be given access to all the relevant information.

As if this weren't sufficient, there is the fact that to be useful, an assessment must be accessible; gathering dust on shelves or languishing in password-protected or otherwise insulated archives is as good as not existing in the first place. After all, the assessment has to actually be accessed by the relevant parties who are supposed to heed the lessons. (Assuming, of course, that they are open to doing something better, and differently than in the past.) And finally, the lessons must be acted upon. This is the hardest step of all, especially for bureaucracies, whose legendary inertia is exceeded only by the number of congressional committees assigned to oversee them. To be sure, none of these obstacles, however daunting, amount to logical impossibility. Each is potentially rectifiable. But it takes imaginative and concerted effort, seriously enforced.

The agency usually considered responsible for seeking to avert the danger of war while serving America's national interest is of course the US Department of State. Unfortunately, it also appears to be among the least inclined to mend its ways. A search on www.state.gov for "lessons learned," for example, will bring up numerous odd entries, the latest on lessons from the Everest earthquake in Nepal, followed closely by a link to "Teaching English to Mothers of Visually Impaired Children" (undated). Anyone wondering whether any lessons were learned from Benghazi will be routed to the testimony of State officials William J. Burns and Thomas Nides before the Senate Committee on Foreign Relations, from December 2012, when both officials promise that a report will eventually be released. Four years later, no such report is mentioned; if the State Department has learned any lessons, from Benghazi or anywhere else, is mostly left to Congress to figure out.

It seems that lessons never do make much of an impression on the State Department. Several years earlier, in 2007, for example, the Government Accountability Office had concluded that State's "Evacuation Planning and Preparations for Overseas Posts Can Be Improved." The reasons were stated plainly:

> State's evacuation preparations are constrained by the lack of a systematic process to collect, analyze, and incorporate evacuation lessons learned. Almost 60 percent of posts evacuated in the past 5 years said they did not produce an evacuation 'after action' report, as required. Further, State has no entity to ensure posts are producing after action reports and no formal review process to analyze and incorporate

lessons learned from these reports into guidance and training. Although State has developed some documents on evacuation lessons learned and distributed them to all U.S. overseas posts, the documents are sometimes vague and can be overlooked by posts due to the volume of material they receive. Limited institutional memory of prior evacuations at posts reinforces the need for a process to collect, analyze, and disseminate lessons learned from evacuations to all post staff.[7]

Lack of interest in evaluation at State evidently extends even to the investigation of criminal cases. As Stuart W. Bowen, SIGIR, told Congress:

> [O]ne of my investigators, working jointly with the FBI on a criminal case, recently was refused information by the State Department regarding a potential subject (who is a State employee). State directed my investigator to use the "audit process" to obtain this investigative information. Worse, he was challenged as to whether the information, which he had requested in good faith, was even related to "reconstruction funding." This development is just the latest quandary in a predicament-filled year, during which the State Department has repeatedly raised fallacious objections to varying SIGIR requests.[8]

This is unacceptable. It is high time that State evaluate itself seriously; the results, in turn, must have follow-up—which requires presidential leadership as well as congressional support.

This is how former NSC official Kori Schake, now Research Fellow at the Hoover Institution, describes DOS's inability to self-evaluate: "Sadly, the culture of the State Department is not attuned to the importance of after-action reviews that roughly critique performance."[9] Not that it doesn't have some idea of its shortcomings: DOS's own QDDR, released in 2010, admits that it has reacted to "each successive conflict or crisis by reinventing the process for identifying agency leadership, establishing task forces, and planning and coordinating U.S. government agencies,"[10] which amounts to little more than an assertion of failure and inability to work with others. Schake is right to wonder: "yet they believe they should lead the interagency process."[11]

For years, studies and reports have produced substantive, useful, and sympathetic recommendations that could lead to reform. But they have been ignored—as indeed have the department's own promises from the 2010 QDDR. It seems that all DOS ever does is ask for more money and an increase in staff—though too often without specific justification for either, demonstrating a spectacular inability to reach out to Congress to make its case. Redressing the deficiencies affecting the nation's foreign affairs professionals should be a top priority for the national security community, but it clearly isn't. Although since 2003 three secretaries of state have increased the number of diplomats, there is no evidence of improved performance. Schake explains: "This connects back to the department's culture. It is assigning personnel to the functions it values rather than the functions for which the personnel were justified and funded."[12]

Not that the functions DOS has traditionally valued are necessarily what its own employees consider paramount, now or ever. No one quite knows, because no one ever asks them. DOS's prospective employees too aren't queried; despite a huge interest in serving abroad, with a ratio of 16 applicants per one hire, DOS "does not survey their attitudes. There is no market research of the kind that assists military recruiting efforts. . . . it surveys only the composition of its hires (race, gender, education, years of work experience), not their motivations."[13] Nor are these attributes tracked at the outset; and mid-career hires don't help much, especially since more experienced people "from the outside" are deemed to have difficulty working successfully in the foreign service.[14]

If only the foreign service, and the civil servants who are supposed to complement their expertise, were doing such a great job; but they appear to have been set up for failure by DOS's own culture. For no matter how capable and motivated they may have been at the outset, DOS provides its hardworking and often underappreciated employees practically no additional training. The American Academy of Diplomacy (AAD), which consists of retired diplomats who seek to help their fellow professionals, has determined that the "traditional means of learning the skills of the diplomatic profession—on-the-job training and guidance from more senior officers—have lost much of their effectiveness."[15] The AAD reports that the deficiencies of, foreign service officers include:

> foreign language fluency, advanced area knowledge, leadership and management ability, negotiating and pre-crisis conflict mediation/resolution skills, job specific functional expertise, strategic planning, program development, implementation and evaluation, and budgeting.[16]

The fault is not individual but systemic: the State Department's inability to adapt to changing circumstance is one of the most important reasons why the United States lost the peace in Iraq. The verdict of the SIGIR in 2009 was that this "experience illustrates the extent to which civilian agencies do not have the capacity to project power abroad."[17] By then, his staff had already uncovered a great deal of waste and fraud, the result of incompetence and dysfunctional contract oversight by both DOS and USAID. Worse was yet to come, at staggering rates, resulting in incalculable damage to Americans and our allies, to say nothing of escalating terror at home and abroad.

In his introduction to the AAD report, Air Force Lt. Gen. (Ret.) Brent Scowcroft urges that "a thorough recalibration of the instruments of American international engagement is overdue."[18] But the recalibration will require not only the will and ability to provide additional training for the skills that used to be valued decades ago; at least as important is a reassessment of which skills are required in the twenty-first century. A very good illustration was inadvertently provided by the unauthorized release of a quarter million diplomatic cables: it turned out that most of them revealed relatively little new information, indicating that it was already available in open sources. Obviously, as Schake notes, "the enormous investment of time and effort in reporting by diplomatic posts is surely less valuable now that information is widely available by non-governmental means."[19] Few diplomats would not welcome a lighter reporting burden; but bureaucratic inertia stands in the way. Is everybody asleep at that switch? Would you please make the requisite update?

Maybe there is still hope. On February 3, 2016, DOS announced the opening of a Center for the Study of the Conduct of Diplomacy, based in Arlington, Virginia; the mission is to allow diplomats "to benefit from lessons learned and best practices" of the profession.[20] What sounds like good news, however, was dampened by the comments of former Deputy Secretary of State William Burns, now president of the Carnegie Endowment, who crowed that "our diplomats are delivering," citing the Iran deal, opening of relations with Cuba, among other similarly "controversial"[21] initiatives that critics have cited as excessively beneficial to the other side. "But we can't afford to rest on our laurels," added Burns. Now the next step is to learn not so much from our alleged—and highly dubious—"laurels" (what, exactly, did we get in return for opening relations with Cuba?) as from our mistakes. Though Ambassador Burns admitted that we'll have "to ask what we got right and [also] what we got wrong," it remains to be seen whether the Center admits there is anything in the latter category—let alone do something about it. It is highly encouraging that input will reportedly be sought not only from former diplomats but also from corporations, academia, policy groups, and philanthropy organizations. Let's hope it will be evenhanded; and, if so, even heeded.

All the criticism of DOS applies in spades to USAID, about which more in the next chapter. At bottom, the inability to assess our own resources and performance, listen to our staffs and understand what they need in order to do their jobs better, what works and what doesn't, is perhaps our biggest challenge. What makes it especially infuriating is that it wouldn't take that much effort; indeed, it would save money, lives, and—most critically—help secure the peace. Unfortunately, Bureaucracy (capitalized for emphasis and opprobrium) has its own momentum, and it has become a mill about the nation's neck that threatens to strangle it.

Do other agencies fare better? The military at least has a rather more impressive repository of studies and evaluation. For example, the United States Army Combined Arms Center (USACAC), headquartered at Fort Leavenworth, Kansas, in 2014 started offering a five-day course on Lessons Learned designed to train a target audience to include not only members of the military but also, pending space availability and approval, civilians, contractors, and even selected foreign military partners.[22] Perhaps such a course can be expanded throughout the nonmilitary sector, since the facilities at Fort Leavenworth cannot possibly accommodate all those who could profit from it.

Professional education is obviously important. Strategic communication, however, is never just about getting the message "right." Or, to put it differently, messaging connotes monologue, it is intrinsically one-way rather than interactive, while what we must do first and foremost, by contrast, is *listen*. It isn't something at which we Americans tend to excel, but it isn't rocket science.

A list of simple commandments in listening follows:

(1) Thou shalt find who your enemies are.
(2) Thou shalt not hesitate calling either an individual or a group 'an enemy.' It won't deter him (it) from being one.
(3) Thou shalt seek to understand the enemy's strategic thinking—and obviously engage the civilian world in this endeavor.
(4) Thou shalt gauge how enemies communicate their intentions, and how those messages are being received.
(5) Though shalt try to understand what resonates with their audiences, and why.
(6) Thou shalt not hesitate calling either an individual or a group 'an enemy,' and whether they might want to cooperate.

(7) Thou shalt assess what portion of your enemies' message contains any kernel of truth, and how much is stark disinformation susceptible to refutation.

(8) Thou shalt cultivate long-term assets through genuine good will and personal contact.

(9) Thou shalt network. And network some more.

(10) Thou shalt not let down your friends. If you are a good friend, you will have good friends. For that reason, be careful whom you befriend; distinguish between temporary alliances and solid friendships. The latter are few and far between, but they do exist.

Though listening does not imply either acquiescence or sympathy, it must include the ability and willingness to commit the cognitive leap needed to grasp the nature of the enemy's ideological and operational narrative. Nothing will sabotage listening more effectively than wishful thinking and mirror-imaging—the illusion that others think along the same lines as we do. It is not a sign of condescension, racism, or any other politically incorrect "ism" to face the reality that people approach the world with a wide variety of preconceived ideas. On the contrary: ignoring those ideas is a form of not-listening, which is presumptuous and disrespectful. If we believe those preconceptions to be wrong, it behooves us to take the time to learn how we might be able to correct and change them—at least, if we get a chance, before our enemies deny us the opportunity by unceremoniously obliterating us.

No part of the government is better equipped to listen than the intelligence community—and thank heavens for that—except that too much of what it listens to is not actual human beings, at least not directly, but through electronic or other indirect communications. This is much to be regretted. For as Sun Tzu pointed out, there is nothing quite as useful as "living agents," defined as people "who return with information" about a potential enemy—as well as, one might add, a potential friend. Adds the ninth-century Sun Tzu commentator and poet Tu Mu: "You must know the men employed by the enemy. Are they wise or stupid, clever or clumsy? Having assessed their qualities, you prepare appropriate measures."[23]

Human intentions (yes, *intentions*, subjectivity and all) are not only very important, they constitute arguably *the* most important relevant facts in analyzing social interactions that should interest policymakers. Intentions are obviously never easy to gauge, and we sometimes miss the mark. It is for that and many other reasons, that policymakers, no less than analysts, are tempted to resort to numbers, signals, and the like; after all, we are all products of the times. As Robert Baer, former CIA case officer, wrote in his autobiography, "few things are more satisfying for a policymaker than to hold in his hand a clean, glossy black-and-white satellite photo, examine it with his very own 3D viewer, and decide for himself what it means. Not only could he do without analysts, he could do without agents too. And thank goodness. Agents were messy. They sometimes got things wrong, even occasionally lied. And they definitely had the potential to cause ugly diplomatic incidents."[24] (This last danger is particularly likely when the agents know they are right, and could (indeed, in Baer's case, did) present evidence proving that the policymakers mishandled, or even deliberately ignored, security threats, an affliction that seems to cut across party lines.)

While Baer agrees that individual judgment is not without risk, he also believes, along with a good number of his colleagues, that personal experience, and well-honed intuition, cannot and should not be eliminated. If what we are after is understanding human behavior and motivation, "you've got to have human intelligence to do it—people on the ground, agents, access agents, a network of traitors, and a case officer willing and able to work it."[25] Someone, in other words, like Baer himself, who will do whatever it takes; or one like Henry Crumpton, who in 2005 became US Coordinator (with rank of ambassador) for Counterterrorism. Such people join the intelligence community (IC) for the right reasons, and will not shirk from the challenges.

It is no coincidence that Crumpton admired Sun Tzu for having "placed as much emphasis on self-awareness as on knowing the enemy. So did the ancient Greek philosophers, but I learned one important self-awareness lesson not from any writer or intelligence expert, but from an African boy."[26] Crumpton understood that valuable insight into human nature can be gained from even (perhaps, especially) the most modest sources. This is not to deny the value of theory. Quite the opposite: Crumpton later in his book expresses his gratitude to the Johns Hopkins School of Advanced International Studies (SAIS) for permitting him to learn and think at a more theoretical level. He nevertheless deemed Sun Tzu's focus on self-knowledge to be the most important part of his legendary admonition to "understand the enemy as well as oneself," as did the little African boy. Though it makes for a nifty bumper sticker, that saying is unfortunately seldom heeded.

In order to be able to influence, to affect someone else's mind, let alone heart, you must first understand your own. In their excellent study on "Cultural Knowledge for Intelligence Analysts," for example, three scientists specializing in cognition found that knowing oneself is a prerequisite first step to understanding others, especially at a deeper level. They note that what they call "cultural sensemaking" begins with having a solid general understanding of one's own culture and patterns of thinking so as to recognize differences from another's, and using that self-knowledge "as a basis for asking questions about another"— to be followed by identifying and using additional cultural mentors.[27] Self-knowledge, however, is elusive. Seeing oneself requires stepping outside of one's self—a rare skill set mastered by few.

Knowledge obviously includes far more than just spying. It includes both information and analysis that are widely available, in addition to understanding which can only be attained through experience. Sun Tzu would be appalled by the intelligence community's condescending attitude toward information available through open sources. The elaborate security clearance process (which, perhaps not coincidentally, still manages to let slip by the likes of Charles Snowden) exacerbates the apartheid culture pitting the lofty *Classified* against the lowly *Unclassified*, not to mention the very lowliest caste of *Non-Classified*. This is at best unfortunate, as General Mike Flynn charges in his no-holds-barred seminal article "Fixing Intel: A Blueprint for Making Intelligence Relevant in Afghanistan": "The Cold War notion that open-source information is 'second class' is a dangerous, outmoded cliché."[28]

In the same article, Flynn cites the estimate of his predecessor, former DIA Director Lt. Gen. Samuel V. Wilson, to the effect that "[n]inety percent of intelligence comes from open sources. The other 10 percent, the clandestine work, is just the more dramatic. The real intelligence hero is Sherlock Holmes, not James Bond."[29] Flynn thus proposes that the US Intelligence Community (USIC) undertake important cultural changes. Analysts, he writes,

> must embrace open-source, population-centric information as the lifeblood of their analytical work. They must open their doors to anyone who is willing to exchange information, including Afghans and NGOs as well as the U.S. military and its allies. As General Martin E. Dempsey, commander of the U.S. Army Training and Doctrine Command, recently stated, ". . . [T]he best information, the most important intelligence, and the context that provides the best understanding come from the bottom up, not from the top down."[30]

This is just another version of the lesson that Crumpton had learned about self-knowledge from the African boy. He also learned a great deal from other ordinary folks, and some not so ordinary—businessmen, university presidents, scientists, and such—in his capacity as chief of the little known and little resourced but vastly important National Resources (NR) division at the CIA. A relatively recent addition, NR's mission was to debrief Americans about a limitless range of topics. Despite (or . . . because?) of its minimal cost, "the rewards [were] sometimes astounding."

Though far less glamorous than hard-core spying operations, partly because far less dangerous, Crumpton discovered, to his surprise, that debriefing Wall Street executives required great skill. But it was eminently worth it; for he found that the US private sector is so far ahead in many areas that they are able to help the government "see new gaps and develop new intelligence requirements." Given their contacts and deep, long-term immersion in foreign societies, "some private sector partners, in fact, were recruiting foreign nationals for us."[31] To his surprise and delight, he also found that, far from having to be forced, "most Americans wanted to help the CIA, at least to some degree." It is time to seriously reconsider the chasm between the intelligence community and the rest of the nation.

An astute intelligence professional who has thought long and hard about the problems plaguing the community, Robert Davis Steele believes that the answer lies right under our noses, with each one of us. And he's known it for twenty years:

> In 1994, I realized that it is not possible to have smart spies in the context of a dumb nation, and in 2006, working with Congressman Rob Simmons (R – CT), I realized that 50 percent of the dots which need to be connected to prevent the next September 11, 2001 (9/11), or to respond to a natural disaster such as Katrina, will be bottom-up dots from citizens and police on the beat. Those dots have no place to go today in 2010, 9 years after 9/11. We need unclassified state-based fusion centers in which sensitive information from all eight tribes can be processed.[32]

Steele is not naïve about the need for secrecy—in fact, he thinks that even presidents should be punished for revealing classified information.[33] But secrecy can hurt us far more than it helps. The nation has become deaf and dumb: we fail to understand both ourselves and the world, and are lulled into complacency by the illusion that our elected representatives are doing their jobs.

Ultimately, it is our job as citizens of a democracy to educate ourselves sufficiently to know at least what to expect our representatives
to do. Once again Steele diagnoses the problem accurately:

> America today needs multiple forms of healing, from how we elect
> our leaders to how we govern ourselves, to how we preserve and
> protect the Republic. In every single instance, it will be HUMINT, not
> some arcane collection of technologies, that discovers, discriminates,
> distills, and delivers education, intelligence (decision support), and
> research—whether from direct human observation or with support
> from technologies—for the benefit of humanity.[34]

It is no coincidence that Steele's own work was inspired by Sun Tzu's
dictum that unless we know ourselves we are in trouble.[35] The blame,
he finds, rests with us: "The greatest strategic error we have made
has been to neglect the education and the civic engagement of our
public, a public that has grown out of touch with global realities, less
competitive in the international marketplace, and virtually oblivious
to the corporate, federal, state, and local miss-steps enacted in our
name."[36] His solution, for the US Army to become "the brain group for
global interagency and combined operations that leverage information
peacekeeping,"[37] has much to be said for it. Certainly a lack of intelligence coordination among the Allies hampers the common effort. Such
coordination, unfortunately, faces significant challenges.[38]

That said, it is—and must be—enhanced if we are to succeed in what
is a global engagement to defend the peace. For starters, it would be
a good idea to take more seriously the contributions of NATO allies
who are much smaller but arguably sometimes smarter than even we
are. This is what Military Intelligence Officer Adam Maisel found when
overseeing a task force tasked to advise and assist Afghan security
forces in Parwan Province:

> The Polish intelligence team that I worked with consisted of a colo-
> nel, first lieutenant, and civilian linguist. Based on numbers alone, it
> wouldn't be difficult to discount the value of collaborating with such
> a small section, especially given that I worked in a 70-personstrong
> intelligence support element. But this three-person shop offered capa-
> bilities that U.S. forces couldn't replicate. Despite its size, the Polish
> intelligence cell was able to maintain a robust source network that
> provided information on insurgent activity in neighboring districts and
> provinces where NATO forces had since retrograded. This intelligence
> helped to plug some of the "black holes" we received from traditional
> collection methods, and extended the reach of reporting to areas with

no U.S. or NATO presence. The Poles also used their small size to their advantage, running source meets and atmospheric patrols off base by simply walking out of the gate with four or five personnel and getting to work. For the majority of NATO forces on post, this wasn't even an option, with ground movements outside the base usually being highly scripted affairs with platoon-sized elements and vehicle support.[39]

In brief, Goliath is well advised to make use of more nimble Davids. He might also take seriously the advice of former Air Force Officer Williamson Murray to go back to school. In reference to a study reported in *The Washington Post* several years ago that less than 20 percent of the CIA's analysts speak a foreign language, Murray observes:

> A general ignorance of history and culture characterizes much of the personnel who make up the American intelligence effort. The inane system of recruitment seems to aim at numbers rather than quality. And perhaps most significantly, the security barriers that are presently in place prevent most of those with the language skills and cultural knowledge to understand our potential enemies from being recruited, as many such individuals possess relatives in the targeted countries. Finally, in the depressing litany of how not to build effective intelligence agencies, my view is that these agencies rarely reach out to the extensive numbers of foreign area experts scattered throughout American academia, not because the intelligence agencies possess such brilliant insights into the external world, but most probably because they are afraid that the U.S. public might discover that the intelligence emperor has no clothes.[40]

This devastating indictment should not be taken lightly. But arguably even more important is the long-overdue need for accountability: people should not be getting away with incompetence and neglect of duty. It would constitute the single most effective reform—with the added advantage of cost-effectiveness and added safety. Fix whatever has to be fixed to help people be their best: it will save money and lives in the end.

Thus Jamestown Foundation Fellow Peter Mattis, after exposing several common misguided assumptions about the best way to reform the IC, argues that "perhaps the best path for reform is to reduce the bureaucratic impediments for cooperation across analysis and operations, as well as across the intelligence-policy divide rather than undertaking wholesale reorganization of the sort that gave us the post-9/11 Directorship of National Intelligence." Instead, "focus on creating a culture of accountability among intelligence officers to their peers and to decision makers may be the best reform of all."[41] Accountability could be a whole new experience. Imagine that: being evaluated on the quality of one's work.

No matter how much money is poured into the Intelligence Community, no matter how many reorganizations are undertaken, there is no substitute for good old accountability. The worst problems, after all, have come from massive intelligence failures due to poor spycraft—and sweeping it under the rug only insures that it will continue. According to former CIA Officer Benjamin B. Fisher, "[d]uring the Cold War, the Central Intelligence Agency bucked the law of averages by recruiting double agents [foreign nationals recruited by a spy service that are secretly loyal to another spy agency] on an industrial scale; it was hoodwinked not a few but many times."[42] The failure, he concludes, "wreaked havoc" on the agency. Fischer also notes, however, that the failure to prevent the double agent deception was dismissed by the CIA as insignificant, and that congressional oversight committees also did not press the agency to reform its vetting processes.

This is business-as-usual in the intel world—and has been, for decades. According to intelligence expert Bill Gertz, as early as "1995, the CIA admitted that for eight years since 1986, it produced highly classified intelligence reports derived from 'bogus' and 'tainted' sources, including 35 reports that were based on data from double agents, and 60 reports compiled using sources that were suspected of being controlled by Moscow."[43] This resulted in false information being fed to three presidents: Ronald Reagan, George H. W. Bush, and Bill Clinton. The CIA's inspector general then urged reprimands for several senior CIA officers, as well as directors William H. Webster, Robert M. Gates, and R. James Woolsey. Yet they all argued that they should be exempt from blame because—what else?—they had been unaware of the problems. But . . . wasn't that just the point? And if not them, then who? We cannot leave these questions unanswered and still expect to win the peace.

The CIA had too often reacted to one problem by adding another, exacerbating both: as agency officers failed to successfully conduct direct recruitments of agents to work for the agency, they relied on "walk-ins," or volunteers, which obviously increased the vulnerability to foreign double agent operations. Clearly, the agency had ignored Sun Tzu's admonition that "he who is not sage and wise . . . cannot use secret agents" (*AoW* XIII. 13); the agents turned out to be sagacity-challenged and unwise. Fischer blames the bureaucratic culture and careerism at CIA for the failure to prevent double agent disaster, among others.

Indeed, especially unheeded was the cautionary advice by Mei Yao-ch'en, Sun Tzu's contemporary and commentator: "Take precautions against the spy having been turned around."[44] The CIA appears to have treated this mindset with ridicule in recent years, evidently overreacting to the notorious paranoia of its counterintelligence bureau's legendary founder, James Jesus Angleton. But Angleton didn't have a mental illness. Unless it was posttraumatic stress disorder suffered upon learning that his good friend Kim Philby, to whom he had unwisely shared extremely valuable information, had been the USSR's most prolific and faithful spy. British historian Ben MacIntyre describes the disaster in his spellbinding *A Spy Among Friends: Kim Philby and the Great Betrayal*: "Everything that Angleton had ever told Philby, and thus the precise human and political cost of their friendship, was on paper, stored in an archive under the direct control of the chief of CIA counterintelligence, James Angleton. Years later the CIA conducted an internal search for these files: every single one has vanished. 'I had them burned,' Angleton told MI5 officer Peter Wright. 'It was all very embarrassing.'"[45]

Thus according to Fischer, beginning in the 1970s, many in the CIA criticized counter-spying, which often involved questioning the loyalties of intelligence personnel, as "sickthink." So it happened that CIA officer Aldrich Ames, who had sent the Russians from 1986 until 1993, allowed them to unmask and arrest almost all CIA recruited agents during the 1980s.[46] Consider the enormity of the situation: our principal enemy during the Cold War knew all our intimate secrets, while they were feeding us disinformation. Robert Baer dubs him one of the great traitors of all time, on a par with Benedict Arnold: "the CIA would never live down Ames. He had ratted out our crown jewels, the reason we existed.[47]

Nor was Congress blameless: "The intelligence failure was covered up by the congressional intelligence oversight committees, according to Fischer, who quotes former CIA officer Brian Latell. In East Germany, all the recruited CIA agents working there were found to be double-agents working secretly for the Ministry of State Security spy service, also known as the Stasi."[48] Yet Fischer's criticism of the CIA's handling of the Ames case earned him mistreatment instead of accolades. To make matters even worse, Congress's subsequent reaction proved exactly wrong: it called on the FBI to investigate to the hilt—forgetting that the two intelligence agencies had been rivals from the very beginning. But the FBI excelled beyond even J. Edgar Hoover's wildest dreams, succeeding in record time to set the fear of God into just about everyone at the CIA. As Baer describes it, during the 1990s "the FBI was eviscerating the CIA." Meanwhile, "Robert Hanssen was giving away the FBI's own secrets in a trashbag."[49] In many ways, the Hanssen story mirrors that of Ames: in both cases, the agencies failed to pick up on signals that in many ways stared them in the face, had they only bothered to pay attention. Lesson learned: too harsh is as bad as not harsh enough—and learning the wrong lessons is as bad as not learning any lessons at all.

Internal intelligence breaches are close to catastrophic. Sun Tzu's recipe for dealing with intelligence compromise is drastic: "If plans relating to secret operations are prematurely divulged, all those to whom he spoke of them shall be put to death" (*AoW* XIII. 15). Given the enormous importance of secret intelligence at all times, dealing with treason incompetently is a form of self-sabotage that does not get enough attention, even by congressional oversight committees, let alone the IC itself. Gertz cites Kenneth E. DeGraffenreid, former senior White House intelligence official: "What we thought was true from the Cold War spy wars was largely wrong, and that says that the counterintelligence model we had was wrong. . . . And therefore because we've not corrected that problem we're in bad shape to deal with the current challenges posed by terrorists and spies from Iran, Russia, China and others."[50]

The first thing to do when addressing any problem is to root out incompetence. We may not need Sun Tzu to tell us that, though his reminders are eminently useful. But it appears that we do need a president who is able to emulate George Washington, and is willing to enforce such a common sense principle. We need as well a vigorous free media to expose corruption more effectively, and robust legislative action that should avoid knee-jerk, overcompensating measures that might make good headlines but do more harm than good. Any intelligence reform should be taken only after extensive deliberation with as wide a variety of experts as possible, including people outside the community.

At the end of the day, the strategic dialogue has to begin inside the body politic itself.

Notes

1. Griffith *Sun Tzu - The Art of War*, 87.
2. Ibid., 79.
3. Richard Holbrooke, "Get the Message Out," *Washington Post*, October 28, 2001. http://www.washingtonpost.com/wp-dyn/content/article/2010/12/13/AR2010121305410.html
4. Christopher Paul, *Strategic Communication: Origins, Concepts, and Current Debates* (Santa Barbara, CA: Praeger, 2011), 3. (Italics in the original; bold added.)
5. Susan Epstein, "U.S. Public Diplomacy: Background and the 9/11 Commission Recommendations," CRS Report for Congress, October 5, 2004.
6. Paul, *op.cit.*, 168.
7. *Evacuation Planning and Preparations for Overseas Posts Can Be Improved*, GAO-08-23, Oct 19, 2007. http://www.gao.gov/products/GAO-08-23
8. Statement of Stuart W. Bowen, Jr., Inspector General, Office of the Special Inspector General for Iraq Reconstruction before the Subcommittee on National Security, Homeland Defense, and Foreign Operations of the Committee on Oversight and Government Reform, United States House of Representatives, December 7, 2011. http://oversight.house.gov/wp-content/uploads/2012/01/12-7-11_NatSec_Bowen_Testimony.pdf
9. Kori Schake, *State of Disrepair: Fixing the Culture and Practices of the State Department* (Stanford, CA: Hoover Institution Press, 2012), 89.
10. QDDR, 123.
11. Schake, op.cit., 90.
12. Ibid., 29.
13. Ibid., 35.
14. Ibid.
15. The American Academy of Diplomacy, *Forging a 21st Century Diplomatic Service for the United States through Professional Education and Training*, Stimson Center, 2011, 11.
16. Ibid., 21.
17. *Hard Lessons: The Iraq Reconstruction Experience* (US Government Printing Office, 2009), 336.
18. Ibid., 6.
19. Schake, op.cit., 69.
20. Charles S. Clark, "State Department Leaders Inaugurate New 'Lessons Learned' Center," February 3, 2016. *Government Executive*, http://www.govexec.com/management/2016/02/state-department-leaders-inaugurate-new-lessons-learned-center/125673/#disqus_thread
21. Ibid
22. http://usacac.army.mil/cac2/call/ll-course.asp
23. Griffith, *Sun Tzu - The Art of War*, 148.
24. Robert Baer, *See No Evil* (New York: Random House, 2002), 139–40.
25. Ibid., 81.
26. Henry A. Crumpton, *The Art of Intelligence: Lessons from a Life in the CIA's Clandestine Service* (New York and London: Penguin, 2012), 60.
27. Dr. Louise J. Rasmussen, Dr. Winston R. Sieck, and Dr. Robert R. Hoffman "Cultural Knowledge for Intelligence Analysts: Expertise in Cultural Sensemaking," *American Intelligence Journal* 31, no. 2 (2013): 34.

28. Major General Michael T. Flynn, USA Captain Matt Pottinger, USMC Paul D. Batchelor, DIA, *Fixing Intel: A Blueprint for Making Intelligence Relevant in Afghanistan*, Center for a New American Security, January 2010, p. 23.

29. Reported by David Reed, "Aspiring to Spying," *The Washington Times*, 14 November 1997, Regional News: 1.

30. Excerpt from a speech by General Martin E. Dempsey, "Our Army's Campaign 15 of Learning," delivered on 4 October 2009 at the Association of the United States Army's Chapter Presidents' Dinner in Washington, DC, and published in *Landpower* (Institute of Land Warfare: No. 09-3, November 2009).

31. Crumpton, *The Art of Intelligence*, 286–7.

32. Ibid., 52.

33. "I have long believed that Presidents and other senior elected and appointed officers should not be beyond penalty for such disclosures, and that no President should be allowed to pardon one of their own staff for high crimes and misdemeanors whether directed by the President or not. We are long overdue for a massive reduction of secrecy and a draconian increase in the penalties for disclosing truly precious secrets." Ibid., 83. Fair enough.

34. Ibid., 53.

35. "In Sun Tzu's terms, it is safe to say that today he would suggest that we do not know our enemy, we do not know ourselves, and we are thus at very high risk of failure." Ibid., xvii.

36. Ibid., xv–xvi.

37. Ibid., xvi.

38. See the excellent article by Anna-Katherine Staser McGill and David H. Gray, "Challenges to International Counterterrorism Intelligence Sharing," *Global Security Studies* 3, no. 3 (Summer 2012): 76–86.

39. Adam Maisel, "NATO at the Tactical Level," *War on the Rocks*, September 15, 2015. http://warontherocks.com/2015/09/nato-at-the-tactical-level/?utm_source=WOTR+Newsletter&utm_campaign=9747532b65-WOTR_Newsletter_8_17_158_15_2015&utm_medium=email&utm_term=0_8375be81e9-9747532b65-60136989

40. Williamson Murray, "The Ignorance of Intelligence Agencies," *War on the Rocks*, October 26, 2015. http://warontherocks.com/2015/10/the-ignorance-of-intelligence-agencies/?utm_source=WOTR+Newsletter&utm_campaign=e203c8b511-WOTR_Newsletter_8_17_158_15_2015&utm_medium=email&utm_term=0_8375be81e9-e203c8b511-60136989

41. Peter Mattis, "Four Assumptions That Need to Go," *The National Interest*, February 2, 2015. http://nationalinterest.org/feature/4-us-intelligence-assumptions-need-go-12165?page=show

42. "Doubles Troubles: The CIA and Double Agents during the Cold War," *International Journal of Intelligence and CounterIntelligence* 29, no. 1 (2016). http://www.tandfonline.com/doi/full/10.1080/08850607.2015.1083313

43. Bill Gertz, "CIA Fooled by Massive Cold War Double-Agent Failure," *Washington Free Beacon*, December 28, 2015. http://freebeacon.com/national-security/cia-fooled-by-massive-cold-war-double-agent-failure/

44. Griffith, *Sun Tzu - The Art of War*, 147.

45. Ben MacIntyre, *A Spy among Friends: Kim Philby and the Great Betrayal* (New York: Broadway Books, 2015), 275.

46. Sandy Grimes and Jeanne Vertefeuille, *Circle of Treason: A CIA Account of Traitor Aldrich Ames and the Men He Betrayed* (Annapolis, MD: Naval Institute Press, 2012).
47. Baer, *See No Evil, l*229.
48. Gertz, "CIA Fooled by Massive Cold War Double-Agent Failure."
49. Baer, *See No Evil,* 231.
50. Ibid.

15

Development Engagement

Aid is just a stopgap. Commerce [and] entrepreneurial capitalism take more people out of poverty than aid.
—Bono, Nov. 13, 2012, Georgetown University

It is one of the beautiful compensations of this life that no one can sincerely try to help another without helping himself.
—Charles Dudley Warner, *Backlog Studies*, 1873

Though known best for advocating "deception," Sun Tzu stressed the importance of moral influence and "command" in prevailing over adversaries, the latter embracing the qualities of wisdom, sincerity, humanity, courage, and strictness, as already mentioned in previous chapters. Sun Tzu commentator Tu Mu explains that someone who is humane, for example, "loves mankind, sympathizes with others, and appreciates their industry and toil."[1] *Mankind* referring to the species, this sentiment is emphatically not restricted to one's own community. Sympathizing with others is deemed a good in itself, bound to enhance a leader's prestige. By implication, an attitude of openness and trust, appreciation and respect for industry and toil, and willingness to engage, are evidently considered assets. It is critically important to remember the fundamental idealism at the center of the Chinese strategist's thinking. It is key to understanding the Art of Peace.

It also tracks well, albeit less obviously, with one of America's most important founding principles, which is the preeminence of commerce, along with the widely held, perhaps excessively sanguine, assumption that free trade is bound to enhance global peace. Trust in Adam Smith's (and we might also add, Sun Tzu's) Invisible Hand has generally been our lodestar, even during Democratic administrations which have tended to be more amenable to government restrictions on commerce. Engagement is, on the whole, America's default mode in the sense that we tend to appreciate industry and toil, and do not wish to harm others who themselves do not wish to harm us.

The business community certainly knows that global economic engagement is here to stay—a fact captured in the title of a study by Dartmouth professor of international business Matthew Slaughter, titled *American Companies and Global Supply Networks: Driving U.S. Economic Growth and Jobs by Connecting with the World.* The study reports that in 2010, for example, globally engaged US companies employed 28.1 million Americans, performed $253.8 billion in R&D, made $587.3 billion in capital investments in the United States and bought more than $8.0 trillion in goods and services from US suppliers. Indeed, US companies of all sizes are increasingly more globally engaged and are vigorously pursuing new customers in the global marketplace. Though big players predictably dominate, no less than a quarter of all United States–based multinational companies are classified by the US government as small businesses. International operations of US companies primarily serve foreign markets—with over 90 percent of the foreign production by US companies sold to foreign customers—and are not imported back to the United States.[2] The trend continues.

Commercial investment and trade are clearly vital to the creation and maintenance of a peaceful and prosperous world. All things equal, engagement of every kind, commercial as well as cultural, educational, diplomatic, and such, tends to promote greater understanding and hence, at least in principle, diminished chances for conflict and hostility. But do investment and trade count as "engagement"? alongside the cultural and educational variety? If so, aren't they of a completely different kind? They seem diametrically opposed because commercial relations are considered profit-oriented, while noncommercial engagement is thought of as mainly of a humanitarian nature. But that impression is not entirely accurate—especially as it relates to what is sometimes called "foreign aid," or "development assistance."

There is of course no provision in the US Constitution for government-sponsored charitable expenditures, and with good reason: ours was meant to be a limited federal government, with Congress being allowed to exercise no more than eighteen (18) enumerated powers, with all the rest retained by the people. A revolution had been fought, after all, to preserve the right of private property. "Taxes" have often joined "death" in the same breath as equally inevitable and, for some, almost as obnoxious. In keeping with its free trade principles, therefore, the United States has traditionally preferred to let private voluntary organizations (PVOs) and individuals engage in charitable giving, rather than using taxpayer funds for humanitarian assistance.[3] That said, benevolent engagement beyond the borders has never been shunned—quite the contrary. For it is clearly not only an expression of generosity and good will (which is also of great value, particularly if astutely, and subtly, leveraged); it may indeed benefit US national security, whether directly or indirectly.

It was World War II that changed things most radically, as the US government recognized the massive contribution of PVOs during wartime and established a number of close collaborative relationships. In 1946, President Harry Truman set up an Advisory Committee on Voluntary Foreign Aid (ACVFA) to work alongside the Department of State, and in 1948, the Economic Cooperation Act provided transportation subsidies for relief shipments to Europe by US PVOs registered with the ACVFA. It was not until 1960 that President John F. Kennedy at last established the two government agencies most closely identified with foreign assistance to underdeveloped nations: the Peace Corps and USAID.

The charter of the former is "to help promote a better understanding on the part of the peoples served, and a better understanding of other peoples on the part of American people," by sponsoring volunteers who go to disadvantaged, often dangerous, communities, learning the local languages and help build schools, repair roads, and do other back-breaking work.[4] USAID, for its part, describes its role as involving "two complementary and intrinsically linked goals: ending extreme poverty and promoting the development of resilient, democratic societies that are able to realize their potential."[5]

Kennedy's rationale for the creation of these agencies through the Foreign Assistance Act of 1961 was explicitly altruistic, based on America's good fortune, which he believed to have imposed upon it certain responsibilities to the poor:

> There is no escaping our obligations: our moral obligations as a wise leader and good neighbor in the interdependent community of free nations—our economic obligations as the wealthiest people in a world of largely poor people, as a nation no longer dependent upon the loans from abroad that once helped us develop our own economy—and our political obligations as the single largest counter to the adversaries of freedom.[6]

While the massive foreign assistance program known as the Marshall Plan, which the United States initiated immediately after World War II, had been fueled, in the words of DOS's Office of the Historian, "by the fear of Communist expansion,"[7] President Kennedy appealed to Americans' goodwill, a feeling that only grew with time. By the 1970s, international foreign aid stressed providing "basic human needs" such as food and health. Even during the Reagan years when emphasis was put on free markets, employment, and economic growth, the link of USAID's activities to US national interests was seldom articulated.

Though American humanitarian assistance was designed "to help countries improve their own quality of life," in reality, what influenced Congress, all too often, were individual constituencies rather than pure altruism, let alone a larger national strategy. For example, in the early 1950s, agricultural interests lobbied successfully for expanding overseas distribution of US government food commodities—which included dairy products, wheat and wheat products, corn, and cornmeal—in order to keep prices high at home. If there lurked any benevolent impulse within their souls, its virtue was eclipsed by the pecuniary, which was only too evident; strategic purpose, by contrast, rather less so.

For most of the past several decades, foreign-aid appropriations have revealed no clear criteria for setting priorities, for sending money to one country rather than another. Liberia, for example, has long been one of the largest recipients of humanitarian assistance. In 2004, it peaked at $186 million, when it was the eighth largest recipient. Most of that aid has been directed "off-budget," meaning that it goes directly to NGOs and contractors. In many ways, this is wise, given that much government-to-government aid ends up in politicians' pockets. But that is only part of the picture; to gauge the true impact on both Liberia's and America's interests, there is another factor that must be considered: the effect on people's attitudes toward their own nation, their leadership, and themselves. In "The Elusive Quest for Effective Aid Management in Liberia," Brad Parks and Nakul Kadaba point out that "when voters get all of their development 'goodies' (e.g., food, water, health, education) from donor-funded projects via off-budget aid, recipient governments risk the appearance of impotence and losing public support."[8] Paradoxically, though predictably, US aid has done more to undermine than to boost Liberians' sense of self-sufficiency.

The old adage about the road of good intentions leading to the underworld, in fact, applies to the vast majority of state-sponsored foreign assistance. Aside from mostly questionable effects on poverty eradication, political modernization, and cultural integrity, the presumed potential benefits to America's global standing are not borne out by the facts. Slowly but irrevocably, what has emerged over time is a radical differentiation between two opposed, seemingly irreconcilable, modes of thinking about advancing the national interest of the United States: on the one hand, through coercive, threatening military strength and on the other, through benevolent, disinterested charity. The hard power–soft power divide strikes again. And it isn't helpful.

Nothing demonstrates the point that foreign assistance is viewed primarily as charitable contributions, without definable and measurable strategic consequences, than this statement from the study of Congressional Research Service (CRS) specialist Marian Leonardo Lawson, entitled "Does Foreign Aid Work? Efforts to Evaluate U.S. Foreign Assistance":

> In most cases, the success or failure of U.S. foreign aid programs is not entirely clear, in part because *most aid programs have not been evaluated for the purpose of determining their actual impact.*[9]

Taxpayers should be outraged. And they would be, if they only knew. But foreign-aid oversight and evaluation does not make for bedtime reading (except as a cure for insomnia). After all, how many people would ever read "Aid Programs Impact Not Determined?" We all just assume those programs are doing some good to somebody, and go on with our business. But the topic is more important than it might look.

In a commendable analysis of the most egregious "don'ts" of US foreign assistance, Clare Lockhart distinguishes between humanitarian assistance offered in times of dire need and what she calls "development engagement," which

> can be low-budget, and should be designed to move a needy country toward self-sufficiency—so that the state can collect its own revenues and the people can support their own livelihoods—as soon as possible. Many recipient countries have enormous untapped domestic resources, and with some effort devoted to increasing those revenues and building the systems to spend them, could assume much more of the responsibility of meeting their citizens' needs.[10]

What Lockhart grasps is that "there is no substitute in the long term for unleashing a society's domestic potential of human, institutional, and natural capital through a well governed country." In the first place, foreign aid is not merely inefficient but sometimes counterproductive in the extreme, as incentives become skewed. For example, a large-scale World Food Program wheat distribution in Afghanistan in 2003 managed to collapse the market so that farmers threw up their hands and simply let their crops rot. "Nor is it only farmers who are affected by thoughtless charity. Every time solar panels, water pumps, tractors, or cell phones are handed out for free, a local supplier can no longer sell and install his inventory, and a small business that might have long-range prospects for hiring and supporting several people is smothered."[11] Yet the main purpose of development assistance is to facilitate self-reliance, not foster dependency.

Perhaps the most famous convert to the value of supporting self-reliance instead of just handing out donations is none other than the renowned rock star Bono, who told an incredulous, largely liberal audience at a Georgetown University Global Social Enterprise Event held on November 13, 2012: "Commerce [and] entrepreneurial capitalism take more people out of poverty than aid. . . . It's not just aid, it's trade, investment, social enterprise. It's working with the citizenry so that they can unlock their own domestic resources so that they can do it for themselves. Think anyone in Africa likes aid? Come on."[12] He was asking not for sympathy but for action. "Your heart is not going to solve these problems," he told the students. Empathy is nice, but not enough. It may not even be necessary.

Lockhart may have coined the term *development engagement*, but the idea is hardly new. She invokes the Economic Cooperation Act (ECA) of 1948 as an excellent framework that has worked quite well, premised on the idea of facilitating "the achievement by the countries . . . of a healthy economy independent of extraordinary outside assistance." What most people do not realize is that the Marshall Plan, invariably cited as the post-conflict development-assistance model to emulate, having been enacted under the ECA, was designed to reduce the need for aid rather than perpetuate it. It didn't happen by chance. She notes too that "George Kennan, in a now-declassified memo from 1947, argued that 'it is absolutely essential that people in Europe should make the effort to think out their problems and should have forced upon them a sense of direct responsibility for the way the funds are expended. Similarly, it is important that people in this country should feel that a genuine effort has been made to achieve soundness of concept in the way United States funds are to be spent.'"[13]

Even more important, however, is that the best development initiatives are directed not by governments but by the private sector and its use of market mechanisms. Lockhart gives several examples of such projects, which she aptly calls "Fish for a Lifetime" approaches—all "designed to unlock and leverage the value from within the society, state, and market. They all start with the operating principle of co-designing programs with the citizens and leaders from the country concerned. Where there is a market, they do not seek to use grant capital. Once the initial intervention is over, success is judged by whether or not the innovations designed for the crisis are sustainable."[14]

Lockhart fully appreciates how taxpayers in the United States and elsewhere in the developed world could be turning against foreign aid with disgust and anger. This is unfortunate, and unnecessary. Rather than throwing money at poverty, there are plenty of market-based, highly effective ways of engaging in a low cost, mutually beneficial manner. Altruism and self-interest, once again, are not only not mutually exclusive but mutually reinforcing.

In fact, unsurprisingly, a large percentage of the public is eager to help people in need. While the US government could certainly play at least a supportive, coordinating role alongside the private sector to alleviate misery and instability in poor countries, there is no reason why the private sector should not be the principal agent. The benefit, moreover, redounds not only to the recipients but to us as a nation. As Admiral James Stavridis, now Dean of the Fletcher School of Law and Diplomacy, told Senators on March 26, 2015:

> What is the price tag for a better, safer world? I would argue that the non-military aspects of our power bring a strong return on our investment, both in the public as well as the private sector. The funds we allocate to foreign aid, diplomatic security, humanitarian relief, education, and the many other international programs can save us from spending far more to put boots on the ground in troubled regions. It's exceptionally cost-effective. By bolstering funding for our presence in the world, we reduce the burden on our men and women in uniform.

He adds: "We are very good at launching missiles—we must improve at launching ideas."[15] Strategic engagement, which includes the launching of ideas, is what those "non-military aspects of power" are all about, and they are indeed "exceptionally cost-effective."

Calls for allocating more funds for foreign aid and humanitarian relief, however, should not be the first but the last resort. As our Founders knew better than most of us today, the most powerful idea in development is the near-miraculous efficiency of the Invisible Hand.

Indeed, one of the most effective tools in assisting poor countries is not to do more but less: specifically, stop putting barriers to imports. Writes development expert Steven Radelet: "Although the United States is generally open to trade, its policies toward poor countries are strikingly protectionist: it charges high tariffs on many products from developing countries (such as textiles, shoes, and apparel) and tightly restricts the imports of a range of agricultural products (including dairy, peanuts, and sugar."[16] He recommends extending duty-free and quota-free access to the world's poorest countries.

Another important way to help poor countries is to encourage governments to reduce barriers to development and cut down on regulations. As economists Peter Bower and J. Svensson, among others, have shown, "pro-market economic policies have been as important as anything we know of in fostering economic development. Yet foreign aid, by relaxing the budget constraint of the government, in many instances has the effect of delaying the introduction of such good policies. In the 1980s and 1990s, the donors tried to address this problem by linking aid to policy reform,"[17] but were essentially unsuccessful, either because the client governments were unresponsive or because conditionality was shunned for "interfering with sovereignty." There are promising indications that direct foreign aid to governments might be giving way to other, more effective, forms of assistance.

Lifting barriers to poor nations' selling their wares is economically speaking the most obvious; it is also most problematic politically, as lobbyists for various domestic industries work hard to justify their hefty salaries by strong-arming members of Congress to secure privileges for their clients. Though special interests, not only domestic but, even more alarmingly, foreign, are hard for cash-strapped politicians to resist, a concerted effort to monitor donations to minimize corruption is worth undertaking. It is much to be hoped, for example, that recent revelations regarding the Clinton Foundation's role in facilitating deals whose effect on national security has been highly dubious[18] will lead to some serious reforms. Hearings on this sort of corruption, along with well-informed and well-researched analysis, taking into consideration best practices, are long overdue.

Whenever government gets involved in foreign aid to other governments, there is trouble. Radelet offers an interesting recommendation, to the effect that "aid agencies should develop innovative ways to promote private investment," and could "encourage local banks to provide loans to promising entrepreneurs, as does the Development

Credit Authority, a small program within USAID,"[19] which he believes should be expanded. There are many other models of assistance; some of the most ingenious are outlined in Hudson Institute's Center for Global Prosperity's (CBP) Index of Philanthropic Freedom (formerly the Global Philanthropy Index).[20]

Unfortunately, USAID is plagued by inefficiency and suffers from an especially acute form of SDS, clearly a birth defect. Former USAID official Carol Adelman and AEI Senior Fellow Nick Eberstadt charge that "like many other bureaucratic organizations, foreign aid institutions are geared to fighting the last war—in this context, to meeting the development challenges of a world we no longer inhabit."[21] Not that the old model ever really worked; recent research carried on all over the world, for more than half a century, has been "inconclusive" regarding the question of whether and to what extent foreign aid helps countries grow. That is, if that was indeed their goal. To the unaided eye it looks more like political grandstanding, whether ideologically motivated nor not.[22] When Sun Tzu praises a humane attitude, which consists of sympathy for others, he is not referring to a mere appearance of sympathy. That has always been known by a very different name: hypocrisy.

One small step in the right direction would be to drastically reduce if not discontinue altogether Congressional earmarks for USAID programs that are driven mainly by special interest constituencies. Admittedly, the chances of such a reform are slim to none. Politically more palatable is reduced dependence on public funding for humanitarian assistance altogether. Thus an agency such as USAID, which has been plagued by monumental waste,

> should [instead] provide for regular, substantive consultations with private-sector players involved in global development, including foundations, charities, corporations, religious organizations, universities and colleges, and individuals. (Beyond the philanthropic sector, millions of migrants throughout the world are sending more than $200 billion in remittances back to their low-income home countries every year—a sum double all donors' annual official development assistance commitments.) USAID must not only be aware of but also work with the vast array of new players in global development who are transforming the ways in which resources are reaching low-income regions.[23]

Only by showing regard for the people most directly affected, namely, the local communities who are supposed to be helped, can there be productive, strategic development engagement that truly promotes their interests as well our own national interest, through genuine peace with liberty. As an example of creative departure from the traditional tried-and-failed approach, Adelman and Eberstadt specifically mention the Global Development Alliance, which has successfully leveraged government funds with contributions from private companies, foundations, charities, and universities, but there are many others.

Another example of a growing move toward private and away from public funding for development is the USAID partnership with private voluntary organizations (PVOs)—in a salutary reboot to an earlier era. Some 650 PVOs have registered with USAID as of August 1, 2015, allowing the agency to respond to global needs by relying on these partners. It should be noted that less than 40 percent of the PVO's funding comes from USAID. But one of the most useful, if underappreciated, aspects of this partnership involves the data collected during the registration process, including specific expertise and geographic presence, which may be found online at the PVO Registry, www.pvo. usaid.gov/usaid/. The latest Report of Voluntary Agencies, released in November 2015, includes not only United States–based but also international PVOs along with US Cooperative Development Organizations (CDOs).

In recent years, USAID has instituted a number of initiatives, such as Local Solutions, aimed to support local innovations and local systems to festering problems throughout the world. The premise for the relationship between USAID and PVOs, according to the Report, is this:

> Top-down processes are giving way to more collaborative and locally based approaches where various actors from the private sector—corporations; foundations; nongovernmental organizations (NGOs), including PVOs; universities; local businesses; civil society organizations; and diaspora groups— provide and draw on resources from a variety of sources and work in concert.[24]

A similar organization, the Advisory Committee on Voluntary Foreign Aid (ACVFA), also organizes meetings, held two times a year, that provide opportunities for information exchange and consultation between USAID and private organizations, representatives from universities, US businesses, and government, multilateral, and NGOs (nongovernmental organizations). These meetings are valuable not primarily as opportunities to find ways to access government funds—which in any event constitute but a relatively minor portion of the NGOs' budgets—but for networking, and learning who does what where, and what lessons have been learned. There are not nearly enough such opportunities.

Networking among individuals and organizations engaged abroad serves many other important functions besides improved development engagement. Among the most important is the creation and maintenance of myriad personal connections, which help deepen understanding of conditions on the ground and provide resources for influencing that are far more reliable than online ads or the small number of US government assistance recipients. Too often, those recipients tend to be English speakers with connections to the diplomatic community, who are atypical in many ways. These are often, predictably, resented by no-less-deserving ordinary people, but who usually do not speak foreign languages. As a result, good will is unnecessarily eroded, and the best projects fail to see the light of day.

Finally, development engagement comes with the most important bonus of all: knowledge and thus, yes, intelligence. A telling example was revealed by Dr. Bernard Fall, who was killed in Vietnam in 1967, in an article published that same year, recently reprinted in the September-October 2015 issue of *Military Review* to underscore its continuing relevance. In that article, Fall points out that as early as 1957 it was already clear that French and Vietnamese officials had failed to recognize that the "peace," which had presumably been secured two years earlier, in 1955, was nothing of the sort. This he learned by noticing an alarming increase of obituaries for village chiefs, clustered in particular areas. They turned out to coincide with the numbers and locations of Communist cells operating in South Vietnam at the time. He also revealed that, had anyone at the time bothered to take a look, tax returns figures obtained by USAID in 1963 would have shown that in twenty-seven provinces the Communists were formally collecting taxes with bonds, receipts, and tax declarations[25]—further proof that they were a power not to be underestimated.

From such data and his own observations, Fall could see early on that Vietnam could not be won by the military. Did that mean that Vietnam was doomed to fall to the Communists? To him the more relevant question was: "Can we in Vietnam, or anywhere else, save (or improve) the administrative or governmental structure? The answer is obvious, and there is no other effort really worth doing. We have tried this with the 'strategic hamlets' and that literally failed."[26] The answer was not that we should have forgotten about Vietnam; it does, however, suggest that we proceeded based on erroneous premises.

By not undertaking a thorough analysis of the situation, by failing to evaluate properly what Sun Tzu called "initial estimates," not looking at what was really going inside the country, and not taking advantage of contacts and locally available information, we were all but guaranteed to fail.

Though global "engagement" sounds benign enough, however, it is not a good-in-itself. This is even true of benign-sounding causes, such as refugee support. Exhibit A is the case of the UN Refugee and Works Agency—UNRWA—which targets Palestinians, with an annual budget of some $1.5 billion. Since its inception in 1950, the United States has been its single largest contributor. Though originally intended to help genuine refugees from war-torn areas, it currently handles services for some 5.4 million children, grandchildren, and great grandchildren of people who left Palestine. . . . in 1948!

Indeed, UNRWA has stopped being an independent relief agency long ago, and is deeply engaged in aggressive anti-Israeli politics, having become closely aligned with the terrorist group Hamas. According to Congressional findings included in a "Sense of Congress Resolution," HR 3829,[27] introduced before the House Committee on Foreign Affairs on October 27, 2015:

> * The curriculum of UNRWA schools, which use the textbooks of their respective host governments or authorities, has long contained materials that are anti-Israel, anti-Semitic, and supportive of violent extremism.
>
> * UNRWA staff unions, including the teachers' union, are frequently controlled by members affiliated with Hamas.
>
> * The curriculum of UNRWA schools, which use the textbooks of their respective host governments or authorities, has long contained materials that are anti-Israel, anti-Semitic, and supportive of violent extremism.
>
> * Despite UNRWA's contravention of United States law and activities that compromise its strictly humanitarian mandate, UNRWA continues to receive United States contributions, including $408,751,396 in 2014.
>
> * Assistance from the United States and other responsible nations allows UNRWA to claim that criticisms of the agency's behavior are unfounded. UNRWA spokesman Christopher Gunness has dismissed concerns by stating that, "If these baseless allegations were even halfway true, do you really think the U.S. and [European Commission] would give us hundreds of millions of dollars per year?"

* Former UNRWA general counsel James Lindsay noted in a 2009 report the following:

> (A) "The United States, despite funding nearly 75 percent of UNRWA's national budget and remaining its largest single country donor, has mostly failed to make UNRWA reflect U.S. foreign policy objectives ... Recent U.S. efforts to shape UNRWA appear to have been ineffective. . . ."

> (B) "[T]he United States is not obligated to fund agencies that refuse to check its rolls for individuals their donors do not wish to support."

UNRWA is also used to stockpile armaments for Hamas:

> * On July 29, 2014, UNRWA confirmed that, for the third time in less than a month, a stockpile of Hamas rockets was found in one of its schools in Gaza, establishing a pattern of Hamas weapons being stored in UNRWA facilities, and calling into question UNRWA's claim of being caught unawares to Hamas' actions.

> * On July 30, 2014, three Israeli Defense Force soldiers were killed in an explosion at a booby-trapped UNRWA health clinic, which was housing the opening to one of Hamas' underground tunnels.

> * On July 30, 2014, John Ging, head of UNRWA from 2006–2011, when asked if Hamas has been using human shields and using United Nations schools and hospitals to store weapons and as a shelter from which to launch missiles into Israel, stated in an interview, "Yes, the armed groups are firing their rockets into Israel from the vicinity of UN facilities and residential areas. Absolutely."

Why, then, is the United States continuing to find UNRWA? HR 3829 recommends that all bona fide Palestinian refugees become the responsibility of the UNHCR—the UN High Commissioner for Refugees. A Heritage Foundation backgrounder by senior research fellows Brett D. Schaefer and James Phillips, released on March 5, 2015, concludes:

> The U.S. could advance the long-term prospects for peace by fundamentally shifting U.S. policy to encourage reform and replacement of UNRWA to facilitate its original purpose: ending the refugee status of Palestinians and facilitating their integration as citizens of their host states, where most were born and raised, or resettling them in the West Bank and Gaza where the Palestinian government can assume responsibility for their needs, as must occur as part of any final Israeli–Palestinian peace agreement.[28]

UNRWA is by no means the only, or even the most egregious, example of bone-headed development assistance—and no, it is not development "engagement," for the United States's role is basically limited to writing checks, while UNRWA's employees busy themselves indoctrinating children. Development engagement must be strategic to be considered a national security asset.

USAID does, at least nominally, purport to have strategic goals—five, to be exact:

1. Strengthen America's Economic Reach and Positive Economic Impact

2. Strengthen America's Foreign Policy Impact on Our Strategic Challenges

3. Promote the Transition to a Low-Emission, Climate-Resilient World while Expanding Global Access to Sustainable Energy

4. Protect Core U.S. Interests by Advancing Democracy and Human Rights and Strengthening Civil Society

5. Modernize the Way We Do Diplomacy and Development[29]

But do any of these goals indicate how USAID is supposed to achieve them and why? Having a positive economic impact is certainly better than having a negative economic impact, unless of course the target is to weaken our adversaries. And what about the fact that goal 3 might conflict with goal 1, since transition to low-emission energy is far more expensive than the alternative? Some might argue as well that goal 3 is not immune to the charge of self-contradiction, if low-emission fuels turn out to have no effect on reducing climate change.

Similarly, Goal 4, which purports to protect core US interests by advancing "Democracy and Human Rights and Strengthening Civil Society," raises more questions than it answers. In the first place, what if among the core US interests is stabilization of conflict-torn areas that are far from ready for "democracy" as we define the concept (never mind that there is no univocal, widely accepted definition). The same may be said of human rights. As for "strengthening civil society," one of the big problems with that concept is the murky world of what some call "liberation groups" which others consider "terrorists." While attempts have been made to protect "good" civil-society groups from being exploited by "bad" civil-society groups,[30] there are no iron-clad rules for differentiating the two. Indeed, most scholars agree that "the term is used differently according to political predilections and inherited understandings.[31]

The least helpful "strategic goal," however, is the last, which is to "modernize" the way we do diplomacy and development. I suggest that we have "modernized" to the point that we lost altogether the sense of direction we once had. In any case, modernize *to what end*? It's that pesky SDS (strategic deficit syndrome) acting up again. When Sun Tzu praises humanity as love for mankind and sympathy with others, he doesn't have to add that one's own nation has to come first; yet that does not exclude empathy for mankind as such. "Sympathizing with others" may not exclude anyone, but those who wish to harm others—and specifically ourselves—deserve no sympathy whatever.

Notes

1. Griffith, *Sun Tzu - The Art of War*, 65.
2. Matthew Slaughter, *American Companies and Global Supply Networks: Driving U.S. Economic Growth and Jobs by Connecting with the World* (Washington, DC: Business Roundtable, December 6, 2012). http://businessroundtable.org/media/news-releases/globally-engaged-u.s.-companies-essential-to-american-growth-and-job-c
3. Brian H. Smith, *More Than Altruism: Politics of Private Foreign Aid* (Princeton, NJ: Princeton University Press, 2014), 54.
4. http://www.peacecorps.gov/media/forpress/news/283/
5. http://www.usaid.gov/who-we-are/mission-vision-values
6. http://www.usaid.gov/who-we-are/usaid-history
7. https://history.state.gov/milestones/1945-1952/marshall-plan
8. Brad Parks and Nakul Kadaba, "The Elusive Quest for Effective Aid Management in Liberia," *AidData BETA*, October 20, 2010. http://aiddata.org/blog/the-elusive-quest-for-effective-aid-management-in-liberia
9. Marian Leonardo Lawson "Does Foreign Aid Work? Efforts to Evaluate U.S. Foreign Assistance," February 13, 2013. Congressional Research Service R42827.
10. Clare Lockhart, "Fixing US Foreign Assistance: Cheaper, Smarter, Stronger," *World Affairs Journal*, Jan–Feb 2014. http://www.worldaffairsjournal.org/article/fixing-us-foreign-assistance-cheaper-smarter-stronger
11. Ibid.
12. Bono's speech is at https://www.youtube.com/watch?v=PUZFgBqcYt8
13. Lockhart, "Fixing US Foreign Assistance."
14. Ibid.
15. Testimony for Senate Appropriations Subcommittee for State, Foreign Operations and Related Programs Admiral James Stavridis, USN (Ret), Dean, The Fletcher School of Law and Diplomacy, Tufts University Supreme Allied Commander at NATO (2009–13), Commander US Southern Command (2006–09) Co-Chair, US Global Leadership Coalition National Security Advisory Council March 26, 2015.
16. Steven Radelet, "Prosperity Rising," *Foreign Affairs*, January/February 2016, 94.
17. Andrei Shleifer, "Peter Bauer and the Failure of Foreign Aid," *Cato Journal* 29, no. 3 (Fall 2009): 385.

18. Peter Schweitzer, *Clinton Cash: The Untold Story of How and Why Foreign Governments and Businesses Helped Make Bill and Hillary Rich* (New York: Harper Publishers, 2015).

19. Radelet, "Prosperity Rising," 95.

20. http://www.hudson.org/policycenters/13-center-for-global-prosperity

21. Carol C. Adelman and Nicholas Eberstadt, "Foreign Aid: What Works and What Doesn't," AEI No. 3, October 08. https://www.aei.org/publication/foreign-aid-what-works-and-what-doesnt/

22. "Inconclusive" is academese for the following: "In other words, it has not been demonstrated that official development assistance makes a regular and predictable contribution to overall macroeconomic growth." Ibid.

23. Ibid.

24. Alfonso E. Lenhardt, Charles North, and Rolf Anderson, eds., *2015 VOLAG Report*, 4. https://www.usaid.gov/pvo/volag-report

25. Bernard B. Fall, PhD, "The Theory and Practice of Insurgency and Counterinsurgency," *Military Review*, September–October 2015, 46. http://usacac.army.mil/CAC2/MilitaryReview/Archives/English/MilitaryReview_20151031_art001.pdf

26. Ibid., 48.

27. H.R.3829—UNRWA Anti-Incitement and Anti-Terrorism Act, https://www.congress.gov/bill/114th-congress/house-bill/3829/text

28. Brett D. Schaefer and James Phillips, *Time to Reconsider U.S. Support of UNRWA*, The Heritage Foundation, Backgrounder #2997, March 5, 2015. http://www.heritage.org/research/reports/2015/03/time-to-reconsider-us-support-of-unrwa

29. *FY 2014—2017 Department of State and USAID Strategic Plan* April 2, 2014. http://www.state.gov/documents/organization/223997.pdf

30. Eric Rosand, Alistair Millar, and Jason Ipe, *Civil Society and the UN Global Counter-Terrorism Strategy: Opportunities and Challenges* (Washington, DC and New York, NY: Center on Global Counterterrorism Cooperation, September 2008). http://www.icnl.org/research/library/files/Transnational/civil.pdf

31. Helmut Anheier, Marlies Glasius, and Mary Kaldor, *Global Civil Society 2004/5* (London: Sage Publications, 2006), ch. 1, "Introducing Global Civil Society," http://is.muni.cz/el/1423/jaro2007/SOC711/3608937/3610178/2001chapter1.pdf

16

Peace-Building Reboot

The war is over. Now the real fighting begins.
—Afghan proverb

It is more difficult to make peace than it is to make war.
—Colin S. Gray, *Fighting Talk: Forty Maxims on War,*
Peace, and Strategy, 2007

Sun Tzu was keenly aware of the ravages that war inflicts on the civilian population, and the heavy price of the ensuing devastation. Hence he admonishes: "The worst policy is to attack cities. Attack cities only when there is no alternative" (*AoW* III. 7). One gathers that, regardless of German perfidy, he would most likely have deplored the Allied carpet-bombing of Dresden in World War II. Sun Tzu also warns against underestimating the difficulty of understanding an alien land, which argues against foolhardy foreign escapades: "Those who do not know the conditions of mountains and forests, hazardous defiles, marshes and swamps, cannot conduct the march of an army" (*AoW* VII. 10). Local guidance is indispensable: "Those who do not use local guides are unable to obtain the advantages of the ground" (*AoW* VII. 11). And those guides, needless to say, must be verifiably reliable. Twelfth-century Sun Tzu commentator Ho Yen-hsi asks, rhetorically: if "we hasten to unfamiliar land where cultural influence has not penetrated and communications are cut, and rush into its defiles, is it not difficult?"[1] You cannot expect to muscle your way into another world unless you have taken the time to learn about it. But that has to happen before you are compelled to intervene. Indeed, if you are far-sighted and clever enough, you may even be able to avoid that contingency altogether—if, that is, you can become a master peace builder.

Though Sun Tzu does not deal with peace building, his perspective allows us to infer that he would support preemptive measures to discourage enemy attacks, including averting state failure. Its (posthumously bestowed) title notwithstanding, there is nothing in *The Art of War* that in any way glorifies warfare in the manner of ancient Greek—most notably, Spartan—culture; Sun Tzu's concern appears to be essentially defensive. This is underscored by his repeated emphasis on winning against the opposing strategy of the offensive enemy, rather than on the battlefield. Sun Tzu consistently supports peace fare over warfare: he prizes planning over firepower, commends savvy over gunpowder, and advocates using every instrument of power preferably instead of the military, if at all possible, in order to prevail. What is more, coercion is deemed inferior to noncoercive methods of influence.

With all due respect to Joseph Nye, coercive nonmilitary instruments of power might not be "soft," and they may not be especially "smart" in some cases, but they are important. These include trade embargos, visa restrictions, financial sanctions, and other measures that could be seen as modes of warfare, given that they are principally hostile, but they do fall short of hard power and are commonly used during periods most people consider quite peaceful indeed. Closer to the other end of the engagement spectrum and more to Nye's liking, the more traditional modes of peace fare involve a whole slew of humanitarian activities such as raising hospitals and building schools, providing medical care, and conducting reconciliation seminars, which are designed primarily to win friends rather than attack enemies.

This method of classification, however, is obviously overly simplistic. For some activities that at first blush appear entirely benign, such as strengthening civic institutions and empowering small entrepreneurs, may threaten some in positions of authority who see their own power eroded as a result. Since such civil society-building activities, therefore, are often subtly subversive of existing leadership, and may even facilitate regime change, whether we describe them as forms of warfare or peace fare depends on your strategic perspective.

It should be fairly obvious that given the potential of all these forms of engagement, which are far short of war, to preempt violence, they are well worth the small price tag of such relatively minor actions. Yet given that supporting groups and individuals abroad may cause repercussions sooner or later, particularly if the assistance is effective, they are bound to cause controversy at home and abroad, and might have to be undertaken covertly. For this reason, they have traditionally been undertaken by the CIA: the best known cases during the Cold War included the support of radios such as Radio Free Europe, which targeted Eastern Europe (where I was honored to speak on occasion, in Romanian) and the Russian-language Radio Liberty,[2] along with funding and disseminating translations of books like *Doctor Zhivago*, which contributed enormously to exposing the truth about the USSR.[3]

The broader CIA's initiative was likened to a "Mighty Wurlitzer" by its orchestrator, Frank Wisner. The boast, however, referred mainly to his lofty aspiration—that the operation should create the tunes to which the rest of the world would dance. The reality was in fact far less sinister. As historian Hugh Wilford painstakingly demonstrates in his bestselling *The Mighty Wurlitzer: How the CIA Played America*, the notion that CIA "puppet masters," whose recipients were simple marionettes, is not only inaccurate, but highly misleading.[4] Rather, the centerpiece of the effort, the Congress for Cultural Freedom (CCF), brought together prominent thinkers, funding superb journals such as *Encounter, The New Leader, The Partisan Review*, and others, enabling them to continue work they had been doing all along. Patrick Iber describes it as

> an opportunity to guarantee that anti-Communist ideas were not voiced only by reactionary speakers; most of the CCF's members were liberals or socialists of the anti-Communist variety. . . . [The] CCF ran lectures, conferences, concerts, and art galleries. It helped bring the Boston Symphony Orchestra to Europe in 1952, for example, as part of an effort to convince skeptical Europeans of American cultural sophistication and thus capacity for leadership in the bipolar world of the Cold War.[5]

The relationship between journals that published articles illustrating the real nature of Communist subversive "active measures" is illustrated by my own experience. The journal *Survey*, under the editorship of the highly respected Polish journalist Leopold Labedz, in 1983 published an article I had written on the Soviet Union's uses of the United Nations, specifically including espionage and disinformation.[6] Five years later, I saw it again—this time, in still-Communist Poland though just days before its collapse, where I was participating in a (privately funded) seminar on democracy at Kraków's famous Jagiellonian University. It was a Polish translation, part of a tiny book the size of a cigarette pack, printed in infinitesimally small font by the New York–based Committee in Support of Solidarity in 1985, then reprinted again in Kraków in 1987. As it happens, there is no evidence the funding came from either the CIA or the AFL–CIO, which was famously and commendably helping the dissident Polish trade union. (As it happens,

I had received no honoraria at any point.) But *Survey* was no different from *Encounter*; they published most of the same authors, and were equally independent.

Clearly, such activities do not have to bear the CIA's stigma, unfortunately not undeserved in light of the agency's far-less-savory covert activities whose damaging aftershocks did more harm than good. Disseminating accurate news about America, engaging in cultural diplomacy, and supporting genuine artistic efforts in totalitarian countries, was also part of the mission of the USIA. Some of the funding for such activities and other kinds of civil society support might have been tasked to USAID, at least in principle. In reality, however, that was not an option. It would have been completely against USAID's entrenched organizational culture.

The people who originally joined USAID were anything but national security minded. Most had been attracted by its avowedly altruistic, humanitarian, peace-building mandate predicated on the notion that rich countries had a duty to relieve poverty all over the world. For many of these folks to be asked, during the 1990s, after the fall of the Soviet bloc, during the 1990s, to engage in what came to be known as *democracy assistance*, had to come as something of a shock. Implementing the rule of law, holding free and fair elections, and improving political processes, such as party-building, strengthening civil society, and establishing free associations, training journalists and supporting independent media, encouraging economic self-sufficiency, and conducting civic education, though interesting and exciting, was not what they had bargained for. Understandably, USAID had no expertise on these issues; but that its employees were offered virtually no training was unconscionable. The result was that USAID never saw itself—nor was capable of acting—as a national security organization at the very time when its work took on new importance. Once USAID's democracy building work came under the ominous rubric of "nation-building," however, the civilian-military rift that had already been in place for some time became a chasm.

But enough, as they say, is enough. A reconciliation between these opposing realms will simply have to take place, preferably sooner than later, for like it or not, nation-building, or stabilization operations (SO), or whatever we want to call such work, is unlikely not to be required of us again. Some of our allies, notably Canada, the United Kingdom, and the Netherlands, none of which comes close to the United States in power and resources, have nevertheless proven capable and willing to establish impressive organizational structures to deal with this critical set of activities that, in the long and even short run, should make for a safer world. We, by contrast, aren't anywhere near. At a conference held on September 17, 2015, at the National Defense University (NDU), several high-level speakers assigned to different offices participating in SO concluded that while recent history "has demonstrated the military's ability to execute SO across the conflict continuum. . . . DoD must temper its expectations of the IA [meaning, the interagency, i.e., the civilian agencies]."[7] In other words, let's face it: if the military doesn't rise to the occasion it, the civilians surely won't. So we need to suck it up and do the best we can.

Giving up on the IA, however, is tantamount to capitulating, to accepting that the US government's peacetime agencies are incapable of applying their skills (if any) to tasks that should in fact belong to them. Nor is it merely a matter of resources. We have allowed ourselves to rely on people who are trained for war to conduct peacetime activities. But as war and peace become increasingly blurred, as more conflict takes place in what has been called "the gray zone," both language and practice are militarized. As the military does more things for which it hasn't been trained, the civilian sector atrophies. But the civilian sector has an enormous reservoir of talent and expertise that should not be left untapped.

The NDU seminar participants were not overly optimistic. Having determined that "the most likely recurring SO challenges will fall into the category of conflict prevention and deterrence" expected to occur in a "gray zone in an environment short of war, which undermines stability," the importance of undertaking governance assistance is obvious. Yet "the gray zone lacks an effective planning construct, as the US government has yet to define what is a 'tolerable' level of instability." But "without an IA planning construct collaboration, unity of effort and a whole of government approach to conflict mitigation will prevent the attainment of policy objectives and protection of national interests." No relief is in sight. Indeed, "the current state of acceptance by U.S. senior policy makers is insufficient"[8]—which is another way of saying that the national security system is broken and likely to stay that way.

"Gray zone" conflicts are but one way of describing a confusing array of circumstances that make it hard to operate in the New World Disorder. Other modes of conflict or "war" are protracted, ambiguous, and hybrid—the latter having become particularly popular since the

305

Russian invasions, first in Georgia, then Ukraine, and most recently Syria. Though not new in every respect, Victor Morris of the US Army Europe's joint Multinational Readiness Center explains, we are still trying to wrestle with how to describe it:

> Contemporary *hybrid warfare, hybrid threat* and *hybrid aggression* have all been used to describe potent and complex variations of warfare in the 21st century. Although this type of warfare is not new, contemporary threat actors are redefining the application by employing 21st century technologies and combinations of diplomatic, intelligence, militaristic, economic, and humanitarian means, and in various domains that are overlapped by cyberspace. What further complicates this form of warfare is the persistent fluctuation and manipulation of political, informational, and ideological conflict—key aspects of hybrid warfare which extend past traditional coercive diplomacy and unconventional war.[9]

Put differently, hybrid war is also a kind of hybrid peace, given that all instruments of power are being manipulated at all times by savvy actors throughout the world. It all depends how you choose to look at it, and, more to the point, how you want others to look at it. Emphasizing the belligerent component creates a sense of urgency; taking account of the normalcy that prevails in peacetime, however, allows taking advantage of the many ordinary interactions that provide opportunities to enhance communication and trust-building, improving alliances, and strengthening the resilience of civil society. But whatever words we may choose to describe it, a hybrid or "gray" situation calls for a mixture of approaches and tools. So once again, the simplistic dichotomy of hard power [coercive and strategic] as against soft power [attractive and nonstrategic] falls short. The complex reality of our times demands a more robust language to both describe theoretically and implement operationally a unified national interest through all the instruments of power.

Our enemies tend to approach the gray zone from an offensive perspective, having demonstrated an impressive array of techniques that fall roughly under the rubric of "political warfare" (rather than peace fare), with China arguably leading in imagination and scope. As Timothy Walton, a Delex Systems analyst, points out in his Special Report on China prepared for a 2012 conference on US strategy toward China, in 2003 the Chinese Communist Party approved a concept that the People's Liberation Army calls "Three Warfares" (san zhong zhanfa, 三种战法), which "is aimed at preconditioning key areas of competition in its favor."[10]

As defined by DOD in its 2011 *Annual Report to Congress on Military and Security Developments Involving the People's Republic of China*, these three warfares include:

- **Psychological Warfare** seeks to undermine an enemy's ability to conduct combat operations through operations aimed at deterring, shocking, and demoralizing enemy military personnel and supporting civilian populations.
- **Media Warfare** is aimed at influencing domestic and international public opinion to build support for China's military actions and dissuade an adversary from pursuing actions contrary to China's interests.
- **Legal Warfare** uses international and domestic law to claim the legal high ground or assert Chinese interests. It can be employed to hamstring an adversary's operational freedom and shape the operational space. Legal warfare is also intended to build international support and manage possible political repercussions of China's military actions.[11]

These distinct though related warfares are all, in turn, subordinated to what is more broadly known as Information Warfare—none of it secret. Walton observes that "in its 2009, 2010, and 2011 annual reports on the military power of China, DOD has noted the development of Three Warfares. However, the U.S. has taken little action to counter or mitigate the effects of this adversarial concept."[12] When it comes to nonlethal engagement, the United States is at best flat-footed. This is one reason for applauding the release in 2015 of a White Paper on *Special Operations Forces Support for Psychological Warfare* (SOFSPW), which points out that Special Forces have been engaged for decades in this kind of business, however politically incorrect the term may be.

While the SOFSPW White Paper did not make headlines in the popular media, it certainly provides a highly useful summary of coercive yet nonlethal instruments that the United States has available, should it choose to use them. Once again, it underscores the need to obliterate a rigid distinction between war and peace, reinforcing what Sun Tzu has called "indirect" rather than "direct" actions. And it is solidly grounded in a grand-strategic context:

> Political Warfare emerges from a Whole-of-Government approach to international diplomatic and security engagement, with agencies beyond DOD performing critical, if not leadership, roles. The overall Political Warfare effort relies on the synchronized and evolving combination of capabilities possessed, enabled, or supported by

SOF. They include coercive diplomacy, economic coercion and engagement, Security Sector Assistance, Unconventional Warfare, and Information and Influence Activities.[13]

These are all essentially hard-power-centric tactics. *Coercive diplomacy* is generally defined as "diplomacy presupposing the use or threatened use of military force to achieve political objectives,"[14] which boils down to a reminder that military force will indeed be used unless political objectives are met. In other words, it's notifying the intended target that a gun is being pointed in its direction, ready to be fired. The oxymoron is only apparent: the only way such "diplomacy" can fail to persuade is if the target either does not believe the threat (and hence is not actually "coercive"), or is—whether consciously or subconsciously—suicidal, which renders most forms of "diplomacy" moot anyway.

The paper goes on to describe in considerable detail how the Special Operations Forces would mobilize in the service of the overall Political Warfare effort, while simultaneously defining that effort as relying "on the synchronized and evolving combination of capabilities possessed, enabled, or supported by SOF." Which seems like a roundabout way of saying that political warfare is what SOF do. And since SOF are "ideally suited to advocate for, integrate, and synchronize the *military* components of Political Warfare," it stands to reason that they seek "to strengthen the whole-of-government network by acting as its connective tissue."[15] Circularity aside, the SOFs' proven record of excellence renders them the most capable segment of the US national security community to operate in the newly rediscovered gray zone between war and peace.

The question, however, remains: does the whole-of-government effort involve just, or even primarily, the *military* components of political warfare? If not, how can the SOF provide the connective tissue in those other—presumably nonmilitary—activities? Either political warfare is essentially a military function, in which case the civilians are secondary, or it is not, in which case the SOF as "connective tissue" for those other functions ends up being a lame figure of speech, mostly speech without much figure. Even though the SOF are better prepared than any other organization for the challenge of coordinating whole-of-government, nonlethal activities designed to create a sustainable peace consistent with democratic values should ideally be conducted by nonmilitary agencies.

The White Paper recognizes this. For while the SOF have developed well thought-out organizational initiatives and are ready to hit the ground running, all these political-warfare efforts require a lead organization that has to be outside DOD if civilian agencies are to be included. The paper's recommended solution is for the National Security Council (NSC) to assign a political-warfare coordinator who would "ensure the coordination and synchronization" of all the government-wide efforts. The problem is: the NSC has no operational authority. The solution offered by the White Paper simply reopens a long-festering wound that has been lurking inside the US government's organization structure for decades.

The White Paper recommends having the State Department (DOS) be the nominal agency in charge, with the NSC sending out the e-mail invites, ensuring that the effort is "a whole-of-government, civilian-led Political Warfare campaign." Meanwhile, SOF "will emerge as a key, central element of Political Warfare integration and execution"[16]—in other words, they basically do the work.[17] In many ways, this is quite ingenious. That DOS could take the lead in these activities, at least in theory, is true. In an unpublished study prepared by an Interdepartmental Committee consisting of representatives of DOS (who chaired it), DOD, Treasure Department, CIA, and USAID, drafted by the distinguished strategic analyst, Dr. D. Robert Worley, argues that, given its traditional responsibility in foreign affairs, DOS is eminently suited "to provide policy guidance and coordination of political warfare programs. . . ."[18] This study provides an excellent model for a whole-of-government effort to combat hybrid or "unconventional" tactics currently embraced by Russia, Iran, and China, not to mention non-state, terrorist organizations.

The good news is that the US Congress is beginning to listen, finally recognizing that the United States has a strategy gap between peace and war. Introduced by with Congressman William "Mac" Thornberry (R-TX), Section 1097 of the National Defense Authorization Act of 2016 directs the Secretary of Defense to develop a strategy and to bring new and creative thinking to the national security challenges we face. But that is also the bad news. You guessed it: why hasn't the Secretary of State been asked to collaborate? Writes David Maxwell: "I know we are deathly afraid of terminology such as political warfare and unconventional warfare. I often hear from military personnel that the civilian leadership and congress do not look favorably on such terms as people recall the friction over the reinvention of irregular warfare post 9-11."[19]

It goes without saying that this friction continues; but we cannot afford to succumb to the status quo. Now that Congress has gotten into the act, Maxwell challenges our leaders to decide: "Are we as [both] a nation and government . . . going to get comfortable"[20] in the gray zone, and take the necessary measures to prevail? Though harboring no illusions, at the end of the day, he is unfailingly optimistic: "We can move from a tactical focus to a strategic focus and as Sun Tzu would have us do, attack the strategies of our adversaries." We can, in principle. Now if we could only take care of those satanic details.

The bottom line, for Maxwell, is that America may be "well equipped for the gray zone is not well prepared"—and the reason is not that we haven't gotten the weapons; rather, "the foundation of being prepared is the ability to 'do' strategy' in the gray zone." He continues:

> We have tactics, techniques, and procedures, we have the units and organizations, we have the ability to campaign in the gray zone and we have the instruments of national power. The question is whether we are prepared to orchestrate all these tools, organizations, and elements as part of a holistic strategy with balance and coherency among ends, ways, and means. And a fundamental question is who (a singular person and a specific organization) is responsible for developing and executing the strategy to address the conditions that exist in the gray zone. I would submit that it is not SOF and it is not in DOD. There has to be a national level organization that must be responsible. The question is do we have national security structure capable of operating in the gray zone?[21]

The short answer: we absolutely do not. But again, it isn't only about bureaucracy, and about who ends up leading the effort. Even if political warfare is largely implemented by SOF, with DOS as the lead coordinator and DOD playing a key strategic role,[22] much is still left undone. For as Maxwell rightly points out, national security is not only a whole-of-government function but indeed a *whole-of-society* concern. An American whole-of-society effort must extend far beyond warfare—political or otherwise. Because the political side itself constitutes at most half the proverbial battle; the other half is actually no battle at all, but seeking to establish mutually beneficial activities that enhance human understanding and cooperation whenever possible. It is a form of gray, or maybe lukewarm, peace.

We might end up calling it *political peacefare, strategic engagement,* or just plain *peace-building.* Semantics notwithstanding, over the course of time words acquire connotations that are nearly impossible to shed. So it is with political warfare: the offensive, belligerent meaning is inescapable. We may—and probably should—use it for specifically military-oriented activities. But that doesn't go far enough. Given that America has always sought to be seen as a peaceful power—sovereign and proudly powerful, but fundamentally benign—the gray zone has to be tackled by working with, rather than against, the common grain, the default-benign consensus. We have to make the case that engagement in the gray zone is everybody's business. Warmongers we are not. That said, Texas has it about right when it draws the line at "Don't mess with us."

We have always been a welcoming nation, provided the newcomers are willing to join us in our great experiment. The torch held high by the Statue of Liberty is famously not a warning to intruders to stay away. Its main message is not that enemies will be met with fire if they dare to attack us; on the contrary, it was intended as a beckoning presence—a beacon of peace. Her official name, "Liberty Enlightening the World," conveys a generous message, to which the nation has been remarkably faithful since its inception. What she holds in her right hand is a *tabula ansata*—a keystone-shaped tablet used to evoke the concept of law - on which it is inscribed "JULY IV MDCCLXXVI"—July 4, 1776. The implication cannot be missed: the United States was founded on the self-evident truths that we are all created equal, with inalienable rights to life, liberty, and the pursuit of happiness, which implicitly accuses anyone who violates those rights of breaking the most fundamental law of all. Even as her size and determined countenance connote power and unflinching commitment to those truths, whose defiance should expect no mercy, her message is serenely, confidently positive.

Not that the Statue of Liberty is the Goddess of Open Borders, notwithstanding the lines from the poetry of Emma Lazarus engraved on the statue's bronze feet, welcoming the world's "huddled masses." Nor would it make sense that it should be, since sovereignty implies a nation's right to define who may be considered a citizen, and hence, too, who may *not*. Yet her formidable demeanor is welcoming, reflecting America's ideal self-image. The country that at its birth was perhaps more firmly committed to global free trade than any other, America continues to be home to people hailing from every corner of the earth. Though an island, we are not insular: we have family ties everywhere. Most of us may not have mastered many foreign languages, but our own is spoken more widely than any other, its range continuing to expand, partly because of technological inventions and cultural products that freedom nurtures.

Humanitarian assistance aside, the United States has not traditionally embraced the notion that building government institutions, national economies, and civil society abroad was worth the money—a sentiment that only grew after the demise of the USSR. According to a 2012 Congressional Research Service (CRS) study by Nina M. Serafino, "[d]uring the 1990s, many policymakers considered the establishment of new institutions in troubled countries to be an overly expensive, if not futile exercise"[23]—evidently unable to see the strategic value of such activities. This translates into relatively meager funding appropriated for projects that sometimes fell under the rubric of democracy building. Those—highly controversial—projects suffered the added misfortune of having to be disbursed by underprepared, overworked, and reluctant USAID employees who saw themselves as humanitarian "development" professionals rather than implementers of US foreign policy. They did not always get help from their equally harassed State Department colleagues, who often failed to coordinate their parallel activities, sometimes working at cross purposes.

Despite some positive results and increased appreciation for the utility of assisting fragile states in strengthening their ability to engage in effective self-government, the message didn't get back to either policy makers or the public at large. Though Congressional calls for abolishing USAID by having it absorbed into the State Department (as happened to USIA in 1999) eventually failed, "foreign aid" remained the black sheep of the appropriations agenda, its reputation as a largely irrelevant boondoggle hard to shed.

In 2006, Secretary of State Condoleezza Rice outlined a new foreign-policy strategy focusing on the "'intersections of diplomacy, democracy promotion, economic reconstruction and military security' and involving extensive changes in government to carry that strategy out."[24] Eager to embrace the idea, the expert community responded in record time, with thoughtful studies containing useful recommendations.[25] One especially prominent feature, as Nina Serafino points out in her CRS Report, "was a recommendation to develop rapidly deployable civilian forces to undertake state-building functions, particularly those related to rule of law, even before hostilities had ceased."[26]

The idea of creating a Civilian Reserve Corps (CRC) similar to the army reserve had first been presented to the president at a meeting on January 13, 2005, which had included Vice President Cheney, Secretaries Rice and Rumsfeld, and Stephen Hadley who was deputy to Rice, by DOD's Doug Feith. As Feith writes in *War and Decision*, it had been on a trip to Baghdad where he saw a soldier, who also happened to be a lawyer, explaining that he would soon be installing a large underground water tank for the neighborhood, so that people would no longer have to wait for the daily deliveries. Surely there is a better way, thought Feith:

> The United States is full of people who are knowledgeable about water systems. Wouldn't it be better if this soldier were performing tasks for which he was actually trained—and a civilian expert were responsible for the water system?[27]

The proposal presented to the president, which would eventually be assigned to the State Department, would involve a database consisting of volunteers with relevant skills needed in reconstruction—including municipal administration, civil engineering, hospital management, and the organization of legal systems. They would be paid to train for their missions and, modeled on the military reserves, would deploy as needed.[28] At issue, however, was not merely—or even primarily— funding; it was, and continues to be, a lack of imagination. As Robert Gates memorably told an audience at Kansas State University in 2007:

> Both the President and Secretary of State have asked for full fund- ing for this initiative. But we also need new thinking about how to integrate our government's capabilities in these areas, and then how to integrate government capabilities with those in the private sector, in universities, in other non-governmental organizations, with the capabilities of our allies and friends—and with the nascent capabilities of those we are trying to help.[29]

That is exactly right. It is called whole-of-society strategy, and we don't have one.

The idea of a CRC is still alive, though barely. The Obama admin- istration has proposed an Expert Corps consisting of an active roster of technical experts, which "could be composed of current temporary hires who have served successfully in Iraq, Afghanistan, Pakistan, and elsewhere, as well as other civilians with critical skills who have not been previously deployed."[30] But a president committed to global dis- engagement rather than engagement, who has admitted that he always wanted to focus on "nation-building here at home" rather than abroad,[31] could not be expected to push this initiative through Congress.

Nevertheless, there is still support for the notion of mobilizing civilian experts "with critical skills" willing and able to work alongside military and diplomatic personnel. Fortunately, the United States is not alone struggling with such problems, particularly since other nations, no less concerned about global security, are themselves experimenting with cost-effective solutions, which to them is even more critical given their considerably smaller national budgets. A case in point is Finland, which has recently formulated a Security Strategy for Society, which is based on collaboration between the Finnish government, the business community, civil society organizations, and individual citizens. It is truly a whole-of-society effort. And though principally directed toward the homeland, it is not so exclusively, but is oriented toward regional partnership, especially in the cyber domain.[32]

There is no reason why such an idea could not be adapted on an international scale, starting small to work out the details. This is anything but an authoritarian-style public mobilization; on the contrary, it being predicated on voluntary participation. But a whole-of-society effort would be far more effective in implementing the art of peace than were the job put solely in the hands of the government. As Colonel Michael R. Eastman notes in his aptly entitled article "Whole of Government is Half an Answer," reform hardly ever happens merely by creating a new position here and there, adding to bureaucratic overhead, or shifting and consolidating bureaus. From his own experiences with peace-building in Iraq and Afghanistan, Eastman finds that "such approaches overlook the vast potential in synchronizing government oversight with private, civil, and nongovernmental organizations already performing a great deal of work in post-conflict environments."[33]

To do a better job of synchronizing all the instruments of power, however, we must first engage in some official housekeeping. The least we can expect from our leadership is that it be capable of articulating a unified and effective grand strategy and making sure it is implemented. The current bicephalous monster with one civilian and one military head, each in turn consisting of several additional appendages, should be helped to evolve into some kind of viable creature that can tackle twenty-first-century threats more credibly. After all, the interagency challenge has always been a difficult issue. But why is it that, over the years, instead of getting better, the congenital bicephaly has grown only more grotesque?

One problem is expecting too much of the National Security Council. As Edward Marks, director of the Simons Center for Interagency Cooperation, writes in the fall issue of the journal *InterAgency*, the National Security Council (NSC) was originally created to provide the president with an interagency coordinating body, but at President

Harry Truman's insistence, ended up as a purely advisory body. The need for interagency coordination, however, didn't go away—and with it, the illusion that the NSC could undertake it. Over the years, the NSC ended up playing various roles depending on the desires of the incumbent president; some NSC advisors and staff were more influential than others. But it could never authorize action; the final power rested with the president, who could not delegate it to the NSC even if he had wanted to.

It was left to the hapless State Department, the agency whose job it is to formulate foreign policy, to try to coordinate as best it could, at least in the field. As Marks explains, at the moment,

> [t]he American embassy is arguably the only formal whole-of-government institution in the U.S. government besides the White House. Yet State shares interest and responsibility for all of these interests with other departments who each have the advantage of focus and constituency support. State is in a sense responsible for managing the traffic flow, but a traffic cop without arrest authority—and no one really likes the traffic cop.[34]

Meanwhile, however, over the decades, the military gained in stature; and while "participat[ing] in embassies as defense attaches and military assistance teams, [they] have also created a parallel inter-governmental system."[35] DOD's gradual ascendance, however, has put DOS in a very difficult situation. To be sure, the United States in not unique in this regard. Continues Marks:

> Foreign Affairs Ministers no longer hold a monopoly over foreign affairs, as the process of international relations now includes domestic agencies and important non-state actors as major participants. This process, beginning early in the 20th century, became more dominant after the Cold War when the bipolar political and economic architecture of that period fractured into disparate interests and great fluidity in international relations. Today, with a multiplicity of economic, social, and ideology factors in addition to the traditional competition for political influence, ministries of foreign affairs are no longer the exclusive channel for international contacts.[36]

But this is not a viable situation, especially given the meteoric rise of non-state actors after 9/11. With each agency having its own international contacts, State's coordinating role has become increasingly more important in principle, but not in fact. Meanwhile, DOD is operating, with a budget that makes State's look like small change. Next to its civilian little brothers, DOD is the mammoth elephant in the room. As the two agencies have evolved side by side, in any given country the US government now has two senior representatives: the ambassador and the combatant commander. Marks explains that as a result, "with the existence of these two parallel 'foreign policy' bureaucracies, coordination is heavily dependent on personal relations or very high-level coordination in Washington." The profound depth of the grand divide between these two important agencies would be on full display in the disastrous peace-building operations after the military interventions in Afghanistan and Iraq.

To be sure, recommendations have arisen galore, from both government and private think tanks, pundits and practitioners, how to improve the nation's ability to prevent war, win the peace beyond the battlefield, and helping other nations stay safe. They range from interesting and thought-provoking to self-serving and utopian. Most entail taking serious steps for which the political will is severely limited. Yet a good many are neither far-fetched nor outlandish, and involve changes in institutional structure, education, and the private sector well worth considering.

In the first place, Congress should at least take a look at the findings of the Project for National Security Reform, which it had itself mandated, in 2006, and the recommended improvements to the US national security system. It was a good idea then to examine the problems and seek solutions; it still is. Why not take advantage of all that research? Over three hundred of the nation's best national security experts from think tanks, universities, federal agencies, law firms and corporations, were able to produce a report in less than two years. That report, *Forging a New Shield*, offers concrete recommendations which deserve serious appraisal by the House and Senate. In a few words, the nearly three hundred-page report concluded that

> the basic deficiency of the current national security system is that parochial departmental and agency interests, reinforced by Congress, paralyze interagency cooperation even as the variety, speed, and complexity of emerging security issues prevent the White House from effectively controlling the system. The White House bottleneck, in particular, prevents the system from reliably marshaling the needed but disparate skills and expertise from wherever they may be found in government, and from providing the resources to match the skills. That bottleneck, in short, makes it all but impossible to bring human and material assets together into a coherent operational ensemble. Moreover, **because an excessively hierarchical national security**

system does not know what it knows as a whole, it also cannot achieve the necessary unity of effort and command to exploit opportunities.[37]

Perhaps the most urgent overhaul is needed by the one agency without a domestic constituency: The State Department itself. One option, recommended by Marks is to rename it and indeed replace it with a "Department of Foreign Affairs Coordination," where policy and resource integration directed at the White House or cabinet level would be implemented in a coordinated fashion at the regional assistant secretary level, and then at each embassy's country-team level, headed by the respective ambassador. This may sound far-fetched and radical, and will (inevitably) be opposed by the Sir Humphreys[38] of the department, but it is eminently reasonable.

One other interesting suggestion has been advanced by Air Force General (Ret.) Richard Myers:

> The issue to date, and certainly through my tenure in the Joint Chiefs of Staff, is that below the President there is no one person, head of a department, or head of an agency who has been tasked with or is responsible for the strategic direction and integration of all elements of national power, so the United States can properly execute a strategy for Iraq, Afghanistan, or a global counterinsurgency. And while there are people who are tasked to do parts of this job, nobody brings it all together. In particular, nobody has the authority and influence needed across the whole U.S. government to be responsible, and held accountable, for strategic planning and execution. We need some new constructs and some new matrixed organizations.[39]

Were Alexander Hamilton alive today, it would be the perfect job for him.

But maybe the not-so-civil war between DOD and DOS did not have to become so virulent, especially in the last two decades, had it been handled better. This, at least, is what NDU's Christopher Lamb, concludes in his article "How System Attributes Trumped Leadership," included in the fine new NDU study, *Lessons Encountered: Learning from the Long War.* Disagreements between DOS and DOD, argues Lamb, "were not reconciled and the success of the postwar mission was compromised—not because of opportunistic assumptions about Iraqi sentiments but because differences between strong departments were not managed well."[40] (The report's title adopts the British equivalent of "lessons learned," highlighting the gaping distinction between mere encounter and actual response.)

Examples abound of presidential guidance being ignored, misunderstanding about who had "the lead" on operations, and a whole slew of "impediments to unified effort at three levels—decisionmaking at the national level (meaning between the White House staff and organizations constituting the National Security Council); within departments and agencies, particularly the Pentagon; and in the field (that is, Afghanistan and Iraq)."[41] This applies to both Republican and Democratic administrations. To some extent, this is sheer incompetence; reading Sun Tzu—or anything else for that matter—won't make much difference. But at another level, it's what happens when even perfectly intelligent, hardworking, well-meaning people are not given proper training. And for that, the right reading and the right guidance, though no panacea, can most certainly make a difference.

Few would disagree that greater emphasis is needed on continuing, ongoing education—across the board, for people serving throughout the entire national-security apparatus, but especially for the civilians who do not have access to the plethora of schools and programs available to the military community. That goes for people at all levels, but specifically, writes Lamb, "[s]enior leaders [who] need to better appreciate the limits of the current system's ability to understand foreign social and political structures—and the fact that this kind of knowledge cannot be generated quickly or organized well on the fly. Leaders must act in advance to institutionalize an effective and expandable sociocultural knowledge base. New organizations to provide sociocultural knowledge seem expensive until the alternative is considered, something the past 15 years of war should have made painfully clear."[42]

Sociocultural education in particular is lacking in both the military and civilian sectors—and it isn't something that can be turned on and off with a spigot. NDU's Frank G. Hoffman and G. Alexander Crowther, writing in the same volume, observe that "DOD's education programs should be adapted to better prepare officers to accept that reality and work in a more iterative way rather than expect the current school model of progressive and deductive reasoning"[43]—in other words, seek to transcend the linear model of reasoning. On the other end of the organizational spectrum, "Civilian political officials will often explore an array of options without defining a firm political endstate. They may be more comfortable exploring the art of the possible and examining political factors and risks differently. They may be more comfortable with ambiguity, political elements, and other intangibles."[44] Their intellectual strengths notwithstanding, it is absolutely imperative for civilian leaders to learn how to define "a firm political endstate," which Hoffman and Alexander recognize: "Policymakers are not generally school-trained in the military decisionmaking process or educated to follow linear planning processes. Instead, they are inclined to search iteratively for general options and reverse-engineer specific objectives."

There are excellent educational programs ready and available in Washington, DC, besides NDU along with the National War College, including Georgetown University's Center for Security Studies, USIP, and the Daniel Morgan Academy, and George Mason University's program on International Security. Certainly there are many outside the capital—notably Fort Leavenworth's impressive Kansas campus, the Center for Stabilization and Economic Reconstruction at the University of North Carolina's Institute for Defense and Business, the Naval Postgraduate's programs in International Relations and Diplomacy, Political-Military Studies, Public Affairs, Religious Studies, and others, which involve a number of "approved" affiliated schools such as Stanford, Tufts, Johns Hopkins, Georgetown, Duke, Trinity Evangelical Divinity School, Emory, Boston, and Princeton Theological Seminary. Additional programs that offer interagency education and cultural knowledge are Air University's Culture and Language Center in Birmingham, Alabama, and Marine Corps University's Center for Advanced Operational Culture in Quantico, Virginia, among others. The list is long, but whether the assets are well distributed, the most appropriate students enrolled, and the best suited subject matter taught, is another question—well worth exploring.

As Secretary Gates has pointed out, we must engage the enormous and entirely underutilized private sector, which more than anything will help this country emerge from the current confusion and lack of direction. One example is the Global Development Alliance (GDA), which combines the assets and experiences of the private sector—corporations, foundations, nongovernmental organizations (NGOs), universities, local businesses and Diaspora (immigrant) groups—leveraging their capital and investments, creativity and access to markets to solve various complex problems facing governments, businesses, and communities. The organization describes itself as "more than just philanthropy or corporate social responsibility, [since] GDAs leverage market-based solutions to advance broader development objectives.... [They] are co-designed, co-funded, and co-managed by all partners involved, so that the risks, responsibilities, and rewards of partnership are shared. They work best and have the greatest development impact when private sector business interests intersect with USAID's strategic development objectives."[45] Who knows, perhaps with a little luck, those objectives really will be strategic one of these days. By all accounts, we're not there yet.

George Washington, Alexander Hamilton, Ben Franklin, those peerless Adamses, all our exemplary Founders—where are you when we need you?

Notes

1. Griffith, *Sun Tzu – The Art of War*, 105.
2. Arch Puddington, *Broadcasting Freedom: The Cold War Triumph of Radio Free Europe and Radio Liberty* (Lexington: University Press of Kentucky, 2003).
3. Peter Finn and Petra Couvee, *The Zhivago Affair: The Kremlin, the CIA, and the Battle Over a Forbidden Book* (New York: Vintage Books, 2014).
4. Hugh Wilford, *The Mighty Wurlitzer: How the CIA Played America* (Cambridge, MA: Harvard University Press, 2009).
5. Patrick Iber, "Literary Magazines for Socialists Funded by the CIA, Ranked," *The Awl*, August 24, 2015. http://www.theawl.com/2015/08/literary-magazines-for-socialists-funded-by-the-cia-ranked
6. Juliana G. Pilon, "The United Nations: Shattered Illusions," *Survey* 27, no. 118/119 (Autumn–Winter 1983): 90–111.
7. Scott Braderman, AUSA Hosts "The Future of Stability Operations" Panel, September 17, 2015, *PKSOI Journal* 6, no. 1 (November 2015). file:///C:/Users/Owner/Documents/Soft%20weapons/Foreign%20Assistance/Peace_Stability_Journal_Volume6_Issue1_reduced.pdf
8. Ibid.
9. Victor R. Morris, "Grading Gerasimov: Evaluating Russian Nonlinear Warfare through Modern Chinese Doctrine," *Medium*, May 14, 2015. https://medium.com/@Doctrine_Man/grading-gerasimov-8089ea595851
10. Timothy Walton, "China's Three Warfares," Delex Special report-3, Delex Systems, Inc., January 10, 2012. file:///C:/Users/Owner/Documents/Soft%20weapons/Soft%20power%20-%20PD%20SC/Three%20Warfares.pdf
11. Office of the Secretary of Defense (DoD), *Military and Security Developments Involving the People's Republic of China 2011*, Annual Report to Congress (Washington, DC: DoD, 16 August 2011), 26. http://www.defense.gov/pubs/pdfs/2011_CMPR_Final.pdf
12. Ibid., 4.
13. SOFSPW White Paper, 11.
14. Carnes Lord, "The Psychological Dimension in National Strategy," with comments by Paul A. Smith, Jr., and Richard G. Stilwell, in Barnett and Lord, eds., *Political Warfare and Psychological Operations* (Washington, DC: National Defense University Press, 1989).
15. Ibid., 28.
16. Ibid., 32.
17. The White Paper thus adopts, giving full credit to, the recommendations by Max Boot and Michael Doran in their earlier cited CFR study released in 2013.

18. D. Robert Worley, "United States Political Warfare Policy," Jan. 2015 (unpublished), p. 24. https://David S. Maxwelldl.dropboxusercontent. com/u/6891151/2015,03,14%20PWP.pdf

19. David S. Maxwell, "Congress Has Embraced Unconventional Warfare: Will the US Military and the Rest of the US Government?," *Small Wars Journal*, December 29, 2015. http://smallwarsjournal.com/jrnl/art/congress-has-embraced-unconventional-warfare-will-the-us-military-and-the-rest-of-the-us-go

20. Ibid., word as well as emphasis added.

21. David S. Maxwell, News from the Associate Director, Security Studies Program, "Paradoxes of the Gray Zone by Hal Brands," February 6, 2016. http://maxoki161.blogspot.com/2016/02/paradoxes-of-gray-zone-by-hal-brands.html?utm_source=feedburner&utm_medium=email&utm_campaign=Feed%3A+NewsFromTheAssociateDirectorSecurityStudiesProgram+%28News+from+the+Associate+Director%2C+Security+Studies+-Program%29

22. Among the most effective ways to promote peace are effective military exchanges: "In its attempt to promote stability and prevent conflict, one of the more effective ways America exerts influence is by building partnerships with the armed forces of potential allies. Not only do these relationships open channels of communication and reduce opportunities for miscalculation, but they also tend to have a professionalizing effect on the militaries involved." Michael R. Eastman, "American Land power and the Middle East of 2030," *Strategic Studies Institute*, Autumn 2012. http://strategicstudiesinstitute.army.mil/pubs/parameters/Articles/2012autumn/Eastman.pdf

23. Nina M. Serafino, Specialist in International Security Affairs, *Peacekeeping/Stabilization and Conflict Transitions: Background and Congressional Action on the Civilian Response/Reserve Corps and other Civilian Stabilization and Reconstruction Capabilities* (Washington DC: Congressional Research Service, October 2, 2012), 3.

24. Taken from a speech delivered by then-Secretary of State Condoleezza Rice. Remarks at Georgetown School of Foreign Service, January 18, 2006. http://www.state.gov/secretary/rm/2006/59306.htm

25. Among the reports are: (1) *Play to Win: The Final Report of the Bi-partisan Commission on Post-Conflict Reconstruction*, Center for Strategic and International Studies (CSIS) and the Association of the US Army (AUSA), 2003 (a booklength version was published in mid-2004, Robert C. Orr, ed., *Winning the Peace: An American Strategy for Post-Conflict Reconstruction*); (2) Clark A. Murdock, Michèle A. Flournoy, Christopher A. Williams, and Kurt M. Campbell, principal authors, *Beyond Goldwater-Nichols: Defense Reform for a New Strategic Era Phase I Report*, CSIS, March 2004; (3) Hans Binnendijk and Stuart Johnson, eds., *Transforming for Stabilization and Reconstruction Operations*, National Defense University Center for Technology and National Security Policy, April 2004, (4) *On the Brink: Weak States and US National Security, Center for Global Development*, May 2004; Office of the Under Secretary of Defense for Acquisition, Technology, and Logistics. *Defense Science Board 2004 Summer Study on Transition to and From Hostilities*, December 2004; and *In the Wake of War: Improving*

U.S. Post-Conflict Capabilities, Washington, DC: Council on Foreign Relations, Report of an Independent Task Force, July 2005.

26. Serafino, *Peacekeeping/Stabilization and Conflict Transitions*, 3.

27. Feith, *War and Decision*, 451.

28. Ibid., 512.

29. Robert M. Gates, Landon Lecture, 11-26-07 https://www.k-state.edu/media/newsreleases/landonlect/gatestext1107.html

30. Serafino, *Peacekeeping/Stabilization and Conflict Transitions*, 29.

31. Stephen Sestanovich, George F. Kennan Senior Fellow for Russian and Eurasian Studies at Columbia University, wrote that "at the start of the Obama administration, it was of course not certain how far disengagement would go." Stephen Sestanovich, "Obama's Focus Is on Nation-Building at Home," *New York Times*, March 11, 2014. http://www.nytimes.com/roomfordebate/2014/03/11/weakness-or-realism-in-foreign-policy/obamas-focus-is-on-nation-building-at-home

32. Aapo Cederberg and Pasi Eronen, Strategic Security Analysis, "How Can Societies Be Defended Against Hybrid Threats?" *Geneva Centre for Security Policy*, September 2015, No. 9.

33. Michael R. Eastman, "Whole of Government Is Half the Answer," *Interagency Journal* 3, no. 2 (Summer 2012). http://thesimonscenter.org/wp-content/uploads/2012/08/IAJ-3-3-pg31-39.pdf

34. Edward Marks, "The State Department: No Longer the Gatekeeper," *Inter-Agency Journal* 6, no. 4 (Fall 2015). http://thesimonscenter.org/wp-content/uploads/2015/11/IAJ-6-4-Fall-2015-3-15.pdf

35. Ibid.

36. Ibid.

37. http://www.worldcat.org/identities/lccn-no2008147273/

38. The consummate bureaucrat from the incomparable BBC series "Yes, Prime Minister," played to astonishing perfection by Nigel Hawthorne.

39. Richard Myers and Malcolm McConnell, *Eyes on the Horizon: Serving on the Front Lines of National Security* (New York: Simon & Schuster, 2009), 302.

40. Christopher J. Lamb with Megan Franco, *Lessons encountered*, 184–5.

41. Ibid., 189.

42. Christopher J. Lamb with Megan Franco, *Lessons Encountered*, 250.

43. Frank G. Hoffman and G. Alexander Crowther, "Strategic Assessment and Adaptation: The Surges in Iraq and Afghanistan," *Lessons Encountered*, 142.

44. Ibid., 144.

45. https://www.usaid.gov/gda

17

Exceptionalism as *Realpolitik*

*Let us replace sentimentalism by realism, and dare to uncover those sim-
ple and terrible laws which, be they seen or unseen, pervade and govern.*
—Ralph Waldo Emerson, *Worship*, 1860

*The choice is not between moral principles and the national
interest, devoid of moral dignity, but between one set of moral
principles divorced from political reality, and another
set of moral principles derived from political reality.*
—Hans J. Morgenthau, *In Defense of the National Interest*, 1951

Sun Tzu was an expert strategist, not a *consigliere* to some National
Godfather ruthlessly bent on plunder. In *The Art of War*, he explains
how to defend a state committed to survival against attack and how to
prevail against its enemies most efficiently. In that sense, he is a realist. But Sun Tzu's signature principle, which is to seek victory without
firing a shot, underscores his conviction that genuine success entails
a commitment to values that transcend mere survival. If that also
makes him an idealist, then so he was—albeit no utopian. Sun Tzu's
conception of international affairs is not Hobbesian or even Machiavellian: there is no suggestion in his writings that mankind is doomed
to endless cutthroat competition among states in a chaotic world with
no imperial global policeman to impose order. Though it would be left
to future Taoists to elaborate on the qualities of good statesmanship,
Sun Tzu clearly suggests that a government whose civilian and military
leadership follows his advice would be considered exemplary—and in
that sense at least, "exceptional." Every state, of course, is potentially
capable of it, though in reality, few make the grade.

Genuine realism demands scrupulous respect for the facts, and the
courage to rely on reason rather than wishful thinking. Far ahead of his
time, when most fellow *Homo sapiens* still trembled before imaginary
demons, Sun Tzu was adamantly opposed to all irrational practices. In

addition to noting that "foreknowledge" in foreign affairs cannot be elicited from spirits nor from gods but from solid intelligence obtained by "men who know the enemy situation" (*AoW* XIII. 4), Sun Tzu declared unequivocally that a good general "*prohibits* superstitious practices" (*AoW* XI. 44). The rules of conflict being rational, they are theoretically accessible to anyone. The only exceptional thing about a society that obeys those rules is that it assiduously seeks to shun unrealistic illusions.

It is mainly in this relatively unremarkable sense—demonstrating a healthy, if rare, respect for empirical facts—that most Americans have traditionally believed their nation to be special. While the early settlers strove to have their actions conform to the Laws of God, they also thought them Laws of Reason, and did not rely on miracles to defeat their enemies. With the exception of the pacifist Quakers, the early colonists did not shrink from battle, but neither did they especially go looking for it. They had braved the treacherous seas to make a life in what they thought would be mostly virgin territory, or at any rate virgin enough, and to raise families. Notwithstanding occasionally irreconcilable theological disagreements with their kinsmen across the Atlantic, the early settlers owed a great deal to the venerable intellectual tradition that had shaped their thinking.

Historian Walter McDougall argues persuasively that the Founders essentially borrowed their strategic principles from British Whig statecraft—and for the most part, even if only most, he is right. The first of those principles "was unshakeable unity at home, which meant suppressing all particularism"[1] on the part of various ethnic groups— although the rationale for the British was principally to prevent foreign powers from meddling in the nation's internal affairs; England had not quite set out to become a "melting pot." A second principle was "the constant pursuit of a favorable peace through aloofness toward the continental powers when possible and temporary alliances in emergency," which allowed England the luxury of a relatively independent foreign policy. Again, McDougall is right to point out that "indeed, such a maritime grand strategy was even more promising for the United States than it had been for the United Kingdom and United Provinces because the America was so much larger, remoter, and more richly endowed than the lands of the British and Dutch."[2]

Yet he glosses over an important difference between the colonies and the Mother Country when he observes that geographic distance "enabled the British to cultivate from offshore a balance of power in Europe while they pursued unfettered expansion, navigation, and commerce with all countries."[3] While the British were less inclined than the rest of Europe to engage in power politics (as the world's supreme maritime power, they could afford it), the Founders were outright opposed to the practice. That said, when circumstances forced the colonists to take advantage of European kings' machinations, they ended up performing splendidly, if grudgingly—to everyone's astonishment, including undoubtedly their own. With their lives and freedom at stake, the Yankee diplomats proved more than up to the task.

What is more, as we saw in chapter 5, unlike their British kin, the Founders did not seek to pursue "unfettered expansion"—certainly not beyond the Continental boundaries they deemed necessary to accommodate their anticipated demographic growth and the security of frontiers. Instead, it was unfettered navigation and commerce that Americans especially treasured, in truth, even more than did their Mother country, Great Britain. Actually, not to quibble, but it had been Scotland, home to Adam Smith, that had principally fueled the American passion for free trade. In later years, the United States would prove itself more faithful to that passion than nearly every other nation on earth, despite the occasional lapse, which it often came to regret.

American defense of naval commercial travel has been, over the years, the most important, if insufficiently recognized or appreciated, immeasurable service to global security. According to a *Fact Sheet* released by DOD's Freedom of Navigation Program,

> Since the founding of the nation, the United States has asserted a vital national interest in preserving the freedom of the seas and necessarily called upon its military forces to preserve that interest. . . . [T]hree months before the United States entered World War II, President Franklin Roosevelt delivered one of his fireside chats to the American people, in which he declared, 'Upon our naval and air patrol . . . falls the duty of maintaining the American policy of freedom of the seas.' As history shows, this U.S. national interest and policy for preserving the freedom of the seas are long-standing in nature and global in scope.[4]

Rather than an example of imperialist overreach, this constitutes a priceless public good provided free of charge to the world, because it benefits the United States as much as it does everyone else, and because no one but the United States has either the means or will to rise to the challenge. As the *Fact Sheet* points out, the Program encompasses all of the rights, freedoms, and lawful uses of the sea and airspace available to all nations under international law, and is administered with regard to the nature of maritime claims rather than to the identity of the coastal nations asserting those claims. This means that "U.S. forces challenge excessive claims asserted not only by potential adversaries and competitors, but also by allies, partners, and other nations." The United States, in brief, plays fair.

Thus the most important difference between the two Anglican nations is left unstated by McDougall, even though it holds the key to America's peculiar—and yes, exceptional—nature. Unequalled among strong nations, the New World has demonstrated with almost improbable consistency for more than two centuries a decided lack of appetite for world domination. As already indicated, Sun Tzu's spirit is in sync with the American: nowhere in *The Art of War* is conquest for its own sake prescribed; the enemy is assumed to be a source of threat, absent which there would be no reason for unprovoked belligerence. Nowhere does Sun Tzu suggest attacking an enemy merely because his presence might offend one's sensibilities, for aggrandizement *qua* "honor," to please our Creator, or for sheer plunder, however couched in euphemisms.

The Chinese Master did not encourage or even countenance imperial ambitions, and recommended the shortest possible military engagement, if any. "For there has never been a protracted war from which a country has benefited" (*AoW* II. 7). European-style colonialists would have found no fan in Sun Tzu. It has been equally foreign to the United States for most of its history, the few lapses at the turn of the last century mere deplorable exceptions that, as the saying goes, prove the rule. American exceptionalism is not imperialist.

To underestimate this deeply entrenched feature of American foreign policy is to misunderstand what motivates this nation's vision of its role in the world. It is admittedly no easy task to reconcile a generally robust American patriotism with almost complete lack of hegemonic ambitions. But so it is, hard as it may be for most people outside and even inside the United States to appreciate: when questioned, most foreign respondents assume the opposite. For example, a survey conducted by the Pew Research Center cited by Andrew Kohut and Bruce Stokes in their 2006 book, *America Against the World: How We Are Different and Why We Are Disliked*, found a pervasive cynicism about American motives in the fight against terrorism. In seven out of eight nations surveyed, majorities believed that "America's ultimate aim is nothing less than world domination."[5]

In a little-noticed but highly revealing study, three Canadians affiliated with the University of Toronto's Massey College actually set out to find out whether Americans' consistently high opinion of their country is tied to imperialist ambitions or is merely a case of unremarkable—because ubiquitous—ethnocentricity. Neil Seeman and two colleagues, noting the paucity of data on whether Americans considered themselves more exceptional than do other nationalities, decided to conduct a survey using new cloud-based technology developed by RIWI, a Canadian innovation called "random domain intercept technology." The technology is able to capture data from respondents at the same time, living anywhere in the world where Web-enabled devices exist.[6] The results were surprising indeed.

The researchers asked a very simple question, targeting more than 18,000 English-speakers from around the world: *Do you agree or disagree with the statement "The world would be better if it were run by people from my country."* What they found was that Americans generally, with no statistical difference between Republicans and Democrats, were actually *considerably less likely* (at roughly 40 percent) than people from other English-speaking countries (at more than 50 percent) to answer yes. Whatever the reasons for these results, and the authors do offer a few tentative speculations, they deflate the presumption that American exceptionalism is inexorably linked to a desire to rule the world.

Those findings happen to match the results reported by Kohut and Stokes: "Most important, contrary to widespread misconceptions, Americans' pride in their country is not evangelistic."[7] While nearly 70 percent of the American public believes in promoting US-style democracy, it "evidences no missionary zeal for this task." Quite simply, the Pew surveys demonstrate the public's total "lack of imperial aspirations."[8] None. Zero.

Then again, maybe we are missing the point—at least, according to Harvard historian Niall Ferguson. He believes that the United States is suffering from a serious disease he calls "imperial denial," an affliction so widespread, it is nothing short of a "national condition."[9] Ferguson's diagnosis is dire: unless America stops being in denial, and is willing to step up to the global plate, in order to assume the imperial mantle (or is it the imperial bat?) so obviously meant for it at this point in history, we are all doomed to fall into a dark age that will make the previous version look as bright as noon in the Sahara.

He warns against a US withdrawal from Iraq and Afghanistan "before their economic reconstruction has been achieved," invoking the image of the Terminator who "finally admits, 'I won't be back.'"[10] The End. The curtain falls on a world left unrescued. Whether or not Ferguson is proved right in the long run, the fact remains that Americans would rather go home and, frankly, not be back. In a compelling new book, journalist Bret Stephens expresses great concern about an *America in Retreat*—the book's title. The subtitle, *The New Isolationism and the Coming Global Disorder*, is not a conjecture but a prediction. Stephens defends it with alarming success.

There are ample signs, however, that Americans are growing increasingly worried that a policy of retreat, much as many or even most people might like to see it in some ideal world, is not in the nation's interest. According to a survey conducted by the Chicago Council on Foreign Relations released in September 2015, a sizeable majority of Americans now "widely agree that the United States should be actively engaged abroad, with 64 percent of Americans saying the United States should play an active role in world affairs, an increase of six percentage points from last year."[11] That still hardly translates into imperial ambitions. For while nine in ten Americans say that strong US leadership in the world is desirable, a whopping 63 percent "prefer a shared rather than a dominant leadership role."[12] Playing an active role is not synonymous with world policing.

Ferguson may certainly be forgiven for believing that the United States would do what any sensible nation that has the power to keep the peace would, which is to exercise that power, in order to save Civilization (the title, incidentally, of another splendid Ferguson bestseller). Conceding that the Colossus/Goliath/America may be congenitally allergic to calling itself an "empire," Ferguson is palpably impatient to the point of condescension:

> I don't mean to say that the existence of an American empire should instead be proclaimed from the rooftop of the Capitol. All I mean is that whatever they choose to call their position in the world—hegemony, primacy, predominance or leadership—Americans should recognize the *functional* resemblance between Anglophone power present and past and should try to do a better rather than a worse job of policing an unruly world than their British predecessors.[13]

But no matter how functional that resemblance may be, the fact remains that America's ethos is now and has always been very different from

Britain's. After all, Pax Britannica, which lasted roughly from 1815 to 1914, was made possible not only by British naval and economic supremacy—and here the resemblance is admittedly more than just functional—but by the obvious comfort of an ancient monarchy, steeped in centuries-old aristocratic values, with taking on the task of civilizing a world it considered woefully in need of guidance. At this point, the resemblance fades. For though some of the British colonies were not governed directly by the Colonial Office in London but indirectly, through local rulers supervised behind the scenes by British advisors, this was hardly out of respect for local, native self-government—merely a question of cost.

The clearest expression of that attitude was expressed by Prime Minister Robert Salisbury in his astonishingly candid response, penned in 1901, to a suggestion that Britain annex a troublesome Zanzibar and be done with it. Not an option, replied the prime minister:

> The condition of a protected dependency is more acceptable to the half civilised races, and more suitable for them than direct dominion. It is cheaper, simpler, less wounding to their self-esteem, gives them more career as public officials, and spares of unnecessary contact with white men.[14]

Lord Salisbury then added: "we have to deal with Moslems, and Arabs who hate us and our religion and our special notions with a particular hatred." Bloodshed could be avoided, he opined, by working through the puppet Sultan, who "at his dearest, could be very cheap compared to direct government from Downing Street."[15] The British prejudice against those Moslems deemed "half-civilised" did not prevail in early America. As Benjamin Franklin proudly noted in his *Autobiography*, published in 1791, "even if the Mufti of Constantinople were to send a missionary to preach Mohammedanism to us, he would find a pulpit at his service."[16] And, he might have added, an audience in the pews that would be left unmolested.

While Lord Salisbury's pragmatism (bordering on cynicism) may have contributed to a welcome, century-long European respite from bloodshed, the world wars that followed should give us all pause. For their aftershocks are still with us, so many of the old animosities and ideological fault lines having been left unaddressed. One cannot but wonder if a Pax of that kind may not command too steep a price.

Ferguson, like Stephens, is right to fear a world descending into chaos if a nation like America doesn't step up to the plate and enforce an order of a sort that Russia, China, or Iran may not be trusted to bring about. That said, the British Empire is not an apt model for us, however similar it may be to our own. America has to take a different approach, based on its own values. Whereas Britain was condescending, America must be egalitarian. In fact, Ferguson himself stumbles on the answer: "In learning from the history of earlier empires, Americans will learn not arrogance but precisely that humility which, as a candidate for the presidency, George W. Bush once recommended to his countrymen."[17]

Back to basics, again– to wit, humility. Franklin knew it well enough. But it is harder for a hegemonic superpower, whose very size and apparent strength makes even the most strenuous efforts to minimize its own pride hard to sustain, let alone convince others of it. When Uncle Sam says he wants YOU, he may only mean to enlist you in the great army of global consumers, but the rest of the world cannot be expected to get that message the way we do. Not when all about them are ruthless strongmen who will exercise their power, mercilessly, whenever they can, a wrathful-looking man pointing a finger at you, however figuratively, doesn't look humble. He looks threatening.

Never mind that many people may also not wish to take up Sam's exhortation on his terms in the first place. Yet they often find they have no choice in the matter, having to decide between what to them look like two equally bad options: be-global or be-gone. We should recognize the fact that modernity is not always victimless—its benefits unevenly spread, long-standing habits broken, and self-confidence undermined for those who are unwilling or unable to join the bandwagon. These are not trivial concerns. At the very least, it will take a serious effort to prevent American economic preeminence from being misunderstood.

The humility problem to which Ferguson alludes, however, is not so much that the forty-third president proceeded to ignore his own advice—especially compared with his successor, who need never fear being accused of excessive meekness. Rather, it's that genuine humility on the global stage requires undoing some deeply entrenched bad American habits. Over the decades, the magnanimous United States seems to have become mesmerized by the self-evidence of its own good intentions and the universal applicability of its sociopolitico-economic model. No, not everyone trusts us. For while it is true that we have always been, and undoubtedly always will be, a generous people, who believe that every human being has the right to pursue happiness, and that helping others in need is the highest virtue, that is by no means obvious to everyone.

For one thing, it is only partly true. Call it idealism, altruism, Christian charity, or just plain charity (considering that no religious sect has a monopoly on kindness), American generosity is not necessarily disinterested. Nor should it have to be. It is actually possible to be simultaneously the most realistic and the most idealistic nation in the world. Altruism can coexist with self-interest. This might sound surprising if someone motivated by self-interest is thought to be heartless, while altruists are defined as self-less almost to a fault, often being branded as unrealistic bleeding hearts and starry-eyed *idealists*. The problem, again, is not human nature so much as semantics. With apologies for a lexical detour, we can't settle this problem without defining some terms.

We should have plenty to choose from, considering that the total number of words in the English language has been estimated by the Global Language Monitor to have surpassed one million as of June 10, 2009.[18] But despite this embarrassment of riches, there seems to be no good word to describe someone who is motivated by self-interest yet whose conception of self-interest *includes* compassion and generosity. The antonyms for "selfish" include self-sacrificing, self-effacing, even selfless—which is defined as "having *no* concern for self." Altruism is sometimes thought to imply even going *against* your own interests to help someone else. Psychologists have recently coined an interesting hybrid concept, meant to explain battlefield selflessness: "parochial altruism."[19] The pejorative "parochial," however, connoting partiality to a subgroup of "buddies," seems to makes the sentiment sound arguably less "pure" than the standard non-parochial variety, which embraces even people you've never met.

Overly rigid dichotomies, unfortunately, can obscure the myriad nuances of human motivation, about which science knows little, though brain imagery is beginning to throw some light on the complexity of neurological activity we associate with one feeling or another. Sun Tzu's comfort with opposites applies here, in spades; long before fMRI scans, he had understood that human emotions are magically, tantalizingly paradoxical. We are all selfish and unselfish, idealists and realists, frightened and brave—and like us, so are the nations we inhabit. The secret to understanding human motivation is not to oversimplify it, but to set it in the proper context. It also helps to use well defined terms that help clarify rather than obfuscate, without fear of ambiguity but being aware that it exists.

In international affairs, the altruism-selfishness dichotomy exactly mirrors that of idealism-realism. Realism is sometimes used interchangeably with the Prussian concept, *Realpolitik*, coined in 1853 by politician and writer Ludwig von Rochau to reflect the understanding that "the law of power" governs the world of nations like the law of gravity does in the physical world. The term later became associated with the ruthless policies of German Chancellor Otto von Bismarck, becoming increasingly more pejorative and closer in meaning to "power politics." Before long, *Realpolitik* came to "suggest a pragmatic, no-nonsense view and a disregard for ethical considerations. In diplomacy it is often associated with relentless, though realistic, pursuit of the national interest."[20]

If realism as *Realpolitik* (as it had come to be used) connotes outright "disregard for ethical considerations," its exact opposite, idealism, is tantamount to living with your head in the clouds, The average undergraduate who is assigned a textbook like, say, *Dynamics of International Affairs*, learns that "realists anticipate conflict and war; idealists, cooperation and peace. Realists focus on what is good for the state; idealists think more about the good of humanity."[21] So: realists are selfish, idealists are altruists. Ridiculously oversimplified as it may be, this description appears in a popular college text; no wonder it infects the public discourse.

Not that more education necessarily translates into greater wisdom. Academic discussion (of which there is no shortage) regarding these concepts fails to enlighten, or worse. The *Stanford Encyclopedia of Philosophy*'s entry on "Political Realism in International Relations"[22] deplores the effect of fruitless debates about the relative values of classical versus neorealism expressed in abstract scientific and philosophical terms, which "have made the theory of international politics almost inaccessible to a layperson" and useless even to diplomats, let alone lawmakers and the public. Realism, which is "ultimately judged by its ethical standards" that stand outside its scope, is supposed to merely remind us that practical considerations come first and tells us nothing about what goals to pursue, or why. On the other side of the conceptual divide lie utopian ideologies "that lose touch with the reality of self-interest and power."[23] So take your pick. What will it be? Un- or perhaps trans-ethical realism that is all about self-interest and power? Or losing touch with reality? Such are the pitfalls of ivory-tower dialectics.

In a valiant attempt to reconcile realism and idealism, which she admits are "fiercely contested" among academics, former State Department official Anne-Marie Slaughter suggests that "it is usually inappropriate to see them as rivals over some universal truth about world politics."[24] But even if not outright rivals over "some universal truth," the two ideologies are seen as mutually exclusive approaches, and portrayed as opposites, because that is how the terms have traditionally been used over the course of many decades. Idealism appeals to our generosity and empathy, it inspires and uplifts, though is deemed perhaps insufficiently attuned to the real world. On the opposing side, realists are often portrayed as heartless. So when American foreign policy pundits urge a more "realist" approach, they mean we should look to our immediate national self-interest rather than pursue vague and idealistic "values."

The trouble with those "realists," who think they are practicing *Realpolitik*, is that they haven't taken a close enough look at that term in its original incarnation. To the rescue comes a fine new book about this much-misunderstood concept by British historian John Bew. Bew not only felicitously restores Rochau's true intent in coining *Realpolitik* but does one better: he carefully explains both its subsequent distortions and its current importance. Dismissing caricaturized versions of this "much used but little understood" German word by self-described international relations pundits as the intellectual equivalent of food fights, he laments that its true meaning "remains occluded by the partisan way the word has been used in Anglo-American political discourse."[25] (His observation that the word "has become an accoutrement of sophistication, intended to signify one's worldliness and to distinguish oneself from dunderheaded ideologues," far from just off-handedly supercilious, is not left undocumented.[26]) Neither driven by a priggish concern to restore the term's pristine etymology, nor eager to "revive a cult of *Realpolitik*," Bew nevertheless warns that the distortions "opened the door to great misunderstanding and, worse still, wrongdoing."[27] Semantics, as if we needed reminding, is much more than word-play; its real-world implications are often, if not always, momentous.

Instead of either "a theology or a science of statecraft," Rochau had meant *Realpolitik* to describe a way of thinking, which involved looking at any given situation on three levels: the existing distribution of power within a state (as distinct from who merely claims to do so); the social and economic conditions that underlie the political system, and the prevailing cultural context.[28] Above all, Bew points out, "for Rochau, ideas mattered"[29]—hardly an earthshaking revelation; yet he was also a critic of utopianism, as distinct from idealism—"a crucial distinction, often missed by those who claim the mantle of realism today."[30] Indeed! Forget idle theories; look at the world first. Bew argues persuasively that "real *Realpolitik*" (*RealRealpolitik*?) would help in today's complex environment, for it emphasizes "the importance of thinking synthetically and holistically, based on an assessment of all the information before us."[31]

This may sound like "basic common sense," but it is not. Were it to have been applied to the enormously complex situation in the Middle East in recent years, argues Bew, the result would have been

> a more textured analysis—a sense of patterns, interactions, and connections—than by new theories. Such an approach to the Arab spring, for example, would have told us to examine the specific circumstances in each country where it was taking place—but not to dispense with a sense of the connections between each. It would have helped us to distinguish between pure and elegant ideas of freedom—that resonated with our own, or appealed to our sense of symmetry—and those with real social weight and revolutionary force. . . . He would have cautioned us against thinking that one political system could supplant another overnight, or that people would always act in their own interests.[32]

Not that Rochau was in any way an apologist for authoritarianism—quite the contrary. He knew that "authoritarian regimes were inherently unstable, particularly in the age of democracy," indeed altogether "anachronistic." The point is to be clear about what is and what could be; what we want to be true and what *is* true. The idea of freedom is both pure and elegant, and should be pursued if at all possible; but it will not take root simply because we want it to do so—and it certainly won't happen with the speed we try to impose on it when the circumstances aren't ripe.

Somewhat surprisingly, Bew finds that the most enlightened application of *Realpolitik* would not take place in Germany. He cites a Berlin-based professor, who told then-*New Republic* editor Walter Weyl, in 1916, that Germans "'write fat volumes about *Realpolitik* but understand it no better than babies in a nursery,' while Americans, he added with a hint of envy, 'understand it far too well to talk about it.'"[33] Unfortunately, since 1916, American theorists seem to have become more like Germans and babies. It would be well to revisit the common sense idealistic realism, or perhaps realistic idealism, of our Founders, which some have called "exceptionalism." They may not have talked about it, but they certainly practiced it.

"Exceptionalism" too, as noted in chapter 8, has been abused, distorted, and exploited, for it constitutes a mighty appealing rhetorical tool: politicians of all stripes are wont to invoke it by pandering to the multitudes. To be sure, that is what pols do for a living; no one expects them to define their terms. But the academy is no less divided, as scholars, true to form, debate its meaning: many experts believe that America's original mission had been conceived in political, rather than purely religious, terms, while others disagree. Some see it as pointing toward isolationism, while others are convinced it reflects a crusader mentality.

Henry Kissinger, ever the maverick, straddles the two camps, arguing that the United States is systematically ambivalent on the issue: it goes from one extreme to the other. In comparing American and Russian forms of exceptionalism, Kissinger argues that "the openness of each country's frontiers was among the few common features" they both shared. But unlike Russia, whose sense of its specialness was expressed through military adventures, "America's exceptionalism led it to isolationism alternating with occasional moral crusades."[34] Kissinger appears to believe that isolationism is no less an expression of exceptionalism than is "Wilsonianism." Yet he, along with most foreign affairs experts, seems to lean toward the latter as rather more closely associated with exceptionalism, particularly in recent years: "Wilson was the embodiment of the tradition of American exceptionalism, and originated what would become the dominant intellectual school of American foreign policy."[35]

The reason why "Wilsonianism" emerged in World War I, argues Kissinger, is that the ailing president, who had originally promised during his campaign to keep America out of war, later repudiated that pledge, at last having "grasped the mainsprings of American motivation, perhaps the principal one being that America simply did not see itself as a nation like any other. It lacked both the theoretical and the practical basis for the European-style diplomacy of constant adjustment of the nuances of power from a posture of moral neutrality for the sole purpose of preserving an ever-shifting balance."[36] But this claim is highly problematic. Kissinger's suggestion that the United States is incapable of appreciating European-style diplomacy with its power-politics is unfairly condescending. Though Americans have indeed tended to shun what Kissinger calls "moral neutrality," this is perhaps because they recognize that the concept is meaningless: all action, after all, including neutrality, has moral consequences. Moral neutrality is a luxury mostly denied to self-conscious, cogitating creatures. And

Americans have generally cared about acting morally; they have sought to be a force for good, at least as they saw it.

It is this kind of "moral exceptionalism," coupled with the notion that America indeed has been the source of more "good" than any other nation that especially irks its self-described realist opponents on the nation's campuses. Harvard political scientist Stephen Walt, for example, accuses the United States of

> talk[ing] a good game on human rights and international law, but it has refused to sign most human rights treaties, is not a party to the International Criminal Court, and has been all too willing to cozy up to dictators—remember our friend Hosni Mubarak?—with abysmal human rights records.[37]

Never mind that signing putative human rights treaties is not exactly equivalent to actually *respecting* rights. Remember that the UN's Human Rights Commission includes such pillars of tolerance as Algeria, Cuba, China, Kazakhstan, Ethiopia, and Russia, along with a few other noxious regimes. As for Mubarak, does the real world not occasionally oblige us to settle on unsavory allies, who can still provide some help in difficult circumstances? Was his successor, Muslim Brotherhood's Mohammed Morsi, that much of an improvement? That we sometimes have to put up with second or even third best does not amount to moral equivalence with thugs.

Yet that is often the tactic of America's detractors, specifically in the academy. Agreeing with Walt, University of North Carolina professors Aseem Hasnain, Josh King, and Judith Blau summarize the standard left-of-center anti-exceptionalist position as follows:

> We pose our questions within the framework of American Exceptionalism, because the assumptions that underlie that term have never been *empirically examined*. Can we conclude on the basis of this analysis that America, when compared with other countries, advances human rights? *No.* Can we conclude on the basis of this analysis that America, when compared with other countries, is a Decent Society? *No.* Can we conclude on the basis of this empirical analysis that America, when compared with other countries, is Exceptional? Destined to promoting liberties and freedoms around the world? *No.*[38]

The authors go on to cite an earlier study that traces the roots of this mindset "to greed, intense competition, and fierce individualism."[39] In sum, America should first become itself "a Decent Society," and start

(!) "advancing human rights;" forget about presuming to be "destined to promote" whatever.

This is not a conversation but a harangue. It's the "Blame America First" crowd,[40] comfortably ensconced within the hallowed cathedrals of Higher Learning. What Walt and too many of his colleagues find most irritating is what they see as self-righteous arrogance, implicit in the American self-image as first among nations—not merely militarily and economically, which is hard to refute, but morally, which all but invites such vicious polemics. The anti-exceptionalists are leery of the "crusader" mentality that they believe animates their opponents, arguing instead for what they call a "realistic" assessment of America's place in the world as not just another nation, but worse, because governed by greed. Writes Walt:

> Far from being a unique state whose behavior is radically different from that of other great powers, the United States has behaved like all the rest, pursuing its own self-interest first and foremost, seeking to improve its relative position over time, and devoting relatively little blood or treasure to purely idealistic pursuits. Yet, just like past great powers, it has convinced itself that it is different, and better, than everyone else.[41]

It is not clear whether pursuing self-interest "first and foremost" is supposed to be good or bad. The rhetoric does imply a certain degree of cynicism: self-interest might be pursued "first," but perhaps "foremost" makes it seem as if higher values are shunned. If Walt does not explicitly say so, he does seem to charge that the United States has devoted "relatively little blood or treasure" to what Walt specifically deems "purely idealistic" pursuits. But is there no middle ground? Can't one pursue one's interests in service of idealistic values? Obviously no national leader should presume to spill blood or even waste any treasure over anything that is "purely" idealistic—by implication, devoid of any benefit to the nation (lest, presumably, it ceases being quite "pure"). A nation with such leadership won't be "exceptional" for long: it will stop being altogether. What Walt sets up is what is known in informal logic as the straw man fallacy. In plain English: he's shadow boxing.

Naturally, there is more than a grain of truth in the charge that a self-righteous presumption of moral, economic, or military superiority might inspire a dangerous interventionism—dangerous both to the intervener and the putative beneficiary. But no fruitful conversation about the proper nature of American foreign policy is possible so long as one side demonizes the other by hurling about a word like "exceptionalism" that is simply too emotionally charged. For that reason, historians like Walter A. McDougall prefer to dispense with the term altogether, for being "more trouble and probably even more danger than it's worth: it either means nothing at all or altogether too much."[42] Were it possible to implement, this is good advice.

As it happens, the word itself was not coined until the Cold War—and it did not actually catch on until after the demise of the Soviet Bloc, a mere quarter century ago. According to sociologist Jerome Karabel, print media references to American exceptionalism increased from a mere two (yes, two!) in 1980 to a stunning 2,580 through November 2011.[43] How can that be? McDougall is undoubtedly correct when he appeals to what he calls "my historian's instinct [which] tells me the question itself is the answer: the Cold War was over, globalization and multiculturalism were the new trends, and American identity got contested as never before."[44] We sure seemed, looked, and sounded exceptional. But at bottom, we were wondering just who, exactly, are we? Are we really special?

The question transcends etymology; at issue is nothing less than a search for America's soul. No serious attempt to define the direction of American foreign policy can take place without fully grasping the depth of the nation's identity crisis. We cannot cogently articulate a vision of peace without having a coherent self-image, and it seems that "exceptionalism" does capture a core element of who we are. Perhaps we could call it "post-bipolar exceptionalism." In any event, the nature and purpose of American global engagement has to be articulated in a manner consistent with the nation's tradition. We seem unable to decide whether to be overly humble, apologizing for our transgressions—as President Obama seemed rather overly predisposed to do throughout his tenure—or, on the contrary, overcompensate with an outraged sense of unrequited gratitude for all the blood and treasure this nation consistently doles out for the benefit of other people. Hasn't America shown more un-parochial altruism than any other country on earth?

Humility, however, is not incompatible with acknowledging our strengths; that is what effective leadership is about. In fact, humility is a prerequisite: bombast nearly always backfires. Being able to listen wisely, and considering alternative ways of responding to whatever a situation requires, a true leader will not hesitate to act: hesitation is less a sign of humility than of plain indecisiveness, which is a weakness that can harm no less than would deliberate wrongdoing. Having taken into consideration as many of the relevant factors as is humanly possible, a good leader will proceed cautiously yet firmly to articulate his strategy in an appropriate manner, with each target audience duly provided with the clearest, most relevant, and comprehensive explanation of the purpose and rationale of the anticipated course of action.

Over time, unfortunately, we have slowly permitted ourselves to forget our founding principles. Two centuries after the Revolutionary War, we are uncertain, confused, and seem to be learning the wrong lessons. Mostly, we are depressed. As Timothy D. Hoyt of the Naval War College puts it, for the past fifteen years, "vast military resources have failed to achieve long-term US objectives—regional stability, a shift toward democratic governance, and eroding support for trans-national terrorism." This despite the fact that "for a generation, the United States has, at great expense, attempted to impose stability on the Middle East, using all the tools of national policy."[45] Definitely depressing. But is it true? Vast resources have been spent, yes—on both military and civilian such attempts. Not so the claim that "all the tools of national power" have been used. Far from it. This widespread impression is tragically, exasperatingly inaccurate. And there's the rub: never mind leading everybody else, America is in dire need of leadership itself.

No, not some knight in the proverbial shining armor but the people themselves. American exceptionalist leadership is not about whether or not "to intervene" on behalf of those age-old American objectives that Hoyt rightly identifies. George Washington and his fellow Founders would always be respected for their learning, eloquence, and cour-age, but they would not be deemed great leaders if countless, mostly anonymous, colonists had failed to secure their own independence and subsequently built the institutions required to preserve it. It will take everything we've got: education, diplomatic engagement, networking, a renewed energy and trust in self-reliance, a free market, and a generous open heart to all who believe in freedom and tolerance. And it will take vigilance. We should do all we can to avoid overreacting militarily, but not demonize hard power. It is our best deterrent.

We must be cautious, of course; but caution is no excuse for timidity. So Hoyt's conclusion should give us pause. "Our inability to convert dominant military force into meaningful strategic success in both Iraq and Afghanistan," says Hoyt, "provides little reason for optimism that expanded intervention in Syria will have quick, decisive success."[46] He is right, but not in the way he meant it: what Iraq and Afghanistan have proved is that military force, no matter how dominant, cannot be converted into meaningful "strategic success," certainly not quickly. Does this imply that we should not even try to achieve those objectives? Of course not. A suggestion: "quick" should be dropped from the strategic vocabulary; it's a nonstarter.

Theories, semantics, and etymology aside, nothing captures American exceptionalism like first-hand experience of its effect in the real world, when the going gets especially rough. In a moving article describing her conversation with Iraq veterans at Fort Hood, Texas, the British-born and educated military advisor Emma Sky, currently at Yale, related her feelings about the time she was in Iraq during the Surge, when she had witnessed commanders on the ground pacify their areas by protecting the population, reaching out to insurgents, brokering cease-fires and carefully targeting irreconcilables. Sky had been full of hope:

> "From 2007–09, we had, for the only time during the whole war, the right strategy, leadership and resources. The violence dropped dramatically. What our soldiers did was real. It made a difference," I said. And for a moment, I was carried back to battlefield circulation with Odierno, visiting units camped out in the middle of nowhere; and Odierno assuring the assembled soldiers, who were exhausted and filthy from patrol, that what they did mattered, that their tactical successes contributed to the overall strategy.
>
> It had been real. All the indicators at the time pointed in a positive trajectory. We and the Iraqis thought the civil war was behind us and that the country was headed in a positive direction. But then it all went wrong.[47]

She diagnoses the problem with pitch-perfect accuracy:

> Things fell apart because of the politics: Iraqi politics and our politics. In our rush for the exit, we gave up our role of "balancer," of moderator, of protector of the political process. We failed to broker the formation of government after the closely contested 2010 elections, thus providing Iran with the opportunity to heavily increase its influence by guaranteeing Iraq's then-Prime Minister Nouri al-Maliki a second premiership on the condition there would be no follow-on security agreement with the U.S. We did not transition from a military-led to a civilian-led relationship with Iraq. We gave up our soft power as we withdrew our hard.

What "soft power"? Until America faces the fact that we have no adequate system for mobilizing those sorts of weapons, however plentiful they may be, until we recognize that managing the political process, at home and abroad, is far more difficult than we would like to imagine, until we face the fact that we cannot simply throw money at problems without the requisite knowledge, sophistication, and human engagement worthy of a responsible, generous, and realistic superpower, we might as well throw in the proverbial towel. Pax Americana will have evaporated for want of self-knowledge and imagination.

It had indeed been real. Can it be again? It seems inconceivable that America is incapable of resurgence. But how? I cannot resist continuing to cite the simple eloquence of Emma Sky:

> I wish politics and media in America were less polarized. I wish more was done to generate consensus on America's role in the world and how to strengthen the capacity of institutions to implement that vision. I wish there would be a bipartisan commitment to learn lessons from the Iraq experience. It is the best way that we can honor those who gave their lives in this war. I wish our civilian and political leadership would try to learn how to better set achievable objectives and make rational assumptions; how to develop an overall national strategy; and how to use military means not as an end in itself, but as a tool to achieve political outcomes.

She adds that "despite its faults, the Army does at least try to learn and improve, to understand the utility of force and its own limitations." The same cannot be said of the Department of State, USAID, National Security Council, or for that matter any of the other nonmilitary government agencies, including Congress. Whose fault is that? In part, of course, there's the matter of leadership. But blaming presidents goes only so far: in a democracy, the people will have the commander-in-chief they deserve. That said, it is also too facile to blame the strategic deficit on democracy as such; though democracies are notorious for operating with a strategy deficit of a political, rather than military, nature.[48]

The wars in Afghanistan and Iraq have surely been life-changing for everyone who has been touched by them, in ways no one could have imagined. Faced with horror and pain, often feeling helpless before enemies that defied our ability to understand, who hated us more than they loved the civilians among whom they lived and even themselves, we learned what we had hoped never to have to learn. As people return from those god-forsaken places, civilians and soldiers alike see their own country in a new way, appreciating its freedom and its goodness, yet frustrated by our collective inability to articulate what makes this nation so truly special, and a beacon of hope.

In the midst of the most awful circumstances, what Emma Sky remembers is the "friendships formed on the battlefield through sweat and tears, and loss and loss and loss, in an effort to give Iraqis the hope of a better future—the only purpose that made any sense as to why we were there." That, above all, is what America's vision is all about. "When I think back to the war," she writes, "I remember our dedication to each other, the commitment to the mission, the selflessness, the trust, the better angels of our nature." Just this simple—and this sublime—is the secret to America's *tao* of peace.

Notes

1. Walter A. McDougall, "American Exceptionalism...Exposed," FPRI, October 2012. http://www.fpri.org/print/868
2. Ibid. See also McDougall, "History and Strategies: Grand, Maritime, and American," Center for Naval Analysis Conference Report (November 2011). http://www.fpri.org/articles/2011/11/history-and-strategies-grand-maritime-and-american
3. Ibid.
4. *Fact Sheet*, US Department of Defense Freedom of Navigation Program, March 2015. http://policy.defense.gov/Portals/11/Documents/gsa/cwmd/DoD%20FON%20Program%20--%20Fact%20Sheet%20(March%202015).pdf
5. Andrew Kohut and Bruce Stokes, *America against the World: How We Are Different and Why We Are Disliked* (New York: Times Books, Henry Holt & Company, 2006), 174. The countries surveyed were Great Britain, Russia, France, Germany, Pakistan, Turkey, Morocco, and Jordan, alongside the United States.
6. Neil Seeman, Alex Mosa, and Alexander Osei-Bonsu, "American Exceptionalism Revisited," *Options Politiques*, Nov.–Dec. 2014, 50–4.
7. Kohut and Stokes, *America Against the World*, 71.
8. Ibid.
9. Niall Ferguson, *Colossus: The Rise and Fall of the American Empire* (New York: Penguin Books, 2005), vii.
10. Ibid., 299.
11. Dina Smeltz, Ivo Daalder, Karl Friedhoff, and Craig Kafura, *America Divided: Political Partisanship and US Foreign Policy*, (Chicago, IL: The Chicago Council on Global Affairs, 2015), 2.
12. Ibid., 12.
13. Ferguson, *Colossus*, 301–2.
14. Andrew Roberts, *Salisbury: Victorian Titan* (Essex: Faber and Faber, 2006), 529.
15. Ibid.
16. Benjamin Franklin, *Autobiography of Benjamin Franklin: 1706–1757* (Carlisle, MA: Applewood Books, 2008), 160.
17. Ferguson, *Colossus*, 302.
18. http://www.languagemonitor.com/number-of-words/number-of-words-in-the-english-language-1008879/

19. See J. K. Choi and S. Bowles, "The Coevolution of Parochial Altruism and War," *Science*, October 26, 2007. http://www.ncbi.nlm.nih.gov/pubmed/17962562

20. http://www.britannica.com/EBchecked/topic/493161/realpolitik (Emphasis added).

21. Walter C. Clemens, Jr., *Dynamics of International Relations: Conflict and Mutual Gain in an Era of Global Interdependence* (Lanham, MD: Rowman & Littlefield Publishers, 2004), 25.

22. "Political Realism in International Relations," *Stanford Encyclopedia of Philosophy*, revised April 2, 2013. http://plato.stanford.edu/entries/realism-intl-relations/

23. Ibid.

24. Anne-Marie Slaughter, "International Relations, Principal Theories," published in *Max Planck Encyclopedia of Public International The Law*, ed. R. Wolfrum (Oxford: Oxford University Press, 2011), 28.

25. John Bew, *Realpolitik: A History* (Oxford: Oxford University Press, 2015), 4.

26. Ibid., 5.

27. Ibid., 7.

28. Ibid., 300.

29. Ibid., 302.

30. Ibid., 303.

31. Bew, ibid., p. 304.

32. Ibid., 304.

33. Ibid., 308.

34. Henry Kissinger, *Diplomacy*, 142–3.

35. Ibid.

36. Ibid., 44.

37. Stephen M. Walt, "The Myth of American Exceptionalism," *Foreign Policy*, October 11, 2011. http://foreignpolicy.com/2011/10/11/the-myth-of-american-exceptionalism/

38. A. Hasnain, J. King and J. Blau, "'American Exceptionalism'—On What End of the Continuum?" *Societies Without Borders* 7, no. 3 (2012): 326–40. (Bold emphasis added; italics in the original.)

39. Ibid. The study is Judith Blau and Alberto Moncada, *Human Rights: Beyond the Liberal Tradition* (Lanham, MD: Rowman & Littlefield, 2006).

40. Michael Barone, "The Blame-America-First Crowd," Real Clear Politics, March 19, 2007. http://www.realclearpolitics.com/articles/2007/03/the_blameamericafirst_crowd.html

41. Walt, "The Myth of American Exceptionalism."

42. Walter A. McDougall, "American Exceptionalism . . . Exposed," FPRI October 2012. http://www.fpri.org/print/868

43. Jerome Karabel, "'American Exceptionalism' and the Battle for the Presidency," *Huffington Post*, updated February 21, 2012. http://www.huffingtonpost.com/jerome-karabel/american-exceptionalism-obama-gingrich_b_1161800.html

44. Ibid.

45. Timothy Hoyt, "Can Obama Take Advice? Reflections on the Middle East and American Strategy," *War on the Rocks*, October 22, 2015. http://warontherocks.com/2015/10/can-obama-take-advice-reflections-on-the-middle-east-

and-american-strategy/?utm_source=WOTR+Newsletter&utm_cam-paign=99beb45a24-WOTR_Newsletter_8_17_158_15_2015&utm_medi-um=email&utm_term=0_8375be81e9-99beb45a24-60136989

46. Ibid.

47. Emma Sky, "Looking Back on Iraq So We Can Move Ahead, *Army Magazine*, October 19, 2015. http://www.armymagazine.org/2015/10/19/looking-back-on-iraq-so-we-can-move-ahead/

48. J. D. Crouch II and Patrick J. Garrity, *You Run the Show or the Show Runs You: Capturing Professor Harold W. Rood's Strategic Thought for a New Generation* (Lapham, MD: Rowman & Littlefield Publishers, 2014).

Conclusion:
Medicine for a Sick World

So, then, it seems that we are back to where we started: the nation wants a strategy, in both senses of that word—it both lacks and wishes it. General James Mattis painted the broad outline to the senators who listened to him on January 27, 2015:

> The international order built on the state system is not self-sustaining. It demands tending by an America that leads wisely, standing unapologetically for the freedoms each of us in this room has enjoyed. The hearing today addresses the need for America to adapt to changing circumstances, to come out now from its reactive crouch and to take a firm strategic stance in defense of our values.[1]

Do we still remember what those values are? And do we know how to "bring to bear all our nation's resources" to defend them? The operative word here is "defend"—not impose them on anyone who is unable, let alone unwilling, to live by them. Nor is the "firm strategic stance" a euphemism for warmongering. It is simply a statement of resolve to defend who we are and what we stand for—assuming that we still know, and have the courage to assert it.

It is not too late to reexamine the nation's founding principles, and seek to reapply them in a new world which, though perhaps more complex than it used to be, is still governed by the same simple rules. Ours is a republic based on the notion that all men are created equal, with the right to life, liberty, and the pursuit of happiness. True, it would take another century to extend that lofty principle, which arguably underlies all the Abrahamic religions,[2] to African-Americans. So too, not for another half century were women allowed to vote; and it would take still half a century longer to extend civil rights to virtually everyone. Yet the Founders accomplished as much as could be expected in their day, given the monumental challenges, to set the

345

fledgling United States on the path to liberty. The nation had been blessed with unmatched leadership: the Founders were all brilliant visionaries, realistic, shrewd, brave, and devoted, who used all the elements of statecraft with stunning skill to prevail despite dauntingly minimal odds of success.

They were also eminently rational and clear-headed. In a splendid, if little known, article that appeared in the Autumn 1967 issue of *Harvard Today*, George F. Kennan praised the Founders (to whom he referred as "the Federalist statesmen," though he undoubtedly meant to also include the Republicans) for being guided by "clear and coherent elements of *concept*"—what today we might call *strategic goals*. One of those concepts was the rounding out of the American territory to include most of North America; another was the Monroe Doctrine, which Kennan rightly describes as "more of a principle than a purpose."[3] These concepts were admirable, he says, because they

> had their foundations in evident and concrete interests of our society. They bore a rational relationship both to the needs of our society's internal life and to the circumstances of its external environment. They were directed to obvious considerations of national security.[4]

In other words, they were rooted simultaneously in our interests, needs, values, and the real world. Imagine that. As the millennials like to say, what a concept!

Perhaps the "concrete interests" of our society are no longer as evident as they once were; too many of the nation's ideals have been sacrificed on the altar of political correctness, semantically castrated to near-oblivion. So too have "rights" proliferated, far beyond the Founders' wildest dreams (or nightmares), far beyond the self-evident, for which the Revolution had been fought, which had all been captured simply and clearly in one word grasped by everyone: *liberty*. As America's power increased, so did its self-regard, encouraging politicians to adopt a grandiosity that flatters the cheering crowds at the expense of clarity. Gaudily clad in the attire of grandiloquent patriotism, a messianic rhetoric cheapens the truly great rational principles for which the nation had been painstakingly established.

Kennan deplores this strident *faux* idealism, which has long infected American ideas about foreign policy with a kind of "histrionic note—a note of self-consciousness, or pretension. There was suddenly a desire not just to *be* something but to *appear* as something: to appear as something greater perhaps than one actually was."[5] Americans found they actually enjoyed being as grand as their territorial expanse appeared to justify, and their leaders didn't mind fueling that vanity.

As we became inebriated with our own sanctimonious image, we overpromised and overextended beyond what served even our own interests, let alone those of people we sought, or at least wanted to think (or appear) that we sought, to help. The crusading streak in American foreign policy that found its apex in World War I under President Woodrow Wilson was further exacerbated by a genuinely well-intentioned naivety, fueled by a heavy dose of ignorance. The problem was not so much that the United States came to the assistance of the Allied powers against Germany, which had to be defeated; it was the abysmal lack of preparation and strategy.

The president had preached Congress:

> [T]he right is more precious than peace, and we shall fight for the things which we have always carried nearest our hearts—for democracy, for the right of those who submit to authority to have a voice in their own governments, for the rights and liberties of small nations, for a universal dominion of right by such a concert of free peoples as shall bring peace and safety to all nations and make the world itself at last free. To such a task we can dedicate our lives and our fortunes, everything that we are and everything that we have, with the pride of those who know that the day has come when America is privileged to spend her blood and her might for the principles that gave her birth and happiness and the peace which she has treasured.[6]

One awaits the "Amen"—except the rhetoric sounds not so much theological as vaguely delusional.

We are all at liberty to carry "the right of those who submit to authority to have a voice in their own governments" as close to our hearts as we wish, but no president should dedicate the loves and fortunes of the nation, indeed "everything that we are and everything that we have," in the name of such a utopian vision. Nor is attaining "a concert of free peoples as shall bring peace and safety to all nations and make the world itself at last free" anything but bizarre. The United States is a deeply idealistic nation, and proud of it; but without a grounding in reality, when that idealism morphs into utopianism, it can bury us. Our Founders were not delusional, and they were not martyrs, but men and women of sense—*common* sense. They practiced *Realpolitik* at its best.

It didn't start with the liberal scion of Princeton, Woodrow Wilson; its origins were Progressive, championed with aplomb and patrician—yet intensely and sincerely populist—flair by the quite Republican Teddy Roosevelt. Finding itself among the great powers at the dawn of the twentieth century, America seemed incapable of resisting imagining itself the steward of world peace, if not by (righteous) warfare then through international organizations and agreements. Kennan calls this too a "concept," though grudgingly, for it was "founded on a rather childish view of world realities, founded also, I suspect, on a certain gratification of our self-esteem. We saw ourselves as high-mindedly devoted to the enthronement, in international affairs, of the principles of law and order."[7] Kennan grasps with uncanny precision the dangerous mix of our immaturity in matters of foreign affairs—the unsurprising result of geographic isolation and relative peace at home—and a barely conscious inferiority complex that has always lurked behind the notorious American bluster and ostentatious directness. Add to that the genetic self-righteousness of idealism and the trouble looms large.

True, Wilson's plans for the United States to join a newly created League of Nations, his lame brainchild (or lamebrain figurative child), which famously failed to prevent World War II, did not materialize in 1919, in part due to his political clumsiness in alienating Republican senators. But the concept lurked into the background. Once that second apocalypse was ended with a bang to end all bangs, a building would be raised on Turtle Bay to host an organization whose birth was celebrated by nearly everyone (with the exception of New Yorkers stuck in worse traffic) with fanfare that would have warmed the cockles of Wilson's visionary heart. It was now official: America had become ineluctably inebriated by visions of conflict resolution.

And indeed, why not give the conference table a chance? After all, the League ended up not including the United States —which led many to hope that, with us in the room, peace wouldn't be far behind. Why not give it a try? Reinvented as the *United* Nations—as if saying so would make it so, after another devastating war once again reviving the utopian vision of perpetual peace, the organization now serves to feed the illusions of a new generation. It is disconcerting to watch the naïve join the cynical in praising the virtues of a mythical "world community," ignoring the fact that the bulk of UN diplomats speak for elites of patently unfree governments, whose interests are largely confined to personal power and fortune. In sheer demagoguery, we don't hold a candle to any of them: American bluster is risible kid's play next to the dictators' bald-faced, murderous lies.

But all that hot air is not without serious fallout here at home, where it fuels toxic divisions that tear us apart. Those high on the elixir of morally equivalent internationalism, on the one side, are condemned by hard-core militarists whose zeal is fueled by far more explosive stuff, at the other extreme. The reality, as always, defies easy dialectic: opposites, when intractable, detract. The *ying* and *yang* of the world as it is, rather than as we wish it to be, cannot dispense with at least some international agreements, strictly enforced. But it must be done without illusions, fully recognizing that incentives for peace have never been as effective as deterrence. On the other hand, hard power requires the application of sophisticated peace fare, best wielded before conflict deteriorates to the point that blowing things up remains the only option. Avoiding the extremes in foreign policy isn't merely squishy and wishy-washy centrism; it's our only option in a complex world that demands both knowledge and wisdom. Properly communicated, such a vision should inspire sustained, cautious, yet hopeful and uplifting engagement.

Above all, we should try not to stumble our way in the world without paying close attention to all the relevant facts, most of which are hiding in plain sight. Vietnam is a perfect example. Writing in 1967, Kennan presciently predicted that the war was doomed from the outset, considering how we got into it:

> Everyone knows that our entry into the Vietnam involvement did not come as a result of national reflection—that it was rather the result of a long exercise in national inadvertence, of a long series of partial decisions, none of them taken with any clear comprehension of the depths of involvement to which they were bringing us.[8]

There are no *ad hominem* invectives here against this or another war-thirsty Dr. No impersonator. It is a measured, almost resigned assessment of the pathetic inadequacy of the national security decision-making apparatus behind that tragic, misconducted, and ill reported incursion. If we don't understand how to win the peace, we shouldn't stumble into war by what he calls, with exquisitely off-handed precision, a sort of "national inadvertence." But this is by no means a hysterical antiwar slogan; Kennan doesn't say that we should not be involved at all. It is a plea for *clear comprehension*.

These words could have been applied to the two wars that shook the world during the past decade, whose aftershocks continue to reverberate, and even earlier, to the Gulf War, which few people criticize but whose consequences are dire. Colonel Mike Pietrucha, an irregular warfare operations officer, calls this a symptom of America's "victory disease:" "The Gulf War, which we often view as occurring at a time of our choosing, was in reality born in the confusion and surprise surrounding the unexpected occupation of a friendly country and the imminent threat of further incursions to follow." And consider the current environment: "Indeed, the danger may be greater now than ever that we might back into conflict without really wishing to do so."[9] Left untreated, festering strategic deficit syndrome often manifests itself in full-blown American victory disease, which can be terminal.

During the half century since Kennan wrote his prophetic article, the national security structure of the United States has practically metastasized, but the predilection for histrionics, simplistic slogans, and inadvertence, shows no sign of abating. All the while the world has become more diverse, more "complex," leading to confusion among the American people, who, seemingly rudderless, oscillate between wanting to demonstrate strength—"just get the job done"—and wishing the rest of the world would go away and leave us to our iPods. After all, what's so hard to get about everybody playing in their own sandboxes while we play in ours? We leave you alone, so you leave us alone; we'll send some foreign aid on occasion, and streaming hard rock. Deal?

No deal. The analogy isn't meant to be deprecating, to dismiss the desire for nonengagement as merely childlike. Children, in truth, have far more common sense than all too many adults. They get "this is mine, not yours," and they also get "leave me alone or I'll show *you.*" That would be a healthy world—we should be so lucky to live in such a one. Instead, the world is as sick as ever: psychopaths run countries, killing their own citizens with chlorine and mustard gas—never mind showing any mercy to innocents abroad—and thugs, emboldened by quasi-religious quackery, butcher children for fun and profit, when they don't merrily blow themselves up for promised pleasures in the afterlife. But you don't treat a sick world with kid gloves, pun (more or less) unintended.

America's strategic deficit syndrome must be seen in that context: we flounder just as the global scene becomes murkier, ideologies being spawned to add a justificatory veneer to the age-old impulse to plunder, pillage, and kill. Flabbergasted by the inability of our military to deliver quick, clear-cut victories so we can get back to the business of business, we seem lost. Obviously "attractive" soft power is a nonstarter against those whom it repels—for whom everything America stands for is anathema. So what's to be done? Is SDS a slowly degenerating terminal disease for which there is no cure, not even a palliative? As with any other disease, surely the first step is to recognize it as such.

Fortunately, that is, slowly but fairly surely, happening—and not a moment too soon. In NDU's report *Lessons Encountered*, editors Richard D. Hooker, Jr., and Joseph J. Collins conclude bluntly that "we were not intellectually prepared for the unique aspects of war" in either country. As a result, "our lack of understanding of the wars seriously retarded our efforts to fight them and to deal with our indigenous allies, who were often more interested in score-settling or political risk aversion than they were in winning the war."[10]

That lack of understanding is the product of dysfunction that tends to take place during peacetime. No one is exempt from blame: "Neither national-level figures nor field commanders fully understood the operational environment, including the human aspects of military operations" because none of that was deemed relevant. When the military scrambled to put together such programs as the Human Terrain Teams and the Afghan-Pakistan Hands Program, these "came too little and too late." Astonishingly, even the much-resourced repository of information, "our intelligence system[,] was of little help here primarily because the Intelligence Community did not see this as its mission. The need for information aggregation stands as an equal to classical all-source intelligence."[11] Gen. Mike Flynn has to be smiling, though sadly.

Hooker and Collins recognize that "understanding the operational environment calls for a whole array of fixes, such as improving language training, predeployment training, area expertise, and reforming the intelligence/information apparatuses," urging that "the renewed emphasis on the human domain and human aspects of military operations should be reinforced and sustained over time."

But then they add: "There can be no substitute for excellent joint professional military education, reinforced by dedicated self-study by career officers and noncommissioned officers. For senior officers and advisors, every dollar spent on civilian graduate education in policy sciences and history is returned many times over." This must bring tears to the eyes of the civilians toiling inside the State Department and USAID, who eye with envy all those dollars—and there are *many*—spent on the fortunate officers. Why aren't there similar "lessons encountered" gathered for the civilian agencies? For in truth, they are the ones who need it most.

This is no mystery. We could never win the peace with the civilians we had: for "there are few assets in the State Department or USAID inventory to mentor and assist a host government in political development. In collateral areas, such as humanitarian assistance, development, rule of law, and reconstruction, State and USAID have more assets, but far fewer than large-scale contingencies require." Nor was it only a matter of scale, but a national deficiency in mobilizing and preparing the resources that we do have. Instead of just throwing people in the middle of a conflict zone, "before they deploy, advisors must be educated culturally and politically to organize ministries and/or train forces that fit the operational environment and local needs"—and that goes not only for the military but for the civilians.

Worst of all is the government's inability to communicate what it needs. Hooker and Collins' verdict is that a diagnostic session is overdue before the patient is too far gone to recover:

> As former National Security Advisor Stephen J. Hadley notes, there needs to be a national discussion on these critical issues. Strategic communication was [note: after which I would add "and emphatically continues to be"] a weak point in our performance in Washington, DC, and in the field. Making friends, allies, and locals understand our intent has proved difficult. At times, the situation on the ground will block good messaging. However, our disabilities in this area—partly caused by too much bureaucracy and too little empathy—stand in contradistinction to the ability of clever enemies to package their message and beat us at a game that was perfected in Hollywood and on Madison Avenue. War crimes and clear evidence of abuse of locals or detainees have further hobbled our efforts, especially when every person with a cellular phone is a photojournalist. This is not a psychological operation or public affairs issue. Strategic communications is a vital task for commanders and senior policymakers at every level.[12]

Amen. You might think this would be a loud enough clarion call—but will it be? Consider this modest suggestion: "Ideally, the United States should have a civilian response corps (CRC), but the urge to develop whole-of-government capabilities is waning."[13]

The ability to work together is admittedly difficult, but can we afford *not* face the problem head on? Again, Hooker and Collins:

> Whole-of-government efforts are essential in irregular conflicts. The military must improve its efforts to reach across departmental divides.

The Department of State and U.S. Agency for International Development (USAID) have improved over time but need to work harder on planning for expeditionary activities. Unfortunately, emphasis on working whole-of-government issues is fading across the U.S. Government, except in the field of joint concept and doctrine development.[14]

The thrust of these comments is war-centric, but the implications go far beyond that context. SDS has attacked the nation after its national immune system had already been weakened by Vietnam when the unravelling of the Soviet bloc dealt an additional blow to the remaining shred of direction. Despite its military's outstanding performance on the battlefield, the nation failed to win the peace: "When conventional warfare or logistical skills were called for in Iraq and Afghanistan, the Armed Forces generally achieved excellent results. At the same time, the military was insensitive to needs of the post-conflict environment and not prepared for insurgency in either country. Our lack of preparation for dealing with irregular conflicts was the result of a post-Vietnam organizational blindspot."[15] That blind spot is not in the military, or certainly not *just* in the military: it is in the nation at large.

In fact, SDS is at heart an autoimmune disorder, which happens when the immune system attacks healthy cells in your body by mistake. No one is sure what causes such painful, and even lethal, diseases like rheumatism and arthritis. Medications do not cure them. But that doesn't mean we are totally helpless against them. That applies equally to our security; we would do well to turn to our Founders for some homespun remedies.

Alexander Hamilton, for his part, warned against forgetting "that of those men who have overturned the liberties of republics, the greatest number have begun their career by paying an obsequious court to the people; commencing demagogues, and ending tyrants."[16] Though acknowledging that in a democracy—or, more precisely, a democratic *republic*—the people's interests are preeminent, Hamilton distrusted the impulse, prevalent among politicians, to demonstrate "unqualified complaisance to every sudden breeze of passion or to every transient impulse which the people may receive from the arts of men, who flatter their prejudices to betray their interests."[17] To put it in medical terms, the medicine that people need may not be what tastes best. Beware of demagogues peddling snake oil in containers of overheated rhetoric.

Jefferson would have agreed. Preferring to allow the body politic to heal itself, he wrote to James Madison from Paris on December 20, 1787, that the nation's health, ordinarily known as "peace[,] is best preserved by giving energy to the government or information to the people. This last is the most legitimate engine of government. Educate and inform the whole mass of people. Enable them to see that it is their interest to preserve peace and order, and they will preserve them. And it requires no very high degree of education to convince them of this. They are the only sure reliance for the preservation of our liberty."[18]

Indeed all the Founders believed, with all their heart, that education holds the key to the nation's spiritual well-being. Not that the truth will suffice to set us free. But it's a start. Self-deception, by contrast, is sure to set us on a dangerous path. Equally dangerous is being unprepared for attack, or lacking what Sun Tzu called "foreknowledge." His wisdom on this score transcended the superstitions of his age and those of many centuries hence, having warned that foreknowledge cannot be elicited from ghosts and spirits. He also advised against easy analogies with past events, and against overreliance on "calculations"—a predilection that is currently most popular. For history, as Sun Tzu knew, never quite repeats itself, and the impressive mathematical formulae of political scientists (some of whom seem to suffer from physics-envy) tend to be overrated. Nor, we may add, should simplistic ideology be relied upon to substitute for hard facts. Foreign policy cannot be properly conducted in the absence of solid empirical evidence, supplemented by intimate understanding of human beings which, adds Sun Tzu, "must be obtained from men who know the enemy situation" (*AoW* XIII. 4).

But it will not be enough to have good sources of information: we must have the ability to use it, to ask the right questions and process their wisdom. For, continues Sun Tzu, "he who is not sage and wise, humane and just, cannot use secret agents. And he who is not delicate and subtle cannot get the truth out of them" (*AoW* XIII. 13). Explains Sun Tzu commentator Tu Mu (802–852): "Among agents there are some whose only interest is in acquiring wealth without obtaining the true situation of the enemy, and only meet my requirement with empty words. In such a case, I must be deep and subtle. Then I can assess the truth or falsity of the spy's statements and discriminate between what is substantial and what is not."[19] It takes extensive, intelligent engagement during peacetime to develop this kind of relationships. And it takes effective coordination at all times among all the instruments of power, particularly the power of information, alongside the hard weapons of the military, to seek to avoid violent confrontation if at all possible.

For a final piece of wisdom, let's turn to the ancient poet Chuan Tzu, the chief authentic historical spokesman for Taoism during the third- and fourth-centuries BC, whose work has been revived by the much loved American poet and Trappist monk Thomas Merton. In Tzu's poem "Advising the Prince," the powerful Prince Wu is said to have asked the wise recluse Hsu Su Kwei: "I want to love my people, and by the exercise of justice to put an end to war. Is this enough?"

The answer follows:

> "By no means," said the recluse.
> "Your 'love' for your people
> Puts them in mortal danger.
> Your exercise of justice is the root
> Of war after war!
> Your grand intentions
> Will end in disaster!
>
> If you are out to 'accomplish something great'
> You only deceive yourself.
> Your love and justice
> Are fraudulent.
> They are mere pretexts
> For self-assertion, for aggression.
> . . .
>
> Abandon your plan
> To be a 'loving and equitable ruler.'
> Try to respond
> To the demands of inner truth.
> Stop vexing yourself and your people
> With these obsessions!
> Your people will breathe easily at last.
> They will live
> And war will end by itself!"[20]

Prince Wu's descendants, unfortunately, are all around us: their pretended "love for the people" have led to untold calamities. The recluse has it wrong: war will never end "by itself," any more than will disease and death evolve away. The best we can do is make our brief interlude on this earth as respectful of one another as possible.

Is there no answer, then, no respite, no remedy? We have yet to figure out a strategy for preserving the peace in a complex world. But we still have our faith in ourselves, in our unique, confused, but great nation, providentially nestled between two oceans. One of Chung Tzu's other poems has Confucius saying: "Look at this window: it is nothing but a hole in the wall, but because of it the whole room is full of light. So when the faculties are empty, the heart is full of light. Being full of light it becomes an influence by which others are secretly transformed."[21]

Oh yes. Like a shining city, on a hill. . . .

Notes

1. Mattis, "A New American Grand Strategy."
2. Juliana Geran Pilon, *Soulmates: Resurrecting Eve*. Piscataway, NJ: Transaction Publishers, 2012.
3. George F. Kennan, "The Quest for Concept," *Harvard Today*, Autumn 1967, 11.
4. Ibid.
5. Ibid., 11–12.
6. Woodrow Wilson, Message to Congress, Feb. 3, 1917, *War Messages*, 65th Cong., 1st Sess. Senate Doc. No. 5, Serial No. 7264, Washington, DC, 1917; p8, http://wwi.lib.byu.edu/index.php/Wilson's_War_Message_to_Congress
7. Ibid., 12.
8. Ibid., 16.
9. Mike Pietrucha, "America's Victory Disease Has Left It Dangerously Deluded," *War on the Rocks*, November 18, 2015. http://warontherocks.com/2015/11/americas-victory-disease-has-left-it-dangerously-deluded/?utm_source=WOTR+Newsletter&utm_campaign=ea51dd82e3-WOTR_Newsletter_8_17_158_15_2015&utm_medium=email&utm_term=0_8375be81e9-ea51dd82e3-60136989
10. Richard D. Hooker, Jr., and Joseph J. Collins, eds., Richard D. Hooker, Jr., and Joseph J. Collins, *Lessons Encountered : Learning from the Long War* (Washington, DC: National Defense University, September 2015), 11–12.
11. Ibid.
12. Ibid., 15.
13. Ibid.
14. Ibid., 9.
15. Ibid., 13.
16. Hamilton, Madison, and Jay, *Federalist 1*.
17. Hamilton, Madison, and Jay, *Federalist 71*.
18. http://www.let.rug.nl/usa/presidents/thomas-jefferson/letters-of-thomas-jefferson/jefl66.php
19. Griffith, *Sun Tzu - The Art of War*, 147.
20. Thomas Merton, *The Way of Chuang Tzu* (New York: New Directions, 1965), "Advising the Prince," 139–40.
21. "The Fasting of the Heart," Ibid., 53.

Bibliography

Books

Adams, John. *The Works of John Adams, Second President of the United States: with a Life of the Author, Notes and Illustrations, by his Grandson Charles Francis Adams*. Boston, MA: Little, Brown and Co., 1856. 10 volumes. Vol. 6.

Aldrich, Chris. *The Aldrich Dictionary of Phobias and Other Word Families*. Bloomington, IN: Tratford Publishing, 2002.

Amster, Randall, Laura Finley, and Edmund Pries, eds. *Peace Studies between Tradition and Innovation*. Cambridge: Cambridge Scholars Publishing, 2015.

Anheier, Helmut, Marlies Glasius, and Mary Kaldor. *Global Civil Society 2004/5*. London: Sage Publications, 2006.

Arendt, Hannah. *On Revolution*. New York: Penguin Books, 1965.

Armistead, Leigh, ed. *Information Operations: Warfare and the Hard Reality of Soft Power*. Washington, DC: Potomac Books, 2004.

———. *Information Warfare: Separating Hype from Reality*. Washington, DC: Potomac Books, 2007.

Bacevich, Andrew J. *The New American Militarism: How Americans Are Seduced by War*. Oxford: Oxford University Press, 2013.

Baer, Robert. *See No Evil*. New York: Random House, 2002.

Bauerlein, Mark, and Adam Bellow, eds. *The State of the American Mind*. West Conshohoken, PA: Templeton Press, 2015.

Becker, Carl. L. *The Declaration of Independence: A Study in the History of Political Ideas*. New York: Vintage Books, 1942.

Bell, Daniel. *The Coming of Post Industrial Society: A Venture in Social Forecasting*. New York: Basic Books, 1973.

Bemis, Samuel Flagg. *American Foreign Policy and the Blessings of Liberty: And Other Essays*. New Haven, CT: Yale University Press, 1962.

Berkowitz, Bruce. *The New Face of War: How War Will be Fought in the 21st Century*. New York: The Free Press, 2003.

Bernays, Edward. *Propaganda*. Brooklyn, NY: Ig Publishing, 1928.

Billington, James H. *Fire in the Minds of Men: Origins of the Revolutionary Faith*. New York: Basic Books, 1980.

Binnendijk, Hans, and Stuart Johnson, eds. Transforming for Stabilization and Reconstruction Operations, National Defense University Center for Technology and National Security Policy, April 2004.

Blau, Judith, and Alberto Moncada. *Human Rights: Beyond the Liberal Tradition*. Lanham, MD: Rowman & Littlefield, 2006.

Bond, Brian. *Lidell-Hart: A Study of His Military Thought*. New Brunswick, NJ: Rutgers University Press, 1977.

Boyd, John. Organic Design for Command and Control, unpublished manuscript, 1987.

Bryen, Stephen D. *Technology, Security, and National Power: Winners and Losers.* Piscataway, NJ: Transaction Publishers, 2015.

Byron, John. *Cain and Abel in Text and Tradition: Jewish and Christian Interpretations of the First Sibling Rivalry - Themes in Biblical Narrative.* Leiden and Boston: Brill Academic Publishing, 2011.

Caputi, Robert J. *Neville Chamberlain and Appeasement.* London: Associated University Presses, 2000.

Carr, Edward Hallett. *The Twenty-Years' Crisis 1919-1939: Introduction to the Study of International Relations.* New York: Palgrave, 2001.

Ceaser, James W. *Reconstructing America: The Symbol of America in Modern Thought.* New Haven & London: Yale University Press, 1997.

Chandrasekaran, Rajif. *Imperial Life in The Emerald City: Inside Iraq's Green Zone.* New York: Alfred A. Knopf, 2012.

Chappell, Paul K. *The Art of Waging Peace: A Strategic Approach to Improving Our Lives and the World.* Westport, CT: Prospecta Press.

Chesterton, C. K. "The Bluff of the Big Shops," *The Collected Works of G.K. Chesterton*, Vol. 5. San Francisco, CA: Ignatius Press, 1987.

Clary, David A. *Washington's First War: His Early Military Adventures.* New York: Simon & Schuster, 2011.

Clausewitz, Carl. *On War*, edited and translated by Michael Howard and Peter Paret. Princeton, NJ: Princeton University Press, 1992.

Clemens, Jr. Walter C. *Dynamics of International Relations: Conflict and Mutual Gain in an Era of Global Interdependence.* Lanham, MD: Rowman & Littlefield Publishers, 2004.

Coram, Robert. *Boyd: The Fighter Pilot Who Changed the Art of War.* New York: Hachette Book Group, 2002.

Crouch II, J.D., and Patrick J. Garrity, *You Run the Show or the Show Runs You: Capturing Professor Harold W. Rood's Strategic Thought for a New Generation.* Lapham, MD: Rowman & Littlefield Publishers, 2014.

Crumpton, Henry A. *The Art of Intelligence: Lessons from a Life in the CIA's Clandestine Service.* New York and London: Penguin, 2012.

Daigler, Kenneth A. *Spies, Patriots, and Traitors: American Intelligence in the Revolutionary War.* Washington, DC: Georgetown University Press, 2014.

Davidson, Philip. *Propaganda and the American Revolution 1763–1783.* Chapel Hill, NC: University of North Carolina Press, 1941.

———. *Vietnam at War, The History 1946–1975.* New York and Oxford: Oxford University Press, 1988.

Dempsey, Gary T., and Roger W. Fontaine. *Fool's Errands: America's Recent Encounters with Nation Building.* Washington, DC: Cato Institute, 2001.

Diggins, John P. *John Adams: The American Presidents Series: The 2nd President, 1797–1801* New York: MacMillan Press, 2003.

Dudziak, Mary L. *War Time: An Idea, Its History, Its Consequence.* Oxford: Oxford University Press, 2012.

Dueck, Colin. *The Obama Doctrine: America's Grand Strategy Today.* Oxford: Oxford University Press, 2015.

Easterly, William. *The White Man's Burden: Why the West's Efforts to Aid the Rest Have Done So Much Ill and So Little Good.* New York: Penguin Press, 2006.

Feith, Douglas J. *War and Decision.* New York: Harper Collins, 2008.

Ferguson, Niall. *Colossus: The Rise and Fall of the American Empire.* New York: Penguin Books, 2005.

Field Manual 6-22. *Army Leadership.* Washington, DC: Government Printing Office, 2006.

Fitzpatrick, John, ed. *The Writings of George Washington,* Vol. 1. Washington, DC: Government Printing Office, 1931–44.

Freedman, Laurence. *Strategy: A History.* Oxford: Oxford University Press, 2013.

Galtung, Johan. *Theories of Peace: A Synthetic Approach to Peace Thinking.* Oslo, Norway: International Peace Research Institute, September, 1967.

Gates, Robert. *Duty: Memoirs of a Secretary at War.* New York: Vintage, 2015.

General McChrystal, Stanley, Tantum Collins, David Silverman, and Chris Fussel. *Team of Teams: New Rules of Engagement for a Complex World.* New York: Penguin Group, Portfolio, 2015.

Gertz, Billl. *The Failure Factory.* New York: Random House, 2008.

Gillis, John R. *Commemorations: The Politics of National Identity.* Princeton, NJ: Princeton University Press, 1994.

Gopal, Anand. *No Good Men Among the Living: America, the Taliban, and the War Through Afghan Eyes.* New York: Henry Holt and Co., 2015.

Gorka, Sebastian, ed. *The Islamic State and Information Warfare: Defeating ISIS and the Broader Global Jihadist Movement.* Washington, DC: The Threat Knowledge Group, January 2015.

Gray, Colin S. *The Future of Strategy.* Cambridge: Polity Books, 2015.

Griffith, Samuel B., trans. *Sun Tzu - The Art of War.* Oxford: Oxford University Press, 1982.

Grimes, Sandra, and Jeanne Vertefeuille. *Circle of Treason: A CIA Account of Traitor Aldrich Ames and the Men He Betrayed.* Annapolis, MD: Naval Institute Press, 2014.

Grotius, Hugo. *The Law of War and Peace: De jure belli ac pacis.* New York: Classics Club, 1949.

Hamilton, Alexander, James Madison, and John Jay. *The Federalist Papers, with an introduction by Clinton Rossiter.* New York: The New American Library, 1961.

Hammond, Grant T. *The Mind of War: John Boyd and American Security.* Washington DC: Smithsonian, 2001.

Handel, Michael I. *Matters of War: Classical Strategic Thought.* London: Frank Cass Publishers, 2006.

Hard Lessons: The Iraq Reconstruction Experience (US Government Printing Office, 2009).

Hayek, Friedrich A. *The Constitution of Liberty.* Chicago, IL: University of Chicago Press, 1978.

Heuer, Richard. *Psychology of Intelligence Analysis.* Washington, DC: CIA, 2007.

Höhn, Karl Hermann. *Geopolitics and the Measurement of National Power.* Hamburg: University of Hamburg, 2011.

Hollander, Paul, ed. *Understanding Anti-Americanism: Its Origins and Impact at Home and Abroad.* Chicago, IL: Ivan Dee, 2004.

Holt, P. F. *The Reluctant Superpower: A History of America's Economic Global Reach.* New York: Kodansha America, Inc, 1995.

Hooker, Jr. Richard D., and Joseph J. Collins, eds. *Lessons Encountered: Learning from the Long War.* Washington, DC: National Defense University, September 2015.

Horne, Alistair. *Hubris: The Tragedy of War in the Twentieth Century*. New York: Harper Books, 2015.

Horowitz, Irving Louis. *The Idea of War and Peace: The Experience of Western Civilization*. New Brunswick, NJ: Transaction Publishers, 2007.

Howard, Michael. *The Invention of Peace: Reflections on War and International Order*. New Haven, Conn: Yale University Press, 2001.

Hutchinson, John, and Anthony D. Smith, eds. *Nationalism*. Oxford: Oxford University Press, 1994.

Huyn, Thomas, annotated. *The Art of War – Spirituality for Conflict*. Woodstock, VT: Skylight Paths, 2009.

Jones, Ishmael. *The Human Factor: Inside the CIA's Dysfunctional Intelligence Culture*. New York: Encounter Books, 2010.

Jullien, Francois. *Treatise on Efficacy: Between Western and Eastern Thinking*. Honolulu: University of Hawaii Press, 1994.

Kagan, Robert. *Dangerous Nation*. New York: Alfred Knopf, 2006.

Kaplan, Fred. *The Insurgents: David Petraeus and the Plot to Change the American Way of War*. New York: Simon & Schuster, 2013.

Karl Popper's The Open Society and its Enemies (1945) and The Poverty of Historicism (1967).

Kass, Leon. *The Beginning of Wisdom: Reading Genesis*. Chicago, IL: University of Chicago Press, 2003.

Keegan, John. *A History of Warfare*. New York: Alfred A. Knopf, 1994.

Kissinger, Henry. *Diplomacy*. New York: Touchstone Books, 1994.

Kohut, Andrew, and Bruce Stokes. *America Against the World: How We Are Different and Why We Are Disliked*. New York: Times Books, Henry Holt & Company, 2006.

Kurkland, Philip B., and Ralph Lerner, eds. *The Founders' Constitution*. Chicago, IL: University of Chicago Press and the Liberty Fund, 1987.

LaFeber, Walter. *The American Age: U.S. Foreign Policy At Home and Abroad - 1750 to the Present*, 2nd ed. New York: W.W. Norton & Company, 1994.

Ledeen, Michael A. *Machiavelli on Modern Leadership: Why Machiavelli's Iron Rules Are As Timely And Important Today As Five Centuries Ago*. New York: St. Martin's Press, 2000.

Lidell Hart, B. H., ed.William T. Sherman, *From Atlanta to the Sea*. London: The Folio Society, 1961.

Lowenthal, Mark. *Intelligence: From Secrets to Policy*, 5th ed. Washington, DC: CQ Press, College, 2011.

Lucas, George. *Anthropologists in Arms: The Ethics of Military Anthropology*. Lanham, MD: AltaMira Press, 2009.

Lutrell, Marcus with Patrick Robinson, *Lone Survivor: The Eyewitness Account of Operation Redwing and the Lost Heroes of SEAL Team 10*. New York: Back Bay Books, 2007.

Martel, William C. *The Making of Future American Grand Strategy*. Cambridge: Cambridge University Press, 2015.

McCullough, David. *John Adams*. New York: Simon & Schuster, 2001.

McDonald, Forrest. *Alexander Hamilton: A Biography*. New York: W. W. Norton, 1982.

McDougall, Walter. *Promised Land, Crusader State*. Boston, MA: Houghton Mifflin, 1997.

McNeilly, Mark. *Sun Tzu and the Art of Modern Warfare*. Oxford: Oxford University Press, 2001.

Merton, Thomas. *The Way of Chuang Tzu*. New York, NY: New Directions, 1965.

Murawiec, Laurent. *The Mind of Jihad*. Cambridge: Cambridge University Press, 2007.

Morgenthau, Hans. *Politics Among Nations: The Struggle for Power and Peace*. New York: Alfred A. Knopf, 1967.

Morgenthau, Hans J. *In Defense of the National Interest: A Critical Examination of American Foreign Policy*. Lanham, MD: University Press of America, 1982.

Myers, Richard, and Malcolm McConnell. *Eyes on the Horizon: Serving on the Front Lines of National Security*. New York, NY: Simon & Schuster, 2009.

Neff, John U. *War and Human Progress*. Cambridge: Cambridge University Press, 1950.

Nye, Joseph S. *Soft Power: The Means to Success in World Politics*. New York: Public Affairs, 2004.

Offenson, James R., ed. *Adam Smith, Selected Philosophical Writings*. Charlottesville, VA: Imprint Academic, 2004.

Orr, Robert C., ed. Winning the Peace: An American Strategy for Post-Conflict Reconstruction (reprint of the 2003 report "Play to Win: The Final Report of the Bi-partisan Commission on Post-Conflict Reconstruction," Center for Strategic and International Studies (CSIS) and the Association of the U.S. Army (AUSA), 2004)

Osinga, Frans P. B. *Science, Strategy and War: The Strategic Theory of John Boyd*. New York: Routledge, 2007.

Paine, Thomas. *Common Sense and Other Political Writings*. Indianapolis, IN: Bobbs-Merrill, 1953.

Palmer, Dave Richard. *The Way of the Fox: American Strategy in the War for America 1775–1783*. Westport, CT: Greenwood Press, 1975.

Paul, Christopher. *Strategic Communication: Origins, Concepts, and Current Debates*. Santa Barbara, CA: Praeger, 2011.

Philbrick, Nathaniel. *Mayflower: A Story of Courage, Community, and War*. New York: Penguin Books, 2007.

Pillsbury, Michael. *The Hundred-Year Marathon: China's Secret Strategy to Replace America as the Global Superpower*. New York: Henry Holt and Co., 2015.

Pilon, Juliana Geran, *Soulmates: Resurrecting Eve*. Piscataway, NJ: Transaction Publishers, 2012.

Pilon, Juliana Geran. *Why America is Such a Hard Sell: Beyond Pride and Prejudice*. Lanham, MD: Roman & Littlefield, 2007.

Rice, Condoleezza. *No Higher Honor: A Memoir of My Years in Washington*. New York: Crown Publishers, 2011.

Robert Worley, D. *Orchestrating the Instruments of Power: A Critical Examination of the U.S. National Security System*. Sterling, VA: Potomac Books, 2015.

Roberts, Andrew. *Salisbury: Victorian Titan*. Essex: Faber and Faber, 2006.

Rodgers, Daniel T. *The Age of Fracture*. Cambridge, MA: Harvard University's Belknap Press, 2012.

Romerstein, Herbert, and Eric Breindel. *The Venona Secrets: The Definitive Exposé of Soviet Espionage in America* (Cold War Classics). Washington, DC: Regnery History, 2014.

Ronis, Sheila R., ed. *Forging an American Grand Strategy: Security a Path Through a Complex Future, Selected Presentations from a Symposium at the National Defense University*. Washington, DC: Strategic Studies Institute and U.S. Army War College Press, October 2013.

Sawyer, Ralph D. *The Tao of Deception: Unorthodox Warfare in Historic and Modern China*. New York: Basic Books, 2007.

Schake, Kori. *State of Disrepair: Fixing the Culture and Practices of the State Department*. Stanford, CA: Hoover Institution Press, 2012.

Schlesinger, Arthur M. *Prelude to Independence: The Newspaper War on Britain 1764–1776*. New York: Random House, 1965.

Schweitzer, Peter. *Clinton Cash: The Untold Story of How and Why Foreign Governments and Businesses Helped Make Bill and Hillary Rich*. New York: Harper Publishers, 2015.

Sherman, William T., ed. *Thomas Merton, The Way of Chuang Tzu*. New York: New Directions, 1965.

Smeltz, Dina, Ivo Daalder, Karl Friedhoff, and Craig Kafura. *America Divided: Political Partisanship and US Foreign Policy*. Chicago, IL: The Chicago Council on Global Affairs, 2015.

Smith, Brian H. *More Than Altruism: Politics of Private Foreign Aid*. Princeton, NJ: Princeton University Press, 2014.

Smith, Rupert. *The Utility of Force: The Art of War in the Modern World*. New York: Vintage, 2008.

Stanton Evans, M., and Herbert Romerstein. *Stalin's Secret Agents: The Subversion of Roosevelt's Government*. New York: Threshold Editions, 2013.

Tocqueville, Alexis de. *Democracy in America*. New York: Signet Classics, 2010.

Unger, Harlow Giles. *John Quincy Adams*. Philadelphia, PA: Da Capo Press, 2012.

Varg, Paul A. *Foreign Policies of the Founding Fathers*. Baltimore, MD: Penguin Books, 1970.

Walling, Karl-Friedrich. *Republican Empire: Alexander Hamilton on War and Free Government*. Lawrence: University Press of Kansas, 1999.

Waltz, Michael. *Warrior Diplomat: A Green Beret's Battles from Washington to Afghanistan*. Omaha, NE: Potomac Books, 2014.

Wheelan, Joseph. *Jefferson's War: America's First War on Terror 1801–1805*. New York: Carrroll & Graf Publishers, 2003.

Whipple, Edwin P. The Great Speeches and Orations of Daniel Webster (1923) June 13, 2004 eBook #12606.

Wilford, Hugh. *The Mighty Wurlitzer: How the CIA Played America*. Cambridge, MA: Harvard University Press, 2009.

Wise, David. *Spy: The Inside Story of How the FBI's Robert Hanssen Betrayed America*. New York: Random House, 2003.

Wood, Gordon S. *The Americanization of Benjamin Franklin*. New York: Penguin Press, 2004.

Yuen, Derek M. C. *Deciphering Sun Tzu: How to Read The Art of War*. Oxford: Oxford University Press, 2015.

Zakharia, Fareed. *The Future of Freedom: Illiberal Democracy at Home and Abroad*. New York: W. W. Norton, 2007.

Zhen-yu, Mi, ed. *History of Chinese Military Scholarship*, Vol. 1. Bejing: People's Liberation Army Publishing House, 2008.

Monographs and Articles

Adelman, Carol C., and Nicholas Eberstadt. "Foreign Aid: What Works and What Doesn't," AEI No. 3, October 2008.

Anheier, Helmut, Marlies Glasius, and Mary Kaldor. *Global Civil Society 2004/5.* London: Sage Publications, 2006.

Anonymous, "The Mystery of ISIS," New York Review of Books, August 15, 2015.

Armitage, Richard L., and Joseph S. Nye, co-chairs. *CSIS Commission on Smart Power: A Smarter, More Secure America.* Washington, DC: CSIS, 2007.

Barone, Michael. "The Blame-America-First Crowd," Real Clear Politics, March 19, 2007.

Blackwill, Robert D. "Media Call: The 2015 National Security Strategy." February 10, 2015.

Boone Bartholomees, Jr. J. *Theory of War and Strategy,* 4th ed. Carlisle, PA: Strategic Studies Institute, July 2010.

Boot, Max, and Michael Doran. "Political Warfare," Policy Innovation Memorandum #33, Council on Foreign Relations, June, 2013.

Bowen, Jr. Stuart W. "No More Adhocracies: Reforming the Management of Stabilization and Reconstruction Operations." Prism 3, no. 2 (2012). https://www.ciaonet.org/catalog/24668

———. Statement before the Subcommittee on National Security, Homeland Defense, and Foreign Operations of the Committee on Oversight and Government Reform, United States House of Representatives, December 7, 2011.

Bozeman, Adda. "War and the Clash of Ideas." *Orbis,* Spring 1976.

Braderman, Scott. "AUSA Hosts 'The Future of Stability Operations' Panel, 17 Sept. 2015." *PKSOI Journal* 6, no. 1 (November 2015).

Brands, Hal. *The Promise and Pitfalls of Grand Strategy.* Carlisle, PA: Strategic Studies Institute, August 2012.

Brook, Tom Vanden. "Army Kills Controversial Social Science Program." *USA Today,* June 29, 2015.

Brooks, Rosa. "There's No Such Thing as Peacetime." *Foreign Policy,* March 13, 2015.

Bryen, Stephen. "No High Level Military Participation in Iran Deal." *Technology and Security,* July 29, 2015.

Carafano, James J. "Here's a Blueprint for Not Wasting the Win." *Army Magazine,* October 19, 2015.

Carothers, Thomas. "Democracy Aid at 25: Time to Choose." *Journal of Democracy* 26, no. 1 (January 2015): 59-73.

Cederberg, Aapo, and Pasi Eronen. "How can Societies be Defended against Hybrid Threats?" Geneva Centre for Security Policy (GCSP), September 2015.

Choi, J. K., and S. Bowles. "The Coevolution of Parochial Altruism and War." *Science,* October 26, 2007.

Clark, Charles S. "State Department Leaders Inaugurate New 'Lessons Learned' Center." *Government Executive,* February 3, 2016.

Cohen, Craig, and Josiane Gabel, eds. *2012 Global Forecast - Risk, Opportunity, and the Next Administration* (Washington, DC: CSIS, April 11, 2012).

Col. Murphy, Dennis, U.S. Army, Retired, and Lt. Col. Daniel Kuehl, PhD, U.S. Air Force, Retired. "The Case for a National Information Strategy." *Military Review,* September–October 2015.

Cordesman, Anthony H. "The QDDR: Concepts Are Not Enough." *CSIS*, December 21, 2010.

Cull, Nicholas, and Juliana Geran Pilon. "The Crisis in U.S. Public Diplomacy," in *Project on National Security Reform – Case Studies Working Group Report*, Vol. II, ed. Richard Weitz. Washington, DC: U.S. Army War College Strategic Studies Institute, 2012.

Deni, John R. *The Real Rebalancing: American Diplomacy and the Tragedy of President Obama's Foreign Policy*. Carlisle, PA: Strategic Studies Institute and U.S. Army War College, October 2015.

Department of State and USAID Strategic Plan, FY 2014–2017, April 2, 2014.

Dilegge, Dave. "Stability Operations: DOD Instruction 3000.05." *Small Wars Journal*, September 17, 2009.

Dobbins, James. "Nation-Building: Un Surpasses U.S. on Learning Curve." *Rand Review*, Spring 2005.

Doran, Michael. "The Tectonic Shift in Obama's Iran Policy." *Mosaic Magazine*, April 22, 2015.

Douglas, Walter. "Public Diplomacy for a New Era." in *2012 Global Forecast - Risk, Opportunity, and the Next Administration*, eds. Craig Cohen and Josiane Gabel. Washington, DC: Center for Strategic and International Studies, 2012.

Earle, Edward Mead. "American Interest in the Greek Cause, 1821–1827." *The American Historical Review* 33, no. 1 (1927): 44–63.

Eastman, Michael R. "Whole of Government is Half the Answer." *Interagency Journal* 3, no. 2 (Summer 2012). http://thesimonscenter.org/wp-content/uploads/2012/08/IAJ-3-3-pg31-39.pdf

Edelman, Eric. "Response: The Obama Doctrine." *Mosaic Magazine*, February 16, 2015.

Edelson, David M., and Ronald R. Krebs. "Delusions of Grand Strategy: The Problem with Washington's Planning Obsession." *Foreign Affairs*, November/December 2015.

Elkus, Adam. "CSI: Pentagon – Who Killed American Strategy?" *War on the Rocks*, October 12, 2015.

Ellena, Katherine, and Rebecca Lorenz. "Cultural Intelligence: Archiving Lessons from Afghanistan." *CTX* 3, no. 1 (February 2013).

Epstein, Jason. "The CIA and the Intellectuals." *The New York Review*, April 20, 1967.

Epstein, Susan B. "U.S. Public Diplomacy: Background and the 9/11 Commission Recommendations." *CRS Report for Congress*, October 5, 2004.

———. Foreign Aid Reform, National Strategy, and the Quadrennial Review, CRS R41173, February 15, 2011.

Evacuation Planning and Preparations for Overseas Posts Can Be Improved, GAO-08-23, Oct 19, 2007.

Fall, Bernard B. "The Theory and Practice of Insurgency and Counterinsurgency." *Military Review*, September–October 2015.

Fassihi, Farnaz. "The U.S. Is Still Iran's Great Satan." *Wall Street Journal*, July 17, 2015.

Fisher, Max. "Americans vs. Basic Historical Knowledge." *The Wire*, June 4, 2010.

Freedman, Lawrence. "Ukraine and the War of Exhaustion." *War on the Rocks*, August 11, 2015.

Freeman, Jr. Chas. K. *Arts of Power: Statecraft and Diplomacy*. Washington, DC: U.S. Institute of Peace, 1997.

Friedman, Thomas. "Iran and the Obama Doctrine." *New York Times*, April 5, 2015.

General Dempsey, Martin E. "Our Army's Campaign 15 of Learning." *Landpower Essay* (Institute of Land Warfare: No. 09-3, November 2009).

General McMaster, H. R. "Discussing the Continuities of War and the Future of Warfare: The Defense Entrepreneurs Forum." *Small Wars Journal*, October 14, 2014.

General Petreaus, David, USA. "Learning Counterinsurgency: Observations from Soldiering in Iraq." *Military Review* (January–February, 2006).

Gertz, Bill. "House Armed Services Chief: Intel Losses, Including Clinton Emails, Caused Serious Damage." *Washington Free Beacon*, September 10, 2015.

Goble, Paul. "Lies, Damned Lies and Russian Disinformation." Jamestown Foundation.org, August 13, 2014.

Goldstein, Aaron. "Iran Deal Represents a 21st Century Munich Agreement." *American Spectator*, July 14, 2015.

Goodman, H. A. "On Foreign Policy, Bernie Sanders Is the Democrat and Hillary Clinton Is a Republican." *Huff Post*, November 3, 2015.

Goodson, Jeff. "The Myth of the $43-Million Gas Station in Afghanistan." *War on the Rocks*, November 18, 2015.

Gottlieb, Stuart. "Four Reasons ISIS Is a Threat to the American Homeland." *The National Interest*, September 20, 2014.

Gray, Colin S. *Hard Power and Soft Power: The Utility of Military Force as an Instrument of Policy in the 21st Century*. Carlisle, PA: Strategic Studies Institute, April 2011.

Gray, Colin S. *Irregular Enemies and the Essence of Strategy: Can the American Way of War Adapt?* Carlisle, PA: Strategic Studies Institute (SSI), March 2006.

———. "The Strategist as Hero." *Joint Forces Quarterly*, Issue 62, 3d quarter 2011.

———. *Tactical Operations for Strategic Effect: The Challenge of Currency Conversion*. Tampa, FL: Joint Special Operations University, 2015.

Greenspan, Rachel. "Public Diplomacy in Uniform: The Role of the US Department of Defense in Supporting Modern-Day Public Diplomacy." American Diplomacy: Foreign Service Dispatches and Periodic Reports on US Foreign Policy, March 2011.

Guiding Principles for Stabilization and Reconstruction. Washington, DC: USIP Press, September 2013.

Hasnain, A., J. King, and J. Blau. "'American Exceptionalism' - On What End of the Continuum?" *Societies Without Borders* 7, no. 3 (2012): 326–40.

Hoffman, Frank G. "The Contemporary Spectrum of Conflict: Protracted, Gray Zone, Ambiguous, and Hybrid Modes of War." *2016 Index of Military Strength*. Washington, DC: The Heritage Foundation, 2015.

Holbrooke, Richard. "Get the Message Out." *Washington Post*, October 28, 2001.

Hornblow, Michael. "Not the Quiet City on a Hill." *American Diplomacy*, May 2007.

Horowitz, Jason. "Events in Iraq Open Door for Interventionist Revival, Historian Says." *New York Times*, June 15, 2014.

Hoyt, Timothy. "Can Obama Take Advice? Reflections on the Middle East and American Strategy." *War on the Rocks*, October 22, 2015.

"Hybrid Warfare: Who Is Ready?" Munich Security Report 2015 (Munich, 2015).

Hyman, Gerald. "Lessons for the 2014 QDDR." September 23, 2014, Center for Strategic & International Studies.

Iber, Patrick. "Literary Magazines for Socialists Funded by the CIA, Ranked." *The Awl*, August 24, 2015.

Ibrahim, Raymond. "Islam's Doctrines of Deception." *Middle East Forum*, October 2008.

In the Wake of War: Improving U.S. Post-Conflict Capabilities. Washington, DC: Council on Foreign Relations, Report of an Independent Task Force, July 2005.

Japanese Ministry of Defense, Defense of Japan 2010 (Annual White Paper).

Jentleson, Bruce W. "Strategic Recalibration: Framework for a 21st-Century National Security Strategy." *The Washington Quarterly* 37, no. 1 (2014). https://www.ciaonet.org/catalog/30497

Kaiser, Frederick M. "Interagency Collaborative Arrangements and Activities: Types, Rationales, Considerations." Congressional Research Service, May 31, 2011.

Kant, Immanuel. Perpetual Peace: A Philosophical Sketch, First Supplement, "Of the Guarantee for Perpetual Peace." https://www.mtholyoke.edu/acad/intrel/kant/firstsup.html

Kaplan, Robert D. "Nile Water Wars?" *Stratfor Analysis*, September 24, 2014.

Karabel, Jerome. "'American Exceptionalism' and the Battle for the Presidency." *Huffington Post*, February 21, 2012.

Kasparov, Gary. "Springtime for America's Enemies." *The Daily Beast*, July 22, 2015.

Katzman, Kenneth. "Afghanistan: Current Issues and U.S. Policy Concerns." Congressional Research Service, November 15, 2001.

Kennan, George F. "Peaceful Coexistence: A Western View." *Foreign Affairs*, January 1960.

———. "Policy Staff Planning Memorandum." May 4, 1948.

———. "The Quest for Concept." *Harvard Today*, Autumn 1967.

Kennedy, David M. "Rogue State." *Washington Post*, October 29, 2006.

Kimball, Roger. "Susan Sontag: a Prediction." *The New Criterion*, December 28, 2004.

Kimenyi, Mwangi S., and John Mukum Mbaku. "The limits of the new 'Nile Agreement.'" Brookings Institution, April 28, 2015.

Lawson, Marian Leonardo. "Does Foreign Aid Work? Efforts to Evaluate U.S. Foreign Assistance." February 13, 2013. Congressional Research Service, R42827.

"Leading Through Civilian Power -The First Quadrennial Diplomacy and Development Review," 2010.

Lenhardt, Alfonso E., Charles North, and Rolf Anderson, eds. 2015 VOLAG Report. https://www.usaid.gov/sites/default/files/documents/1866/Volag2015.pdf

Lidell Hart, B. H. *Foreword to Sun Tzu – The Art of War.* Translated by Samuel Griffith. Oxford: Oxford University Press, 1963.

Lockhart, Clare. "Fixing US Foreign Assistance: Cheaper, Smarter, Stronger." World Affairs Journal, Jan–Feb 2014. http://www.worldaffairsjournal.org/article/fixing-us-foreign-assistance-cheaper-smarter-stronger

Londono, Ernesto. "Report: Iraq Reconstruction Failed to Result in Lasting, Positive Changes." *Washington Post*, March 5, 2013.

Lord, Carnes. "The Psychological Dimension in National Strategy," with comments by Paul A. Smith, Jr., and Richard G. Stilwell, in Barnett and Lord, eds., *Political Warfare and Psychological Operations.* Washington, DC: National Defense University Press, 1989.

Lowenthal, Mark M. "Intelligence Education: Quo Vadimus?" *American Intelligence Journal* 31, no. 2 (2013).

Lt Col Sparling, Bryan. Joint Advance Warfare School (National Defense University) thesis. *Coming of Age: Information Operations and the American Way of War*. Norfolk: JAWS, 2010.

Luehrs, Christoff. "Provincial Reconstruction Teams: A Literature Review." *Prism* 1, no. 1. Washington, DC: National Defense University.

Maddox, Thomas H. "Dangerous Nation: Review." *H-Diplo*, April 29, 2007.

Maj Sirard, Jonathan, Lt Col Steve Walden LTC, and Joseph El Hachem. "Redefining Information Operations (IO): Applying Rand Corporation's Analysis of Army IO to Joint IO." *IOSphere*, Winter 2014.

Major General Flynn, Michael T., USA Captain Matt Pottinger, and USMC Paul D. Batchelor, DIA. Fixing Intel: A Blueprint for Making Intelligence Relevant in Afghanistan, Center for a New American Security, January 2010.

Marks, Edward. "The State Department: No Longer the Gatekeeper." *InterAgency Journal* 6, no. 4 (Fall 2015).

Martel, William C. "The Making of Future American Grand Strategy." *The National Interest*, January 27, 2015.

Mastapeter, Craig W. *The Instruments of National Power: Achieving the Strategic Advantage in a Changing World*. Monterey, CA: Postgraduate Naval War College, 2008.

Mattis, General Jim. "A New American Grand Strategy." *Defining Ideas - A Hoover Institution Journal*, February 26, 2015.

Mattis, Peter. "4 U.S. Intelligence Assumptions That Need to Go." *The National Interest*, February 2, 2015.

Maxwell, David S. "Counterinsurgency is Not a Substitute for Strategy." *Small Wars Journal*, May 6, 2014.

McCarty, Kevin. "Can Kennan Shake us Out of Our Strategic Groundhog Day?" *War on the Rocks*, November 9, 2015.

McClay, Wilfred M. "History, American Democracy, and the AP Test Controversy." *Imprimis* 44, no. 7/8 (July/August 2015).

McCloskey, Megan, Tobin Asher, Lena Groeger, Sisi Wei, and Christine Lee. "We Blew $17 Billion in Afghanistan. How Would You Have Spent It?" *ProPublica*, December 17, 2015.

McCoy, Alfred W. "Can Anyone Pacify the World's Number One Narco-State? The Opium Wars in Afghanistan." *TomDispatch*, March 30, 2010.

McDougall, Walter A. "American Exceptionalism . . . Exposed." *FPRI*, October 2012.

McGill, Anna-Katherine Staser, and David H. Gray. "Challenges to International Counterterrorism Intelligence Sharing," *Global Security Studies* 3, no. 3 (Summer 2012): 76–86.

Mehta, Aaron. "Mixed Reaction to US National Military Strategy." *Defense News*, July 12, 2015.

Miller, Aaron David. "The Risks If Iran Doesn't Become More Moderate With Nuclear Deal." *Wall Street Journal*, September 9, 2015.

Moran, Daniel. *Strategic Theory and the History of War*. Monterey, CA: Naval Postgraduate School, 2001.

Moran, Michael. "Obama's Secret Iran Strategy." *Mosaic*, February 2, 2015.

Morris, Victor R. "Grading Gerasimov: Evaluating Russian Nonlinear Warfare through Modern Chinese Doctrine." *The Pendulum*, May 14, 2015.

Murdock, Clark A., Michèle A. Flournoy, Christopher A. Williams, and Kurt M. Campbell, and principal authors. Beyond Goldwater-Nichols: Defense Reform for a New Strategic Era Phase I Report, *CSIS*, March 2004.

Murray, D. W. "Transposing Symbolic Forms: Actor Awareness of Language Structures in Navajo Ritual." *Anthropological Linguistics* 31, no. 117 (1989): 195–208.

Naylor, Sean D. "Out of Uniform and Into the Political Fray." *FP*, June 19, 2015.

Niles, Hezekiah, ed. Niles' Weekly Register, Vol. 20. Baltimore, MD: 1821.

Nossel, Suzanne. "Smart Power." *Foreign Affairs*, March/April 2004.

Nunberg, Geoffrey. "And, Yes, He Was a Great Communicator." *The New York Times*, June 13, 2004.

Nye, Joseph S. "What China and Russia Don't Get About Soft Power." *Foreign Affairs*, April 29, 2013.

Obama, Barack. "The President's News Conference in Strasbourg." The American Presidency Project.

On the Brink: Weak States and US National Security, Center for Global Development, May 2004; Office of the Under Secretary of Defense for Acquisition, Technology, and Logistics. Defense Science Board 2004 Summer Study on Transition to and From Hostilities, December 2004.

Palau, Rainer Gonzalez, Stefanie Nijssen, and Steven A. Zyck. "Stabilisation & Reconstruction: Definitions, Civilian Contribution & Lessons Learnt," Civil-Military Fusion Center, September 2011.

Parks, Brad, and Nakul Kadaba. "The Elusive Quest for Effective Aid Management in Liberia." AidData BETA, October 20, 2010.

Pietrucha, Mike. "America's Victory Disease Has Left It Dangerously Deluded." *War on the Rocks*, November 18, 2015.

Pilon, Juliana Geran. "Up in Arms, or at Arm's Length?" *International Journal of Intelligence Ethics* 1, no. 1 (Spring 2010).

Pomeranetz, Peter, and Michael Weiss. *The Menace of Unreality: How the Kremlin Weaponizes Information, Culture and Money*. New York: institute of Modern Russia, 2014.

Pomerantsev, Peter. "Inside Putin's Information War." *Politico*, January 4, 2015.

Pondiscio, Robert, Gilbert T. Sewall, and Sandra Stotsky. Shortchanging the Future: The Crisis of History and Civics in American Schools, A Pioneer Institute White Paper, No. 100, April 2013.

Radelet, Steven. "Prosperity Rising." *Foreign Affairs*, January/February 2016.

Rasmussen, Louise J., Winston R. Sieck, and Robert R. "Hoffman Cultural Knowledge for Intelligence Analysts: Expertise in Cultural Sensemaking." *American Intelligence Journal* 31, no. 2 (2013): 28–37.

Rauscher, Frederick. "Kant's Social and Political Philosophy." The Stanford Encyclopedia of Philosophy (Summer 2012 Edition).

Reed, David. "Aspiring to Spying." 16 *The Washington Times*, November 14, 1997.

Rice, Condoleezza. Remarks at Georgetown School of Foreign Service, January 18, 2006.

Rodgers, Daniel T. "American Exceptionalism Revisited." Raritan 24 (2004).

Rosand, Eric, Alistair Millar, and Jason Ipe. *Civil Society and the UN Global Counter-Terrorism Strategy: Opportunities and Challenges*. Washington, DC and New York: Center on Global Counterterrorism Cooperation, September 2008.

Rothkopf, David. "Operation Charlie Foxtrot." *Foreign Policy*, March 27, 2015.

Schadlow, Nadia. "Peace and War: The Space Between." *War on the Rocks*, August 18, 2014.

Schaefer, Brett D., and James Phillips. Time to Reconsider U.S. Support of UNRWA, The Heritage Foundation, Backgrounder #2997, March 5, 2015.

Schindler, John R. "Obama Fails to Fight Putin's Propaganda Machine." *Observer*, November 5, 2015.

Schmitt, Eric. "In Battle to Defeating ISIS, U.S. Targets Its Psychology." *New York Times*, December 28, 2014.

Seeman, Neil, Alex Mosa, and Alexander Osei-Bonsu. "American Exceptionalism Revisited." *Options Politiques*, November–December 2014.

Serafino, Nina. *Peacekeeping/Stabilization and Conflict Transitions: Background and Congressional Action on the Civilian Response/Reserve Corps and other Civilian Stabilization and Reconstruction Capabilities*. Washington, DC: Congressional Research Service, October 2, 2012.

Sestanovich, Stephen. "Obama's Focus Is on Nation-Building at Home." *New York Times*, March 11, 2014.

Shleifer, Andrei. "Peter Bauer and the Failure of Foreign Aid." *Cato Journal* 29, no. 3 (Fall 2009): 379–90.

Slaughter, Anne-Marie. "International Relations, Principal Theories." *Max Planck Encyclopedia of Public International Law*, edited by R. Wolfrum. Oxford: Oxford University Press, 2011.

Slaughter, Matthew. *American Companies and Global Supply Networks: Driving U.S. Economic Growth and Jobs by Connecting with the World*. Washington, DC: Business Roundtable, December 6, 2012.

Smith, Marion. The Myth of American Isolationism: Commerce, Diplomacy, and Military Affairs in the Early Republic. The Heritage Foundation Special Report from The Kenneth B. Simon Center for Principles and Politics, No. 134, September 9, 2013.

Solomon, Jay, and Maria Abi-Habib. "U.S., Iran Relations Move to Détente." *Wall Street Journal*, October 28, 2014.

Spalding, Matthew. "America's Founders and the Principles of Foreign Policy: Sovereign Independence, National Interests, and the Cause of Liberty in the World." The Heritage Foundation, First Principles Series Report #33 on Political Thought, October 15, 2010.

Stavridis, Admiral James. Testimony for Senate Appropriations Subcommittee for State, Foreign Operations and Related Programs, March 26, 2015.

Stearman, William L. "Lessons Learned from Vietnam." *Military Review*, March–April 2010.

Steele, Robert David. *Human Intelligence (HUMINT): All Humans, All Minds, All the Time*. Carlisle, PA: Strategic Studies Institute, May 2010.

Stephanson, Anders. "Cold War Origins." Encyclopedia of American Foreign Policy, 2002.

Stillings, Major Kris J. USMC, General George Washington and the Formulation of American Strategy for the War of Independence, Marine Corps Command and Staff College, April 2001.

Takyeh, Ray. "The Iran Deal Is a Big Bet on a Revolutionary Outlier." *Washington Post*, August 6, 2015.

The American Academy of Diplomacy, Forging a 21st Century Diplomatic Service for the United States through Professional Education and Training, Stimson Center, 2011.

The Commission on the Intelligence Capabilities of the United States Regarding Weapons of Mass Destruction, *Report to the President of the United States.* Unclassified. Washington, DC: US Government Printing Office, 2005.

The U.S. Army Operating Concept: Win in a Complex World - 2020-2040, TRADOC Pamphlet 523-3-1, October 7, 2014.

Thomas, Timothy. "Russia's Military Strategy and Ukraine: Indirect, Asymmetric—and Putin-Led." *Journal of Slavic Military Studies* 28, no.3 (2015): 445–61.

Tomes, Peter R. "On the Politicization of Intelligence." *War on the Rocks*, September 29, 2015.

———. "Toward a Smarter Military: Socio-Cultural Intelligence and National Security." *Parameters* 45, no. 2 (Summer 2015).

Ulin, Bob. "About Interagency Cooperation." *Interagency*, No. 10-01, September 2010.

"USIA – An Overview." http://dosfan.lib.uic.edu/usia/usiahome/oldoview.htm#overview

U. S. Department of Defense, "Military and Security Developments Involving the People's Republic of China 2011." *Annual Report to Congress.* Washington, DC: August 16, 2011.

U.S. Department of Defense, Quadrennial Defense Review Report, February 2010.

United States Special Operations Command White Paper, The Gray Zone, September 9, 2015.

US Army, Field Manual 3-13, Inform and Influence Activities, January 2013.

US Army, Field Manual 3-38, Cyber Electromagnetic Activities, February 2014.

Van Puyvelde, Damien. "Hybrid War – Does It Even Exist?" *Nato Review Magazine*, May 2015.

Vandiver, John. "SACEUR: Allies Must Prepare for Russia 'Hybrid war.'" *Stars and Stripes*, September 4, 2014.

Vershbow, Ambassador Alexander. Remarks at the Meeting the Strategic Communications Challenge, Public Diplomacy Forum 2015.

Voelz, Glenn J. *The Rise of iWar: Identity, Information, and the Individualization of Modern Warfare.* Washington, DC: Strategic Studies Institute and U.S. Army War College Press, October 2015.

Walt, Stephen M. "The Myth of American Exceptionalism." *Foreign Policy*, October 11, 2011.

Walton, Timothy. "China's Three Warfares." Delex Special report-3, Delex Systems, Inc., January 10, 2012.

Waltzman, Rand. "The U.S. Is Losing the Social Media War." *Time*, October 12, 2015.

Weeks, William E. "Dangerous Nation Roundtable." *H-Diplo*, April 29, 2007.

Wilson, Woodrow. Message to Congress, February 3, 1917, War Messages, 65th Cong., 1st Sess. Senate Doc. No. 5, Serial No. 7264, Washington, DC, 1917.

Index

A

Abel (*see also*, Cain), 177–182

Academy (also Universities), 8, 195–196, 293–294, 313, 316, 319, 335–336
American Academy of Diplomacy, 269
academic(s), 83–85, 159, 167, 235, 332

Action(s), 9, 13, 15, 39, 47, 49, 56, 64–74, 86, 104–107, 140–141, 158, 162–3, 182–3, 196–198, 210, 217, 220, 243, 248–9, 290, 297, 307, 315, 324, 339
covert, 110, 212, 219, 263–265
military, 14–15, 162, 244, 307

Active measures (also, Taquiyya; *see also*, Disinformation), 40–42, 303

Adams, John, 79, 83, 104, 116–120, 136–138, 148

Adams, John Quincy, 95–96, 117, 142, 146

Adams, Samuel, 79, 90–91, 103–111, 133, 243

Adapt, 38, 53, 59, 66, 74, 92–94, 116, 123, 148, 160, 213, 257, 266, 269, 314, 318, 345

Adelman, Carol C., 293–294

Advice, 35, 58, 64, 69, 85, 95, 109, 118, 125, 136, 138,179, 227, 279, 323, 330, 338
advise, 33, 51, 65, 110, 132, 136, 213, 214, 221, 276–7, 354
ill-advised, 132, 180, 183, 189,

Afghanistan, 153, 159, 161, 185–200, 206, 220, 228–229, 233, 236–237, 246, 255, 274–276, 290, 313–318, 328, 339, 341, 351, 353

Africa(n) (also, African-American), 93, 134, 141, 188, 195, 235, 273, 290, 345

Agency/agencies, 208–210, 218, 221, 237, 267–268, 309, 317
Central Intelligence Agency (CIA), 189, 199, 278–279, 304

Defense Advanced Research Projects Agency (DARPA), 248
Defense Intelligence Agency, 198
National Security Agency, 194
U.N. Refugee and Works Agency (UNRWA), 196–197
U.S. Agency for International Development USAID), 160, 293–294, 353
U.S. Information Agency, 207
interagency, 227–228, 234–235, 237–238, 268, 276, 305, 3140–315, 319
(*See also*, Defense, State)

Agent(s), 34, 109, 110, 112, 143, 145, 199, 218, 250, 272–279, 291, 354
double-agent(s), 108, 278–179

Al Qaeda (*see also*, Osama bin Laden), 153, 187–189, 195, 222, 252, 256

Allah (also, Mohammed(anism)), 41, 253, 329

Alliance(s), 6, 12–13, 69, 91, 93, 107–108, 116–117, 126–127, 140, 181, 217, 252, 265, 272, 306, 324

Altruism (also, Compassion, Unselfish (ness)), 288–291, 314, 331, 338

America (*see* United States)

Analysis, 10, 15, 47, 48, 60, 67, 91, 161, 182, 184, 200, 210, 232, 238, 274, 277, 289, 292, 296, 334, 336

Anti-Americanism, 169–171, 195

Antithesis, 31, 88

Arab(s)(ic) (also, Arab Spring), 32, 37, 40, 188, 249, 253

Arendt, Hannah, 87–89

Armistead, Leigh, 211

Army, 249, 255, 264, 271, 274, 276, 301, 306, 312, 330, 341

Arrogance, 35, 250, 330, 337
hubris, 35, 56, 94, 131

Articles of Confederation, 137
Asia/Central Asia, 9, 186
Assessment, 18–19, 46–47, 59, 89, 115, 128, 160, 166, 198, 227, 266–267, 270, 334, 337, 349
Asset(s), 28, 48, 52, 76, 199, 211, 221, 252, 272, 285, 298, 316, 319, 352
Authority, 72, 107, 124, 196–198, 214, 302, 309, 315, 317, 347
Authoritarian (also, Semi-authoritarian, Autocratic), 180, 213, 233, 314, 334
Aware (awareness) (also, Self-awareness), 7, 13, 49–50, 58, 109, 124, 164, 170, 179, 188, 254, 266, 273, 293, 301, 331, unaware, 13, 257, 278, 297

B

Baer, Robert, 272–273, 279–80
Barbary, 134–135, 138
Bartholomees, Jr., J. Boone, 13, 18
Bauerlein, Mark, 165
Belief(s), 10, 81, 86, 89, 133, 135, 139, 180, 207, 216, 252
Bellow, Adam, 165
Bemis, Samuel Flagg, 140
Benefit(s), 15, 18, 30, 73, 94, 128, 133, 135, 142, 170, 215, 228, 249, 270, 276, 287, 289, 291, 325–326, 330, 337–338
Blackwill, Robert D., 156
Border(s) (also, Frontier(s)), 10–11, 180, 216, 231, 247, 250, 257, 287, 311, 325, 335
Boyd, John, 51–52
Bozeman, Adda, 5
Brands, Hal, 17–18
Bryen, Stephen D., 238
Britain (also, England, Great Britain, United Kingdom, Mother Country), 79, 83, 87–88, 90–91, 99, 100–101, 118–119, 121, 136–138, 304, 324–325, 329–330
Bureaucrat(s)(ic) (also, Bureaucracy(ies)), 59, 148, 161, 193, 199, 208–209, 220, 228, 257, 265–267, 270–271, 277, 279, 293, 310, 314, 316, 352
Burke, Edmund, 79, 99–102, 111

C

Cain (see also, Cain), 177–179, 213
Capabilities, 45, 145, 184, 210, 231, 254, 276, 307–308, 313, 352
Capitalism, 31, 40, 285, 290
Carothers, Thomas, 229–230

Carr, Edward Hallett, 207
Casualties, 16, 17, 110
Ceaser, James. W., 139
Chandrasekaran, Rajif, 192, 228
Chappell, Paul K., 4
Charity, 33, 261, 281, 290, 331
China, 249, 280, 306–309, 330, 336
Christian(s) (also, Christianity), 10, 33, 56, 182, 331
Civil Society, 294, 298, 302, 304, 306, 312–313
civilian(s), 301, 304–305, 308–309, 312–313, 316, 318–319, 323, 329, 340–341, 351–352
Civilization, 17, 32, 88, 101, 133, 178, 216, 238, 328–329
Clausewitz, Carl von, 15–17, 51, 66–69, 218
Clinton Administration (also, Clinton years), 186, 199, 217
Bill, 188–189, 278
Foundation, 292
Hillary, 160, 197
Coalition, 232–234
Coercion, 7, 94, 136, 147, 213–217, 302, 308
Cold War, 10, 13, 40, 159, 171, 196, 207–208, 274, 278–280, 302–303, 315, 338
Collaboration (see also, Cooperation), 19, 234, 305, 314
Collins, Joseph J., 351–352
Colonies, 76, 79, 83, 87, 89–96, 99–101, 103–108, 131, 133, 137, 142, 181, 229, 324–325, 329
Colonialism (see also Imperialism), 262, 326
Combat(ant)(s), 3, 16, 33, 41, 59, 67, 168, 193, 232, 253, 255, 307, 309, 316
Command(er) (see also, General, Leader, Ruler), 13–14, 17, 46–49, 63–72 110, 140, 155, 157, 203, 210, 218–219, 245, 251, 261, 264, 274, 285, 316–317, 351–352
Commander-in-chief (see also, President), 124–125, 132, 238, 244, 341
Committees of Correspondence, 104–105
Communication(s) 25, 51–52, 102, 105–106, 110, 164, 178, 220, 243–253, 256, 263, 272, 301, 306
Strategic communication (see also Influence), 28, 47, 79, 104, 264, 271, 352

Communism/communist, 8, 33–34, 40–41, 102, 171–172, 183, 212, 288, 295, 303, 306

Complex(ity), 9, 12, 25, 30, 32, 35–38, 48, 52–53, 58, 60, 64, 74, 89, 92, 99, 106, 124, 153, 158, 167, 170, 172, 178–179, 185, 189, 192–194, 199, 209, 227, 316, 319, 331, 334, 345, 349–350, 355

Conflict, 5, 10, 13, 25–31, 34–35, 39, 41–42, 46, 51, 58–59, 65, 68–76, 96, 108, 123, 153, 171, 182, 191, 197, 200, 206, 219, 233, 254, 266, 268, 286, 298, 305–306, 324, 332, 349–353

    Military (also, Armed, Battle-ground, High Intensity), 11, 19, 38, 42, 88, 94, 99, 232, 255

    Resolution (also Prevent(ion) (ing), End(ing), Post-Conflict), 99, 157, 171, 233, 261, 269, 290, 305, 314, 348

Congress, 84, 87, 95, 107, 119, 123, 124, 126, 138, 141, 142, 144, 146, 156, 159, 161, 166, 186, 199–200, 220, 235, 237, 251, 267–268, 279–280, 286, 288, 292, 296, 309, 313, 316, 341, 347

    Congressional committee(s), 155, 197, 198, 200, 227, 267, 278–280, 296

Conscious(ly), 64, 87, 214, 249, 257, 308, 348

    consciousness (also, Self-conscious (ness)), 50, 106, 335, 347

    unconscious (also, Subconscious), 52, 56, 195, 198, 214, 255, 308

Constitution(s) (al), 56, 88–89, 116, 142, 144, 255

    U.S. Constitution, 64, 94, 107, 122–125, 137, 144, 286

Continuum, 11, 31, 46, 305

Conservative(s) (also, Neoconserva-tive(s)), 86, 89, 96, 127, 172, 212

Contractor (s) (also, Contracting, Con-tract(s)), 42, 235–236, 270–271, 288,

Control(s) (also, Controlling), 41, 47–50, 59, 70, 74, 87, 92, 93, 102–103, 106–107, 143–144, 158, 161, 207, 215, 221, 231, 246, 278, 279, 296, 316

Cooperation, 141, 160, 179, 200, 228, 235–238, 277, 287, 290, 310, 316, 332

Coordination (see also Synchronization), 235–237, 261, 276, 309, 315–317, 354

Cordesman, Anthony H., 253

Corruption, 94, 231, 236, 262, 280, 292

Counterinsurgency (COIN) (See also, Insurgency), 153, 192, 221, 227–228, 237, 290, 317

Crime/criminal(s), 42, 134, 170, 177, 188, 235–236, 253, 268, 336, 352

Crumpton, Henry A., 197, 273, 275

Culture/cultural, 4, 5, 10, 17, 25, 30–33, 51–52, 70, 79, 100, 102, 128, 135, 153, 164–170, 189, 192, 196, 209, 211, 213, 216, 229–230, 234, 236, 238, 248, 255, 261, 268–269, 273–274, 277, 286, 301–302, 304, 333, 352

    American Culture (also, Culture of the U.S.), 132, 170, 216, 221–222, 303, 311,

    Awareness (also, Acumen, Culturally Attuned, Cultural Knowledge), 28, 184, 319

    bias(es) (also, Lack of Cultural Under-standing), 13, 108, 183

Cyber (also, Cyberspace, Cyber war(fare)), 11, 179, 196, 206, 210, 306, 314

D

Daesh (also ISIS, ISIL), 153, 155, 222, 250, 252, 254, 153, 155, 222, 250, 252, 254

Daigler, Kenneth A., 108, 111

Danger(ous)(s) (also, Endanger(s)(ing)) (see also, Threat(s)), 11–12, 28, 33, 35, 46–47, 49, 51, 53, 58, 65,69, 73, 84, 85, 95, 103, 115, 116, 119, 122, 124, 133, 135, 137, 142, 145, 159, 162, 165–169, 178, 181–182, 188, 194, 196, 198, 200, 206, 214, 216, 222, 252, 255, 267, 273–275, 287, 337–338, 348, 350, 354–355

David (see also, Goliath), 36, 50, 79, 182, 244, 277

Davidson, Philip, 102–103, 105

Deception, 28, 38–42, 70, 74–75, 108–110, 249, 263, 278, 285

    self-deception, 255, 354

Decision(s) (also, Decision maker(s) and Decision-making), 46, 51, 71–72, 90, 103, 123, 135, 138, 160, 163, 166, 184–185, 191, 196, 200, 209, 254, 276, 278, 312, 318–319, 349

Declaration of Independence, 56, 87, 91, 92, 96, 107, 120, 146

Defense, 49, 51, 93, 96, 100, 123, 128, 142, 158, 171, 237, 246–247, 315, 345

Department of Defense (DOD), 42, 157, 160, 198, 200, 208, 220, 227, 237, 309

Definition(s) 12–13, 15, 102, 104, 108–109, 207, 210, 213, 217, 232–233, 298

Dempsey, Gary T., 232–233

Divine (also, Divinely), 6, 14, 55, 66, 71, 83, 131, 177, 205

   God (also, Godlike, Goddess(s), God-given, Demigod), 2, 8–10, 14, 33, 45, 56, 64, 71, 109, 131, 168, 177–178, 205, 280, 311, 323

Democracy, 86, 93, 111, 133, 144, 148, 165, 171, 183, 212, 215, 229–233, 255, 276, 298, 303, 327, 334, 341, 347, 353,

   assistance (also Democracy Aid, Democracy Building, Democracy Promotion), 229–232, 261, 304, 312

Democrat(s)(ic), 164, 191, 230, 285, 318, 327

   Republican(s) (ism) (see also, Federalist(s)), 6, 8, 85, 104, 116, 123, 125, 127, 128, 138, 148, 164, 168–169, 181, 230, 318, 327, 346, 348

Demographic(s), 25, 58, 89, 117, 196, 206, 250, 325

Dutch (also, Holland), 5, 7, 119–120, 126, 134, 324

Deterrence (also, Deter, Deterring, Deterrent), 28–29, 50, 128, 158, 162, 305, 307, 339, 349

Development, 143, 158, 160–161, 171, 200, 209, 230, 232–237, 244, 266, 268–269, 285–299, 307, 312, 319–320, 352–353

DIME (Diplomatic, Information, Military, and Economics), 245

Diplomacy, 4, 18, 28, 69, 85, 91, 96, 110, 115, 117–118, 124, 126, 128, 148, 158, 160–161, 163, 171, 211, 218–220, 230, 261, 265, 308

   Public diplomacy (see also Influence, Strategic Communication) 47, 189, 208, 219–220, 247–248, 251, 253, 265–266, 298–299, 304, 306–308, 312, 319, 332, 335

Disease (also, Illness), 4–5, 11, 28, 279, 327, 350, 351, 353, 355

Disinformation (see also, Active Measures), 108, 179, 207, 249–253, 261, 272, 279, 303

Doctrine, 40, 42, 46–47, 74, 153, 158, 218, 238, 274, 353

Dialectic(s), 9, 12, 15, 30–32, 35, 153, 193, 207, 217, 332, 349

Dobbins, James, 232

Doran, Michael, 218

Dualist/Dualism, 11, 193

Dueck, Colin, 179

E

East(ern), 4, 17, 30, 279, 302

   Middle East, 19, 34, 234, 334, 339

Eastman, Michael R., 314

Education (al), 102, 106, 109, 117, 164–169, 194, 237–238, 248, 269, 271, 276, 286, 288, 291, 304, 316–319, 332, 339, 351, 354

Economy(ies)/economic(s), 12, 13, 15, 33, 42, 56–58, 69, 79, 100, 120–122, 128, 136, 167, 178–179, 200, 206–207, 209, 212, 232, 245, 250, 255, 286–288, 292, 298, 304, 306, 312, 315, 328–330, 333, 337

   economic assistance, 147, 229–230,

   warfare (also, Economic Sanctions, Economic Coercion, Boycott(s)), 79, 105, 124–126, 128, 137, 212–213, 308

Education(al), 102, 106, 109, 117, 164–169, 194, 237–238, 248, 269, 271, 276, 286, 288, 291, 304, 316–319, 332, 339, 351, 354

Electronic(al), 48, 207, 210, 253, 272

Element(s), 12, 13, 19, 46–47, 80, 118, 147, 148, 199, 247, 250, 276, 277, 338, 346,

   of national power, 158, 207–211, 217, 245, 309–310, 317

Elkus, Adam, 162

Empathy (also, Empathetic, Altruism) 52, 71, 106, 193, 216, 228, 287–291, 299, 304, 331–333, 338, 352

Empire, 9, 76, 80, 84, 86, 89–90, 99–101, 123, 125, 133–134, 137, 144, 168, 206, 328, 330

   Imperial(ist) (also, Imperialism), 85, 93–94, 127, 133, 139, 233, 262, 323, 325–328

Enemy(ies)/foe(s), 8, 16, 28–29, 35, 37–39, 47–51, 57, 59, 69, 73, 94, 105–109, 137, 143, 180, 182, 184, 190, 192–193, 196–197, 210, 221, 246, 249, 253–254, 256, 261, 263–265, 271–273, 301–302, 307, 324, 326, 354

   friend(ly)(s) (ship), 8, 13, 25, 32, 35, 37, 105, 108, 111, 119, 133, 140, 144,

146, 153, 158, 171–172, 179–182, 190–193, 218, 221, 228, 243, 256, 272, 279, 302, 313, 336, 342, 350, 352

Energy, 40, 49, 59, 67, 251, 298, 339, 354

Environment, 12, 15, 29, 35, 38, 48, 53, 59–60, 67, 74, 75, 109, 158, 181, 183, 189, 192, 194, 200, 209, 217, 231, 251, 261, 266, 305, 314, 334, 346, 350–353

Epstein, Susan B., 161

Equality, 96, 127

Espionage (also, Spy(ing) (craft) (ies)), 108–110, 181, 196–197, 218, 255, 274–275, 278–280, 303

Ethics/ethical, 25, 41, 70–71, 235, 236, 332

Ethnic, 34, 168, 178, 186, 324

Etymology, 2, 3, 333, 338, 340

Europe/European, 3, 34, 52, 86, 91–95, 101, 116, 119, 120, 133, 142, 143, 145, 180, 182, 251, 296, 303, 325, 326, 329, 335

Evaluation/evaluate(d)(ing), 50, 181, 237–238, 264, 266–269, 271, 278, 289, 296

Exceptionalism, (also, American Exceptionalism), 131–132, 138–139, 212, 323, 326–327, 334–338, 340

Executive(s) (see also, Commander-in-Chief, President) 123, 156, 237, 248, 275

Expert(s)/expertise, 4, 18, 70, 157, 160, 179, 183, 184, 194, 195, 196, 228, 229, 232, 233, 234, 250, 265, 269, 273, 277, 278, 280, 292, 294, 304, 305, 312, 313, 316, 323, 335, 351,

F

Fail(ure)(s)(ing), 3, 12, 14, 15, 17, 19, 25, 28, 29, 34, 38, 47–48, 69, 73, 75, 90, 92, 93, 103, 108, 128, 134, 136–139, 159–161, 178, 182–184, 186, 189, 196, 206, 216, 222, 230–231, 235–237, 245, 254, 256–257, 268–269, 275, 278–280, 289, 294–297, 301, 308, 312, 332, 339–340, 348, 353

Fairweather, Jack, 185–186, 190, 192, 229,

Fascism/fascist (also, Nazi(sm), Neo-Nazis(m), Hitler), 1, 33–34, 102, 180, 254,

Fate(ful) (also, Destiny), 1, 9, 88, 133, 139, 142, 143, 145, 170, 178,

Federal(ism), Federalism, 122–123, 136, 168, 209, 227, 233, 276, 286, 316

Federal Bureau of Investigation (FBI), 197, 268, 280

Federalist(s) (also, Federalist Papers), 88, 93, 116–117, 122–123, 138, 346

Feith, Douglas J., 220, 246–248, 312–313,

Finance(s)(d)/financial (see also, Money), 40, 119, 124, 136, 209, 229, 252, 302

Flynn, Michael T., 198, 200, 251, 274

Force(s)(ful), 15–16, 35, 38, 40, 56, 58–59, 67–68, 75, 76, 88, 93, 95, 100, 101, 126, 134, 135, 138, 139, 147, 158, 160, 200, 207, 209, 211, 212, 217, 221, 234, 237, 246, 249, 262, 268, 275–277, 312, 326, 334, 336, 341, 352

Air Force, 51, 270, 317

Military (also, Armed), 15, 18, 40, 138, 157, 158, 183, 189, 206, 212, 216, 232, 308, 325, 339–340, 353

Special Operations, 42, 187, 192, 219, 248, 307–308

Foreign, 13, 93, 108, 118, 123, 124, 127, 128, 134, 135, 139, 170, 179, 181, 185, 193, 210, 215, 220, 229, 233–234, 249, 271, 275, 277, 278, 286, 287, 301, 318, 326

affairs/relations, 115, 166, 171, 207, 208, 227, 248, 309, 311, 315, 317, 324, 335, 348

policy(ies) (also, National Security Policy(ies)), 12, 13, 18–19, 28, 56, 65, 86, 91–92, 95–96, 115, 125, 133, 139–140, 142, 155, 156, 159–161, 163, 170, 195–196, 208, 214, 218, 234, 255, 297, 298, 312, 315, 316, 324, 333, 335, 337, 338, 346–347, 349, 354

assistance/aid, 18, 144–147, 161, 188, 200, 228–238, 257, 286–299, 312, 350

Founder(s), 79–96, 102, 106, 111, 115–119, 122–123, 128, 133–134, 138–140, 142, 144, 148, 153, 163–164, 168–169, 181, 219, 243, 254, 262, 265, 291, 320, 324–325, 334, 339, 345–346, 353–354

founding principles, 285, 339, 345

France, 88, 117, 125, 126–127, 138, 141, 145

French (also, French Revolution), 2, 3, 16, 83, 89–90, 96, 108–110, 118, 120–121, 125–128, 132, 180, 295

Franklin, Benjamin, 79, 83, 89–90, 110–111, 117–118, 121, 145, 181, 254, 320, 329–330

Freedom(s), 2, 7, 32, 79, 96, 101, 110, 127, 128, 132, 135, 139, 145–148, 195, 206, 233, 262, 287, 293, 303, 307, 311, 325, 334, 336, 339, 341, 345

liberty, 56, 79–81, 85–86, 88–89, 101, 120, 122–123, 127, 141, 144–145, 147, 169, 231, 238, 294, 311, 345–347, 354
Free Trade, 79, 120–122, 128, 135, 144, 285, 287, 311, 325
Freedman, Laurence, 4, 15–16, 30, 71, 75
Freeman, Chas. K, 219, 249

G

Gates, Robert, 220, 278, 313, 319
General(s)(ship) (see also, Commander, Ruler), 14, 15, 27, 29, 33, 39, 40, 49, 58, 60, 64, 65–67, 71–75, 84, 92, 109, 112, 123, 155, 158, 159, 160, 183, 185, 200, 221, 247, 251, 254, 274, 317, 324, 345,
Genius, 67–71, 79, 89, 94, 117, 118, 122, 124
Geography(ical), 17, 25, 30, 47, 58, 81, 83, 122, 206, 264, 294, 324, 348
German/Germany, 3, 7, 31, 42, 279, 301, 332, 333, 334, 347
Prussia(n), 66, 68, 121, 332
Gertz, Bill, 278–279
Gillis, John R., 167
Global(ly), 8, 37, 41, 58, 79, 139, 142, 146, 155, 171, 210, 235, 248, 250, 252, 253, 256, 262, 266, 276, 285–286, 289, 290, 293–294, 298, 311, 314, 317, 319 323, 325, 327, 328, 330, 350
Goal(s) (also, Purpose(s), Objective(s)), 13, 14, 18, 28, 29, 33, 36, 37, 40, 41, 43, 58, 82, 85, 92–93, 104, 117, 124, 149, 156–157, 160, 162, 181, 183, 189, 191, 214, 215, 218, 230, 234, 236, 245, 253, 261, 266, 287,1 293, 297, 305, 308, 319–320, 332, 339–34
strategic, 261, 298–299, 346
Goble, Paul, 249–250
Goliath (see also, David), 36–37, 50, 79, 108, 182, 243, 277, 328
Gopal, Anand, 190–191
Governance, 47, 149, 231, 233, 255, 305, 339
Government(s) (al), 18, 33, 39, 50, 59, 64, 83, 87, 88, 94, 96, 101, 103, 104, 110, 115, 116, 118, 119, 122–124, 127, 138, 142, 144–145, 147–148, 156, 158, 160, 161, 162, 166, 171, 181, 185, 189, 192, 196, 200, 208, 218, 220, 221, 227, 232, 233, 235–237, 244–248, 251, 261, 265, 266, 268, 272, 275, 285–288, 290–292,

294–297, 305, 309, 310, 313–319, 329, 340, 341, 347, 349, 353–354
self-government (also, Self-governance, Self-rule), 8, 91, 94, 99, 101–102, 148, 168–169, 233, 262, 312, 329
whole-of-government, 219, 227, 233, 305, 307–310, 315, 352–353
Gray, Colin S., 14–15, 27, 30, 157, 215–217
Gray zone, 12–13, 305–306, 308–311
Griffith, Samuel B., 72, 95
Grotius, Hugo, 5–6
Ground, 14, 19, 38, 58, 65, 67, 72, 82, 100, 132, 183, 189, 191, 192, 234, 244, 249, 273, 277, 291, 295, 301, 307, 340, 352
Guerilla(s) (also, Guerilla Warfare), 38–39, 42, 206
Guns, 190, 191, 244, 249, 273, 277, 291, 295, 301, 307, 340, 352

H

Hamas, 296–297
Hamilton, Alexander, 82–83, 88, 93–96, 115–117, 122, 124–128, 137–138, 146, 317, 320, 353
Handel, Michael I., 15, 17, 30, 68–69
Hard power, 118, 163, 182, 210, 214, 216, 238, 264, 289, 302, 306, 339, 349
Hayek, Friedrich A., 56
Health(y), 2, 4–5, 11, 34–35, 50, 110, 192, 288, 290, 297, 350, 353, 354
Hezbollah, 197
History, 1, 5, 11, 13–14, 19, 27, 31, 40–41, 46, 56, 60, 63, 83, 84, 90, 91, 103, 116, 128, 135, 139, 159, 160, 166, 177, 179–186, 191, 195, 208, 251, 277, 305, 325, 327, 330, 351, 354
American, 4, 86, 107, 165–169, 244, 326
Hoffman, Frank G., 318–319
Hollander, Paul, 169
Holbrooke, Richard, 235, 265
Hooker, Jr., Richard D., 351–352
Horowitz, Irving Louis, 32–34
Howard, Edward Lee, 197
Human Terrain (also, Human Domain), 35, 184, 193, 228, 351
Humane, 71, 84, 120, 285, 293, 354
Humanitarian, 42, 187–188, 229, 286, 291, 296, 302, 304, 306
assistance (also, Intervention), 229, 261, 287–289, 293, 312, 352
relief, 236, 287, 291, 296–297

Hybrid, 40, 305–306, 309, 331
   war(fare), 12, 250, 252, 305–306
Hyman, Gerald, 161

I

Ideal(ism) (see also, Utopia(n)(s), Vision,
   Realism), 9, 28, 29, 31–34, 39, 51, 66,
   68, 86, 89, 96, 101, 102, 116, 117, 127,
   132, 135, 139, 144–148, 165, 168, 170,
   201, 230, 262, 285, 308, 311, 316, 323,
   331–337, 346–348
Identity (also, National Identity, American
   Identity), 140, 165, 193, 232, 326, 338
Ideology (also, Ideological, Ideologue(s)),
   8, 96, 164–165, 167, 171, 183, 196, 208,
   222, 235, 238, 247, 265, 272, 293, 329
Ignorance, 19, 35, 82, 165–171
Influence (also, Political Influence), 28,
   69–70, 86, 108–110, 185, 200, 207–210,
   213, 217–218, 220–221, 228, 247–248,
   253, 264, 273, 301–302, 308, 315, 317,
   356
   in colonial times, 92–93, 102–112, 181,
   moral, 46, 95, 264, 285
Information(al), 25, 42–43, 47–48, 52, 58,
   64, 69, 73, 169, 170, 182, 184, 193–196,
   200, 207, 219, 244–246, 248, 261, 265,
   267–279, 296, 306–308, 334, 351, 354
   in colonial times, 103–105, 108–110,
   118, 143, 153, 164
   operations, 28, 208–211, 248
   warfare, 40, 79, 249, 251–253, 307
Institution (s), 47, 50, 122, 128, 158,
   164–165, 208, 217–218, 230–233, 289,
   293, 302, 312, 315–316, 339, 341
Insurgency (also, Insurgent(s)), 186, 191,
   193, 200, 206, 221–222, 246, 276, 340, 353
Intelligence, 28, 42–43, 46–49, 51, 64, 79,
   96, 108–112, 162, 182–187, 194–200,
   209, 261, 265, 274–280, 295, 306, 324, 351
   analyst(s) (also, Officers, Agents, Ex-
   pert(s), Professional(s), Intelligence
   Community), 52, 194, 197, 200, 209,
   248, 251, 255, 272–277, 279–280, 351
   counterintelligence, 108–109, 197,
   279–280
   human (HUMINT), 196, 199, 273, 276,
   open source (see also, All-source), 47,
   185, 274, 275, 351
   (see also, Central Intelligence Agency,
   Defense Intelligence Agency)

Interest(s), 13, 18–19, 25, 28, 33, 60,
   65–66, 92–96, 106, 111, 116, 120–123,
   132, 136, 140, 142–144, 148, 158–159,
   161, 172, 180–181, 187, 193, 196,
   207–208, 214, 217, 230, 257, 262, 267,
   288–289, 292–293, 298, 306–307,
   315, 320, 325, 328, 331, 346–347, 349,
   353–354
   self-interest (also, Selfish), 6, 70, 91, 190,
   291, 331–334, 337
International organizations, 34, 348
Internet, 45, 109, 207, 245, 248, 252
Intervention(ism)(ist)(s), 25, 65, 86,
   99–100, 134, 184–185, 187, 212, 229,
   233, 291, 316, 337, 339
Intuition/intuit(ive), 25, 51–53, 70, 218,
   273
   counterintuitive, 35, 39, 164
Invisible Hand, 18, 55–60, 100, 121, 285,
   291
Iraq, 153, 159, 161–163, 184–192, 198,
   206, 220–221, 232, 235–236, 255–256,
   313–318, 328, 339–340–342, 353
Iran, 11, 34, 163, 180, 238, 249, 270, 280,
   309, 330, 340
Islam(ic) (see also, Muslim), 10, 34, 40–41,
   198, 246, 252
Islamist/Islamism (also, Jihad(ism)), 7,
   34, 40–41, 178, 188, 218, 247, 249,
   252–253, 256
Isolation(ism) (ist)(s) (also, proto-isola-
   tion(ist)(m)), 65, 80, 84–86, 91, 133,
   139–140, 146, 172, 195, 328, 335, 348,
Israel/Israeli (s), 34, 296–297

J

Jefferson, Thomas, 85, 87, 96, 105, 115,
   117–118, 123, 125–127, 134–138,
   141–142, 146, 169, 353
Jew(s)/Jewish, 1, 56, 212
Jones, Ishmael, 199–200

K

Kant, Immanuel, 6–7
Kagan, Robert, 84–86, 91, 133–4, 136,
   138–139
Kaplan, Fred, 221, 228
Kasparov, Gary, 180
Kennan, George F., 7, 13, 179, 218, 290,
   346, 348–350

Kennedy, David M., 86
Kennedy, John F., 244, 287–288
Kimball, Roger, 170
Kissinger, Henry, 91–93, 96 115–116, 119, 125, 335
Knowledge, 5, 25, 35, 48, 52, 59, 75, 106, 119, 143, 165–167, 169, 183, 190, 192–196, 200, 210, 222, 229, 254, 266, 269, 274, 277, 295, 313, 318–319, 341, 349
  foreknowledge, 109, 324, 354
  self-knowledge, 170, 273–274, 341
  tacit, 67–68
Kohut, Andrew, 326–327

L

LaFeber, Walter, 123–124
Language(s), 3, 7, 15, 17, 27, 31, 33, 50, 52, 79, 146, 192, 218, 219, 245, 263
Law(s)(yer(s))/Legal 5, 30, 46, 50, 55, 59–60, 87, 90, 94, 101, 103, 104–107, 115, 126, 131, 134, 143–144, 162, 208, 209, 229, 245, 248, 296, 304, 307, 311, 313, 316, 324, 332, 336, 348, 352
Leader(s) (ship) (see also Commander, General, Ruler), 12, 14, 17, 19, 25, 46–47, 58, 60, 63–76, 81–82, 85, 91–92, 95–96, 104–107, 111, 142, 145, 158, 182–183, 185, 188–189, 192, 196, 212, 220–221, 245, 247, 249–250, 256, 264–265, 268–269, 276, 285, 287–288, 291, 302–303, 307, 309–310, 314, 317–319, 323, 328, 337, 339–341, 346–347
Learn(ed)(ing), 25, 59, 88–89, 100, 109, 121, 128, 135–136, 164, 178, 183–184, 196, 197, 229, 231, 234, 235, 238, 244–245, 266–271, 273, 280, 287, 294–295, 317, 330, 337, 339, 341, 352
Legitimate (also, Legitimacy, Legitimize(ing)), 34, 39–40, 86, 100, 162, 170, 205, 214–215, 217, 219, 230, 244, 354
  illegitimate (also, Illegitimacy), 102, 249
Liberal(s), 170–171, 290, 303, 348
Liberalism, 40, 41, 50, 85, 90, 96, 121
Lidell Hart, Sir Basil H., 16–17
Locke(ian), John, 90, 96
Lockhart, Clare, 229, 289–291
Logic(al)(ally), 14, 18, 30–31, 43, 45, 46, 65, 67, 90, 156, 216, 218, 228, 267, 337
Logistic(al)(s), 14, 15, 66, 69, 193, 353
Luttrell, Marcus, 191, 246

M

Madison, James, 96, 115, 117, 123, 125–127, 134–135, 138, 142,
Mankind, 1, 7, 33, 56, 71, 89, 106, 120, 127, 132, 138, 145–146, 217, 285, 299, 323,
Mao Tze Tung, 57, 70
Martel, William, 18, 159
Marx, Karl (also, Marxism, Marxist(s), neo-Marxist, pre-Marxist), 7–8, 31, 34, 40–41, 70, 96, 167, 170, 207
Mattis, James, 155, 159, 345
Mattis, Peter, 198, 277
Maxwell, David S., 221, 309–310
McChrystal, George, 58, 60, 72, 74,
McClay, Wilfred M., 167–168
McDougall, Walter, 139
McMaster, HR, 160, 221
McNeilly, Mark, 57, 196
Measures/measurement, 13, 28, 36, 40, 42, 96, 106, 119, 127, 207, 209–211, 217, 219, 272, 280, 301–303, 310, 349,
Media, 109, 155, 160, 171, 189, 195, 220, 244–252, 280, 304, 307, 338, 341
  newspaper(s), 107
  radio (also, Radio Free Europe/Radio Liberty), 191, 248, 252, 302–303,
Merton, Thomas, 355m
Message(s) (also, Messaging), 104, 106, 126, 145, 210, 211, 244, 245, 247, 253, 256, 265–266, 271–272, 311–312, 330, 352
Metaphor, 9, 34, 57–59, 67, 131, 139,
Militia(s) (men), 79, 10, 12, 13
Mind (also, Mindset), 7, 12, 17, 25, 31, 32, 33, 34, 37, 43, 46, 48–51, 55, 56, 63, 82, 85, 89, 93, 104, 133, 139, 149, 162–164, 165, 179, 182, 191, 209, 219, 220, 252, 255, 265, 273, 279, 336
Mission(s), 47, 91, 104, 110, 139, 186, 187, 189, 193, 207, 208, 214, 218, 229, 231, 232, 235, 270, 275, 304, 313, 317, 335, 342, 351
Monarchy (also, Quasi-monarchy), 123, 125, 144, 329
Money, 48, 79, 90, 120, 136, 172, 186, 190, 199–200, 211, 229, 235, 251, 268, 271, 277–278, 288, 291, 312, 341
Monroe, James, 95, 142, 145, 147
  Monroe Doctrine, 86, 92–95, 143, 346

Moral(ism) (also, Morality), 91–92, 95–96, 99, 116, 120, 141, 145–148, 198, 214, 235, 255, 264, 285, 287, 335–337, 349

Morale, 107, 110, 243, 264

Moran, Daniel, 67

Morgenthau, Hans J., 207, 211

Motivation (also, Motivate, Motivator) 15, 25, 36, 51, 91, 133, 135, 165, 194, 254, 269, 273, 293, 326, 331, 335

N

Narrative, 45, 85, 167, 178, 250, 254, 272

Nationalism/nationalist, 81, 178
Internationalism(ist(s)), 140, 349

Navy (ies) (also, Naval, Navigate, Navigation)), 12, 15, 47, 83, 110, 118, 122, 134, 136–138, 141, 145, 190, 245, 246, 319, 324–325, 329, 339

Network/networking, 193, 261, 272–273, 276, 286, 294, 295, 308, 339

Nongovernmental Organizations (NGOs), 158, 294, 314, 319

Nonstate actors, 153, 197

Norm(s) (also, Normative, Values), 11, 28, 33, 37, 50, 76, 82, 100, 108, 154, 161, 164, 168–171, 182, 194, 212, 214–216, 229, 231, 237, 252–253, 269–270, 287, 290–292, 308, 312, 323, 329–330, 332–333, 337, 345–346

Nye, Joseph S. 153, 212–217, 302

O

Obama, Barack (also, Administration), 155, 162–163, 179, 185, 198, 230, 236, 238, 248, 251, 256, 313, 338

Objective(ly) (also, Objectivity), 57–58, 83, 181, 206, 253, 264, 266

Observation(s), 17, 52, 56, 89, 101, 109, 145, 166, 179, 234, 276, 295, 333
Empirical, 55, 100, 216, 324, 336, 354

Obstacle (s), 25, 58, 82, 211, 267

Occupation, 16, 94, 250

Offensive, 47, 72, 92, 110, 127, 213, 217, 302, 306, 310

Officer(s), 17, 27, 40, 68, 108, 110, 183, 192, 193, 199, 200, 222, 237, 247, 250, 269, 273, 276–279, 318, 350–352
official(s), 157, 161, 198, 200, 218, 220, 222, 227, 228, 236, 238, 244, 247, 251, 267, 268, 280, 293, 295, 318, 329, 332

Operation(s)(al), 13, 14, 28, 40, 42, 72, 73, 108, 110, 141, 144, 145, 153, 157, 158, 160, 206, 208–211, 219, 221, 232, 233–234, 237, 191–193, 248, 272, 275–278, 280, 286, 303, 306–310, 316, 318–319, 350–352

Osama, bin Laden (see also Al Qaeda, Terror), 11, 57, 187–189, 222, 246, 256

Osinga, Frans, 52

P

Paine, Thomas, 106–107, 121, 132

Palmer, Dave Richard, 87, 92, 128

Paradox(ical)(ly),10, 32, 36–39, 63, 68, 69, 87, 122, 125, 132, 158, 164, 169, 170, 211, 254, 288, 331

Passive (also, Passivity, Inaction, Inactive(ity)), 51, 65, 86, 105, 110, 213–214, 243, 263

Patriot(s) (ism), 82, 93, 138, 165, 169, 326, 346

Pattern(s), 30, 32, 45, 50, 52–53, 274, 297, 334

Paul, Christopher, 104, 265–266

Peace
building, 192, 231–234, 261, 301–320
definition, 1–20
peace fare, 2–3, 13, 231, 302, 306, 310, 349

Perception(s) (also, Misperception(s)), 75, 213, 215, 219, 230, 244, 249, 255, 264

Personal(ize), 41, 47, 48, 67–68, 79, 83, 84, 107, 110, 111, 147, 163, 193, 195, 206, 207, 254, 255, 272, 273, 295, 316, 349

Personality(ies), 29, 37, 79, 106, 119, 179, 180, 190

Perspective, 6, 30, 32, 46, 47, 75, 86, 90, 99, 119, 126, 147, 180, 207, 233, 255, 301, 302, 306

Persuasion/persuade/persuasive

Petreaus, David, 185

Phillips, James, 297

Physical, 16, 25, 28, 29, 31, 42, 49, 66, 68, 81, 82, 147, 198, 206, 208, 332,
metaphysical, 31, 50, 57

Pillsbury, Michael, 70

Plan(s)(ed) (also, Planning, Planner(s)), 18, 28, 38, 39, 48–50, 59, 63, 66, 69, 74, 91, 104, 105, 111, 118, 124–125, 133, 137, 142, 157, 160, 161, 194, 200, 218, 230, 232, 236, 246, 264, 266–269, 280, 288, 290, 302, 305, 317, 319, 348, 353, 355

Plato(nic)(nist), 55, 88, 164

Pluralism (Pluralist) (also, Tolerance, Tolerant), 7, 33, 34, 41, 238, 336, 339

Poland (also, Polish), 276, 303

Police (man)(men)(ing), 40, 275, 323,

Policy (see also Foreign Policy), 120, 122, 125, 126, 127, 138, 143, 161, 166, 179, 185, 190, 194, 198, 215, 216, 218, 220, 230, 233, 237, 249, 265, 271–273, 277, 292, 297, 301, 305, 309, 312, 319, 325, 328, 339, 351, 352

Politics, 15, 17, 33, 40, 65–66, 70, 91–92, 96, 116, 119, 139, 140, 163, 166, 167, 179, 207, 212, 296, 325, 332, 333, 335, 340, 341

  geopolitics (Geopolitical), 28, 93, 171

  political correctness

Pomerantsev, Peter, 250, 252

Population(s), 2, 39, 47, 79, 89–91, 100, 107, 111, 119, 146, 158, 183, 185, 186, 187, 190, 206, 219, 221, 228, 229, 246, 257, 274, 301, 307, 340

Power

  hard, 118, 163, 210–217, 238, 264, 302, 306–308, 339

  national, 76, 153, 158, 206, 209–211, 219, 239, 246, 310, 317

  soft, 45, 153, 205–221, 265, 289, 306, 340, 351

Practical (also, Practice(s)), 3, 4, 14, 17, 35, 38, 40, 41, 58, 64, 68, 82, 89, 92, 104, 119, 123, 125, 127, 128, 132, 140, 159, 160, 171, 194, 208, 218, 233, 257, 262, 266, 270, 292, 305, 323–325, 332, 333, 335, 348,

  impractical, 137, 247

  theoretical(ly) (also, Theory), 45, 55, 67–68, 70, 85, 89, 120, 123, 139, 169, 206, 207, 231, 257, 273, 306, 309, 324, 332, 335

Presidency, 141, 164, 330

Priority(ies), 18, 159, 161, 185, 235, 243, 248, 261, 265, 268, 288

Progress(es) (ivism), 41, 127, 166, 170, 218, 318, 348

Project(s), 50, 74, 160, 200, 216, 228, 229, 234–237, 288, 291, 295, 312, 316

Propaganda, 13, 50, 71, 96, 102–104, 109, 207, 180, 219, 245, 249, 251–252, 265

Property, 29, 31, 101, 122, 134–135, 142, 286

Protection(ism), 124, 128, 177, 292, 305

  Mercantile (Mercantilism, Mercantilist(s)), 107, 118, 120, 124, 126

Psychology (also, Psychological), 28, 32, 35, 48, 50, 57, 66, 68, 70, 198, 252, 254, 255

  operations (PSYOPS), 218–219, 352

  warfare, 13, 265, 307

Putin, Vladimir, 34, 40, 180, 194, 213, 250–251

Q

Quality(ies)/qualitative, 9, 11, 14, 47, 53, 56, 63–66, 69, 70–71, 73–74, 106, 165, 187, 190, 214, 229, 233, 264, 272, 277, 278, 285, 288, 323

Quantity(ies)(Quantitative), 11, 157, 194, 206, 209

R

Radelet, Steven, 292

Race(s) (also, Racial, Racism, Racist(s)), 34, 132, 167–169, 178, 269, 272, 329

Rauscher, Frederick, 6

Reagan, Ronald (also, Reaganesque), 136, 212, 233, 245, 278, 288

Realism (also, Realist), 29, 67–68, 70, 75, 92, 91, 105, 122, 138–139, 147, 172, 182, 216, 239, 262, 323–324, 331–337, 341

  Realpolitik, 91, 140, 323, 332–343

Rebel(s) (also, Rebellion), 87, 132, 181, 87, 132, 181

Reconstruction, 159, 203, 228–238, 255, 268, 312–313, 319, 328, 352,

Recruit(s) (ed) (ing) (ment), 110, 253, 269, 275, 277–279

Reform(s) (ing), 148, 197, 229, 232, 261, 265–266, 268, 277–278, 292–293, 297, 314, 316, 351

Reilly, Robert R. 253

Refugee(s), 255, 296–297

Religion(s) (also, Religious, Quasi-religious), 1, 10, 33, 34, 41, 101, 132, 135, 139, 144, 148, 178, 213, 265, 293, 319, 329, 331, 335, 345, 350

  spiritual(ity), 48, 58–59, 67, 71, 101, 133, 354

  theology (also, Theological), 319, 324, 333, 347

Resource(s), 40, 42, 47, 108, 119, 138, 143, 157, 183, 185, 206, 207, 214, 229,

254, 265, 271, 275, 289, 290, 293–295, 304, 305, 316, 317, 339–340, 346, 351, 352

Responsibility, 19, 41, 85, 159, 163, 182, 212, 237, 238, 267, 289, 290, 296–297, 309, 310, 313, 315, 317, 319, 341

Revolution(s) (see American, French)

Rice, Condoleezza, 195, 198, 231, 312

Right(s), 5, 8, 19, 80, 86, 96, 101, 105, 120, 122, 127, 128, 133, 135, 142, 144, 165, 214, 230, 245, 286, 298, 311, 336–337, 345–347
  privilege(d)(s), 127, 245, 292, 347

Risk(s)(y), 8, 12, 69, 74, 91, 142, 158, 162, 221, 231, 254, 273, 288, 318, 351

Ritual(s)(istic), 16, 28, 38, 48, 205

Rothkopf, David, 19

Rule(s), 38, 73, 87, 101, 116, 119, 133, 181, 191, 193, 248, 149, 251, 253, 264, 298, 304, 312, 324, 326, 327, 345, 352

Ruler(s), 7, 28, 64–68, 72, 83, 144, 146, 183, 329, 355

Russia(n)(s) (also, Soviet (Union), USSR), 10, 34, 38, 40–42, 88, 170, 180, 186, 189–190, 196–197, 206–207, 249–253, 256, 279–280, 303–304, 306, 309, 312, 330, 335, 336

S

Sabotage, 3, 47, 74, 122, 168, 171, 197, 272, 280

Sawyer, Ralph D., 70

Schaefer, Brett, D., 297

Schake, Kori, 268–270

Schlesinger, Arthur M., 107,

Secrecy (also, Secret(s)), 36, 40, 47, 79, 92, 108, 110–111, 153, 197, 200, 278–280, 307, 342, 354
  classified (also, De-classified), 47, 108, 153, 171, 196, 274–275, 278, 286,290

Sector(s), 196, 192, 308
  civilian (also, Nonmilitary), 160, 162, 271, 305, 318
  private, 147, 261, 275, 290–294, 313, 316, 319, 329

Security (also, National Security), 4, 7–8, 12–13, 20, 40, 47–48, 90–91, 122–123, 141, 148, 153, 155–160, 171–173, 185–189, 193–195, 209, 215, 218, 221, 227, 231, 237, 262, 274, 277–281, 287, 291, 298, 304, 307–319, 325, 340–353

Selfish(ness), 56, 91, 96, 140, 331, 332

Situation(s) (also, Situational), 2, 19, 25, 29, 31, 35, 37–38, 41, 46–47, 52, 58–59, 69, 72–73, 76, 93, 94, 103, 109, 122, 132, 139, 144, 183, 187, 192, 214, 217, 222, 250, 264, 266, 279, 196, 306, 315, 324, 333–334, 338, 352, 354

Slaughter, Anne-Marie, 332

Smith, Adam, 55–56, 60, 100, 120, 124, 285, 325

Smith, Marion, 141–142, 147–148

Smith, Sir Rupert Anthony, 39

Society
  civil (also, civilized)

Sontag, Susan, 170,

Space (see also, Cyberspace), 5, 12, 27, 32, 45–46, 117, 219, 307

Spalding, Matthew, 140

Spirituality (see Religion)

Stability (also, Stabilize(ing), (zation)), 111, 159, 183, 231–239, 255, 291, 298, 305, 319, 339

Stavridis, James, 291

Stephens, Bret, 328

Stovepipe(d) (ing), 221, 228

Strategy, 1, 4, 13–20, 25–30, 37, 42–43, 51, 58, 64–69, 77–79, 92, 94, 108, 117, 154–162, 189, 193, 209, 221, 234, 247, 256, 263–266, 302, 309–314, 317, 339–341, 345–355
  grand, 13, 75, 79, 92, 141, 156, 237, 314, 324
  national, (also, National Security), 8, 153, 155–156, 158, 209, 211, 215, 288

Success(ful), 14, 15–17, 29, 39, 46, 57, 58, 73, 79, 83, 87, 93, 100, 102, 106, 107, 111, 116, 118, 128, 131, 134, 136, 138–139, 145, 158, 182, 185, 200, 206, 212–213, 219–221, 228, 236, 245, 248, 250, 253, 255, 261, 269, 278, 288–289, 291, 294, 313, 317, 323, 328, 339–340, 346
  unsuccessful, 190, 252, 255, 292

Survive (also, Surviving, Survival, Survivor), 11, 25, 32, 29, 32, 43, 57, 81–82, 91–92, 95, 103, 122–123, 140, 163, 181–182, 191–192, 323

Symbol(s) (ize)(ized)(izing)(ism), 1, 9, 87, 96, 133, 238

Synchronicity (also, Synchronize(d), Synchronization), 210–212, 250, 307–309, 314

Syria(n), 198, 250, 253, 306, 339
System(s) (also, Systematic)

T

Tactic(s)(al)(ization), 8, 12, 14–15, 29–30, 35, 38–42, 59, 69, 72, 82, 92, 103, 104, 106–107, 123, 135–136, 145, 157, 163, 179, 183, 189, 212, 231, 250, 254, 264, 266, 308–310, 336, 340
Target(s)(ed), 28–29, 42, 49, 75, 107–108, 119, 128, 185, 188, 190–191, 193, 200, 214, 249, 252, 261, 271, 277, 296, 298, 302, 308, 327, 339–340
Team(s), 25, 37, 58, 60, 73–74, 83, 111–112, 161, 191, 198, 234, 251, 276, 315, 317, 351
Technical (also, Technician(s), Technocrat(s), Technology(ies)), 8, 17, 19, 28–29, 39, 64, 133, 153, 170, 178, 184, 193–194, 199, 206, 208–210, 218, 233, 276, 306, 310, 313, 327,
Terror (also, Terrorist(s), Terrorism), 11, 45, 135, 150, 179–180, 186, 191–195, 197, 202, 218, 222, 231, 235, 248, 270, 273, 280, 296, 309
Threat(s)(en)(ens) (see also, Danger(s)), 11, 12, 15, 33–34, 42, 47, 60, 69–70, 82, 84, 94, 122, 124, 138, 141, 153, 155, 162, 164, 179–180, 182, 187, 193, 195, 197–198, 212, 217, 231, 246, 252, 271, 273, 289, 302, 306, 308, 314, 326, 330, 350
Time (see also, Space), 5, 17, 18, 27, 28, 41, 45–46, 51, 59, 67, 70, 72, 110, 193, 211, 212, 234, 246, 249, 251, 254, 257, 264, 270, 272, 312, 337, 339, 340, 350–354
Tomes, Robert R., 184–185
Tools (also, Instruments), 7, 12, 18, 28–29, 34, 38, 40, 42, 57, 64, 69, 79, 81, 86, 101, 104, 107, 117, 136, 158, 169, 194, 209, 213–218, 228, 246, 252, 292, 302, 306–314, 339, 354
Train(ing)(er)(ee)(s)) (also, Untrained), 4, 37, 40, 67, 69, 76, 79, 108, 111, 158, 183, 199, 232, 246, 268–271, 274, 304–305, 313, 318–319, 351–352
Transition(s), 88, 229, 230, 232, 298, 340
Tribe(s) (also, Tribal(ism)), 89, 123, 133, 158, 164, 181, 190, 221, 275
Trust(ed) (also, Distrust(ed), Entrust(ed)), 25, 41, 48, 55–56, 70–72, 82, 85, 89, 99, 101, 111, 115, 121, 122, 124, 138, 144,

164, 171, 179, 181, 185, 190, 192, 206, 218, 221, 228, 244, 252, 264, 285, 306, 330, 339, 342, 353

U

United Nations, 34, 297, 303, 348
Unity (also, Unified), 9, 168, 211, 243, 305, 306, 314, 317, 318, 324

V

Van Puyvelde, Damien, 12
Varg, Paul A., 96, 116–117, 120
Vershbow, Alexander, 251–253
Victory (also, Victorious), 38, 41, 51, 57, 59, 63, 84, 100, 108, 124, 134, 186, 189, 212, 231, 264, 323, 350–351
Vietnam, 153, 156, 170, 183–184, 192, 195, 228, 244–245, 255–256, 295, 349, 353
Violence (also, Violent), 1, 3, 4, 11, 25, 28–29, 38, 39, 41, 57, 67, 69–70, 87–89, 100–101, 106, 122, 127, 148, 162, 178, 182, 185, 193, 212, 214, 216, 296, 302, 340, 354
Vision(ary)(ies), 80, 82, 83, 85, 89, 91–94, 96, 118, 122, 124, 133, 137, 141, 156, 158, 160, 166, 235, 238, 326, 338, 341–342, 346–348
Vulnerability(ies) (also, Vulnerable), 39, 42, 47, 49, 51, 82, 178–179, 206, 211, 278

W

Waller, J. Michael, 254
Walling, Karl-Friedrich, 93–94, 116, 138
Walt, Stephen M., 336–337
Walton, Timothy, 306–307
Warfare, 3, 8, 11–16, 21, 28, 38, 39–43, 56–57, 64, 66–68, 74, 79, 94, 103, 124, 128, 157, 160, 179, 184, 191, 206–211, 216–221, 237, 244, 247, 249–254, 264–265, 302, 306–310, 348, 350, 353
Washington (also, DC; nation's capital), 4, 19, 192, 201, 220, 236, 244, 247, 316
Washington, George, 65, 79, 84–86, 91–92, 108–111, 116–117, 123–129, 140, 149, 165, 181, 186, 188, 261, 280, 339
Weapon (s) (ize) (ization), 12, 28–29, 36–37, 39, 57, 63–64, 76, 79, 100, 110,

118, 147, 153, 178, 182–184, 197, 201, 214, 248, 250, 252, 297, 310, 340

Wheelan, Joseph, 135–136, 138–139, 335

Wilson, Woodrow (also, Wilsonianism), 132, 335, 347–348

Wilford, Hugh, 303

Woman (Women), 8, 48, 66, 74, 77, 83, 149, 215, 291, 345, 348

Wood, Gordon S., 118

Worley, Robert D., 209, 309

Y

Yuen, Derek M. C., 30–31, 35–37, 48–49, 52, 58, 75

About the Authors

Dr. Juliana Geran Pilon is Senior Fellow at the Alexander Hamilton Institute for the Study of Western Civilization, having earned her PhD in philosophy from the University of Chicago. Her books include: *Soulmates: Resurrecting Eve*; *Cultural Intelligence for Winning the Peace*; *Why America is Such a Hard Sell: Beyond Pride and Prejudice*; *The Bloody Flag: Post-Communist Nationalism in Eastern Europe—Spotlight on Romania*; and *Notes From the Other Side of Night*. She has also published over 200 articles and reviews on international affairs, human rights, literature, and philosophy, has made frequent appearances on radio and television, and has served on several advisory boards. She has taught at several colleges and universities, including the National Defense University and George Washington University. During the 1990s, she was first Director and later Vice President for Programs at IFES (The International Foundation for Election Systems), where she designed and managed a wide variety of democratization-related projects. She has held post-doctoral fellowships in international relations at Stanford University's Hoover Institution and at the Institute of Humane Studies.

Colonel Michael R Eastman is the Executive Officer to the Commanding Officer of the Army Cyber Command, having previously commanded the 75th Field Artillery Brigade, and deployed to Jordan. As Deputy Brigade Commander for Civil Capacity, he has coordinated economic, political, and civil reconstruction operations across four Iraqi provinces; and in Afghanistan, he was Special Assistant to the Commanding General of the Office of Military Cooperation. His many awards include the Legion of Merit, two Bronze Stars and seven Meritorious Service Medals.